D0394084

THE BOXING KINGS

THE BOXING KINGS

When American Heavyweights Ruled the Ring

Paul Beston

ROWMAN & LITTLEFIELD
Lanham • Boulder • New York • London

Published by Rowman & Littlefield
A wholly owned subsidiary of The Rowman & Littlefield Publishing Group, Inc.
4501 Forbes Boulevard, Suite 200, Lanham, Maryland 20706
www.rowman.com

Unit A, Whitacre Mews, 26-34 Stannary Street, London SE11 4AB

British Library Cataloguing in Publication Information Available

Library of Congress Cataloging-in-Publication Data
Names: Beston, Paul, 1966-
Title: The boxing kings : when American heavyweights ruled the ring / Paul Beston.
Description: Lanham : Rowman & Littlefield, [2017] | Includes bibliographical references and index.
Identifiers: LCCN 2017001989 (print) | LCCN 2017025080 (ebook) | ISBN 9781442272903 (electronic) | ISBN 9781442272897 (cloth : alk. paper)
Subjects: LCSH: Boxers (Sports)—United States—Biography. | African American boxers—Biography. | Boxing—United States—History.
Classification: LCC GV1131 (ebook) | LCC GV1131 .B48 2017 (print) | DDC 796.83092 [B]—dc23
LC record available at https://lccn.loc.gov/2017001989

♾™ The paper used in this publication meets the minimum requirements of American National Standard for Information Sciences—Permanence of Paper for Printed Library Materials, ANSI/NISO Z39.48-1992.

Printed in the United States of America

For my mother, Edna Mae Beston,
and to the memory of my father,
Richard F. Beston

"We have a theory about the heavyweight championship, that somehow each of the great figures to hold the title manages to sum up the spirit of his time. All the great ones are not merely the best pugs of their day but demigods larger than life. It may all be accidental, but the main currents of their period either shape their personalities or their personalities seem wondrously to reflect their times."

—Budd Schulberg, *Sparring with Hemingway:*
And Other Legends of the Fight Game

"If they [heavyweights] become champions, they begin to have inner lives like Hemingway or Dostoyevsky, Tolstoy or Faulkner, Joyce or Melville or Conrad or Lawrence or Proust."

—Norman Mailer, *Existential Errands*

"The boxing ring is the ultimate focus of masculinity in America, the two-fisted testing ground of manhood, and the heavyweight champion, as a symbol, is the real Mr. America."

—Eldridge Cleaver, *Soul on Ice*

CONTENTS

ACKNOWLEDGMENTS

I'm grateful to Stefan Kanfer for his early support for this project and expert advice and to *City Journal*'s editor, Brian Anderson, for his support and—at a very late-running function some years back—for more or less suggesting the idea.

Thanks to Alec Shane at Writers House and to Christen Karniski and Darren Williams at Rowman & Littlefield. And thanks to the Manhattan Institute.

Thanks also to Veronica Delora, David DesRosiers, Loretta Hayes, John and Sylvia Highland, Michele Jacob, Mike Kelleher, Andrew Klavan, Karen Marston, Doug Schoen, Bernadette Serton, Robert Sherwood, Harry Stein, Springs Toledo, and Michael Woods. Thanks always to Wlady Pleszczynski.

I'm deeply indebted to Janice Meyerson for her copyediting and to Matthew Hennessey for giving me invaluable feedback.

Thanks to my wife, Emma, and daughter, Grace, for their love and support.

Thanks to my mother, for too many things to list. And finally, thanks to my three brothers, Rick, Pete, and Dave—fighters all.

INTRODUCTION
The Lineage

He seems everywhere these days—on Broadway, in movies, on talk shows. He mocks himself gently; he weeps easily. He is a damaged human being, he would be the first to say, and somewhere in memory lurks the man who threatened to eat an opponent's children and who, in one of his biggest fights, took bites out of another opponent's ears. But that menacing figure is nowhere to be seen today, and those who feel generously toward Mike Tyson hope that the demon is gone for good, replaced by this devoted family man. He has been a public figure for so long that we have almost forgotten why we first paid attention.

He was the last great heir to the American crown: the last American heavyweight champion who mattered to a world beyond the ring, whose presence transcended sports, who seemed to represent something central about American identity. The last champion, not the first: Tyson brought an end to a lineage that once seemed as if it would go on forever.

For most of the twentieth century, boxing was prominent in American life, and the heavyweight championship—the richest prize in sports, as it was long known—held a special place in the national mind. The champions themselves occupied a public office not unlike the presidency, though they were often better known and better liked than the man in the White House. Like the presidency, the heavyweight championship came with perks, precedents, and boundless opportunity—but also unrelenting criticism, unexpected limitations, and the persistent burden of the past. It was an office both royal and republican, as befit its British and American heritage. The title brought kingly benefits, and its possessors sometimes actually wore a crown. Yet the title could not be given: it had to be earned and, once earned, defended.

The heavyweight champions number among the most memorable figures in our popular culture. Some rank with the greatest boxers ever to step into the ring, while others were more notable for their unusual personalities or for their social significance; a rare few combined all these attributes. Often sparking ethnic, racial, or even national pride, their exploits seemed to mirror broader social trends. The country's best writers interviewed them, profiled them, and analyzed them. They appeared on cereal boxes and *Time* magazine covers, in comedians' monologues, in the conversations of weekday commuters, and probably in our dreams.

It was called the heavyweight championship of "the world," but the title seemed more like a national property. With only a few exceptions, all the champions of the twentieth century came from the United States—American kings in the American century. And then, almost right on schedule, when the century passed, so did they.

Tyson became a huge star in the 1980s, but by then, his sport was struggling to hold on to fans, especially when it left free television for the lucrative but isolating opportunities of cable and pay-per-view. Eventually, the heavyweight title ceased to be an American possession, passing first to Britain—fittingly, as modern boxing started there—and then to Ukraine. Few in America today can name the heavyweight champion, and boxing is not even the most popular combat sport anymore, at least among younger fans, who prefer mixed martial arts.

When the heavyweights moved to distant shores, boxing lost its narrative in America. The sport's great figures—and some remain—are no longer integrated into our cultural fabric. No American champion stands as a reference point in the language, an easy metaphor with which to make arguments about other things. The long prominence of the heavyweight title in this country looks increasingly like a twentieth-century phenomenon, a product of unique and temporary circumstances. That wasn't how it seemed in the 1970s, when boxing seized hold of my young imagination and wouldn't let go.

Around 1976, when I was ten, I started returning home from our local library carting books with titles such as *The Heavyweight Champions* or *A*

Pictorial History of Boxing or *Dempsey*. I'd become drawn to boxing—the sport was all over television back then—and to boxers. These were the waning days of Muhammad Ali, who was by then the most recognized face in the world, though his ring skills were slipping. Most of his late fights were on regular television, and I remember the anticipation of seeing him, along with the carnival atmosphere that often prevailed. But I also found myself compulsively watching matches involving fighters at any weight—middleweights, lightweights, featherweights, bantamweights—unable to pull myself away. Compulsions sent me to books, and soon I had memorized the Dewey decimal call number for boxing: 796.83. Most boxing books at my local library centered on the heavyweight champions, and I sensed for the first time the thrill of historical knowledge, the promise that if I followed the trail back far enough, I could trace a line from the beginning to what had happened yesterday.

Why boxers? It must have had something to do with their solitariness, though if it had been only that, I might have idolized painters or scientists or tennis players or political dissidents. It must have had to do as well with the danger that they courted and the loneliness of it—because fighting another man is about as lonely as it gets, especially when a crowd is watching. I'd already developed a passion for solitude and an aversion to group dynamics. Boxers seemed pure, autonomous.

And then there were the images: the fighters, the gloves and trunks, the roped square surrounded by the collage of faces. Two battlers wearing tights in blurry old photographs, surrounded by crowds of men in greatcoats and hats and, in the distance, stark pine trees; a scowling fighter standing over a dazed opponent who sits on the canvas, clutching the middle rope; a black man lying on his back, arms up, seeming to shield his eyes from the sun, as a white man paces over him and distant spectators seem to leap out of their seats.

I watched it; I read about it; soon enough, I wanted to try it. My brothers and I acquired the necessary equipment and started boxing in our basement, armed with the instructional manual *Inside Boxing*, by former champion Floyd Patterson. I pored over the book's photos showing how to execute various punches and defensive moves. Early on, I mostly boxed with my eldest brother, Rick, who had three years on me and thus did not fight me at full strength. Later, my brother Pete, just a year older, was my main sparring partner.

In the pages of *Ring* magazine, I saw ads for old fight films on Super 8 mm. They were sold through a long-gone company called Ring Classics, based in Hauppauge, New York. The films were silent, almost all shot in black and white, and, projected onto a blank wall or white screen, they transported me to another world. The first two I saw were Joe Louis versus Billy Conn, in 1941, and Rocky Marciano versus Jersey Joe Walcott, in 1952, in which Marciano won the title with a pulverizing right hand. (One of boxing's iconic photographs captures a Marciano punch distorting Walcott's features.) I remember anticipating the climactic thirteenth round in both fights and the whispering sound that the reels made as they turned in the dark.

I took my last punch as a recreational boxer just before graduating from college. My last sparring partner landed a right that sent a thick ring of pain under my jaw and around both ears. I'd gotten headaches before from sparring, but not like this. I decided to conserve my remaining wattage for the challenges ahead.

By then, I'd begun to lose the boxing thread. The sport grew more disorganized and confusing by the year. As I moved into middle age, my affection for it was based in memory. Boxing felt like some habit from youth that I had mostly renounced.

Mostly. I learned as the years passed that boxing wasn't quite done with me, and that its characters—especially the heavyweight champions—formed a gallery in my mind, always accessible and somehow never exhaustible. If we are the sum of our youthful passions, I'll never escape the boxing brand. No use trying to do so, anyway. As Joe Louis said: You can run, but you can't hide.

★

The Boxing Kings tells the story of the heavyweight title in America, examining the lives and careers of the champions, with a special emphasis on the seven who have held a defining place in our culture: John L. Sullivan, Jack Johnson, Jack Dempsey, Joe Louis, Rocky Marciano, Muhammad Ali, and Mike Tyson. The narrative is built around these key figures, though it incorporates the stories of their peers and rivals, all memorable in their own right. The book charts how America changed as the title shifted from one claimant to another and how the major champions developed an uncanny connection with their times.

They came from every point on the American map. Jack Johnson, the first black heavyweight champion, was a native of Galveston, Texas, where his family lost everything in the great hurricane of 1900. Johnson spent much of his public life walking on America's racial fault line: he bested white men in the ring and bedded white women outside it. At a time when black Americans faced enormous adversity, such behavior made Johnson notorious, at least among whites. After the federal government used questionable charges to convict him for violating the Mann Act—a law designed to stop interstate prostitution—he fled the country and lived as a fugitive. Reactions to Johnson from whites and blacks, from critics, and from the law offered a stark glimpse of the country's racial obsessions half a century after Appomattox.

From Colorado came Jack Dempsey, a former hobo whose early life would have fit neatly into a Jack London novel. Dempsey fought in a style never before seen—a swarming, hyperaggressive attack perfectly suited for the sensation-mad Roaring Twenties. So many people wanted to see his fights that special arenas were built to accommodate them. Dempsey met with presidents, shot movies with Charlie Chaplin, earned almost as much money in one fight as Babe Ruth did in his entire career, and helped make Americans sports crazy, as they have remained.

Joe Louis, an Alabama sharecropper's son and the grandson of slaves, fought out of Detroit. He was Jack Johnson's opposite in every way, inspiring blacks and whites during the Depression and World War II with his patriotism, his dignity, and his politically tinged showdown with Hitler's favorite boxer.

When Louis retired, the champion's shoes seemed impossible to fill, but Rocky Marciano, an Italian American from Brockton, Massachusetts, stepped into them. Marciano achieved something that no other champion could claim: he fought an entire career without tasting defeat. Along the way, he embodied the American promise, especially for Italian Americans.

Louisville's Cassius Clay became Muhammad Ali, champion in the 1960s and 1970s, who symbolized an era of protest and social change. Like Johnson before him, Ali inspired black pride and white resentment—not by pursuing white women but by joining a militant black nationalist group, the Black Muslims, and speaking out on racial issues. Like Johnson, Ali squared off against Uncle Sam: in his case, he refused induction into the armed forces for service in Vietnam and was convicted of draft evasion. But Ali had better luck than Johnson, winning a Supreme Court appeal and becoming, by the end of his career, the most celebrated athlete of all time.

Ali's departure left a Louis-like hole; he had called himself "The Greatest" for years, and many agreed with him when he said that boxing would die after he was gone. But Mike Tyson, a troubled young man from Brownsville, Brooklyn's violent streets, proved Ali wrong. Tyson reminded many of a young Dempsey, and his love of boxing history made his rise seem fated—until a different kind of fate intervened.

These men and their contemporaries stood on some of the great stages of the twentieth century, before a public willing to make them rich but usually wanting more in return than they could deliver. Some loved holding the title; some were nearly destroyed by it. None were the same afterward. Sometimes cast as primitives lacking inner lives, they were as complex and flawed and sympathetic as people everywhere. Among them were comics and straight men; blowhards and introverts; prima donnas, hoodlums, and opportunists; workingmen, preachers, and saviors. Like all classic American heroes, they faced their greatest tests alone.

Their story starts long before Tyson and Ali, Louis and Dempsey, and even Jack Johnson. It starts in Boston, with John L. Sullivan, the first of the line. It was Sullivan who made the heavyweight title a commercial property, just as commercialism was becoming an American invention. Sullivan's appeal generated huge public interest in boxing, which was still an outlaw sport. His career symbolized the struggles and triumphs of the Irish, then the nation's largest immigrant group—though he earned sums of money unmatched by anyone below robber-baron status. He may have been the best-known American of his time, his picture hanging in countless homes and taverns, even as he squandered his money and drank himself into health and legal troubles.

One other thing: Sullivan made the title synonymous with America. "There isn't a self-respecting American," he said, "no matter what tomfool ideas he may have about boxing in general, who does not feel patriotic pride at the thought that a native born American, a countryman of his, can lick any man on the face of the earth."[1] He wore a diamond-encrusted championship belt that read: "Presented to the Champion of Champions, John L. Sullivan, by the Citizens of the United States." The belt served as the model for those that his successors would wear; the sentiments represented the quasi-royal authority that heavyweight champions would attain in America. It was that authority—along with unimagined riches—that gave the heavyweight title its special character and that made such different men willing to fight for it.

PROGENITOR

"I can lick any son of a bitch in the world!"[1]

Browse a few pages of any boxing history, and it won't be long before you come across that boast and the man who made it: John L. Sullivan, the Boston Strong Boy, "the man who started it all." Whether photographed or illustrated, he usually appears with close-cropped hair, intense black eyes, and a powerful upper body. Depending on what stage of Sullivan's career is depicted, he might appear paunchy and ponderous, more like a man playing a fighter than being one—this was the Sullivan who had already tasted fame and its delights and whose consumption of food and alcohol would become as legendary as his fighting prowess. Or he might look comparatively lean, ready to have at it—the Sullivan who first rose to national attention in the early 1880s.

That younger Sullivan came along with no precedents for the role he was about to play, which was to become the George Washington of boxing and America's first sports superstar. In 1882, the year Sullivan won what was recognized, at least in America, as the heavyweight championship, the idea of professional sports was in its infancy. Horse racing enjoyed broad popularity, the races that would later constitute its Triple Crown already established. But professional baseball was just coming into existence; the National League had been founded six years earlier. American football was barely a flicker in the eye of Yale's Walter Camp, whose changes to the rugby-based game would lead to the modern sport. Basketball had not yet been invented. As for boxing, it had passionate followers, but even its finest practitioners had to run from the law, and when their fighting days were over, they quickly slipped into obscurity and poverty.

Sullivan would change all this through a pulverizing fighting style and a magnetic personality—the first made people pay attention; the second made them care. He delivered his famous boast to every willing S.O.B. upon entering taverns and other public spots and from countless public stages. Sullivan would turn not only himself but also the heavyweight championship into a money machine. He would become a defining figure of the Gilded Age, an inspiration to millions of Irish immigrants, and a steady source of material for journalists struggling to understand the new phenomenon known as celebrity.

Soon enough, he was known as the Great John L.: shake the hand that shook the hand of the Great John L., men lucky enough to meet him boasted to their peers. Like other American creators, Sullivan seemed to emerge from a void and leave behind a world. And like many of them, little in his origins suggested such a destiny.

★

"There are so many John Sullivans, Jerry Daileys and William O'Briens, who are all made in the same mold," said a Boston census agent in 1845, describing the difficulty of accounting for all the city's foreign-born residents.[2] Irish immigration to the United States was surging; between 1845 and 1860, nearly two million Irish came to the United States, the vast majority of them in the wake of the Great Hunger, also known as the Great Irish Famine. Many others died traveling to America aboard crowded and disease-ridden "coffin ships."

The John Sullivan who would make his own mold was born in Boston on October 12, 1858, the son of parents who had come to the United States a few years earlier. By the early 1850s, Boston was teeming with newly arrived Irish, who already made up about a quarter of the city's population. John Lawrence Sullivan grew up as part of the generation that came of age after the Civil War, when industrial growth and technological advancement began to make the United States a world power. Remarkable inventions, from electric lights to the telephone, were revolutionizing American life, especially in the cities. Average daily wages of American manufacturing and industrial workers rose 50 to 60 percent between 1860 and 1890, making possible a standard of living that was the envy of the world.

Yet the prospects for most working-class Irish immigrants remained limited. Like so many of his fellow Irishmen, Mike Sullivan, John L.'s father, led a life of physical toil, one of legions of Irish in the manual-labor trades. In the brief years in which he lived his father's kind of life, Sullivan got all he wanted of it. He apprenticed as a tinsmith, plumber, and pipe fitter, and he worked on laboring crews, though his hot temper often got him into fights and cost him jobs. His life changed in 1878, when he and some friends visited the Dudley Street Opera House to watch a variety program. A young man named Jack Scannell, having heard of Sullivan's brawling reputation, challenged him to a gloved boxing match. Sullivan accepted and bounded up onto the stage. When Scannell clocked him with a blow, Sullivan rushed Scannell and connected with a roundhouse swing that knocked him into a piano on the stage—or into the orchestra pit, by some accounts. The event caused a stir, and Sullivan soon began considering a career as a prizefighter.

He may as well have planned to become a professional criminal. Prizefighters were seen as lowlifes, ruffians, and barbarians. They practiced an illegal trade and consorted in saloons and gambling dens with gang leaders and political bosses. They generally ended their short lives drunk and destitute. In an era devoted to progress, prizefighting was seen as atavistic.

Boxing was illegal in all thirty-eight U.S. states when Sullivan started out, though most states permitted exhibitions like the one he attended at the opera house—demonstrations of "scientific" self-defense and other principles of the "manly art." Any genuine contest for financial stakes—that is, prizefighting—was against the law. Yet prizefighting had enjoyed a following for decades, its loyalists staging bouts on barges or in out-of-the-way places in order to evade the eyes of the law. They often enjoyed sly cooperation from police and members of the political establishment, many of whom took a financial interest in the outcomes. Fighters, police forces, and political parties blended together in the Northeast during Sullivan's youth, especially in New York, where the Tammany Hall Democratic machine used boxers to work as muscle to convince those who needed political convincing.

Prizefighting, as it had been known up until Sullivan's time, involved battling with bare fists under the 1838 London Prize Ring Rules, which were based on a set of standards drawn up in 1743 by Jack Broughton, the father of modern boxing. (Pugilism's origins trace back to Greco-Roman times, but the British initiated the sport's modern revival.) Under the London Prize Ring Rules, bouts were fought to the finish—that is, until one man could no longer continue. In addition to punching, wrestling holds were permitted, but eye-gouging or hitting a man when he was down was prohibited. Rings were twenty-four feet square and pitched on turf. Rounds had no time limits, ending only when one man went down—whether from a punch, a wrestling toss, or exhaustion—and thus could last a few seconds or much longer. Marathon bouts, fought over dozens of rounds and lasting for hours, were part of the sport's emerging lore. The fighters got thirty seconds' rest before the next round was to begin. If they could not make it out to the "scratch line"—a mark drawn at the center of the ring—they were said to have failed to "come to scratch," and the bout was over.

Under assault from Victorian reformers, prizefighting in Britain declined as the nineteenth century wore on. In America, it surged, achieving prominence not only among the outlaw sport's heavily immigrant working-class fan base but also with a native-born faction not much better off economically. Some in the upper classes felt drawn to the sport as well, attracted by its elevation of strength and heroic action—virtues seen as endangered in a mechanized age. In the United States, the late nineteenth century saw a burst of interest in health and fitness as an expression of revitalization and national strength. "Anything is better than this white-blooded degeneration to which we all tend," Oliver Wendell Holmes wrote.[3]

John L. Sullivan's career would make some worry more about red-blooded than white-blooded degeneration, but the American future would belong to men like him.

$$\bigstar$$

From the beginning, he showed a gift for getting headlines. His name first appeared in the *New York Times*—on the front page, no less—on December 26, 1880, for his win over "Professor" John Donaldson in Cincinnati. The following spring, on a barge floating near Yonkers, Sullivan pummeled a New York City gang tough, John Flood, the Bull's Head Terror. Flood, a hard man in a rough social milieu, could do little against Sullivan's clubbing blows, the likes of which few could recall ever seeing. Sullivan's career built momentum; observers told of how he charged out of his corner, his left arm slapping against his thigh, looking to land knockout blows. His backers clamored for a shot at the heavyweight championship.

That would mean taking on Paddy Ryan, an Irishman from Tipperary who had settled in Troy, New York. Ryan was known as the Troy Giant, though his dimensions—he stood about six feet and weighed 195 pounds—would barely qualify him as a major league shortstop today. He had won the American version of the heavyweight title in his first professional fight. Now he took on the challenge of the Boston Strong Boy, as Sullivan was being called. The two originally planned to fight in New Orleans, but Louisiana authorities chased them out and the battle was moved to Mississippi City, Mississippi (now part of Gulfport).

Ryan and Sullivan squared off on February 7, 1882, in front of the Barnes Hotel. The fight lasted just eleven minutes. Sullivan dropped Ryan with nearly the first blow he threw. The Troy Giant could not contend with Sullivan's strength and ferocity, and Sullivan scored the "fall" in most rounds. Finally, in the ninth round, a Sullivan right dropped Ryan again, and the champion was carried back to his corner, where the battle was conceded. "When Sullivan struck me," the deposed champion said afterward, "I thought that a telegraph pole had been shoved against me endways."[4]

Sullivan had won American laurels under the London Prize Ring Rules, but he was already partial to a newer set of regulations, drawn up by Welsh sportsman John Graham Chambers and attributed to the Marquess of Queensberry. These guidelines stipulated fights with gloves, set three-minute limits for each round with a one-minute rest between, barred wrestling holds, and allowed for bouts to take place inside the modern version of the boxing ring, instead of on turf. With some modifications, these rules govern boxing matches today. Rough as he was, Sullivan preferred the Queensbury Rules.

Not long after beating Ryan, Sullivan set off on a barnstorming tour of cities around the country, offering $250, then $500, and eventually $1,000 to any man who could last four rounds with him in legal "exhibition" bouts with gloves. Only one opponent, the aptly named Tug Wilson, survived the four rounds by clutching Sullivan and falling to the mat at every opportunity in order to avoid damaging blows.

Sullivan's first true test as champion came in New York in May 1883, when he took on Britain's Charley Mitchell, who was really a middleweight, standing only five foot seven and a half and weighing much less than Sullivan. But Mitchell was a clever boxer and hoped to use his guile to outwit and eventually outfight his foe. Every seat in Madison Square Garden—the first of four editions of the sporting mecca—was filled by 8 p.m., but crowds kept streaming in, and the promoters placed settees and then dry-goods boxes, kegs, and milk cans, on which spectators stood. New York's pugnacious police chief, Clubber Williams, had ninety cops on hand for a crowd of about ten thousand, which included luminaries such as Roscoe Conkling, New York's Stalwart, anti-reformist ex-senator, and Tony Pastor, the vaudeville impresario.[5]

The prominence of the attendees and the respectable venue made clear how, in just a few years, Sullivan had become an object of national fascination. His fame was driven by the growing metropolitan press and the swelling readership for sporting weeklies—especially the *National Police Gazette*. The *Gazette*'s editor, a fellow Irishman named Richard Kyle Fox, transformed the paper with his tireless coverage of sports as well as lurid crime reporting and other scandalous material. Fox turned the *Gazette*, which he printed on pink paper, into one of the country's most widely circulated publications. He died a millionaire in 1922, his audacious style tracing a clear line to today's tabloid journalism.

The ascent of Fox was inseparable from the rise of John L. and the interest in boxing that he generated, though the two men were sworn enemies. According to a popular story, Sullivan snubbed Fox's request to join him at his table at Harry Hill's, a New York nightspot popular with the sports crowd, infuriating the proud *Gazette* editor. Whether this really happened is unclear, but Sullivan and Fox prided themselves on bowing to no one and were bound to clash. The feud served both men well. Steady coverage of Sullivan sold papers, and the *Gazette*'s obsession helped make the fighter a national figure.

After entering Madison Square Garden to a raucous ovation, Sullivan, his weight reported at 202 pounds, charged out of his corner and flattened Mitchell with one of his first punches. When Mitchell rose, Sullivan resumed his assault, pinning him on the ropes. Mitchell broke away and landed a blow that sent Sullivan back on his heels and crashing to the canvas. The arena exploded with cheers and shouts. Sullivan scrambled to his feet and pressed Mitchell hard until the bell rang. In the second round, he drove Mitchell into the ropes repeatedly, finally knocking him over the top strand and out of the ring, headfirst. In the third round, Sullivan battered Mitchell around the ring, dropping him several more times. Mitchell kept rising, but Clubber Williams had seen enough. Recognizing that the fight could no longer pass for an exhibition, the police chief entered the ring and stopped the fight.

The Mitchell fight heightened Americans' interest in Sullivan. Unlike his pugilistic predecessors, Sullivan broke through to the swelling middle classes, many of whom had previously opposed boxing as barbaric. He was able to do this not only through his spectacular fighting style but also through his willingness to market the title and himself—and to forge, in the public mind, an identification of one with the other.

In 1883 and 1884, Sullivan embarked on a far more elaborate national barnstorming tour—the most ambitious that any American, including presidential candidates, had made at that time. He traveled with a troupe, or "combination," consisting of preliminary acts and several sparring partners, with whom he gave boxing exhibitions while also taking volunteers from the crowd for the now time-honored test of attempting to last four rounds with the Great John L. Sullivan. The Grand Tour, as it was known, brought Sullivan from New England to California—through the nation's interior, the Southwest and the Midwest, and back again, on the scale of a rock star's concert itineraries. Many of the places that Sullivan visited had never hosted a boxing match; others had barely seen the end of the Indian wars. Some territories, where hostile tribes still roamed, were not safe to travel through. But Sullivan saw much of America, and America saw him.

His timing was right for such a massive undertaking: America's railroad system had been built out dramatically, now exceeding all the rail mileage in Europe. In 1883, the demand for intercity rail transit had become so overwhelming that the United States created four standard time zones to manage it (cities and towns had previously operated on their own time). Sullivan was on tour when, on November 18, 1883, cities and localities across the United States reset their clocks, creating our modern time system.

Through the tours and sparring exhibitions, Sullivan became a wealthy man; he would make perhaps $1 million (in nineteenth-century dollars) by the time his career was finished. Few Americans had earned so lavishly; no working-class immigrant's son, Irish or otherwise, had come within a galaxy of such riches. But Sullivan could hold on to none of it, spending it as quickly as it came in, on business ventures, such as his Boston saloon, but especially on what would become familiar trappings of a champion's lifestyle—an entourage of friends and hangers-on, mistresses, prodigious rounds of food and drink, and a lavish wardrobe. "I've got the prettiest clothes you ever saw," he said. His appetites, especially for food and alcohol, were gargantuan, and his image embodied vigor and excess. Some of it was celebratory: tales of his Bunyanesque strength abounded. It was said that he was so powerful that he had bent a blacksmith's iron bar over his forearm and then bit a piece off; he could blow a silver dollar across a room; he could lift a man three feet off the ground with his handshake; and so on.

But he was a figure of scandal, too. His long benders and frequent scrapes with the law—for brawling in saloons or crashing his carriage, for example—were always dutifully reported, and not just by Richard Kyle Fox. After Herbert Slade, a former opponent who had joined his touring company, decided to quit, an incensed Sullivan found him in a tavern, head-butted him, and kept pounding away until the police arrived. The *Virginia Chronicle* spoke for many when it lamented that the champion "has almost invariably exhibited the brutal side of his character." After another incident, the *Cleveland Herald* declared that "it is about time that press and public 'sat down' on the lionizing of this disreputable individual."[6] Sullivan, another reporter once wrote, was "a son-of-a-bitch of the first water, if he ever drank any."[7]

Indeed, from early in his fighting career, Sullivan fully qualified as an alcoholic, despite his unintentionally hilarious disclaimers: "I don't drink much," he said in 1883. "Say, five or six glasses of ale a day and a bottle for dinner, if I feel like it."[8] One story had it that he downed fifty-six gin fizzes in one hour—unless it was sixty-seven. "We are going to be a long time dead," he said once, "and only a few of us know how to enjoy life as it goes." He richly deserved the designation a critic gave him as one of the great drunkards who had ever lived.

John L.'s ruinous thirsts also destroyed his marriage to Annie Bates, a chorus girl whom he married in 1883 and with whom he had his only child, John Jr. The child died of diphtheria in 1886. By then, Annie had left him and initiated divorce proceedings, alleging "cruel and abusive treatment and gross and confirmed habits of intoxication."[9]

Eventually, his self-destructiveness threatened his fighting career. In June 1884, he agreed to a rematch with Mitchell, again in Madison Square Garden. The New York arena was packed in anticipation. But as Sullivan came down the aisle toward the ring, it was obvious that he was unwell: pale, sweating, and clearly out of condition. Finally, he raised his arm and told the crowd that he could not perform, and made his way back out, to boos. The event was a financial fiasco for the promoters, and the newspapers excoriated Sullivan as a public drunkard. It was one of the low points of his career.

But Sullivan always rebounded from these disasters, as if challenged by public disapproval and the need to refill his dwindling coffers. When he could stick with it long enough, he could get himself into condition to handle any man in the ring, as he did throughout the 1880s. And the American public forgave him his transgressions, not only because he made good copy but also because Sullivan the man was so genuine.

Tales abounded of his generosity to his family and friends, as well as to the poor. He bought the rounds in public alehouses and gave money to panhandlers, old women, and children. Lithographs of Sullivan adorned homes and saloons, and idyllic images of his benevolence graced the pages of the *Police Gazette* and other publications in what scholars would call "the cult of masculinity." The most famous illustration was Charles Dana Gibson's "The Champion," which showed a powerful man in an overcoat and a top hat, cigar in his mouth, mobbed by young boys.

For many, Sullivan would be the emblematic figure of a young nation coming into its strength. "I go in to win from the very first second, and I never stop until I have won," he said, giving early voice to what remains the American sporting creed. "Win I must, and win I will, at every stage of the

"I can lick any son of a bitch in the world!" thundered **John L. Sullivan, who inaugurated the modern line of heavyweight champions and transformed the title into an American franchise.**

game."[10] When he chanced to meet Sullivan in a Manhattan hotel lobby, Ulysses S. Grant told him: "Your style of fighting, Mr. Sullivan, proves the idea I tried to put into operation during the Civil War—that is to carry the battle to the enemy and fight all the time."[11] Sullivan's career also seemed to symbolize the democratic promise—that regardless of social position, one could rise and better one's condition through action.

The Great John L. became America's first working-class, ethnic celebrity, open and unguarded in ways that no American public figure had ever been. In an age when spin and public relations were insinuating themselves into American life, Sullivan was the ultimate straight shooter. He was, he said, always "on the level." He liked to punctuate his statements with "Yours truly, John L. Sullivan," sometimes writing his name in the air.[12]

Sullivan reached the height of his public acclaim in 1887, when he visited the New York Stock Exchange and received a rousing ovation from the trading floor. He also stood in line with other White House visitors to greet President Grover Cleveland. The greatest moment of all came in summer 1887, when Sullivan went to the Boston Theater to accept a championship belt that his admirers and backers had made for him. Valued at $8,000— roughly $200,000 in today's dollars—the belt featured a shield with the flags of the United States, Ireland, and England. In diamond-encrusted letters, the shield's front read, "Presented to the Champion of Champions, John L. Sullivan, by the Citizens of the United States." It was dated July 4, 1887. The belt, fourteen-carat gold and weighing nearly thirty pounds, was almost four feet long. A crowd of more than three thousand attended, including John L.'s father and Hugh O'Brien—Boston's first Irish mayor.

A sober Sullivan stepped forward in formal wear to accept the belt, and Mayor O'Brien fastened it around Sullivan's ample waist. John L. offered his thanks and pledged his love for Boston. And then: "I remain, as ever, your devoted friend, John L. Sullivan." The band struck up a chorus of "Hail to the Chief."[13]

★

High living ensured that Sullivan would always be in need of funds, no matter what his income. In late 1887, he toured the British Isles, conducting boxing exhibitions and giving the English a look at America's version of the world champion. Some British, loyal to their bare-knuckle tradition, were slow to accept Sullivan; others wanted him to take on Charley Mitchell again. But Sullivan earned another high honor when the Prince of Wales, the future King Edward, sent his Scottish Guards with a message that he would like to meet the champion. The prince was impressed with Sullivan, who sparred for him—and asked him when he had last put up his dukes.

Early in 1888, when Sullivan was still in England, his backers met with Mitchell's to arrange a contest. Late-Victorian Britain increasingly frowned upon prizefighting, and so the fighters and their camps headed across the channel to France. On March 10, when Sullivan was visiting the cathedral at Amiens, his people rushed over to tell him that a site had been found for the battle—the estate of Baron de Rothschild in Apremont, near Chantilly—but they had to go there right away, while the baron was not at home.

The Sullivan and Mitchell camps, along with a few dozen spectators and two young American reporters who would go on to long careers—Arthur Brisbane of the *New York Sun* and Stephen Bonsal of the *New York Herald*—boarded trains for Paris and then, to throw off the authorities, disembarked at Criel and got back on. They arrived at the baron's grounds around noon, identified a plot of raised ground near the horse stables, and pitched a ring. The fight would be waged under the London Prize Ring Rules—to the finish, with bare knuckles—before about forty people plus a few of the baron's game wardens, who showed up on the estate midway through the contest and, apparently tolerant of criminal trespassing, stuck around to watch.

What they saw were two men battling the elements as much as each other. A driving rain began falling and increased in strength as the fight wore on. Sullivan, in poor condition but eager as ever, dominated the early action, scoring most of the falls, chasing Mitchell and either punching or tossing him to the turf. Mitchell jabbed at Sullivan and landed some blows of his own, but his main strategy was to tire out the champion. Sullivan's stamina, Brisbane wrote, had vanished "under the double bombardment of French champagne and American whiskey."[14]

Each time Mitchell was knocked down and carried to his corner, he shouted back defiantly at Sullivan, reminding him that the fight wasn't over. Often, he dropped to end rounds before Sullivan could do him much damage, and John L. would deride him. The fighters' partisans exhorted their men from the sidelines. "Nothing was left unsaid," Bonsal later wrote, "to make the affair as brutal and as disgusting as possible."[15]

Mitchell's ceaseless chattering and his hit-and-run tactics puzzled and infuriated Sullivan, and the conditions at Chantilly made the champion's task nearly impossible: as the rounds passed, the turf deteriorated, making footing treacherous around most of the ring. The rain came down so heavily at points that the spectators ducked under the eaves of the horse barn to take cover, but the fighters stayed at it, flailing in the slop. Early on, Sullivan hurt his right arm, which swelled purple in the wind and rain. Mitchell's body was covered with welts from the pounding of Sullivan's blows, while John L. had a bloody nose and bloody shins; Mitchell spiked him whenever they got close. By the time the downpour relented, it was too late to make any difference. Sullivan and Mitchell were imprisoned in a stew of mud.

To Bonsal, Sullivan "seemed to be fighting in a dream." By Round 32, the champion's teeth were chattering and he had developed chills. He seemed dispirited and disgusted, while Mitchell persisted in his fly-evading-the-flyswatter tactics. Four times, by mutual consent, the fighters paused to clean off their mud-caked spikes. The rounds grew longer: Round 32 lasted twenty-seven minutes, Round 35 fifteen minutes, and Round 39 thirty minutes. The two fighters spent much of these long rounds wandering around the ring, baiting each other, only rarely engaging.

Finally, after Round 39, both camps agreed to call the fight a draw. The struggle had lasted over three hours but had produced only frustration. It was the first time that Sullivan had entered a ring and failed to come out the victor, either officially or by general acclamation. In a public sense, it was as if he had lost. The result, Brisbane wrote, "was as crushing to his hopes of international championship as an actual defeat."[16] The *New York World* went further: "The secret is now in everyone's mouth. Sullivan's fighting days are finished."[17]

When Sullivan came home, things got worse.

He spent a good portion of 1888 on a long bender of public drinking and loutish conduct, and his body finally rebelled: he was stricken with what was officially deemed typhoid fever but was almost certainly exacerbated by damage from alcohol abuse. Running a high temperature, covered under blankets in the sweating regimen of the day, Sullivan was said to be near death; a priest visited his bedside. After a few tense days, he rallied. By some accounts, Sullivan's weight had reached 280 pounds before the illness; now he was down near 180. It didn't seem as though much of the old Boston Strong Boy could remain in John L.'s well-abused body.

Meantime, Richard Kyle Fox of the *Police Gazette* had created a heavyweight championship belt of his own and awarded it to his current favorite, a former millworker and national amateur sculling champion named John Killion, who fought under the name Jake Kilrain. In the rugged Kilrain, who had been watching at Chantilly, Fox seemed to have found the man who could beat Sullivan. John L. snorted that Fox's championship belt wasn't fit to put around a dog's neck, but contracts were signed in early 1889 for a summer match.

The battle's terms favored the challenger. It would be waged under the London Prize Ring Rules, with no gloves or time limits and with wrestling holds allowed (Kilrain was a skilled grappler). Though he preferred the Queensbury Rules, Sullivan would wage his most celebrated battle with bare fists, under the same standard observed by the old British champions. In fact, Sullivan versus Kilrain would be the last bare-knuckle championship fight.

★

No sooner had John L. accepted Kilrain's challenge than he resumed his hard-living ways, once again consuming heroic quantities of alcohol. By May 1889, he weighed about 240 pounds. He continued to hit the pubs after his daily exertions, which weren't very exerting, and remained bloated and in poor aerobic shape for the struggle that awaited him.

Finally, those with the champion's best interests at heart got him to hire William Muldoon, a champion Greco-Roman wrestler and physical-fitness fanatic with little tolerance for nonsense. Muldoon was a forerunner to today's hard-body gurus: his understanding of physical conditioning and nutrition was far ahead of his time. So eager was Muldoon for the challenge of getting Sullivan ready that he agreed to work for nothing if John L. didn't win.

Muldoon brought the thirty-year-old champion to his farm in Belfast, a heavily Irish mill town in western New York, on the banks of the Genesee River. He started John L. on a high-protein diet and put him to work alongside his hired hands. A man of the city through and through, Sullivan milked cows, cut wood, and tilled the earth, sweating profusely and cursing Muldoon all the while. Slowly, Sullivan regained his natural strength, and Muldoon, a one-man police state, mostly kept Sullivan away from the booze. John L. learned to hate Muldoon and his cows, which often woke him up early, but the regimen worked. Sullivan approached the eve of battle weighing 205 pounds, in condition to fight hard and long.

The contract between Sullivan and Kilrain called for the fight to take place within two hundred miles of New Orleans, for $10,000 a side. The governors of Mississippi and Louisiana insisted publicly that they wouldn't allow the fight in their states and made elaborate plans to stop it. But everyone knew that it wouldn't be stopped. Nationwide, betting on the fight—wherever and whenever it was going to take place—was massive. Western Union sent dozens of telegraphers to New Orleans to report on the event.

"The city is fighting mad," the New Orleans *Times-Picayune* reported. "Everybody had the fever and is talking Sullivan and Kilrain. Ladies discussed it in street cars, men talked and argued about it in places which had never heard pugilism mentioned."[18] The *New York Times* compared the excitement with that of a presidential election, while the *New York World* opined that Kilrain's fitness and wrestling skills would carry the day. The paper dismissed Sullivan's chances: "According to the history of all such drunkards as he, his legs ought to fail him after 20 minutes of fighting."

A day before the fight, word of the secret location leaked out: just south of Hattiesburg and 105 miles northeast of New Orleans, in Richburg, Mississippi—a hamlet that was really the private fiefdom of Colonel Charles W. Rich, a wealthy young lumberman who owned thirty thousand acres of pineland and ran a prosperous sawmill. On the night of July 7, 1889, thousands flocked to New Orleans's Northeastern Railroad station to board a fourteen-car train that became so mobbed that the police couldn't check tickets. Dozens of men climbed onto the tops of the cars, and the police couldn't get them down, even whacking their legs with nightsticks or firing their rifles into the air. Finally, around 2:30 a.m., the train set off with the men clinging to the top for the overnight journey. Another train followed behind. All told, perhaps three thousand people made the trip from New Orleans—including, some said, chorus girl Ann Livingston, John L.'s mistress, who attended disguised in men's clothes.

The two fighters and their camps were already in Richburg, where they spent the night as Rich's guests. About twenty of the colonel's laborers worked by torchlight constructing the ring out of eight-foot stakes of ash, which they hammered into the parched ground with difficulty. Then they constructed twelve tiers of bleacher seating out of fresh-cut pine, finishing at daybreak. Not long after, the trains began arriving. Undaunted by their long journey, people rushed to the clearing on Rich's property, near the railroad tracks, where the empty ring and bleachers stood. By mid-morning on July 8, the temperature had almost reached 100 degrees.

★

Shortly after 10 a.m., the opposing camps made their way through the crowd. The two contestants threw their hats into the ring in the time-honored gesture of willingness. Clad in bright green tights and white stockings, John L. struck everyone as fit and powerful. Kilrain, wearing dark tights, seemed uneasy, looking "as if he felt that there was hard work before him," a correspondent from the *New York Times* wrote. But Kilrain could take heart from his cornermen: Charley Mitchell, Sullivan's nemesis, was with him, along with two Old West legends—Bat Masterson and Luke Short. The most important man in Sullivan's corner was Muldoon.

The bout began with a slight advantage to Kilrain, who, dodging a jab from Sullivan, rushed in, seized Sullivan in a headlock, and tossed him to the ground, ending Round 1 in about fifteen seconds. Sullivan scoffed and walked back to his corner, where he would refuse to sit for the duration of the fight. In Round 2, he threw Kilrain; in the third, he knocked Jake down with a right hand behind the ear. Round 4 was the longest—fifteen minutes—and it saw Kilrain adopt Charley Mitchell's evasive tactics. As he had in France with Mitchell, Sullivan berated Kilrain to "fight like a man." In the sixth, Sullivan managed to catch up with Kilrain, land a blow to his jaw, and toss him to end the round. Kilrain's backers had their best moment in the seventh, when Jake bloodied Sullivan's ear, drawing the coveted "first blood" milestone—and prompting a flurry of cash exchanges around ringside as bettors covered their wagers. But in the eighth, Sullivan caught up with the fleeing Kilrain and knocked him off his feet to end the round.

Now Kilrain went all-in on the Mitchell philosophy, circling away from John L. and ending many rounds by taking a knee. "You're a champion, eh?" Sullivan snarled. "A champion of what?" Jake got in his blows from time to time, but John L. was the stronger man. The question was whether Sullivan could hold out in the heat against a foe who might be prepared to resist for hours. Muldoon asked him at one point how long he could keep going.

"Till tomorrow morning, if it's necessary," he answered. He spurned sitting down between rounds for the entire fight. "What the hell's the use? I only got to get right up again, ain't I?"

The rounds passed, the fighters becoming covered in red splotches and blisters from the punishing sun, as Sullivan chased and Kilrain retreated. Kilrain hoped that by staying away, he could wear the big man down. In Jake's corner, Mitchell continued to encourage this course of action, remembering Chantilly. But there were no mud puddles in Richburg.

Landing a blow and taking Kilrain into a clinch, Sullivan looked over at Mitchell and said, "I wish it was you I had in here."[19] At another point, watching Kilrain retreat yet again, Sullivan exploded: "You are a god-damned scoundrel and a cur!"[20] He kept pressing.

For some reason, someone in Sullivan's corner slipped him some whiskey mixed with tea. Coming out of his corner to begin Round 44, Sullivan vomited in the center of the ring, leading some who knew him well to joke that he had thrown up the tea but retained the whiskey. It looked as if he might have to concede the match or agree to a draw, but when Kilrain asked him if he would, John L. scoffed, "No, you loafer!"[21] He recovered almost as soon as the fit had seized him, knocking Kilrain down.

In the opposing corner, Kilrain drank whiskey steadily throughout the latter part of the battle. From Round 50 on, his cause seemed hopeless. Though he could not bring himself to quit, he began going down almost instantly at the start of each round. He was deranged with fatigue, his head lolling on his shoulders. Fear mounted that he might fight to the finish—of his life. If that happened, John L. would be deemed guilty of murder under Mississippi's anti-prizefighting law. The penalty was death by hanging.

Finally, after Round 75, a physician visited the Kilrain corner. "If you keep sending that man of yours out there, he will surely drop dead," he warned.[22] Kilrain's chief second, Mike Donovan, who had sparred with Sullivan nearly a decade earlier and recognized his talent, halted the fight before Round 76. The bout had lasted two hours and sixteen minutes, and John L. Sullivan was still champion.

The crowd rushed the ring. "Reporters' desks were splintered, fences went down, and all restrictions were swept aside," as the *New York Times* described it. Those from whom the heat had not sapped all energy began grasping for mementos: the felt hat that Sullivan had thrown into the ring was sold for $50, the buckets that held the ice water for the combatants for $25 each. Like football fans tearing down goalposts, the revelers tore into Rich's lovingly made ring posts, splinters from which were sold for $5 each. The ring ropes were cut up in similar fashion. Even the sod was gathered and taken away.

The two gladiators hustled out of Richburg to evade the malingering arm of the law. (Both would face court dates later.) Kilrain was driven away in a carriage, on the edge of delirium. He was plastered and surely dehydrated, probably had heat stroke, and had taken a two-hour beating. Sullivan boarded a train in haste. He had a near-miss with the law, in which he had to exit one train, hide in a field, and board another, but he made his way back to New Orleans, where he took a room at the Young Men's Gymnastic Club and celebrated with what must have been one of the tightest ones he ever tied on. Like an American king, he tossed cash out his window to adoring boys below.

From a distance of more than 125 years, the seventy-five rounds that the two men battled, the bare knuckles, and the hellfire temperatures mark the event as otherworldly, and closer analysis only makes Sullivan's feat more daunting.

Consider that the seventy-five rounds were fought over two hours and sixteen minutes. From those 136 minutes, subtract the thirty-second rest periods spread over seventy-four rounds (not counting the last one, after which the fight was called). That's thirty-seven minutes taken from the total, bringing it down to ninety-nine minutes of actual fighting. Spread out over seventy-five rounds, that's barely an average of a minute and fifteen seconds per round, and Round 4 notably went on for fifteen minutes, making the average for the others even shorter. But remember that the rest periods were only thirty seconds, compared with sixty seconds today. And the ninety-nine-minute figure means that, compared with our modern twelve-round fights—thirty-six minutes of fighting, maximum—Sullivan and Kilrain battled for nearly three times as long as boxers do today. And they did all this with their bare hands in withering heat.

Boxing's version of Gettysburg, the Richburg fight would enshrine Sullivan in ring annals. The bout's legendary qualities are only heightened by its taking place before the advent of film, though a handful of photos survive. The best is a long shot showing Sullivan standing over a fallen Kilrain in what is said to be the final round. We see a small but eager audience, entirely male, packed into Rich's custom-built bleachers—almost all wearing coats and hats.

Though the Richburg crowd was comparatively small, enough of what happened in the Mississippi field that day was transmitted through word of mouth and newspaper reports to make the event an epochal one. Crucial to spreading the news was the telegraph, which had become a major communications industry. By 1889, all the continents had been wired; messages sent from London could reach New York in ten minutes. Reporters on the White House press beat were even surprised to receive official requests for updates on the fight. A generation later, looking back on the America of his youth, the poet Vachel Lindsay found in the Richburg fight the herald of a new post-Victorian age of strife, energy, and individual freedom:

> When I was nine years old, in 1889,
> I sent my love a lacy Valentine.
> Suffering boys were dressed like Fauntleroys,
> While *Judge* and *Puck* in giant humor vied.
> The Gibson Girl came shining like a bride
> To spoil the cult of Tennyson's Elaine.
> Louisa Alcott was my gentle guide ...

Then ...
I heard a battle trumpet sound.
Nigh New Orleans
Upon an emerald plain
John L. Sullivan
The strong boy
Of Boston
Fought seventy-five red rounds with Jake Kilrain.[23]

In beating Kilrain, Sullivan left no question of his claim to the heavy-weight title—at least in the United States. Overseas, the question was more problematic, and Sullivan to this day is not universally regarded as the first "world" heavyweight champion because the British never recognized him. And then there was the matter of the color line.

When John L. came onto the scene, the United States had just finished withdrawing troops from the South, ending Reconstruction. What lay ahead for black Americans was a long period of retrenchment, marked by the resurgence of white supremacy in both law and deed. It would culminate in the 1896 Supreme Court decision in *Plessy v. Ferguson*, which upheld "separate but equal" public accommodations for whites and blacks. Torn apart by the Civil War, the nation had reunited in large part by emphasizing the fraternity between Northern and Southern whites and their mutual valor on the battlefield. The legacy of slavery and the question of black equality were obstacles to that concord.

Sullivan was a man of his time and milieu: he shared Irish working-class attitudes toward blacks, which were not generous. But he seemed to take it upon himself to draw a color line. As he declared in an 1892 pronouncement to challengers, he would fight any and all men "who are white. I will not fight a Negro. I never have and never shall."[24] (Though it didn't seem to bother him to fight New Zealander Herbert Slade, who was half Maori.) Sullivan's refusal to fight blacks would attain the force of precedent, one that would shape heavyweight boxing and American sports for generations.

The principal black victim of this policy was Peter Jackson of Australia, who may have been the great fighter of the age. Blessed with a marvelous physique, speed, and all-around boxing skills, Jackson sought a championship opportunity against Sullivan for years. Judging by the difficulty that John L. had with Charley Mitchell, it's a fair bet that Jackson could have beaten him. But they would never meet, and Jackson, whose picture hung on the wall in Frederick Douglass's Washington office, became the first in a long line of great athletes whose only mistake was to be born the wrong color.

★

Sullivan now turned his energies toward a career in the theater. He head-lined a melodrama titled *Honest Hearts and Willing Hands*, written espe-cially for him, in which he starred as a blacksmith who vies for the heart of "a girl under a cloud." He had no acting ability to speak of, but audiences loved him anyway, even when, as often happened, he started his soliloquies over at the beginning, whenever he was interrupted with applause.

In 1891, he agreed to a sparring exhibition with a young "dude" from San Francisco named James J. Corbett, who was lean and refined in a way that John L. could never be. The refinements, which included a pompadour hairstyle and a background working as—of all things—a bank teller, also extended to his boxing technique. Corbett excelled at the art of hitting while not getting hit. He'd gotten Sullivan to agree to the sparring session, which took place at one of the theaters where John L. was performing, only on condition that the two men wear evening clothes. This was probably gamesmanship on John L.'s part to minimize Corbett's importance; it may also have had to do with disguising John L.'s girth. While Sullivan regarded the event as a joke, Corbett marked it down to research: he unveiled some of his patented feints, where boxers fake a blow or a movement to reveal an opponent's response. Sullivan bit on every one. Afterward, Corbett told his aides that Sullivan was "made to order for me."[25]

Sullivan's profligate ways forced him to accept Corbett's challenge to de-fend his title. He could not turn down the money: $25,000, winner-take-all. The match was made for New Orleans on September 7, 1892.

It had been ten years since John L. had defeated Paddy Ryan in an "il-legal" bout. Now, thanks to him, the sport was making inroads of social acceptance. The previous year, the New Orleans city council legalized box-ing matches overseen by recognized athletic clubs. Sullivan versus Corbett would be held at New Orleans's opulent Olympic Club, under newfangled electric lights, and fought under the Queensbury Rules, with five-ounce gloves.

Approaching his thirty-fourth birthday, Sullivan could not get himself to train in the manner of the days of 1889, though he managed to cut his weight down to 212 pounds. Still, oddsmakers made him a 4–1 favorite over the twenty-six-year-old Corbett. He remained the champion of the people, and when he traveled from New York to New Orleans on a triumphant rail pilgrimage, crowds lined the way and filled train depots to get a glimpse of him. Newspapers around the country reported so heavily on the fight that one correspondent complained that they had only "scant space to give to the movements and utterances of the Presidential nominees" that year—Benjamin Harrison and Grover Cleveland.[26]

Right up to the opening bell, fans disembarked from excursion trains originating from all over the United States. More than ten thousand spectators in the jam-packed Olympic Club would see the fight, the largest crowd at that time to attend a boxing match, while thousands milled about New Orleans. Around the country, people awaited telegraph updates.

The live crowd at the Olympic Club found it hard to believe what they were seeing. From the opening rounds, Corbett's new style—hit and move, stay out of range—had Sullivan frustrated. John L. charged after Corbett and made vicious, often wild, swings but hit only air. Corbett moved on his toes, peppering Sullivan's face and midsection with left jabs and right hands and, when he judged it safe, standing in front of Sullivan and opening up with punches. One of these combinations, in Round 3, sent geysers of blood from Sullivan's face. Corbett had broken his nose. The crowd cheered Corbett for his skill and verve.

By Round 7, Sullivan was gasping for air, and his face, reddened around the eyes and with blood spurting from his nose, had become a ghastly sight. Sometimes, when taking another combination from Corbett, he would paw at his face and say, "That's a good one, Jim."[27] Considering his poor physical condition, his endurance proved remarkable. He would not quit: he rushed Corbett time and again, nearly falling from missing his punches or running into the ropes empty-handed. Corbett laughed at him.

Finally, in Round 21, Corbett made his move. Sullivan, wide open after yet another wild swing, stood defenseless in front of the challenger; this time, Corbett let him have it with a combination of lefts and rights. Sullivan fell to his knees—and then rose. Corbett unleashed another fusillade, and John L. "fell as falls an oak tree, slowly and majestically," as the *New York World*'s correspondent put it. He rolled over onto his side and tried to make it up but could not. The referee tolled ten, and John L. Sullivan was beaten at last. The Olympic Club fell silent for a few moments. Then spectators rushed the ring, flocking to Corbett, the new champion.

Sullivan's men carried him to his corner. When he came to, he waved his hand, asking for attention, and the crowd quieted. Speaking through bloody, swollen lips, Sullivan said: "All I have to say is that I came to the ring once too often, and if I had to get licked I'm glad that it was by an American. I remain yours truly, John L. Sullivan."[28]

The speech was Sullivan at his best: frank, unpretentious, appealing to the masses as one of them. It also had the sad and prophetic line—"I came to the ring once too often"—that would serve as an epitaph for most of his successors. Later that evening, Sullivan wept for the loss of his title. "What has happened? What'll become of me?" he said to no one in particular.[29] That lament would also echo down through the years, capturing the despair that others felt when the crown—which brought with it an identity and a purpose—was no longer theirs.

The New Orleans fight captivated the nation. In San Francisco, crowds danced in the streets to celebrate Corbett's win. As the *New York Herald* observed, "The odium which rested upon the prize ring and the majority of its exponents a decade or two ago, because of the disgraceful occurrences connected with it, have in a measure been removed, until now the events on hand are of national and international importance."[30] John L. never entered the prize ring again, though he continued to give sparring exhibitions and threatened occasionally to make a comeback. He remained a commanding figure in retirement, spending money as quickly as he made it, drinking to excess and sometimes almost to death, and combining magnanimity with volatility. Eventually, the money ran out: he was forced to declare bankruptcy in 1902 and even to pawn his beloved championship belt, which disappeared forever; it was purportedly melted down at a U.S. mint. A jewelry manufacturer designed an elegant facsimile, which resides today in the Smithsonian's National Museum of American History.

"It is a dollar to a nickel that he is known to more people in this country than George Washington," the *Police Gazette* wrote of Sullivan in 1905.[31] That year, he showed that he had a few thunderbolts left in him. First, in March, he staged an exhibition bout with a credible young fighter, Jim Mc-Cormick, in a Grand Rapids, Michigan, opera house. Looking grotesque at 273 pounds, the forty-six-year-old Sullivan wheezed after McCormick in the first round, with little success. But in the second, he landed the famous right—and McCormick went down for the count. Fans broke chairs and other obstructions in an effort to mob the old champion, as if it were 1889. It was essentially an act of magic, a dramatic illustration of the maxim, common to sports and showbiz, that great ones can sometimes tap their reserves for a final deed.

Whether it was coincidence or the momentum he felt after beating Mc-Cormick, John L. shocked observers again days later by announcing that he would never take another drink—and he never did. He eventually became a temperance lecturer, giving a popular talk whose title evoked the journey that he and others would take: "From Glory to Gutter to God." Enormous of girth, the lion of appetite and impulse now preaching restraint, he made his final public appearance in 1916, at Madison Square Garden, before the heavyweight championship fight between Jess Willard and Frank Moran. The occasion was later memorialized in a George Bellows painting.

Two legends persist about his passing in February 1918: that he died penniless and that the ground had to be dynamited to make way for his body. In fact, he left a very modest estate, but the second legend was true. The ground was so frozen that day that it had to be blasted apart. One didn't need to be a literary student to recognize the aptness of the metaphor.

"Just as John L. would have liked it," said Jake Kilrain on that frigid day.[32] The recipient of Sullivan's bitterest efforts in the ring, Jake was one of John L.'s pallbearers.

★

If John L. originated the archetype of heavyweight champion as warrior king, James J. Corbett, the new champion, created an archetype of his own. Corbett was John L.'s opposite in every respect: where Sullivan brawled, Corbett boxed; where Sullivan gladly accepted punishment, confident that he could land a finishing blow, Corbett avoided punches; where Sullivan lumbered, Corbett danced and moved. Sullivan never had a boxing lesson, while Corbett studied and honed his craft like a dedicated musician. Corbett became the pioneer of modern scientific boxing, an approach relying on strategy, speed, and defense. The sophistication extended beyond the ring: Corbett was fastidious about his appearance, especially clothes, in which his tastes ran to the extravagant. After beating Sullivan, he embarked on his own theatrical tour, in which he starred in a play called *Gentleman Jack*. Corbett went on to forge careers in two fields closely linked in his day: prizefighting and the popular stage. He would be a working actor all his life.

Though he enjoyed a long career as a matinee idol, Corbett never won anything like the acclaim that Sullivan had enjoyed. His more subtle style, both in and out of the ring, seemed to suggest snobbery. Corbett's biggest problem was one that would face some of his successors. As he put it years later: "You can't destroy a public hero without it being resented."[33]

But Gentleman Jim did achieve a boxing feat that eluded John L.: winning recognition across the Atlantic as the one and only heavyweight champion. He did it in 1894, when he needed just three rounds to knock out John L.'s old rival, Charley Mitchell, the recognized British champion. The British, always hedging when it came to Sullivan, granted their blessing to Corbett. For a century afterward, the title would remain almost exclusively an American property.

Corbett spent his title reign more devoted to theatrical pursuits than to fighting. But on March 17, 1897, when he defended his title against Englishman Bob Fitzsimmons in Carson City, Nevada, the bout still attracted enormous interest. Enoch J. Rector of the Kinetoscope Exhibition Company shot the event on nearly 11,000 feet of 63 mm nitrate film stock—and the finished product, over one hundred minutes long, became the first feature-length film. In its surviving portions, the film, with its flickering images and pale hues, its frames hopping and skipping, cannot convey the intensity of the battle. For most of the bout, Corbett retained control: his defensive skills left Fitzsimmons little target, and his pinpoint punching made the challenger's face a crimson mess, even spattering blood onto Fitzsimmons's wife, Rose, who watched from the corner. The Carson City bout marked the first time that women attended a prizefight in substantial numbers. The promoter even set aside a special box for them, cordoned off from the men.

In Round 14, with Rose's exhortations in his ears—some at ringside heard her yell, "Hit him in the slats, Bob!"[34]—Fitzsimmons sidestepped and planted a left to Corbett's belly. On the film, his fist seems to linger there for a moment, as if he is twisting a dagger in. Corbett goes down, writhing on one knee, holding his midsection, gasping for air as he tries to rise. But he cannot, and the referee counts him out. Fitzsimmons, the new champion, raises his arms in triumph, and the film dissolves.

Later, a physician described the knockout blow as landing in the "solar plexus," a fancy anatomical term for the pit of the stomach. After a *New York Journal* reporter used the phrase in his story, the "solar-plexus punch" entered the American vernacular.

Rector's film of the Corbett–Fitzsimmons fight became a sensation. It was shown in theaters, high class and low, across the United States and around the world. Just as they had for the fight in Carson City, women came out to see the film in the United States, despite considerable outcry at their watching nearly naked gladiators—especially Corbett, who wore trunks that left both buttocks exposed.

An ex-champion at thirty-one, Corbett was despondent at his defeat, especially to a man whom he considered his inferior in the ring. But not just anyone could land such a punch on the master boxer. Bob Fitzsimmons may not have been the ring scientist that Corbett was, but he possessed guile and craft that came with long years of battles at varying weights. Unlike Gentleman Jim, he punched with power to bring down much larger men. In fact, he fought Corbett at just 158 pounds—making him a middleweight, a division of which he had already been champion. Fitzsimmons would be the last British heavyweight champion for 101 years (he was born in Cornwall but spent most of his early life in New Zealand). Years later, he became champion of the new light heavyweight class, making him boxing's first three-division titleholder. His middle name, Prometheus, was well chosen: he seemed gifted with a power beyond his body.

They called Fitzsimmons "Ruby Robert" because of his red hair and freckled complexion, but one of his admirers, the American poet Edgar Lee Masters, wrote that much of this was exaggeration. Fitzsimmons's hair was red, yes, but not especially so, and as for the freckles that supposedly covered him, they were barely in evidence. One famous feature about Fitz, however, Masters confirmed: his incredibly broad shoulders, built up through long years of working in a smithy. They sat atop his narrow frame and spindly legs like one of those photos where one puts a head onto the cutout frame of another's body. Fitz's arms, Masters wrote, were like "long symmetrical cables of muscle, like a python's body, like the legs of a large man."[35] Masters, who prided himself on making a lifelong study of pugilists, believed that Fitz was "a fighter with no superior" and "a wonder in every way."[36]

Wonder or not, Fitz was thirty-five when he beat Corbett, and he wouldn't hold the title long. After taking the better part of two years off to play theaters in *The Honest Blacksmith*, Fitzsimmons was coaxed back into the ring to defend his title against James J. Jeffries, a young and burly brawler whom he felt sure he could outbox. "The bigger they are, the harder they fall," Fitz liked to say.[37]

Fitz and Jeffries met at the New Coney Island Sporting Club in New York on June 9, 1899. Outweighed 205 to 167, Fitzsimmons dished out severe punishment to his challenger but could not put away the bigger man. Jeffries seemed impervious to pain, and he had boundless stamina. He caught up with the thirty-seven-year-old champion in Round 11, froze him with a left hook, and then put over a demolishing right hand. The former blacksmith crashed to the canvas and took the ten-count.

★

The arrival of Jeffries, just twenty-four years old, heralded a new chapter in the heavyweight story, at the dawn of a new century. Fitzsimmons and Corbett were well into their thirties now, and the retired Sullivan, though only forty-one, had been called Old John L. almost from the moment he climbed out of the ring in New Orleans. All three champions carried the banner of the Victorian age, even if their public careers symbolized the waning of that age. The evolution of the heavyweight championship from an underground, quasi-mythical title to a commercial property was part of a social revolution, one in which working-class passions—amusement parks like the one on Coney Island, major league baseball, vaudeville, prizefighting—would create a new popular culture in America.

The twentieth century beckoned, and it seemed to hold great promise for boxing. But in the first two decades of the 1900s, boxing would be challenged from every quarter: legal restrictions, allegations of fixed fights and gambling influences, the advent of a global war, and reformers' efforts to stamp out the sport once and for all. Soon enough, boxing would face its ultimate existential crisis: a black heavyweight champion.

PARIAH

America had never seen an Independence Day like July 4, 1910. Nearly half a century after Grant met Lee at Appomattox, the nation would mark a different battle for supremacy—one confined to a boxing ring. In Reno, Nevada, where boxing was proudly legal, James J. Jeffries, a white man, and Jack Johnson, a black man, would fight for the heavyweight championship of the world. It was billed as the Battle of the Century, and to the American public, that description wasn't hype.

Johnson, thirty-two, had won the title two years earlier with a knockout over the Canadian Tommy Burns in Sydney, Australia. Even before its outcome was known, the bout had smashed a precedent established by John L. Sullivan: that black fighters were not to contend for the heavyweight title. Mixed-race contests at lower weights were permissible but not at heavyweight—not when the title had become a symbol of American masculinity. Giving blacks a chance at the prize might send disturbing messages about equality, stir up racial passions, and cause social turmoil, the thinking went. But the money had been too good for Burns to pass up, so he conceded to meet Johnson in the ring. Fourteen rounds later, he had been pounded to a pulp, and a black man was heavyweight champion.

Burns's defeat reminded many whites, even if only subconsciously, of another reason they had opposed interracial heavyweight title bouts: the unspoken fear that the black fighter might win—despite the official line that whites were superior in athletics, as in every other area. In addition to their mental deficits, it was believed, blacks lacked courage. They had a "yellow streak." Yet whites also feared that blacks might hold unfair advantages—their primitive, thicker skulls, some maintained, could shield them from white fighters' punches. Whatever the contradictions of white supremacist logic, the resolution had been plain: a black man must not get near the heavyweight title. Now Burns had gone and ruined everything.

But perhaps the blow would have been softened had the black champion not been a man, like Jack Johnson, so willing to violate social and racial decorum—flaunting his wealth and a sensuous lifestyle, gleefully mocking white fighters in the ring, and, most of all, openly consorting with white women, an act of practically insurrectionary bravado. For someone like this to hold the heavyweight title left many whites feeling as if the world had been turned upside down. Some whites wanted Johnson dead; almost all wanted him defeated.

Thus, from the moment Johnson won the title, calls went up for a white fighter to take it back. Leading the charge was the novelist Jack London, who had watched from ringside in Sydney as Johnson humiliated Burns. Calling the fight a "hopeless slaughter," London concluded his report with an appeal that would echo across America: "But one thing now remains. Jim Jeffries must now emerge from his alfalfa farm and remove that golden smile from Jack Johnson's face. Jeff, it's up to you. The White Man must be rescued."[1] After a year of hesitation, the long-retired Jeffries had heeded the call.

No wonder, then, that extra trains were steaming daily into the small desert city—population just eleven thousand in 1910—where hotel rooms, meals, and all other essentials were soon in short supply. People slept on park benches, in cars, and in poolrooms. Pickpockets, grifters, and common criminals ran free.

Hundreds of reporters were in Reno. Columnists for major metropolitan newspapers wrote tirelessly about the fight, most viewing it as a struggle to confirm white racial supremacy. Black newspapers like the *Chicago Defender* saw the battle as crucial, too, but hoped for a different result. On Independence Day, crowds milled around newspaper buildings and telegraph offices in cities across the country, eager for updates. It was the most widely followed sporting event in American history up to that time. The heavyweight championship had captivated the nation before, but until Jack Johnson came along, the title had never seemed so fraught with meaning.

★

It was no wonder that London and millions of others would look to Jim Jeffries to rescue the title from Johnson. In 1910, Jeffries's image was that of the unconquered gladiator. If anyone could deliver America from the stain of a black champion, he could.

Jeffries was born in 1875 in Carroll, Ohio, and moved to California when still a boy. His schooling days ended as a teenager, and he went to work in the Temecula Copper Mines, where he became the camp wrestling champion. He also worked as a fireman on the Santa Fe Railroad and as a boilermaker at the Lacey Manufacturing Company. He didn't take up boxing until age twenty, but his size and strength were impossible to ignore: standing six foot two and weighing about 220 pounds, thick and muscled with a body covered with hair, Jeffries would come to be known as the California Grizzly Bear. He caught the notice of Billy Delaney, Jim Corbett's trainer, and Delaney brought him to William Brady, Corbett's manager. Big Jeff, as many called him, got a job in the Corbett training camp, helping the champ prepare for his battle with Fitzsimmons.

Brady took Jeffries under his managerial wing, and the youngster won all his fights, though his crudeness concerned his handlers. Eventually, Jeffries developed his famous crouching style: bent at the waist, head tucked under his left shoulder, left arm extended out in front of him, "like the jibboom of a clipper ship," Corbett remembered.[2] The crouch complemented Jeffries's other assets: sledgehammer punching power, bottomless strength and stamina, and an indomitable fighting will. It was too much for Fitzsimmons in June 1899 on Coney Island, where the title changed hands.

Jeffries proved a fighting champion. In November 1899, he put his title on the line against Tom Sharkey, a rugged former sailor. Their twenty-five-round battle on Coney Island became the first boxing match filmed indoors with motion-picture cameras. Murderously hot movie lights hung directly over the ring, close enough for Jeffries and Sharkey to touch; the lights singed their hair, and both started going bald shortly afterward. It felt like "a ball of fire on my head," Jeffries said.[3] His corner gave him champagne and put a block of ice against his head to cool him down. Some in the crowd passed out from the heat, while inside the ring, Jeffries and Sharkey went at it with a savagery rarely equaled. After twenty-five rounds, referee George Siler raised Jeffries's hand and declared him the winner on points.

In May 1900, Jeffries gave his former boss, Corbett, a chance to regain the title, and Gentleman Jim put on the performance of his life before seven thousand spectators packed into a Coney Island firetrap called the Seaside Athletic Club. Fighting as masterfully as he had against John L. Sullivan in New Orleans, Corbett boxed and moved, lacing Jeffries about the eyes with slashing combinations. His footwork amazed ringside observers, as time and again, he left Jeffries lunging. The crowd, puffing cigarettes or cigars so that the ring was only dimly visible through clouds of smoke, filled the aisles in violation of every known fire ordinance.

With a few rounds to go in the twenty-five-rounder, Corbett's old title was within his grasp. But sitting on his stool before the twenty-third round, Corbett heard the taunts from fans and from Jeffries's corner that he was a coward for refusing to fight toe to toe.

"I'm going to mix with him this time," he told his men. "I'll show them I can fight as well as box."[4] They begged him not to.

Jeffries cornered him and needed only one punch, a left hook. Corbett went down, his head heavily striking the canvas flooring. He could not beat the referee's count. Gentleman Jim had proved more valiant in defeat than he had ever been in victory, but his near-miss engendered a long line of former heavyweight champions who tried in vain to regain their lost titles.

Corbett–Jeffries was the third title fight held on Coney Island in a year, but it would be the last. Later in 1900, the New York state legislature passed, and Governor Theodore Roosevelt signed, a repeal of the short-lived Horton Law, which had permitted prizefighting under strict conditions. The locus of the sport shifted west, to California, where anti-boxing laws had long been on the books but were rarely enforced.

Now fighting closer to home, Jeffries continued his dominance. He even gave his two predecessors second chances. The thirty-seven-year-old Corbett got his in 1903, but this time Jeff blasted him out in just ten rounds at Mechanics' Pavilion in San Francisco. It was Corbett's last fight. The previous year, at the Arena in San Francisco, Jeffries gave the forty-year-old Fitzsimmons another shot. A legend persists that Fitz "loaded" his gloves for this fight—perhaps with collodion, a viscous solution used in everything from photographic film to surgical dressings. The former champion sliced apart Jeffries's face, but Jeffries remained steadfast under the assault. As the older man slowed, he closed the distance and cut Fitz down again, this time in the eighth round.

Men of Jeffries's generation considered him the greatest fighter of all time. But he didn't capture the national imagination as John L. or, in a different way, Corbett had. He was the best, and people knew it; this was all.

Still unbeaten in 1905, Jeffries announced his retirement and declared that the winner of a fight that he would referee in Reno between Marvin Hart, a top heavyweight contender, and Jack Root, a former light heavyweight titleholder, would be the new champion. Jeffries held no authority to make such investitures, but neither did anyone else; outside the city athletic clubs, there were no boxing regulatory bodies.

Hart knocked Root out in the twelfth round, and, true to his pledge, Jeffries raised Hart's arm and declared him the new king of the heavyweights. Most Americans didn't accept Hart as champion, though. To them, Jeff still held the office.

But Jeffries was serious about retiring. He settled down on his ranch and farm in Burbank, ran a saloon near downtown Los Angeles, got married, and gained one hundred pounds. The years passed. Except for refereeing fights, he stayed out of the ring. The heavyweight division would have to work out its destiny without him.

Few remaining white heavyweights on the scene regretted Big Jeff's departure; they had either been beaten already by the champion or, like Hart, saw an opportunity to rise in his absence. And Hart himself owned a disputed victory over the only other unconquered challenger, who happened to be a black man: Jack Johnson of Galveston, Texas. Johnson had been agitating for a title fight for years but was still coming into his own as a fighter in 1905, when Jeffries walked away. He had developed a skillful defensive style. His mastery of tactics, including blocking and slipping blows, as well as his artful feinting, made him confounding to hit. Johnson did not always please the fight crowd, which wanted more action, but his opponents saw his ability.

In setting his sights on the heavyweight title, Johnson chose not to acknowledge the color line: perhaps if he ignored it, others would, too. Impatient, he had even confronted Jeffries in a San Francisco saloon, demanding that the champion give him a chance. Jeffries refused. "You've got no name," he said, skirting the racial issue, "and we wouldn't draw flies." But then he offered Johnson a consolation. "I'll tell you what I will do," Jeff said. "I'll go downstairs to the cellar with you and lock the door from the inside. The one who comes out with the key will be the champ." Johnson scoffed, doubting that Jeffries was serious.

"I am," the champ said, "and I'll do it right now."[5]

"I ain't no cellar fighter," Johnson said and walked out.[6] Or so goes the story.

★

The second child and first son of Henry and Tina Johnson, both former slaves, Arthur John Johnson was born in Galveston on March 31, 1878, the year after the last federal troops left the defeated South, bringing an end to Reconstruction. Galveston was then known as the Wall Street of the South.

Famous for its stately mansions and scenic beauty, the city was the nation's second-richest, per capita, in 1900—but that year, the city was hit by a massive hurricane that remains the deadliest in American history: death-toll estimates ranged between six and twelve thousand. Henry Johnson lost his home, as did countless others, but his family somehow made it through the storm and its aftermath.

Though he happened to be at home when the great hurricane hit, Jack Johnson was already well into the roaming life that he would lead to the end of his days. He had long dreamed of distant adventures. Until he was an old man, Johnson told stories about himself, many of them sheer invention, others distortions of real events. Determining the veracity of anything he said requires secondary sources. One of his favorite tales was how, at twelve, he left Galveston to travel as a stowaway on trains up to New York City to meet one of his boyhood heroes, Steve Brodie, a stunt artist famous for surviving a jump off the Brooklyn Bridge. Along the way, Johnson claimed many other exploits, including a battle with a giant shark on a fishing boat. He started boxing as a teenager in Galveston, and as he honed his ability, he began to make money as a prizefighter, both in the port city and elsewhere—Chicago, Denver, Oakland, Los Angeles, San Francisco, Philadelphia. Records of his earliest fights are fragmentary or lost, but it is generally accepted that he began his professional career at nineteen, in 1897—the same year that Bob Fitzsimmons knocked out Johnson's first ring idol, Jim Corbett, in Carson City, Nevada, to win the heavyweight championship.

American race relations were at a low ebb in these years. Johnson was part of the first generation of blacks who were born free but who came of age at a time of racial retrenchment, when the white South had reasserted itself. After the pullout of federal troops, old Confederates took control of statehouses and local governments, imposing literacy tests and poll taxes to disenfranchise blacks at the voting booth. Blacks were abandoned by the federal government to a culture of violent intimidation and segregation.

By the turn of the century, black voices were stirring. The nation's most prominent black citizen was Booker T. Washington, a former slave who had risen to become an educator and founder of the Tuskegee Institute. Washington's gospel of black self-help urged blacks to prioritize education and economic advancement over social and political equality. Other voices challenged Washington's strategy of accommodation, most prominently W. E. B. DuBois. "We claim for ourselves every single right that belongs to a freeborn American, political, civil and social," DuBois wrote. "And until we get these rights we will never cease to protest and assail the ears of

America."[7] Black anger increased as lynching in the South and elsewhere became a national scourge—though many whites didn't see it that way. Among the most popular postage items were postcards containing photos of lynchings from around the country, often accompanied by friendly notes on the back. Only in 1908 did the postmaster general ban "lynching cards" from the U.S. mail.

The year 1908 would be momentous for another reason: Jack Johnson would get his chance to fight for the heavyweight title, against Canadian Tommy Burns, who had won the title from Marvin Hart. When Burns, whose real name was Noah Brusso, beat Hart, few respected his claim on the title—especially since Burns, at five foot seven and barely 180 pounds, was the shortest heavyweight champion in history. So Burns took his disputed crown around the world, beating national champions in Britain, France, Ireland, and Australia and winning genuine, if grudging, recognition as the world champion.

But Burns was a hounded man: the thirty-year-old Johnson was now recognized as the outstanding challenger, black or white. And he was tired of waiting. He took matters into his own hands, joining Burns on his world tour. Wherever the white champion went, the black challenger followed, goading him for a match. Johnson's taunts infuriated Burns, who considered him insolent and vowed that he would never agree to a match. But in the next breath, Burns named his price: $30,000, more money than any boxer had ever made for one fight. He figured that no promoter would pay it.

When an Australian sports entrepreneur, Hugh D. McIntosh—he was called "Huge Deal" McIntosh—came up with the money, Burns was cornered and agreed to terms. The bout was held in Sydney, on Boxing Day, December 26, 1908, when about twenty thousand people came out to Rushcutter's Bay, many arriving on Christmas night and sleeping outside the arena. Though the hostility between the combatants might have created a tense atmosphere, the crowd was well behaved throughout, and the fight gave little cause for acting up. It was among the most one-sided sporting events ever held.

Johnson tormented Burns from the opening bell, dropping the champion in the bout's opening seconds with an uppercut. In the second round, he sent Tommy down with a right. By the fourth, the men were jabbering furiously at each other. Johnson ridiculed Burns's efforts at every turn. "C'mon, Tommy! Swing your right!" he called out.[8] He pointed to his midsection and dared Burns to hit him there—in part to defuse the myth that black fighters couldn't take punches to the body. As the rounds passed, he mocked and denigrated his white foe.

"Poor, poor Tommy," Johnson jeered, "who taught you to hit? Your mother? You a woman?"

"Poor little Tommy, who told you you were a fighter?" Burns could do next to nothing against his black challenger.

After thirteen rounds, Burns's jaw had swelled to nearly twice its size, his mouth was bleeding profusely, and his eyes were closing. In the four-teenth, Johnson beat Burns mercilessly until the champion collapsed to the canvas. The police ordered the fight stopped, and Jack Johnson became heavyweight champion of the world. Johnson's moment of triumph was cut from the fight film after its early screenings, probably to spare the feelings of white audiences. The surviving film concludes just as Burns is about to fall for the final time.

So it had happened: a black man claimed a title that had become synony-mous with national vitality. It was bad enough that Johnson had punished Burns so, but he had taunted him as well. Perhaps most troubling of all was Johnson's persistent smile. Something about it seemed to suggest doom. That's what Jack London, covering the fight for the *New York Herald*, saw as he sat at ringside in Sydney and penned his notorious appeal to Jeffries and the white race.

Johnson considered his victory the culmination of a life's ambition, but he soon found out that others wouldn't share in his joys, even in his old hometown. Galveston canceled a parade in his honor when it became known that he was traveling with Hattie McClay, a white prostitute whom he had not married but called "Mrs. Johnson"—an honorific he gave to others over the years, some his wife, some not. Johnson had a taste for prostitutes, or, as they were often called then, "sporting women." He was at home among them, as he was a "sport" himself—dressing in the finest clothes, frequenting nightclubs and brothels, enjoying fine food and liquor, always seeking a good time. Johnson lived in a style that, in those more socially conservative times, would have been hotly controversial for a white man. For a black man, it was a national scandal, made worse by Johnson's refusal to be discreet. Throughout his years in the public eye, as he traveled the country on vaudeville tours and drove glamorous cars at high speeds, he often drew the attention of the law.

In one story—probably more of a folktale—Johnson was pulled over for speeding in a Southern town. The policeman told him that his fine would be $50 and was surprised to receive a $100 bill from the champion. "Keep the change," Johnson said, "'cause I'm coming back just as fast as I went through."[9]

Johnson was no apostle of Booker T. Washington's: he saw no reason to defer to white sensibilities. In his view, he was an American man and had his rights, regardless of the color of his skin. Yet he was hardly a DuBois exemplar: the idea of a life spent in political engagement for the progress of others held no appeal for him. DuBois and Washington agreed that a black man in the public eye had broader responsibilities to the race. Johnson didn't think so. "I have found no better way of avoiding racial prejudice," he wrote, "than to act in my relations with people of other races as if prejudice did not exist."[10] Individualism was his creed.

Johnson's disregard for social mores made him more hated by whites than he would otherwise have been, and his choice of white women as lovers touched the fault line of the American social order. Many blacks admired his fearlessness, and how could they not? Here he was, insisting on his right to live as he wished in a remarkably hostile racial climate, with no public allies, and at genuine risk to his safety. Some blacks felt that Johnson was at least partly to blame for the hatred he aroused; he didn't have to be so provocative, they reasoned, and they resented his rejection of black women.

However they viewed him, blacks understood that Johnson had become the most famous colored man in America and a source of torment to whites. If nothing else, they could see the cracks in the white order through the mirror that Johnson held up. And the mirror was never more reflective than when it came time for Johnson to face Jim Jeffries. Demand for the fight built inexorably, a sporting version of the Irrepressible Conflict.

★

Jeffries insisted that he was through with the ring. He wouldn't come back, he said, to fight Johnson or anyone else. Find another hitter.

They tried. Johnson took on several white challengers in 1909 without incident—at least until October, in Colma, California, when he fought the middleweight champion, Stanley Ketchel. The two men were friends, and Ketchel, known as the Michigan Assassin, was a draw at the gate, a lethal puncher and colorful personality. In fact, he was something like a white Jack Johnson outside of the ring, charismatic and driven by appetites for women and good times he couldn't always control.

Johnson outweighed Ketchel by thirty-five pounds and toyed with him for most of the fight, even holding him up when he was hurt. He knocked Ketchel down in the second and sixth rounds, yet he seemed to be holding back—probably because the two men had agreed to extend the fight for the full twenty-round distance, since films of a longer fight would be more of a draw in movie theaters. But in the twelfth round, Ketchel got other ideas: seeing an opening, he uncorked his right, and Johnson went down. Everyone in the outdoor amphitheater rose to his feet as Johnson pushed himself up in time to beat the count.

Ketchel charged in, setting himself to throw another right, but before he could, Johnson nailed him with a right uppercut that sent him to the canvas on his back. Ketchel collapsed before Johnson could hit him with a following left, and the force of his blows carried Johnson across the ring, where he fell over Ketchel's prostrate form. The referee tolled the fatal ten over the challenger, who lay motionless, arms spread out.

What really happened between Johnson and Ketchel remains uncertain. The widely accepted story is that the fight was a double-cross gone wrong: that Ketchel had agreed to let Johnson "carry" him for the full twenty rounds but couldn't resist when he saw an opening. Other accounts suggest that a twelfth-round knockout was always the prearranged plan—meaning that the fight was a fraud—but that Ketchel had told Johnson to knock him out for real when the time came, since he doubted his ability to play-act. Whatever the truth was, Ketchel paid the price: it took several minutes to revive him.

By the time Johnson fought Ketchel, Jim Jeffries could feel the clamor building around the country. Letters kept pouring in from people he had never met, urging him to get into training. His country needed him. It was a patriotic duty. Most of all, it was a racial duty. As the black champion vanquished his white challengers—flashing his detested grin, full of gold teeth—the vise tightened.

Jeffries had become the Great White Hope. The phrase endures as a metaphor in American culture, but in Jeffries, it was made flesh. Once, he had been as great a fighter as the ring had seen; now, he had to be something larger, something transcendent. It would be difficult to find a man less suited for the role.

In December 1909, in Hoboken, New Jersey, just across the river from New York—where even meeting to discuss boxing matches was illegal—contracts were signed for a fight, to be held on July 4, 1910, in San Francisco.

Johnson–Jeffries marked the formal entry onto the boxing stage of Missouri-born George Lewis Rickard, known as "Tex," for his adopted state. Rickard had been a cattle rancher in Texas, a gold prospector in the Klondike, and the proprietor of the famous Northern Saloon in Nome, Alaska, where, as the dealer of faro games, he earned a reputation for being as forthright as one could be in his line of work. He was well-known to adventurers and gamblers but not to the general public: the Hoboken event made the name of this unheralded promoter who had managed to outmaneuver more established rivals. Rickard secured agreements with both fighters for a $101,000 purse to be split 60–40 in favor of the winner, plus two-thirds of the film rights. And he threw in a $10,000 cash bonus for each man. The figures were so far above what Tommy Burns had commanded in Sydney in 1908 that they staggered the imagination. Rickard would become boxing's first great promoter.

The Hoboken announcement sparked national celebrations. At last, whites would have their chosen representative in the ring against Johnson and what Jack London called his "golden smile"—and on the nation's birthday, no less. Even the choice of referee became steeped in symbolism. Rickard asked Arthur Conan Doyle, a known fight fan, to officiate, but Sherlock Holmes's creator declined, pleading other commitments. By some accounts, Rickard even asked President William Howard Taft to do the honors. Finally, Rickard named himself referee.

The promoter began constructing an open-air arena out of yellow pine. But three weeks before the fight, disaster struck. California governor James Gillett faced pressure from reformers to cancel the bout from the moment the contract was signed. One campaign delivered a million postcards to the governor's office, reading: STOP THE FIGHT: THIS IS THE TWENTIETH CENTURY.[11] Gillett held out for a time, but when a New York congressman told him that he would lose the Pan-American Exposition for San Francisco if the fight went on there, the governor told Rickard to take his fight and get lost.

Undaunted, Rickard packed up. It wasn't as if he had many alternate sites to choose from. The only real option was Nevada, the most permissive state in the union where prizefighting was concerned. Rickard chose Reno, for its superior rail transport—major East and West Coast train lines ran through the desert city. He ordered his unfinished stadium disassembled and transported. The fighters and their camps followed.

Jim Jeffries faced a daunting task. By the time he stepped into the ring against Johnson, he would be thirty-five years old—and six years removed from his last fight. Johnson was only three years younger but was in his fighting prime. And Jeffries first had to go about the agonies of slimming down and getting himself back into fighting shape. He weighed more than three hundred pounds when he began training.

Through Herculean efforts, he got himself down to 227, and but for his encroaching baldness, he looked like the Jeff of old. But his mind wasn't right, and the insiders in his training camp knew it. Shy and intense, Jeffries had always fled the limelight, but now, under public pressure that few

American men outside the presidency had experienced, he became as congenial as a porcupine. He was short with reporters and visitors; he seemed consumed with agitation. It may have been a dawning realization of what he faced in the ring against Johnson and the cumulative toll of being the White Hope, chosen by the multitude to perform a deed of almost spiritual significance—and sensing that he could not deliver.

Johnson, meanwhile, seemed unperturbed. At his training quarters, the champion entertained observers not just with sparring but also with music, comedy routines, jokes, and banter. His playfulness bewildered white reporters, who fell back on their stereotypes of cheerful darkies, unable to appreciate that Johnson faced even greater pressure than Jeffries: he had not only to redeem the black race but also to contend with the racist insults in the newspapers and a regular stream of death threats. He laughed them off but kept a pistol in his pocket and other guns near his bedside. Outside his camp, Johnson posted an armed guard.

Through the magic of the telegraph, newspapers promised instant or nearly instant fight reports. Leading the way was the *Reno Gazette*, which would provide fight bulletins outside its offices and rush out a late-afternoon edition. Around the country, crowds waited for similar dispatches. Even Booker T. Washington, who disliked Jack Johnson, couldn't ignore the fight: at the Tuskegee Institute, he installed a special telegraph to get updates.

★

The gates to Rickard's arena opened at noon, and people pushed their way in, quickly removing their coats in the July heat, which made the pine-board seating sizzle. More women came out than for any previous fight, many wearing colorful hats. On the arena's west end, about thirty feet from ringside, nine motion-picture cameras would film the fight. The prefight ceremonies seemed to stretch on forever, but finally the ring was cleared. Just before 2:30, well behind schedule, Jeffries made his way to the ring. Johnson followed.

"Cold feet, Johnson!" some yelled, thinking his late arrival symbolic.

"Now you will get it, you black coward!"[12]

A photograph of Jeffries climbing into the ring shows the former champion wearing a stricken expression. Other images show his body clenched, his face severe. By contrast, Johnson was relaxed and smiling. He even applauded with the rest of the crowd when Jeffries was announced. He wore light blue trunks with an American flag as his belt. Jeffries wore purple trunks, also with an American flag. Despite the all-American imagery, the two combatants agreed to waive the prefight handshake, a hallmark of sportsmanship in boxing. That alone made clear that Johnson–Jeffries was not like other fights.

In what resembled a chain of former presidents attending an inaugural, all the past heavyweight champions were in attendance. John L. Sullivan was covering the fight for the *New York Times*, while Jim Corbett had been busy training Jeffries and would be in his corner for the battle. Bob Fitzsimmons and Tommy Burns sat at ringside. The only heavyweight champions not working the fight or watching it were in the ring waging it.

Jeffries moved out to face the champion at the opening bell. They sparred so cautiously that some shouted from ringside that they were carrying each other for the motion pictures. Both smiled, but it was the last time Jeffries would do so.

He could not work Johnson the way he had worked other men: when he tried to get inside, Johnson expertly tied him up, showing no difficulty in matching Jeffries's vaunted physical strength. Worse, as Jeff moved in, Johnson clipped him with short, straight lefts and then, in the clinches, hammered Jeffries with right uppercuts. A common sequence in the film shows the two men walking around the ring close together, locking each other's arms. Rickard made no motion to break these clinches, the way a modern referee would. He mostly stood away from the action, hands on hips, the most passive referee who ever worked a championship fight. The clinching intervals, which took up large portions of the early rounds, were interrupted only by the sight of Jeffries's head snapping back as Johnson nailed him with another uppercut. Johnson stifled Jeffries at every turn—out-feinting, out-blocking, out-clinching, and out-punching him—but his mastery, combined with the older man's impotence, made for a dreary spectacle, except for the banter.

"All right, Jim, I'll love you if you want me to," Johnson said, when Jeffries clinched.[13]

"He wants to fight a little, Jim!" Corbett called out to Jeffries from the corner.

"You bet I do," said Johnson. Corbett kept up a stream of commentary, convinced that he could rattle Johnson, but nothing worked. Jeffries stayed mostly silent, but that didn't spare him from the champion's observations.

"C'mon, Mr. Jeff," the champion prodded. "Let me see what you got. Do something, man. This is for the championship."[14]

In the fourth round, the Jeffries legions, in Reno and across the United States, found cause for hope. Jeffries landed a left, opening an old cut inside Johnson's mouth that the champion had originally suffered in training. "First blood for Jeff!" a telegrapher cabled. Outside newspaper offices in big cities, strangers embraced. But Jeffries couldn't reach Johnson to follow up, and he could not get himself out of the way of Johnson's punches. All he had to offer was his undiminished ability to take punishment.

"Ain't I got a hard old head?" Jeff asked Johnson. He seemed already to be adopting the posture of defiant loser.

"You certainly have, Mr. Jeffries," Johnson replied—and resumed his work.[15]

Sitting in his corner between the fifth and sixth rounds, Johnson spotted John L. sitting nearby. The two men had developed a surprising rapport.

"John, I thought this fellow could hit."

"I never said so," Sullivan replied, "but I believe he could have six years ago."

"Yes," Johnson answered. "Five or six years ago ain't now, though."[16]

Hunched over in his famous crouch, his left arm hanging down to his thigh, Jeffries appeared almost decrepit. His face became a bloody mass, the blood spilling onto his arms and chest as his exhaustion mounted. Desperation mounted in Jeffries's corner. Corbett continued hurling verbal abuse at the champion. Johnson would be the last person to admit whether taunts like these, coming from the champion he had most admired, hurt him. Always, he answered with rejoinders of his own. At one point, he walked Jeffries over to the corner and asked, "Where do you want me to put him, Mr. Corbett?"[17] And he flashed his dreaded grin.

Corbett became more unhinged as the bout proceeded, screaming obscenities at Johnson, spittle forming at the corners of his mouth. "Stand up and fight, you coward!" he called after the champion.[18] Did he remember that John L. had baited him with almost the same words?

Finally, exasperated by Johnson's defense, Corbett yelled, "Why don't you do something?"

"Too clever," Johnson replied. "Just like you."[19]

As the rounds passed, Johnson began asking Jeffries, "How do you feel, Jim? How do you like 'em?"

"They don't hurt," Jeffries snarled.

"I'll give you some more of them now." And he did, snapping Jeff's head back with punches.[20]

Johnson also kept up a dialogue with others at ringside, including Tommy Burns. When he landed a punch to the pit of Jeffries's belly, he looked over at Burns and said, "I didn't show you that one in Sydney."[21] When Jeffries went deep into his crouch, Johnson said, "I'll straighten him up in a minute," and fans at ringside yelled, "He'll straighten you up."[22] But Johnson's uppercut did as promised.

In the tenth round, two Johnson lefts and a right uppercut made Jeffries gasp, "Oh!"[23] In the eleventh, the champion scored repeatedly with his patented uppercuts as Jeff tried wildly to fight back. After the twelfth round, Jeff went back to his corner spitting blood, and in the thirteenth, Johnson lifted one of Jeff's feet off the floor with an uppercut.

Finally, in the fifteenth, Johnson sensed that the time had come. Fighting with rare aggression, he backed Jeffries against the ropes and poured on the punches. Jeffries fell into a sitting position against the ropes. He had never been down before. Johnson stood a few feet away, hands on hips; Rickard pushed him back as Jeffries rose, and Johnson rushed forward and landed a left to the jaw that put the big man down again. This time, he nearly fell through the ropes. Johnson stepped back; Jeffries's handlers, against the rules, rushed to his aid on the ring apron, hoisted him up, and pushed him back into action. Rickard would have been justified in disqualifying Jeffries right there, but Johnson made no protest, only waving his glove at Jeff's seconds, as if to say, "Help him all you like, but you can't protect him." And they couldn't.

"Stop it!" called voices at ringside. "Don't let him be knocked out."[24]

Even Corbett now pleaded with Johnson not to hit Jeffries anymore. When Johnson dropped Jeffries for a third time at the other end of the ring, Jeff's handlers rushed in again—this time to save him. Rickard tapped Johnson's shoulder but did not raise his arm. The fight was over.

"I couldn't come back, boys," Jeffries said as he was led away, as if he were breaking the news to himself. The crowd swarmed the ring. Johnson approached Jeffries to shake hands, but Corbett and others waved him away. When Johnson got back to his corner, John L. Sullivan was among the first to congratulate him.[25]

The newspapers were unanimous in praising Johnson's fighting prowess. Reversing their pronouncements of his racial disadvantages and yellow streak, they now went to the other extreme. "The Black Champion Proves to Be Invincible," read one headline in the *Reno Gazette*. "Sluggish White Champion Is Terribly Beaten by the Cleverness of Ethiopian," read another, using the African designation for Johnson. The *New York Daily Tribune* wrote of the subdued Reno crowd's grudging respect for the champion—"They could not help but admire him, and there was little animosity shown"—and cited Rickard's tribute to Johnson as "the most wonderful fighter that ever pulled on a glove."

Johnson celebrated on a railroad car heading back to Chicago, where his many black supporters were euphoric over his victory. Traveling in this sea of black humanity was, remarkably, Sullivan, who seemed to enjoy Johnson's victory, perhaps because it came at the expense of his old nemesis, Corbett. Johnson's mother was cheered outside her Chicago home. Not long after the fight, a black folk ballad adapted the words of an old spiritual in celebration of Johnson's triumph:

> Amaze an' Grace, how sweet it sounds,
> Jack Johnson knocked Jim Jeffries down.
> Jim Jeffries jumped up an' hit Jack on the chin,
> An' then Jack knocked him down again.
>
> The Yankees hold the play,
> The White man pull the trigger;
> But it make no difference what the white man say;
> The world champion's still a nigger.[26]

"The colored fellow beat me fair and square," Jeffries said afterward, though he maintained that "six years ago the result would have been different."[27] This was an early example of what would become a timeless ex-champion's lament: at my best, I would have won. History, however, has mostly recorded Jeffries saying: "I could never have whipped Jack Johnson at my best. I couldn't have hit him in a thousand years."[28] There is some dispute about whether he really said these words or whether they were attributed to him many years later. With his brooding nature, Jeffries was the kind of man who could have said both things on the same day. Either way, many whites found Jeff's failure difficult to accept. Some claimed that he had been "doped" or that he was suffering from a nervous disorder. In later years, Jeffries himself would revive the doping excuse and disparage Johnson's achievements.

Jeff's bitterness likely stemmed from an awareness of how much the Battle of the Century had cost him. He lost the fight not once but twice: first in the ring to Johnson and then outside it to posterity, which now views him not only as a lesser fighter than Johnson but also a lesser man—judgments far from being self-evident, in either case. Modern discomfort with the White Hope crusade has led some to suggest that Jeffries was elevated beyond his worthiness as a fighter. This is simply untrue. Racial obsessions had their say in 1910 but needed a genuine vessel to bear them, and only Jeffries could have aroused them to the pitch they reached.

Almost from the moment the fight ended, the worst fears of those who had tried to stop it were realized: racial violence erupted in dozens of cities, killing perhaps two dozen people, possibly more, mostly blacks; it was the worst such outbreak before the 1960s. The violence led many cities and

The Battle of the Century, July 4, 1910: Jack Johnson stands over the fallen James J. Jeffries in the fifteenth round, which would be the last.
Granger, NYC—All rights reserved.

states to ban showings of the Johnson–Jeffries fight film, while some others, like New York, went ahead and screened it. Though most of the rioting broke out before the movies were shown, Congress pressed for a ban on interstate sale of fight films. The bill passed in 1912 and stayed on the books for a generation.

The Johnson–Jeffries fight may have been the most public exercising of racial differences in America since the end of the Civil War. Its result was a shattering blow for white supremacy and a momentary boon to black self-confidence—but it strengthened determination among whites to keep the races separate in competitive sports and other endeavors, while giving momentum to boxing abolitionists. "If the unpopularity of Johnson's victory leads to a cessation of prizefighting in the United States it will be no cause for regret," the *New York Times* editorialized. Even Theodore Roosevelt, long a devotee of the manly art, now called for the sport's abolition.

By any competitive standard, the Battle of the Century was not a very good fight. Its trappings—the long buildup, the violent aftermath, the impact on both principals and on American race relations—have always been more compelling than the action in the ring. More than one hundred years on, only one other American sporting event—another heavyweight fight, a generation later—can match its social significance.

★

After Reno, Johnson's life unfolded as a long anticlimax. But his anticlimaxes were most people's crescendos.

Riding high, the champion saw no reason to tone down his personality or his habits, both of which had a way of making news. But while beating white fighters and flaunting his wealth were bad enough, his sex life was the bomb across the bow. By now, the women were always white and usually prostitutes. Johnson seemed to enjoy violating sexual taboos. He even played with white insecurities about black sexual prowess, wrapping his crotch in thick gauze during training.

Promoters continued to seek white challengers who could beat Johnson. In lieu of that great deed, they set up a tournament to determine the White Heavyweight Championship of the World. If few acknowledged the irony of whites creating an alternative prize to compensate for their inferiority, even fewer put much stock in the meaningless white title. Everyone knew who the real champion was.

By 1912, the thirty-four-year-old Johnson was losing interest in the hard grind of being a boxer. He was more devoted to running his new nightclub, the Café de Champion in Chicago, which he appointed with stylish furniture and décor, including walls of red and gold damask, upon which he hung paintings of himself or his new wife, Etta Duryea. Etta was no sporting girl; she had formerly been married to a Long Island financier. She was also, perhaps, clinically depressed, and choosing a life with Johnson would do nothing to alleviate that condition. They often quarreled over Johnson's serial infidelities, and Johnson beat her. She felt herself spurned by both races—hated by whites for marrying a black man and resented by blacks for being Johnson's white trophy.

In September 1912, a despondent Etta committed suicide. Johnson seemed devastated, collapsing with grief, but he rebounded quickly, taking up with an eighteen-year-old prostitute, Lucille Cameron. After Cameron's mother went to the police, claiming that Johnson had kidnapped her daughter into a life of prostitution—he hadn't—Johnson was arrested in Chicago that November on charges of abduction and then released on bail. The government wanted to pursue a case against him under the Mann Act, or White-Slave Traffic Act, a 1910 law that forbade the transport of women across state lines for immoral purposes—mainly, prostitution. But the feds could get nowhere with Cameron, and the charges were dropped. Soon afterward, Johnson married her.

Despite its setback with Cameron, the federal government redoubled its efforts. It found the witness it needed in prostitute Belle Schreiber, a disgruntled former lover of Johnson's. She claimed that Johnson had indeed "transported" her across state boundaries for the express purpose of practicing her trade.

The Mann Act would be the instrument, at long last, to bring Johnson down, and by its broadly worded terms, Johnson appeared guilty. He had traveled with Schreiber, he had sent her money, and he had once even helped her set up her own brothel. Johnson's defenders argued that the government's case was flimsy. Yes, Johnson kept company with prostitutes, but the women he traveled with were his lovers, not his sexual employees. He did not transport women explicitly for prostitution, and none had traveled with him against her will.

But Schreiber's testimony helped persuade an all-white jury to convict Johnson in June 1913. He was sentenced to one year and a day in federal prison but didn't wait around to begin his incarceration, escaping first to Canada and then to Europe. Johnson told various colorful tales about how he got away from the G-men, but the likeliest explanation is that the champion bribed his way out of the country, greasing the palms of enough government agents to clear his path to freedom. He embarked on long years of wandering that, even by his standards, must have been disorienting at times.

★

Johnson claimed that in Europe, he found the racial tolerance missing in the United States, but his reception wasn't all that different from back home. He discovered that the British government was not keen on entertaining an American fugitive, and the French government not much more so. He did his usual routines to generate income, giving boxing exhibitions and performing on stages, and he defended his title against another White Hope: Frank Moran, a Pittsburgher with a right hand he called his Mary Ann. They fought on June 27, 1914, at the Vélodrome d'Hiver in Paris. In a bout that went twenty dull rounds, Johnson won easily, stopping to applaud once when his challenger finally managed to hit him.

The next day, Archduke Franz Ferdinand was assassinated in Sarajevo, and Europe would soon plunge itself into the civilizational suicide of the Great War. For Johnson, moneymaking options on the Continent were drying up. Troops began amassing in the Paris streets amid terror about the approaching Germans.

More than anything, Johnson needed a lucrative fight. In early 1915, the opportunity materialized in the person of Jess Willard of Pottawatomie, Kansas. Willard had never been viewed as a great fighter, but, along with the color of his skin, he had an asset that brought instant public credibility: he was a giant, at least by the standards of the day, standing six foot six and weighing nearly 250 pounds. They called him the Tall Pine of the Pottawatomie or the Pottawatomie Giant.

Born in St. Clere, Kansas, in 1881, Willard had worked as a livery stableman and wagon driver before the White Hope fervor of the Johnson years propelled him into boxing. He had no taste for violence, however, and he almost quit the sport in 1913, after winning a match in California against William "Bull" Young, who died the next day. Though he was acquitted of second-degree murder charges, Willard was horrified by the event and came to hate boxing. Yet through the skillful guidance of Tom Jones, who had guided other fighters to world championships, Willard found himself in a position to challenge Johnson in 1915.

The theme of racial restitution was prominent in the national mind that year. In February 1915, D. W. Griffith's Civil War epic, *The Birth of a Nation*, opened to packed movie houses and ecstatic reviews around the country. The film told the story of Southern Reconstruction from a white Southerner's point of view, portraying Northern racial reformers and free blacks as irresponsible, immoral, and unfit for leadership. It also touched, as Jack Johnson had touched, the unspoken dread of its white audience: interracial sex. Its most lurid scene, in which a lascivious mulatto chases a young white girl until she hurls herself to death from a cliff, remains shocking today. Her death sets off the birth, on film, of the Ku Klux Klan—and in the last frame, the Klan rides triumphant through a Southern town liberated from black rule. History turned to fiction became history again: later in 1915, white Georgians, inspired by Griffith's film, burned crosses on Stone Mountain and founded the modern Klan. By coincidence or not, 1915 would see the most documented lynchings of the century—seventy-nine blacks and forty-six whites.

Since Johnson remained a fugitive from American justice, the Willard bout was made for Havana, Cuba. Johnson stood to make a good payday: about $30,000, along with a percentage of the movie rights, while Willard would earn $10,000. These figures were a far cry from the numbers of the Jeffries fight five years earlier, but as the fight approached, a familiar fever gripped American fans. They lined up outside newspaper offices in cities around the country, waiting to hear the results.

Willard arrived in Havana in peak shape, weighing just 230 pounds. Johnson, by contrast, trained little. His weight was thought to be at least 225 pounds, perhaps more; he had weighed 208 for Jeffries. But he was sure that his superior skill would overcome the untutored challenger.

The bout was held at the Oriental Race Track in Marianao, ten miles outside Havana, on April 5, 1915, before a crowd of sixteen thousand, many of whom arrived when the gates opened at 7 a.m., bringing packed lunches. The weather by fight time, 1 p.m., was about 105 degrees.

Even in the broiling temperatures, and carrying a noticeable paunch, Johnson dominated the action. He outboxed Willard with ease and led more aggressively than usual; in the twelfth round, Johnson backed Willard around the ring with combinations. But his punches, while leaving red welts on Willard's pale white body, didn't bother the huge Kansan. On the old film, one can see Johnson conserving his energy, as always, moving economically and throwing punches with purpose, not merely to "lead." He fought sometimes off his back foot, his left arm cocked at the elbow, showing Willard his feints. Or he raised both gloves in front of his face and stood still, as if to give his challenger target practice. Willard rarely took the bait, and the fight, like most of Johnson's, was only intermittently exciting. Once, in the seventeenth round, when Willard made a rush at Johnson, the champion dropped both arms to his sides and taunted him.

"What a grand old man," Johnson said to the crowd at ringside.[29]

But he was losing heart. He had made a crucial error by agreeing to a forty-five-round distance, which meant, in effect, that the contest was a fight to the finish. Unless he could find a way to knock out his hulking challenger, Johnson was not even halfway through the battle. As the fight approached the twenty-round mark, he made one last effort to knock Willard out. He could not. As Johnson flagged under the sun, Willard pressed the action. In his corner between rounds, Johnson had an aide send a message to Lucille in the stands: get yourself out of here.

In the twenty-sixth round, Willard crossed a right to Johnson's jaw, and the champion collapsed to the canvas, clutching Willard as he fell. The referee, Jack Welsh, counted Johnson out and raised Willard's arm. The mostly white crowd rushed the ring to congratulate the new champion, who began climbing through the ropes, eager to get away. Cuban soldiers held the throngs back with machetes. It seemed fitting that a white giant had been needed to depose the great black champion.

"It was a clean knockout and the best man won," Johnson told a reporter. "It was not a matter of luck. I have no kick coming."[30] In the days afterward, he even suggested that Willard's size would make him unbeatable.

A few years later, Johnson began claiming that he had thrown the fight. He pointed to a famous photo showing him take the ten-count on his back, with his arms crossed over his face, as if he were shielding himself from the sun. He agreed to the fix, he said, after the promoter, Jack Curley, promised to intercede with American authorities to commute his sentence and allow him to return home. Curley denied it, but even if he had made such promises, they wouldn't have amounted to much. Justice Department officials insisted that Johnson serve his time.

Many believed Johnson's claims about throwing the fight, and some still do today. But the weight of the evidence—starting with his own performance— suggests that Johnson lost his title fairly. Against a younger, stronger man, he fought skillfully in punishing heat for twenty-six rounds, a distance more than double the length of today's championship fights. He won most of the rounds and made every effort to finish Willard off. He capitulated only when he could go on no longer. It hardly matters whether he was shading his eyes from the sun; tired men assume different postures, and Johnson's may have

Jess Willard knocks out Jack Johnson and takes the title in Havana, April 5, 1915—though Johnson, seemingly shading his eyes from the sun, would later claim that he threw the fight.

been an involuntary reflex. Perhaps he could have gotten up, but he was
beaten and he knew it. Like John L. and Jeffries, Corbett and Fitzsimmons
before him, he had stayed too long at the party. By insisting that he'd thrown
the fight, he could assert control over the one moment in his boxing career
when control deserted him. In his personal code, losing on purpose was more
honorable than losing honestly.

Willard put it best. "If Johnson throwed that fight," he said, "I wish he
throwed it sooner. It was hotter than hell down there."[31]

★

Life the rest of the way wasn't easy for Johnson. He spent most of the war
years in Spain, where he got some fights, started an advertising agency, and
dabbled in bullfighting. After the war ended, he made his way to Mexico
and, in 1920, crossed the border and surrendered to U.S. authorities. Johnson served a one-year term at Leavenworth, where he worked as physical
director and enjoyed generally soft treatment, though he was sometimes
written up for breaking rules and other times accused of getting special
perks from guards—both eminently believable charges. Released in July
1921, he insisted that he deserved another chance to fight for the heavyweight title. He couldn't grasp that he would never get anywhere near the
crown again.

Johnson never lost the sense of himself as a grand subject and his life
as a modern legend worthy of endless retelling, in which the details could
change as he saw fit. "The more that is written and said concerning one
who has held public interest, the less the public knows about that person,"
he wrote in his 1927 memoir, *In the Ring and Out*.[32] The words must have
made him smile; no one had spread more disinformation than he.

On June 10, 1946, he was driving to New York, on his way to attend the
Joe Louis–Billy Conn fight at Yankee Stadium. Moving at his usual high
speed, he misjudged a turn on U.S. Highway 1 north of Raleigh, North
Carolina, and crashed into a light pole. He was dead at sixty-eight. With the
possible exception of being cashiered by a jilted lover, a more symbolically
fitting end could not have been found. As sportswriter John Lardner put it:
"Jack Johnson died crossing the white line for the last time."[33]

In 2005, *Unforgivable Blackness*, a Ken Burns documentary based on the
identically titled biography of Johnson by Geoffrey Ward, debuted on PBS.
Both film and book portrayed Johnson as the ultimate American individual,
unafraid of challenging social norms. The Burns film culminated a transition in Johnson's reputation from outlaw to idol—the original bad-ass black

athlete. The process had begun a generation earlier, with Howard Sackler's Broadway play *The Great White Hope*, later a feature film. In both, James Earl Jones portrayed a Johnson-like character who somehow lacked all his more troubling qualities. Changing views of Johnson originated in a sense of fairness and sympathy for a man who was ill-treated, as well as the heightening of black racial consciousness after the civil rights movement.

When Johnson died, his ring mastery was acknowledged by boxing historians, but his influence was regarded as almost entirely negative. Today, by contrast, Johnson occupies an honored place in American memory. Once demonized, he is now more often lionized for his defiance of American racism, and his prosecution is generally regarded as unfair. His preference for white women is seen as a radically individualist statement in an America that would deny individuality to blacks; his delight in sensuality and vice seems utterly contemporary in an age when personal license is a badge of honor. In addition to Broadway plays, he has inspired books, movies, jazz scores, documentaries, and academic studies. Sympathy for Johnson has also inspired attempts to right the wrongs of history. Efforts to secure a posthumous pardon for Johnson's Mann Act conviction have gone on for years, with Burns and Senator John McCain, among others, leading the charge.

What this long cycle of redefinition has produced, though, is a heroic image almost as misleading as the original racist caricature. Among all the heavyweight champions, Jack Johnson is probably the most complex. He possessed a kind of genius. His quick study of bullfighting was one example; his patenting of an auto wrench, while in prison, was another. He spoke several languages, was a competent musician, and read widely. And he was surely one of the bravest men of the age.

But he was also profoundly reckless and heedless of the effects of his actions on others. He was brilliant but self-indulgent, resourceful but at least partly deluded. Sure, wrapping his crotch in extra gauze was a "bold" move—as we might say today—but it also reinforced white racists in their views of blacks while putting other blacks in the way of white resentment and even violence. The same could be said for Johnson's constant seeking of physical sensation, from booze to fast cars; his profligate lifestyle; his serial dishonesty and storytelling; and his myriad run-ins with the law, including his conviction under the Mann Act—for which one could argue, Johnson-like, that he was both guilty and not guilty at the same time. And how to overlook that this compelling, impossible man was also a chronic abuser of women, especially of Etta Duryea, who killed herself at least in part because of it?

As a black man living on his own terms—not those of whites, not those of blacks, and not those of Booker T. Washington or W. E. B. DuBois—Johnson had no home in the America of his time. But he didn't have to make the choices he made.

Johnson's prominence in American social history has distracted from his formidable place in boxing history. Nat Fleischer, founder and editor of *Ring* magazine, saw every heavyweight champion from Jim Corbett to Muhammad Ali. "I have no hesitation in naming Jack Johnson as the greatest of them all," Fleischer wrote. "In all-around ability, he was tops."[34] That stood as a famous judgment for years, given Fleischer's influence, though the *Ring* editor had a clear bias for old-timers. Yet even a 2005 poll by the International Boxing Research Organization rated Johnson the third-greatest all-time heavyweight. Boxing historians laud his defensive genius, his mastery of feinting, and his skills at glove and elbow blocking, viewed as lost arts by many today. Historians more skeptical of Johnson's stature point to his weak competition as champion; he drew his own color line, refusing title opportunities to black fighting legends like Sam Langford, Sam McVey, and Joe Jeannette. And perhaps a younger Jeffries, in his fighting prime, would have beaten him. As for how Johnson would fare against modern fighters, it depends whom you ask. Men of Fleischer's generation and some contemporary boxing historians insist that the older fighters, as a rule, were better—a debatable position, given the progress of the modern athlete in every other sport. Still, the arguments continue. Jack Johnson would have enjoyed them.

★

The former heavyweight champions who watched Johnson's greatest victory in Reno felt obliged to protect a heritage that, for all its symbolic power, was barely three decades old. By 1910, the heavyweight title had acquired the cultural potency of a royal lineage. From Jim Corbett on, the champions took backward glances over their shoulders, wondering how they squared with history. But these had all been white men. After Jack Johnson, there would always be a recognizable line of ancestors for subsequent champions, of whatever type—slugger, boxer; hero, pariah; white man, black man. The shadow was now full-size, and its next great inheritor was already traveling under it.

THE MILLION-DOLLAR HOBO

On another Independence Day—Friday, July 4, 1919, in Toledo, Ohio—Jack Dempsey woke early. Today he would have a chance at his life's ambition—to fight for the heavyweight championship of the world—but not until late afternoon, when the temperature would hover around 100 degrees. He prowled his training camp in the broiling early morning hours with nothing to do. His mind entered a realm where the rest of the world fell away, except for one man: heavyweight champion Jess Willard, the Pottawatomie Giant.

Dempsey had been in Toledo since May, winning over the locals and the national press. He conveyed a youthful innocence despite his rugged appearance. His training sessions, in which he inflicted daily punishment on his sparring partners in an outdoor ring, impressed observers. His quickness was compared to that of jungle cats. The doctor for the Toledo Boxing Commission compared his blood pressure to that of a boy and was struck by his remarkably low resting-pulse rate—44.

With the fight imminent, though, Willard betting money still held a slight 5–4 edge. It was natural to defer to the champion. Big Jess, after all, was the man who had beaten Jack Johnson and brought the title back to the white race. And then there was the six-foot-six champion's enormous bulk—he had weighed in at 245 pounds, Dempsey at just 187. If some Dempsey boosters saw the Toledo battle as David versus Goliath, other observers thought of it as man versus boy. Willard himself sometimes referred to

Dempsey as a boy. He even asked promoter Tex Rickard, back in boxing after a stint as a cattleman in South America, for legal immunity in case he killed the challenger. And Rickard worried. "Every time I see you," he told Dempsey, "you look smaller to me."[1]

If these doubts bothered Dempsey, he didn't let on. Being underestimated was nothing new. In the years leading up to the Toledo bout, it had often seemed that the world was opposed not merely to his success but to his existence.

★

The ninth child of a restless, itinerant father and a devout Mormon mother, William Harrison Dempsey was born on June 24, 1895, in Manassa, Colorado, a community of a few hundred Mormons in the San Luis Valley. "I am basically Irish," Dempsey told one biographer, "with Cherokee blood from both parents, plus a Jewish strain from my father's great-grandmother."[2] Or maybe it was Chocktaw blood on his father's side, he suggested elsewhere. Whatever the final mix, it was an inheritance steeped in fighting.

It was Dempsey's mother, Celia, who told him about John L. Sullivan, whose biography she had read after a struggling peddler left it for her in exchange for a meal. Even far out in the Western wilderness, the story of the great John L. circulated. Celia Dempsey felt that "Harry" would be her special child.

In 1911, Dempsey left home at sixteen, with a frontier equivalent of an eighth-grade education. All over Colorado, Utah, and New Mexico—in towns with names like Uncompaghre, Leadville, and Rifle—he lived like a character in a Jack London story, passing through the "hobo jungles," working as a miner, fruit picker, bowling-alley pin boy, janitor, laborer, and brothel bouncer. Money and food were scarce. He couldn't afford to buy a seat on the railroad, so he got around by "riding the rods," wherein the rider ties himself to the brake beams on the bottom of a Pullman car and holds on for dear life.

"There's only a few inches between you and the tracks and roadbeds—and death," Dempsey recalled years later. "If you fall asleep you'll roll off your narrow steel bed and die. If you're so cold you can't hold on any longer, you die. . . . You have to be desperate to gamble like that, but if you weren't desperate you wouldn't be on the rods."[3]

No matter how bleak things got, Dempsey kept pursuing his boyhood dream of being a fighter. From his older brother, Bernie, he learned the basics, along with disciplines like soaking his face in beef brine to toughen the skin and chewing the sap from pine trees to strengthen his jaw. No full tally of his fights is possible; many took place in informal settings such as mining camps, dance halls, and saloons and went unrecorded. Early on, he campaigned under the name Kid Blackie and then began billing himself as "Jack Dempsey," borrowing the fighting moniker of an Irishman who had held the middleweight title in the late nineteenth century. Old-timers called that Dempsey the Nonpareil (the unequaled).

It didn't look like the second Dempsey would come anywhere near such a standard. He made his way to New York in 1916 and fought well but left the city penniless, nursing broken ribs and driven out under a scorned manager's threat to blackball him from fighting in the East. Returning west, he fell into the snares of a piano-playing prostitute named Maxine Cates and proposed to her. The marriage was short-lived; she soon left him and returned to her profession. Dempsey's boxing ambitions seemed to run aground in early 1917, after he was knocked out in the first round of a fight in Murray, Utah, against Fireman Jim Flynn, who had once fought Jack Johnson. The thirty-seven-year-old Flynn made quick work of Dempsey in a bout that historians have long found suspicious. Some believe that Dempsey, broke and desperate, agreed to "lie down" in exchange for a payday.

The humiliating loss left Dempsey with a damaged reputation to go along with his usual hunger and empty pockets, so he was surprised to get a letter from Jack Kearns, a thirty-four-year-old manager, wheeler-dealer, and con artist who had guided one of Dempsey's earlier opponents. Kearns's real name was John Leo McKernan, and his previous occupations read like a parody of a Whitman poem: minor league baseball player, welterweight boxer, cab driver, bouncer, salesman of Bibles and cemetery plots, manufacturer of fire extinguishers. On the Oakland ferry, Kearns impersonated a preacher, offering to perform marriage rites for whatever cash that gullible couples had on hand. As Dempsey put it, Kearns was "a man who connived for success, and any method was good enough just so long as it worked."[4] Kearns rubbed most people the wrong way, but his amorality, shrewdness, and daring would make him a great boxing manager. He just needed a fighter.

Kearns wired Dempsey train fare, put him up at his mother's home in San Francisco, and boosted the half-starved young fighter's confidence, telling him that he could beat anyone. Most inspiring of all, Kearns promised that they would both get rich. Kearns became Dempsey's guru; in tribute, the fighter affectionately dubbed him "Doc."

Under Kearns's guidance, Dempsey began to win. In 1918, he enjoyed the most dominant year of any heavyweight in history, winning nineteen fights, seventeen by knockout—twelve of those in the first round. He put away huge Fred Fulton, who had hoped to challenge Willard, in just twenty-three seconds. He got revenge on Fireman Flynn in one round, destroyed Johnson-era White Hopes like Carl Morris and Gunboat Smith, and beat younger contenders like Billy Miske and Bill Brennan. He fought in a swarming style, swiveling his torso up and down and side to side in a technique known as bobbing and weaving, and kept his chin tucked in close to his chest, making him hard to hit. There had been offensive-minded heavyweights before, but none had ever worked with such speed and uninhibited physical release. With each win, Kearns recruited more sportswriters to their cause, insisting that Dempsey would annihilate Jess Willard—if only Big Jess would give them a chance.

By 1919, memories had grown faint of Willard's defeat of Johnson in Havana four years earlier. He had defended the title only once since then. And world events had made prizefighting an afterthought. In April 1917, in response to German submarine warfare, President Woodrow Wilson asked Congress for a declaration of war, and the nation mobilized to join the European conflict. By late spring 1918, the United States was playing an important role in what would be the climactic battles on the Western Front. Dempsey's knockout run out West didn't arouse much national attention in this climate; but within months of the Armistice ending the war in November, eager talk began of a heavyweight title fight, the first in years, and with the biggest price tag ever: $100,000 for Willard, $27,500 for Dempsey.

★

In the terrible heat—one ringside thermometer registered 120 degrees— the fighters made their way to the open-air wooden arena in Toledo's Bayview Park, on Maumee Bay. Outside, Old West lawmen Bat Masterson and Wyatt Earp, self-appointed security marshals, collected firearms and knives from spectators.

Robe-less, wearing white trunks nearly down to his knees and with a towel slung over his shoulder, Dempsey arrived in the ring, his hair cut into the so-called hobo or brakeman's cut—shaved along the sides and back. His body was deeply tanned. Clad in blue trunks that looked as though they would fit a man twenty pounds lighter, Willard was pale and enormous. To Dempsey, the champion was even bigger than he looked in pictures. A familiar feeling of desperation gripped the challenger. "I wasn't just fighting for the title," he remembered later. "I was fighting for my life."[5]

Shortly before Dempsey entered the ring, Kearns had let him in on a secret: he'd bet $10,000 with a local bookmaker that Dempsey would knock out Willard in the first round. Kearns had gotten the wager at 10–1 odds, meaning that if Dempsey pulled it off, they would earn $100,000, nearly four times their purse. If not, they'd have to cover the bet.

The bell rang for the first round, but it made only a muffled sound, and no one heard it. The rope used to ring the bell had been pulled out of alignment during pre-fight festivities that had damaged the ring. With a stopwatch running, the timekeeper blew a military whistle instead, and the fighters moved out of their corners to begin.

What happened next is well documented in tens of thousands of words from newspaper stories and books. Yet words alone cannot capture the reality of the Toledo fight. It has to be seen to be believed, if not understood, and it can be seen, thanks to the magic of YouTube. Our twenty-first-century eyes behold a spectacle that is archaic in its style and setting but utterly contemporary in its violence.

One notes first the contrast in the fighters' styles. Willard stands straight up, like a nineteenth-century fighter conducting a gentleman's sparring session, whereas Dempsey is constantly in motion. He fights from a modified crouch, darting in and out of reach of the big man, trying to get inside his long arms with heavy punches. Where Willard's stiffness seems to come from the age of the still photo, Dempsey's activity fits the new medium— motion pictures.

In the center of the ring, Dempsey throws a combination to Willard's midsection and then comes up to Willard's jaw with a left hook. The punch turns Willard's head parallel to his shoulder. He drops on the seat of his trunks like someone landing in a dunking tank after the target has been hit. Everyone in the arena stands. For a moment, Willard sits on the canvas, looking up at Dempsey as if to ask him how he did it, and then tries to get up as the referee, Ollie Pecord, counts over him. Dempsey stands a few feet away and then circles around Pecord and rushes Willard as he rises, pinning him on the ropes.

Dempsey lands a series of rights and lefts, and Willard goes down on his hands and knees. Pecord begins to count, but Willard is up quickly. Dempsey again swarms him. Willard seems like a man caught in a sandstorm, looking for a clearing to open his eyes. He turns away from Dempsey, who whips a left hook over his shoulder, and a small white flash appears on the film—Dempsey's bared teeth. Willard collapses in Dempsey's corner.

With each knockdown, Dempsey moves to get around Pecord and position himself above Willard before he can rise. Few fighters had ever done this before; most would stand aside when an opponent was down. Pecord struggles to count over Willard with one hand and hold Dempsey off with the other, but Dempsey continually outmaneuvers him. After Dempsey blasts Willard to the canvas for a sixth time, the champion is left kneeling in an almost fetal position along the ropes. Even on the old film, we can see that his face is dark with welts and blood, especially on the right side. With both gloves, he pulls on the middle rope and raises himself up, resembling the anchorman in a tug-of-war. Having once again glided by Pecord, Dempsey rushes in and throws a right to Willard's ribs and then a shattering right to the side of his jaw. Willard begins falling backward, and Dempsey blasts him into the corner with one more right. Willard's arms are wrapped around the ropes, his head thrown back on his shoulders. It is his seventh trip to the canvas. This time, he does not rise.

When Pecord tolls "ten" over Willard, Dempsey walks to his corner, where Kearns and others have flooded into the ring. They embrace him and then, strangely, Kearns directs him to leave. Why not celebrate? Kearns knows that the timekeeper had blown his whistle to end the round when Pecord was at "seven" in the count, which means that Willard would be "saved by the bell." But the referee didn't hear the whistle over the crowd noise and counted the champion out. Kearns wants that result to stand—he will win the $100,000. He hopes that Dempsey's quick exit will persuade the officials to call the result a first-round knockout.

They don't; instead, realizing their mistake, they tell Kearns to get Dempsey back into the ring or he'll be disqualified. We see Kearns waving his arms and screaming at Dempsey to come back. Having gotten nearly halfway to his dressing room, Dempsey now fights through the crowd to return. The bout resumes for two more rounds.

Though damaged beyond repair, Willard attempts to rally; he does not go down again. Both men are soaked with perspiration and blood. Near the end of the third round, Dempsey lands one last salvo: three straight left hooks to the jaw and then a right, another hook, and a right uppercut. Somehow, Willard takes it and fights back. But before the fourth round, Willard's men toss a towel into the ring, the time-honored boxing signal of surrender. Dempsey walks to the center of the ring, where Pecord raises his hand in triumph. (On his way out of the arena, Willard will tell a reporter: "I have $100,000 and a farm in Kansas."[6])

The ring is filled with gleeful men in boater hats. Many dance around and gesture at the movie camera, an early instance of what will become a national habit. Dempsey is swarmed, the people slapping him on the back and hoisting him up in the air. Someone throws a floppy straw hat over his head, and he floats above the crowd, looking vaguely like a Mexican revolutionary on the shoulders of his minions. The film goes black.

★

The press tried to absorb what it had just seen. The fight was "not a battle, but a slaughter . . . a kind of pugilistic murder," stated the New York Times. "Dempsey worked as a fighter never worked before."[7] "He is a new type," agreed sportswriter and cartoonist Bob Edgren. "He fights like no other champion we ever had."[8]

Willard was gracious in defeat, praising Dempsey for fighting a "grand, fearless battle."[9] But in time, Willard came to believe that Dempsey had won through dirty work: he would allege that Dempsey's gloves had been "loaded," perhaps with cement. Most boxing histories catalog Willard's injuries in lurid terms: a jawbone fractured in thirteen places, multiple broken ribs, and several teeth cracked or missing. The legend of the loaded gloves would become central to the Dempsey mystique. Nearly a half-century would pass before the issue burst out into a public controversy.

"I hadn't realized," Dempsey later wrote, "that my inner fury could do so much damage."[10] Dempsey's inner fury made him a national sensation, a perfect star for the dawning 1920s, in which sports would explode into commercial prominence. His various nicknames—Jack the Giant Killer, the Manassa Mauler—had a folklorish quality. Tex Rickard forgot his misgivings about Dempsey's size and saw fortunes to be made with the new champion's fists. In 1920, New York legalized boxing for good—the city soon became the boxing capital—and during the 1920s, laws against the sport were overturned in state after state. In 1922, Nat Fleischer founded Ring magazine, which became the sport's flagship publication and ratings authority. Boxing would become the nation's leading sport, next to baseball.

Dempsey's timing was auspicious, though it wouldn't have seemed so in July 1919. Though the Great War had ended, the United States seemed in deep turmoil, plagued with labor strikes, race riots, and political violence. A month before the Toledo fight, on June 2, 1919, anarchists exploded bombs in eight American cities, all targeting public officials. Change seemed everywhere: two days after the June 1919 bombings, the Senate passed the Nineteenth Amendment, for women's suffrage. Three days before Dempsey fought Willard, on July 1, 1919, wartime prohibition went into effect in the United States; though the war was over, the order would hold until the troops were fully demobilized. By then, the Eighteenth Amend-ment, establishing prohibition, would come into force. The ensuing decade would play out against the grandest and most futile of all American social experiments.

Yet the Roaring Twenties would be associated not with the forebodings of 1919 but with a joyous welcoming of everything modern—from "liber-ated" women to radio, from the advent of mass consumerism to the birth of the modern entertainment and celebrity culture. Central to both consump-tion and entertainment was the new obsession with professional sports, and it was Jack Dempsey who, in 1919, forged the path that the decade's other giants—Babe Ruth, Bill Tilden, Red Grange, Bobby Jones—would follow.

Soon after winning the Toledo fight, Dempsey was presented with a gold and diamond belt symbolizing the heavyweight championship—the title that John L. Sullivan had forged into the national mind. With his almost ritualistic slaughter of Willard, Dempsey had become the most spectacu-lar heir to that throne since John L. himself, and he had at his command a world of new opportunities to exploit it: not just vaudeville, where he quickly surpassed his earnings in the Willard fight, but also the big screen. Starting years of work in Hollywood, he made a fifteen-episode serial called *Daredevil Jack*, in which he played a traditional hero saving heroines. He became good friends with Charlie Chaplin, Rudolph Valentino, and espe-cially Douglas Fairbanks, and he was linked romantically with Hollywood starlets. But the former hobo would discover that American celebrity was a hard master.

★

In 1921, Dempsey defended his title against the world light heavyweight champion, Georges Carpentier of France, who was also regarded as the heavyweight champion of Europe, though he weighed barely 170 pounds. Carpentier was a skilled boxer with a powerful right hand, but what made Tex Rickard match him with Dempsey was his personal style: he was cul-tured, almost delicate, and, in the best French fashion, a dandy: he owned hundreds of suits and changed clothes six to eight times a day. Rickard could see the possibilities: France versus America, elegance versus brute force, good guy versus villain—because while Carpentier was a French war hero, winner of the Croix de Guerre, Dempsey had become unpopular.

The previous year, Dempsey had endured a sensational, if brief, trial for draft evasion. The charges sprang from allegations made by his former wife, Maxine, who claimed that she had proof that Dempsey had conspired to get out of military service so that he could pursue his boxing career. The irony of the world's toughest man supposedly shirking the Great War was hard to miss, and millions branded Dempsey a "slacker"—a term that, back then, amounted to calling someone half a man. Maxine couldn't substantiate her charges, though, and she made a poor witness. The jury readily acquitted Dempsey, but the slacker stigma would follow him, lessening as the decade wore on but never entirely disappearing. Rickard, who had become fond of Dempsey, knew how much the charges hurt but also understood that powerful contrasts made for compelling fight promotions. Dempsey–Carpentier— or the Battle of the Century, as Rickard billed it, echoing Johnson–Jeffries— became the first great sporting event of the 1920s.

On July 2, 1921, more than ninety thousand people crowded into a custom-built wooden bowl at Boyle's Thirty Acres, a site that Rickard had leased in Jersey City, for the showdown. They paid a total of $1.8 million, boxing's first million-dollar gate, and the event captured global headlines. The French government ordered that news about the fight's result take precedent over all other messages, even diplomatic communications, and arranged for military planes to fly over Paris to flash news of the winner— red lights for Carpentier, white lights for Dempsey. The crowd in Jersey City included a huge sampling of the nation's elite in politics, business, and the arts, along with a host of international dignitaries. How far boxing had come toward social acceptance was symbolized when Rickard himself escorted John D. Rockefeller to his seat. Perhaps two thousand women attended, the most ever at a prizefight. The Radio Corporation of America made its on-the-air debut, transmitting the fight to as many as three hundred thousand people—one of radio's first mass broadcasts and a pioneering moment for the new technology.

With his majestic crowd in place, Rickard had only two worries: that it would rain before the main event and that Dempsey would destroy Carpentier with the first punch he threw, spoiling the day before people got their money's worth. He pleaded with Dempsey to go easy, but the champion never took any opponent for granted. Anxiety played a crucial role in his aggression. He once summed up his fighting philosophy: "The sooner the safer."[11]

When both men were in the ring, observers noted the size difference. Officially, Dempsey outweighed Carpentier, 188 to 172, but Carpentier was probably lighter than that. Even more striking was the contrast in their appearance. Unshaven and scowling, Dempsey wore a battered old maroon sweater into the ring; with delicate features that, for one reporter, suggested Joan of Arc, Carpentier wore a dove-gray robe with black cuffs. He was cheered ecstatically.

After a careful first round, the fight's most memorable moment came in the second, when Carpentier rocked Dempsey with a right hand, bringing most in the arena to their feet. (The arena itself was shaking violently; it had been built with ingenuity and speed, not care.) Carpentier broke his right thumb with the punch but knew that the right was his only chance to keep Dempsey off him, and he kept throwing it in the third. Dempsey ignored the onslaught and pounded Carpentier at every turn with body blows and, in clinches, rabbit punches—illegal blows to the back of the neck that are thought to weaken the nerves. The challenger slumped on his stool at the end of the round.

In the fourth, a series of Dempsey punches put Carpentier down on his side, and he lay there, seemingly content to take the count. Then he leaped to his feet at nine, trading with Dempsey. The champion bludgeoned him to the canvas again; this time, Carpentier took the full count. The Battle of the Century had lasted barely ten minutes, but no one was complaining.

Coverage of the fight the next day was more lavish than any sporting event had ever received. The *New York Times* devoted almost all its first thirteen pages to the fight. Yet plenty of other news was going on. In Raritan, New Jersey—barely fifty miles away—about an hour after Carpentier took the ten-count, President Warren G. Harding signed the Knox-Porter resolution, formalizing the peace terms ending World War I. About thirty people attended the no-frills ceremony. While the war had shaped the promotion of the Dempsey–Carpentier fight and accounted for much of its public appeal, the war itself, at least in America, was no longer a story.

★

Dempsey earned $300,000 for his four rounds' work (about $4 million today), while Carpentier made $200,000. Those sums stunned people in 1921, prompting concern about a materialist culture that showered entertainers with such lavish rewards. Tex Rickard was content to let critics debate such matters; he didn't plan on promoting another Dempsey fight for some time. He believed that Dempsey should fight rarely, allowing Rickard to find the right opponent and build public interest. In the meantime, Dempsey could enjoy his fabulous earning power.

By early 1923, though, Dempsey knew that he needed a fight. Fair-minded observers, like *The Ring*'s Nat Fleischer, wanted him to take on a black fighter, Harry Wills—by most accounts, the leading heavyweight contender. Though he had announced after beating Willard that he would "draw the color line" as champion—reaffirming the standard that had prevailed before

Jack Dempsey in 1922
Associated Press

Jack Johnson—Dempsey reversed himself not long afterward, stating that he would give black challengers a chance. He had fought blacks before winning the title, and a Wills matchup was a good one for him, as Wills, large and lumbering, would make an inviting target for the champion's blitzing assaults. But Rickard feared another divisive promotion like that of Johnson–Jeffries, along with the business risk of seeing the title pass from a bankable property like Dempsey to a black man. The match would never be made.

Instead, Dempsey let Kearns talk him into defending his title against Tommy Gibbons, a defensive specialist, in tiny Shelby, Montana, where oil had been discovered. A group of civic boosters from Shelby were looking to promote their town to investors and newcomers. They hit on the idea of staging a heavyweight championship fight there on the Fourth of July. Kearns, who longed to prove that he and Dempsey didn't need Rickard, named his price: $300,000, the same purse that Dempsey had gotten for Carpentier, to be paid in three installments—$100,000 up front, $100,000 on June 15, and $100,000 before Dempsey got into the ring. The Shelby men agreed, setting the stage for one of boxing's most colorful and desperate episodes. In short order, the Shelby boosters were scrambling to find the rest of the money, and rumors that the fight would be cancelled persisted almost until the opening bell. By drawing letters of credit on banks around the state, and finally by agreeing to pay Kearns the remaining cash out of the gate receipts, the organizers managed to stage the fight—though it turned out to be a grinding, unspectacular contest, won by Dempsey on a fifteen-round decision before a sparse crowd. Kearns and Dempsey had both become deeply unpopular in Shelby by this point, and they hustled out of the arena, where the mood was turning hostile. Within days, the four Montana banks that had helped finance the bout failed.

The Shelby episode did nothing for Dempsey's reputation, but Rickard soon found the perfect opponent for another big-money extravaganza. The new challenger was Luis "Ángel" Firpo, an Argentinean heavyweight who, eight days after the Shelby fight, electrified a crowd of one hundred thousand at Boyle's Thirty Acres by ending the comeback attempt of forty-one-year-old Jess Willard. Six foot two and 215 pounds, Firpo was a crude brawler with no boxing science. He threw clubbing, roundhouse blows; he pushed and mauled; and he bothered little with defense. His best punch was his right, which he used to put Willard down for the count in the eighth round. The crowd loved it. Newspaperman and author Damon Runyon christened Firpo the "Wild Bull of the Pampas."

Rickard booked Dempsey v. Firpo for the Polo Grounds, where the New York baseball Giants played. He threw all his promotional machinery into action, but the contest didn't need much playing up: people knew that they were going to see a fight, not a fencing match. Firpo's absence of caution made him as volatile an opponent for Dempsey as could be imagined. But whatever people did imagine, what they saw on September 14, 1923, exceeded it.

★

Between eighty-five and ninety thousand fans flooded into the Polo Grounds, giving Rickard his second million-dollar gate. By now, Rickard's crowds had acquired a certain character: they were as massive and various as the American population, with workingmen filing in beside Astors and Rockefellers, bankers and politicians and baseball players and Hollywood stars. Those with the better tickets sat on benches along the infield, where the ring was pitched.

Rickard fretted again that Dempsey might win too easily and warned the champion not to knock out Firpo with the first punch. "I hate to think of all them nice millionaires going out of here sore at both of us," the promoter said. Never easygoing before a fight, Dempsey could not maintain a pretense of politeness, even for his friend. "Go to hell!" he exploded.[12]

At the bell, Dempsey charged across the ring, but Firpo, moving backward toward the ropes, clipped him a right on the jaw, and Dempsey went down to one knee. He was up before a count could begin, throwing punches: left hooks to the body and head, rights to Firpo's jaw. A left hook dropped Firpo for a count of two; left hooks at close quarters dropped him twice more for short counts. The Wild Bull rose and charged into Dempsey, who landed a short right to the jaw, and Firpo went down again. It looked like he might stay there.

Firpo just beat referee Johnny Gallagher's count but was barely erect before Dempsey, standing over him, clubbed him back to the canvas with another right. He rose again—and this time, he was ready. As Dempsey rushed in wildly, Firpo nailed him with a right, and Dempsey had to balance himself with both gloves on the canvas to get his bearings. The two were fighting furiously, not only exchanging their best punches but also wrestling for control in the rare moments when they weren't punching.

Twice more, Dempsey put Firpo down; after Firpo crumpled to the canvas for the seventh time, Dempsey stepped over him and stood in the adjacent corner. He wound up his right, as if to hit Firpo before he was up, but then thought better of it and let the challenger get clear. Dempsey would regret that.

Firpo began landing rights again, and Dempsey seemed unable to get out of their way. The challenger pushed Dempsey past ring center and threw a series of rights, each more looping than the last. Two crashed onto Dempsey's jaw, mighty punches that would have finished an ordinary man. Firpo wound up another right, his arm extending high above his head; it, too, came crashing down on the jaw of the champion. As Dempsey absorbed the blow—its impact both punch and push—his body sagged against the ropes. As if in response, the ropes opened wide, and Dempsey launched backward out of the ring.

He disappeared, one reporter later wrote, "as though a trap door had opened and swallowed him," landing on his back on a set of typewriters in the press row.[13] A *New York Tribune* reporter and a Western Union operator pushed Dempsey up onto the ring apron—not to help him, they later insisted, but to get him off them. "Get me back in there, I'll fix him!" Dempsey snarled, reaching for the lower rope.[14] He climbed into the ring as the referee's count reached nine.

While Dempsey struggled, Firpo peered out into the darkness, wondering whether he was about to be crowned the new champion. When he saw Dempsey reemerge, he went for the kill, convinced that he was one punch away from the title. He landed four—two lefts and two rights—square on Dempsey's jaw, yet Dempsey stayed on his feet until the bell rang, ending the most frenzied round in boxing annals.

The Polo Grounds crowd was in delirium. The infield benches toppled over, and men scuffled, among them Babe Ruth, who nearly got into a fray with welterweight champion Mickey Walker. Chaos reigned in Dempsey's corner, too, where Kearns dumped a bucket of cold water over the champion's head and screamed for the smelling salts to his aide, Jerry Luvadis, who could not get Kearns to understand, over the din, that the salts were in his own breast pocket. Dempsey asked them what round it was.

As it turned out, Dempsey needed no help. Showing his recuperative powers, he pressed the attack again in the second round. Firpo was soon on the floor again, and he was wearing down. Still, he came after Dempsey, and the champion found him first with a left hook that drove him backward and then with a finishing right. Firpo crashed to the canvas—it was the ninth time he had been down—and rolled over onto his back. This time, Gallagher counted him out.

"One of the classic fights of all history," the *New York Times* declared. "About the greatest fight in the history of pugilism."[15] What a *Chicago Tribune* columnist called "the greatest battle since the Silurian Age"[16] had lasted just 3 minutes and 57 seconds, but like the Willard fight, it redefined boxing's dramatic possibilities. A few years later, George Bellows's painting immortalized the moment when Firpo knocked Dempsey out of the ring. The sense deepened that Dempsey was, as Bob Edgren had written in Toledo, a "new type."

Some criticized Dempsey, though, for dirty tactics, especially his habit, also seen in the Willard fight, of standing over opponents after he had knocked them down, in violation of the rule that required the fighter scoring a knockdown to retire to the "farthest corner and remain there until the count is completed."[17] If he didn't, the rule said, the referee *may* stop counting over the fallen fighter until he complied. Dempsey, whose early fights took place in the win-or-go-hungry environment of the rural West, wasn't about to give any opponent a breather, but now boxing authorities reworded the rule to *require* that the referee not start counting over the fallen man until his opponent retreated to a "neutral" corner.

The rule change would have a profound effect on Dempsey's career, but not in 1923. Having earned the ungodly sum of $500,000 for the Firpo fight, Dempsey focused again on his ventures outside the ring. At the White House, he called on Calvin Coolidge; Silent Cal had become president after the sudden death of Warren G. Harding. Where John L. Sullivan had waited in a receiving line to shake hands with Grover Cleveland, Dempsey was a guest of honor. He was the greatest sports star in America, if not the world, with the possible exception of Ruth. But there was no comparison between Dempsey and the Babe economically: Dempsey made almost as much in one fight as Ruth made in his career.

All that money made it easier for Dempsey to stay out of the ring. By 1924, he had fallen in love with Estelle Taylor, a screen actress, and the two were married in early 1925. Then Dempsey made news on two fronts: he and Doc Kearns were splitting up, and he had a new nose. The nose job was Taylor's idea—she hated boxing and boxers—but the symbolism of the Manassa Mauler getting prettied up seemed ominous. So did his break with his longtime manager, for even those who disliked Kearns—and that would be most people—could see what he had done for Dempsey. But Kearns wasn't going without a fight. He tied up the champion's money, filing suits and countersuits that would go on for years.

In 1926, with Dempsey's layoff approaching three years and the champion passing his thirty-first birthday, a public clamor went up for him to fight someone—anyone—or announce his retirement. Dempsey accepted Rickard's offer to defend his title that September in Philadelphia against an ex-marine, Gene Tunney, who had fought his way into top contention. Press and public welcomed the news that the Manassa Mauler would return to the ring, and Rickard set to work crafting his storylines and managing his logistics.

★

Gene Tunney had none of Dempsey's ability to generate passion. Tunney was not a slugger but a boxer, and a scientific one, at that—how scientific, Dempsey and Rickard were about to find out.

Tunney hadn't come up in Dempsey's hardscrabble world but had been poor by any other standard. Born in 1897 to Irish parents in Manhattan, he grew up in Greenwich Village and started boxing at Catholic Church fund-raising events. After the United States entered World War I, he enlisted in the Marines, shipping out to France in October 1918, a month before the war ended. The only action he saw in France was in a boxing ring, where, fighting in the American Expeditionary Forces tournament, he won the light heavyweight championship.

He was not a natural fighter and had no special physical assets, but his mind and will proved nearly unmatched. Failing or giving up was unthinkable; setbacks, no matter how devastating, were temporary. In 1922, Tunney endured a fifteen-round bloodletting in his first battle with middleweight Harry Greb, still ranked among the greatest fighters in the sport's history. Greb broke Tunney's nose in the first round and opened up cuts over both of Tunney's eyes, the blood flowing so freely that it stained the canvas and covered both fighters and the referee. Yet Tunney stayed on his feet, losing the decision and two quarts of blood along the way. Defeats like this can ruin a fighter, but the Greb slaughter was Tunney's boxing catechism, and he emerged a true believer. From his hospital bed, he laid plans for a rematch. He would fight Greb four more times and never lose again.

Even before running into Greb, Tunney had set his mind on challenging Dempsey. It became a defining ambition, a nearly decade-long quest, at the end of which he saw not just the heavyweight championship, and not just the wealth to which he aspired, but also a different life—one of learning and culture and possibility. While Dempsey sat idle in the mid-1920s, Tunney kept beating top fighters, including former Dempsey foes Georges Carpentier and Tommy Gibbons. Tunney had grown into a heavyweight— by the standards of the time, anyway, weighing nearly 190 pounds—and had been studying Dempsey's fights for years. He was sure that he could hit Dempsey with right hands, as Carpentier and Firpo had, and that by moving and tying up Dempsey's rushes, he could prevail.

Public anticipation was high for the first heavyweight championship fight in three years. Once again, a Rickard promotion commanded national and international attention. Between his guarantee and a sizable share of the gate receipts, Dempsey would make more than $700,000. Tunney would earn $200,000 and entered the bout as the popular favorite. He had served his country in the war, whereas Dempsey had shirked; he fought cleanly, whereas Dempsey was seen as a rule-breaker; and he was clean-cut and apparently virtuous, while Dempsey had become enmeshed in the world of money, celebrity, and lawsuits.

On Thursday evening, September 23, 1926, as storm clouds gathered over Philadelphia, Tunney donned his marine robe and made his way to the ring in the new Sesquicentennial Stadium (completed that spring, in time for the international exposition marking the 150th anniversary of the Declaration of Independence). Rickard's promotional ability and Dempsey's drawing power were as reliable as ever: 120,000 people, the largest sports crowd in history at the time, paid nearly $2 million to see the fight.

The Dempsey who awaited Tunney was not the Dempsey he had pursued for so long. His body out of tune from years of easy living, the champion seemed uncertain of himself. He had been harried by Doc Kearns's process servers during training, and he had gotten sick to his stomach on the way to Philadelphia. Above all, he had lost what even great champions lose: the spring of youth and the compelling need to be in the ring.

★

Dempsey charged out for the first round, as always, but he was in for a surprise: Tunney aimed to fight him—or, at least, to fight on Tunney's terms, which meant circling and bouncing on the balls of his feet. But from these postures, Tunney took the fight to Dempsey. A minute into the action, he flashed out the right with everything he had on it. It landed high, on Dempsey's cheekbone, but it was the first real punch the champion had taken in three years, and its effects amazed him. Sitting in his corner after the first round, Dempsey thought, "I'm an old man."[18] As if on cue, the sky opened and rain began falling.

Dempsey lived up to his ferocious image in the second round, throwing knockout punches and chasing the challenger around the ring. Tunney was unfazed; he kept Dempsey at arm's length, popping him repeatedly with rights, some thrown as leads, others set up with jabs. Dempsey could not pin Tunney on the ropes, the skill that boxers call "cutting off the ring." Instead, he merely followed, like a dance partner obeying a lead.

The rain soon became a downpour, but the huge crowd wouldn't dream of turning away. At ringside, the soaked sportswriters who had followed Dempsey's career since Toledo could see that he was in trouble. By the middle of the fight, the area around Dempsey's eyes had gone purple, and his battered face became more misshapen in the driving rain. Once, in the sixth, he broke through, nailing Tunney with a left hook to the throat. Tunney would later cough up blood from the punch. But the champion's legs and stamina were gone, and he was lucky that the fight was only scheduled for ten rounds. By the final round, still pressing, Dempsey seemed half-blind. Except for the drama of the title changing hands, the fight was dreary; a sense of inevitability crept in long before it was over.

When the unanimous decision for Tunney was announced—it was the first time a challenger had won the title this way, instead of by knockout—Dempsey grabbed hold of his seconds and said, "Take me to him." Tunney watched as the man he had stalked for the better part of a decade approached. "All right, Gene," Dempsey managed through swollen lips. "All right, good luck."[19] And he threw his arms around Gene Tunney in the rain.

The rain still pounded as the fighters left the ring, but now the cheers came up that Dempsey had longed to hear for so long. In the seven years that Dempsey had been on top, he had often heard more boos than applause. Like Ruth, he aroused great passions that made neutrality impossible; and like Ruth, he was one of the most unaffected men who ever stood in the American spotlight. Won over at last by his bitter courage, the crowd rallied to him.

Dempsey's magnanimity in defeat transformed his public image from that of scowling villain to vulnerable hero. "I have no alibis to offer," he said. Then he added words that, consciously or not, echoed those of John L. Sullivan when he had been beaten: "I lost to a good man, an American—a man who speaks the English language."

He inadvertently introduced a phrase into the language when a reporter overheard Estelle Taylor asking him what had happened. "Honey, I just forgot to duck," he said.[20] The comment hit the papers the next day and, in the unaccountable way of such things, helped bring the public's latent adulation bursting forth. The line itself survived its context; half a century later, on a hospital bed from an assassin's bullet, Ronald Reagan used it to similar effect.

But Dempsey's new stature came at the price of the title he had coveted since he was a boy. In his dressing room after the Tunney fight, he wept, as Sullivan had.

The Dempsey–Tunney fight made news around the world. The *New York Times* devoted a three-tier, six-column front-page headline to the result, along with several supporting stories about the event and the crowd. New York's first heavyweight champion came home to a hero's reception, but the honeymoon was brief. Complicated and aloof, Tunney didn't connect with the sporting public in the way Dempsey had, and his cerebral defensive style left many fans cold. Though a profoundly dedicated boxer, Tunney hated the boxing business and saw most people associated with it as criminals or brutes. Where Dempsey enjoyed mingling with sportswriters, Tunney's distaste was never far from the surface.

Worst of all for Tunney's image, it came out that he liked to read serious literature, including Shakespeare. This discovery might have been acceptable to the fight crowd were it not for Tunney's pretensions. Often, he spoke with an affected diction that suggested a man trying to impress people who weren't in the room. Chiding reporters for a story he disliked, he lectured them: "Your conduct . . . was most unbecoming, when I acted the man, for you to construe, as you did, my actions to your ends. That's the sort of ungentlemanly thing that makes it so difficult for you chaps to get what you want."[21]

Meanwhile, Dempsey, brooding on the loss of his title, decided that he could not live with himself unless he tried to get it back. On July 21, 1927, he entered the ring at Yankee Stadium to fight Jack Sharkey, a leading contender and ex-navy man known as the Boston Gob, with Tunney set to fight the winner. Though it was not a fight for the championship, Dempsey–Sharkey gave Rickard yet another million-dollar gate, as eighty-five thousand fans crowded in, some jumping over the bleachers to have a look.

Talented but temperamental, the twenty-four-year-old Sharkey had the fading former champion on wobbly legs early and outfought him all the way, building a large lead through the first six rounds. But even as Sharkey ripped his face open with cuts, Dempsey pressed the attack, especially to the midsection, hoping to slow the younger man down. Fighting at close quarters in the seventh round, Dempsey dug a series of hard blows to Sharkey's belly. Sharkey broke from Dempsey, dropped his hands, and complained to referee Jack O'Sullivan that the punches were low. Dempsey's left hook landed on Sharkey's chin an instant later. Sharkey dropped to the canvas, and O'Sullivan counted him out.

Another Dempsey fight, another controversy: some critics felt that Dempsey should have been disqualified for fouls, while others objected to his hitting a man who had dropped his hands. Yet Sharkey had violated a cardinal boxing rule: "Protect yourself at all times." As Dempsey put it: "What was I going to do—write him a letter?"[22] There would be a second Dempsey–Tunney fight, in September.

★

Promising to scale tickets up to $40—well above New York's top price of $27.50—Chicago was a logical winner of the Dempsey–Tunney sweepstakes: under the leadership of William "Big Bill" Thompson, who had just regained the mayor's office, the Windy City prized its reputation as a "wide-open town." And Thompson enjoyed the backing of the era's defining gangster, Al Capone. Chicago also offered recently constructed Soldier Field, which was bigger than anything New York could provide. With tens of thousands of field seats added to the giant stadium in Grant Park, Rickard hoped to set an all-time attendance record of 163,000.

The buildup for the Dempsey–Tunney rematch took place against the backdrop of what was, even by 1920s standards, an eventful year. The stock market kept booming, and the miracles kept coming: 1927 saw the first transatlantic phone call and the first demonstration of television. Dempsey's only competitor for sports adulation was Ruth, pursuing his record-setting sixty home runs that season. But neither the Babe nor Dempsey could compare with Charles Lindbergh, who flew his single-engine plane, the *Spirit of St. Louis*, from New York to Paris in May. Lindbergh made the thirty-three-hour flight alone, sometimes navigating by sight. He landed on May 21 at Le Bourget airfield in Paris, the American hero of the decade, bar none.

By September, all eyes were on Chicago and its two complex figures— the one too flawed to be perfect, the other too perfect to be a hero. Dempsey–Tunney II broke all records for gate receipts—$2,658,660—and created the sporting spectacle of the era. Special trains arrived in Chicago from cities around the country; a railroad worker called it "the greatest troop movement since the war."[23] Joining those of modest means were Rickard's coveted people—politicians, entertainers, international royalty, and the financial elite. The swelling crowds filed into Soldier Field on Thursday evening, September 22, 1927. The official paid attendance was 104,943, but contemporary estimates ran as high as 150,000. The throngs would watch a ten-round battle between two men earning the most kingly purses in history: $450,000 for Dempsey, just shy of $1 million for Tunney. It was Rickard's masterwork: the ring posts were made of gold.

Around the United States, millions tuned to the fight via radio, the largest audience that had ever heard a broadcast. Fifty-five American stations around the country carried Graham McNamee's blow-by-blow, and shortwave radio took it around the world. For many, the transmission of the battle's defining moment would be lost in overwhelming waves of noise.

Shortly before 10 p.m., Dempsey arrived in the Soldier Field ring, and referee Dave Barry called the fighters together to review the rules. He placed special emphasis on the last one: "In the event of a knockdown, the man scoring the knockdown will go to the farthest neutral corner. Is that clear, Jack? Is that clear, Champ?" Both men nodded. "In the event of a knockdown," Barry continued, "unless the boy scoring it goes to the farthest neutral corner, I will not begin the count." Then Barry said, "Shake hands and come out fighting."[24]

Dempsey started faster than he had in Philadelphia, his aggression more pronounced, but the rematch soon resembled the first fight. Boxing in the tradition of his ring idol, James J. Corbett, Tunney was choreographing the second fight almost as well as he had the first. Dempsey, though out-generaled, was fighting with even more viciousness than usual, hammering Tunney to the body—sometimes low—and throwing his usual assortment of rabbit punches. After taking a pasting in the fourth, Dempsey fought back in the fifth and sixth.

"Some of the blows that Dempsey hits make this ring tremble," radio broadcaster Graham McNamee told his worldwide audience at ringside, "and the microphone down below it."[25] But after six rounds, Tunney seemed well ahead.

They came out for the seventh, and the usual pattern of circling and pursuit continued. Near the center of the ring, Dempsey landed a right cross to the side of Tunney's face. It was the kind of punch that Tunney had deflected easily in seventeen rounds of battling Dempsey over the past year. This one had gotten through. Following him, Dempsey looped a long left hook and connected again. Now he was nearly upon Tunney's chest, and he landed a short right. Three consecutive punches had found the elusive champion's chin. The third punch forced him into the ropes, but he sprang off, straight into Dempsey and the shortest punch yet, a left hook that landed just above the chin. Tunney's legs deserted him, and he began to fall.

As Tunney descended, Dempsey managed to hit him three more times: a right hand, another left hook, and a finishing right. The seven-punch combination that had begun at ring center sent Tunney to the canvas in a sitting position, his right leg bent backward. The formerly bright eyes of the master boxer, the Shakespeare student and self-willed man, were vacant.

Referee Barry directed Dempsey across the ring, invoking the neutral-corner rule. Dempsey stepped back a few feet behind Tunney—not what the rule required. Barry persisted, trying to move Dempsey over. Dempsey's face was blank, his mind churning. Was this bureaucrat really telling him where to stand? Finally, he shuffled away.

As he fell, Tunney grabbed hold of the middle strand of ropes with his left glove. He sat in a reverie with the roar of one hundred thousand people in his ears, pulling hard on the rope as he steadied himself against the whirlwind in his head. Behind him, Dempsey and Barry negotiated. It was as if a piece of theater had split off into two scenes, leaving the audience to decide which to follow. All this drama—the essence of the fight—transpired in barely five seconds.

Standing over Tunney, Barry looked down to ringside to knockdown timekeeper Paul Beeler, whose job was to toll the seconds the moment a fighter hit the canvas. At this point, Beeler was shouting, "Five." Barry raised his arm and shouted, "One!" He was restarting the count because of Dempsey's infraction. Beeler understood and called back, "Two," and both men counted over the champion in unison. At Barry's count of three—at least eight seconds after hitting the canvas—Tunney raised his head and picked up the count, his eyes coming back into focus. At Barry's "nine," Tunney hoisted himself up, using the middle rope. He had been on the canvas at least fourteen seconds.

Dempsey rushed across the ring to finish the job. Tunney got up on his toes and danced, flicking out jabs and right hands as he went. The punches were mostly perfunctory; the action was in Tunney's legs, which carried him around Dempsey's furious rushes. His superb physical condition—he had practiced running backward in training, thinking precisely of this scenario—restored him to his senses as he glided around the ring, and Dempsey could not catch him.

It didn't take long to see that Dempsey had missed his chance. As if sensing it himself, he beckoned Tunney to come and fight. Nothing doing: Tunney stayed away until just before the bell ending the round, when he landed a right under the heart that left Dempsey gasping. Outside the ring, men were already chattering about how long Tunney had been on the floor.

In the eighth, Tunney dropped a fading Dempsey with a short right. Dempsey rose immediately—no taking of a full count for him. But he had nothing left, and his face was a mess. Tunney now took complete command. The last two rounds resembled the Philadelphia fight, with an exhausted Dempsey, again puffed around the eyes, giving chase in vain. The decision, handed down by referee Barry and two judges, was unanimous for Tunney. He was $1 million richer and still champion.

But had he really won? The debate that surrounds what became known as the Long Count comes down to two questions: Could Tunney have gotten up without the benefit of the extra seconds? And if he had, could he

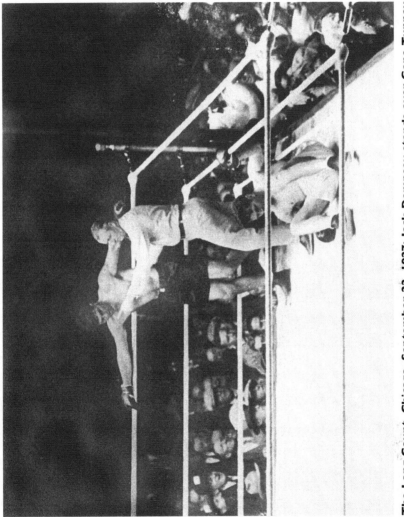

The Long Count, Chicago, September 22, 1927: Jack Dempsey stands over Gene Tunney while referee Dave Barry directs him to a neutral corner—an instruction that Dempsey would take too late.

have survived Dempsey's attack? Tunney insisted that he could have gotten up at the referee's count of three, after about eight seconds had elapsed. Judging from the film, Tunney appears alert enough to rise—but whether he could have evaded Dempsey is impossible to know.

After filing an initial protest of the referee's decision, Dempsey accepted the outcome. The grail had slipped through his fingers. His second loss to Tunney had a poetic character. Dempsey's tragic flaw, it turned out, was that he was so much a fighter that he had forgotten the new, civilizing rules, and this had cost him the title. But he was celebrated for his gracious handling of what many saw as an injustice.

Of course, the fighter in him couldn't resist looking back. "You know, I probably hit him too many times. You can knock a fellow out sometimes and then bring him around with another punch. I've seen it happen more than once."[26] Tunney would also revisit the Long Count: "At the count of two I came to, and felt in good shape. I had eight seconds to go. Without the long count, I would have had four seconds to go. Could I, in that space of time, have got up? I'm quite sure that I could have."[27] They had the rest of their lives to talk about it.

★

Some called for a third Dempsey–Tunney fight, but Dempsey, worried about the damage he'd suffered around his eyes, decided that he'd had enough of the ring. He had plenty of money, and he must have figured that he would never come closer to his old title than he had in Chicago.

After beating Dempsey, Tunney went to collect his $990,445.54 purse from Rickard, but he brought with him a personal check for the difference, thus accepting Rickard's check for an even $1 million, a framed photostat of which would hang in his home for years. He fought once more after Chicago, knocking out Tom Heeney, a rugged but unremarkable contender, in a bout on which Rickard lost money and all concerned felt Dempsey's absence. Then Tunney retired from the ring and announced his engagement to Polly Lauder, a Carnegie heiress to a $50 million fortune. Tunney's life moved inexorably in the directions he had envisioned: now a man of wealth, he read and studied—he once lectured on Shakespeare at Yale—pursued business interests, and mostly maintained his distance from the boxing scene. His connection with Dempsey kept him before the public, though: the Long Count linked them in history, each anniversary providing fodder for retrospectives, and the two became warm friends. In 1964, Dempsey campaigned for Tunney's son John, who was running for Congress. John won and later served as a senator from California. When Tunney died at eighty, in November 1978, William F. Buckley Jr., eulogizing him in *National Review*, wrote: "We meditate, with resolution to emulate, his spirited encounter with life."[28]

Dempsey's encounter with life was just as spirited and far more public. He lost millions in the 1929 stock market crash, and he put the gloves on again and set out on a national exhibition tour, which proved lucrative and briefly tempted him to come back. With a business partner, he opened Jack Dempsey's Restaurant in the mid-1930s. Once it settled in at its Broadway and 49th Street location, it became a New York institution until its closing in 1974, the blueprint for the modern sports bar. Its signature piece of décor was James Montgomery Flagg's massive wall mural of the Dempsey–Willard fight in Toledo. Dempsey himself often occupied a table near the window, where he greeted visitors. He would never be far from boxing, and he was known for being a soft touch for ex-fighters and magnanimous to fans. The cheers that sounded for him in Philadelphia in 1926 never really stopped until 1983, when he died in New York at eighty-seven.

By then, he had resolved most of the loose ends of an eventful life. After the Japanese attacked Pearl Harbor in 1941, the forty-six-year-old Dempsey tried to enlist. The army turned him down, but the Coast Guard commissioned him to lead its physical training program. In 1945, Dempsey went ashore after the liberation of Okinawa. He won plaudits and honors for his patriotic service, which, remembering his "slacker" past, he took pains to downplay.

In 1950, accepting an award as the greatest fighter of the half-century from the Associated Press, Dempsey made peace with his estranged ex-manager, Doc Kearns, crediting Kearns with turning him into a champion. Kearns was grateful, but his gratitude didn't last. In 1963, the ailing Kearns sold a story to *Sports Illustrated* reviving the controversy from the Willard fight: that Dempsey's gloves had been "loaded." Kearns had done the job himself, he claimed, using plaster of paris. Kearns's story was pure fiction, as attempts to duplicate what he described proved. Moreover, *Ring* magazine's Nat Fleischer, as upstanding a figure as existed in boxing for half a century, had watched Dempsey's trainer, Jimmy DeForest, wrap the fighter's hands in Toledo and had seen nothing unusual. Neither had Willard's men, who had also been present.

The punishment that Dempsey inflicted in Toledo—likely exaggerated as the years passed—can probably be explained by DeForest's use of a hardening adhesive tape to wrap his hands. One observer compared it with bicycle tape, which would make Dempsey's hands very hard indeed. The tape was not illegal, at least in Toledo in 1919. Dempsey and Kearns were always looking for advantages. At least one pre-Willard opponent asked to inspect

Dempsey's hand-wraps, and in 1921, before the opening bell in Jersey City, Georges Carpentier's manager, Francois Descamps, insisted that Dempsey remove the adhesive tape on his hands and wear the softer gauze bandages mandated by the New Jersey Boxing Commission. Dempsey complied. Were Dempsey's gloves loaded in Toledo? Yes—but only in comparison with the softer wrappings that modern fighters wear. The foul-play accusations that surround the Willard fight make wonderful lore but poor history. These were different times.

Dempsey's demolition of Willard, his battles against Firpo and Tunney, and his power as a gate attraction explain why he holds a special place in boxing history. But how good was he? Critics cite his inactivity, mediocre opponents, and failure to fight Harry Wills. Defenders point out how Dempsey's swarming, attacking style changed the sport. His ranking tends to split along traditionalist vs. modernist lines.

In the end, it doesn't really matter where Dempsey ranks—as it doesn't for Sullivan or Johnson, either. Like them, he forged something that hadn't existed before. No one could ever be Dempsey again. No one would ever duplicate the Willard massacre; such savagery would never again be permitted. No one would re-create the madness of the Firpo fight, its chaos suggested but surely not fully captured in the jumpy old silent film. No one could restage the Long Count. And the Dempsey archetype—the lean, hungry fighter, stripped of adornment—remains the defining one in boxing, as Mike Tyson would prove nearly sixty years later. Against all this, modern judgments can only say so much.

★

In the first week of 1929, Tex Rickard suddenly died, of complications after an appendectomy. The promoter had been organizing an elimination series to determine the new heavyweight champion. Already, Dempsey's retirement had robbed boxing of its star. Tunney's departure had presented the challenge of anointing a successor. Now Rickard was gone, too.

That fall, Black Tuesday sent the stock market reeling and laid the foundation for the Great Depression. The riotous energies of the 1920s would soon dissipate under a grinding struggle to survive. Soon, the simple things of life would be harder to come by, and people would survive on less than they had ever imagined. The same ethic would apply to the heavyweights. Other men stood waiting now for their chance at the vacated title. They wouldn't remind fans of Dempsey or Tunney, but they were the only available substitutes. Like everything else in the Depression years, they would have to do.

THE SUBSTITUTES

Max Schmeling sat on his haunches before eighty thousand people in Yankee Stadium, holding his groin. He'd been coming to the United States for a few years now, and he'd struck his share of poses: young heavyweight hopeful who looked strikingly like Jack Dempsey; articulate, cultured German, a favorite of Weimar's café society; and genial self-promoter, always happy, when landing again in New York, to answer questions from sportswriters—to whom he often handed bottles of good German beer. But this posture was a new one: victim.

Schmeling had been hit low by Jack Sharkey, his opponent on a June night in 1930, and he collapsed to the canvas. His handlers carried him to his corner like a stricken man. The boss in Schmeling's corner, Joe Jacobs, berated referee Jim Crowley, insisting that Schmeling had been fouled and should be declared the winner. (Unlike today, when most fouls result in warnings or point deductions, in 1930 a single foul could end a fight, with victory awarded to the wronged boxer.) In his other ear, Crowley got the counterargument from Johnny Buckley, Sharkey's manager. The huge crowd waited for Crowley's ruling, on which the heavyweight title rested.

Schmeling and Sharkey were the finalists from a nearly two-year-long series of elimination bouts set up to fill the vacant heavyweight title. Before 1928, only one heavyweight champion, Jim Jeffries, had ever taken the title into retirement—and Jeffries appointed his own successor. When Gene Tunney duplicated this impressive yet somehow inconsiderate feat, he left the task of succession to the New York State Athletic Commission and the National Boxing Association, which regulated boxing outside New York. Two years without a heavyweight champion amounted to a crisis of meaning, and the Yankee Stadium crowd paid $700,000 to see a new champion step into the lineage.

The brief fight was dominated by the twenty-eight-year-old Sharkey, who had reached his fighting peak. Since his ill-fated battle against Dempsey in 1927, he had fought everyone; many felt that Tunney had avoided him. Though he remained unpredictable, he was aggressive and determined against Schmeling, hurting him in the third with several rights. Schmeling looked overmatched. Near the end of the fourth, as the two men came together, Sharkey tried a left hook to the body. His head got caught under Schmeling's arm as the German tried a left hook of his own; Sharkey's torso twisted downward, and his fateful punch landed below the belt.

The two judges scoring the bout were seated at opposite ends of the ring—one had seen the foul clearly, while the other had seen nothing. The beleaguered Crowley was trying to make up his mind when a Hearst newspaperman—Arthur Brisbane, who, as a young man, had covered the John L. Sullivan–Charley Mitchell mud-fest in Chantilly—told him that Sharkey's foul was blatant and that if Crowley didn't name Schmeling the winner, then he, Brisbane, would make sure that Hearst papers ceased covering boxing.

Crowley's indecision vanished. He declared Max Schmeling the winner and new heavyweight champion—the first German to win the title and the only man ever to claim it from a sitting position. If Schmeling's victory struck boxing fans as a strange resolution, they couldn't imagine how strange things were going to get.

★

Born the son of a German sailor in 1905 in Klein-Luckow, Germany, Max Schmeling endured a poverty-ridden childhood that darkened further when Germany lost World War I. More than two million Germans had died, and the country was plagued by food shortages, mass unemployment, political instability, and the burden of paying war reparations as dictated by the Treaty of Versailles (Germany would not settle its World War I accounts until 2010). All the seeds were planted for the rise of political extremism, but for most of the 1920s, the struggling Weimar Republic brought something like democracy to the country. And in Berlin, Hamburg, and elsewhere, science, architecture, literature, and the fine and performing arts flourished, producing a remarkable flowering of creativity.

The sixteen-year-old Schmeling discovered boxing when he saw movies of the Dempsey–Carpentier fight. In 1925, when just a fledgling pro, he had the experience of his young life when he sparred with Dempsey, who was visiting Cologne as part of a European tour. His talents also attracted attention from an unlikely quarter. The artists and intellectuals of Weimar's café society viewed boxing as a unique blend of the primitive and cerebral and also as an expression of modernity, a break from bourgeois cultural traditions. By the late 1920s, Schmeling had become their favorite.

Though he possessed little formal education, Schmeling had a curious mind, and he enjoyed getting to know these creative people, many of them Jews. He crossed paths with actor Fritz Kortner, painter George Grosz, actress and singer Marlene Dietrich, filmmaker Josef von Sternberg, novelist Heinrich Mann, and art dealer Alfred Flechtheim, who, in 1927, invited Schmeling to attend his art salons, thus bringing the fighter into the charmed Weimar circle. As Schmeling left one of Flechtheim's parties, he was asked to sign the guestbook, and he offered a rhymed couplet: *Künstler schenkt mir eure Gunst, Boxen ist doch auch eine Kunst* ("Artists, grant me your favor, boxing is also an art").[1]

In 1928, after winning the German and European heavyweight titles, Schmeling set out for greater fortunes in the United States. The American heavyweight scene was in transition: Dempsey had just retired, and Tunney was about to do the same. And then along came this dark-featured German who actually looked like the Manassa Mauler—and he could fight. The boxing writers called him the German Dempsey or, more dramatically, the Black Uhlan of the Rhine (after the lancers in the German army). Schmeling secured the services of Joe Jacobs, a Jewish fight manager whose leverage and connections earned him the nickname Yussel the Muscle. With Jacobs guiding the way, Schmeling worked his way to the top of the heavyweight ranks.

Capturing the heavyweight championship should have been a glorious moment for Schmeling, but instead it brought him ridicule. He was derided as the "foul champion," and the New York commission, for a time, refused to recognize him—though the decision to award him the title had been made by one of its own officials. (American commissions changed the foul rule shortly afterward.) Even in Germany, Schmeling sometimes found himself mocked.

Another showdown with Sharkey would settle the matter. The two were finally matched again in June 1932, at Madison Square Garden's huge new outdoor arena in Long Island City. This was not a new Garden but a spinoff structure, meant for summer events and known as the Madison Square

Garden Bowl, sometimes called the Long Island City Bowl. Its debut seemed promising: seventy thousand fans came out to see Sharkey–Schmeling II. Millions tuned in to NBC to hear the broadcast over sixty-nine radio stations, the most yet to carry a boxing match.

In the rematch, the roles were reversed. It was Schmeling who fought with direction and purpose, pressing the action, and Sharkey who fought with caution resembling indifference. Neither man was in any danger over fifteen dull rounds. But Schmeling's performance was a confident one—he had mastered Sharkey, it seemed, and answered the doubters.

Then came the decision: Sharkey. He was the new champion.

A despondent Joe Jacobs shouted something about Schmeling being "jobbed" or "robbed," an expression immortalized in American vernacular as: "We wuz robbed!"[2] Many in the predominantly American crowd, unmoved by seeing the title come back home, booed the decision. At ringside, fourteen of twenty-two writers scored the fight for Schmeling.

The second fight reversed roles outside the ring, too. Now Schmeling was the martyr, a champion whose title had been taken from him. And the long-frustrated Sharkey finally had the crown, only to hear that he didn't deserve to wear it. It seemed fitting for a man who had, as one writer put it, "the strangest, most paradoxical career in all ring history."[3]

Even his name was indeterminate. The son of Lithuanian immigrants, he was born Joseph Paul Cukoschay in Binghamton, New York, in 1902—unless he was born Joseph Paul Zukauskus. Even when he died, ninety-one years later, wire-service obituaries used one or the other. Cukoschay/Zukauskus grew up around Boston and started boxing in the navy, quickly becoming the best fighter aboard any ship he sailed on. Starting his professional boxing career, he changed his name to the Irish-sounding Jack Sharkey, not to deceive about his ethnic origins but to honor two of his boxing heroes: Jack Dempsey and Sailor Tom Sharkey, the turn-of-the-century battler who had warred with Jim Jeffries on Coney Island in 1899.

Sharkey mastered a style that combined elements of boxing and brawling, and, with a fiery temperament, he made a formidable opponent. When he squared off against Schmeling in 1930, no one doubted his credentials. It was his psyche that they wondered about.

Sharkey soon became as well-known for his volatile behavior as for his boxing skills. In one fight, he began crying in the ring when it looked like the referee might disqualify him for a low blow. Sportswriters dubbed him the Weeping Lithuanian and the Mad Balt. He could look unbeatable, as he did for six rounds against Dempsey and four against Schmeling in their first fight. Or he could be mediocre and passive, as he was against Schmeling in their return fight. William Muldoon, John L. Sullivan's old trainer, called Sharkey "the best fighter in the world from the neck down."[4] *New York Times* columnist John Kieran wrote that whenever Sharkey entered the ring, the referee should ask, "Who comes there?"[5]

Yet Sharkey was a practical man outside the ring: after each fight, he made large deposits in a Boston bank, and he got special satisfaction out of the $211,000 he dropped in there for fighting Dempsey, his greatest purse. He hoped to settle down soon with his family in Chestnut Hill, Massachusetts, where he planned to open a bar, hunt and fish, and cultivate petunias.

By 1933, he was well on his way to that goal—and was certainly doing better than the rest of the country. The Great Depression had unfolded slowly after Black Tuesday, but a plague of bank failures—more than one thousand in 1930, including the Bank of the United States in New York, and more than two thousand in 1931—made clear that the financial system was unstable. Signs of desperation filled American cities: the infamous "Hoovervilles," shanties and cardboard shacks where displaced people took shelter; beggars coming into restaurants and drawn-looking men selling apples on the street; hoboes thumbing it on the roads and on the trains; and long lines of men applying for scarce jobs or waiting for a piece of bread. On March 4, 1933, when Franklin D. Roosevelt took office as the nation's thirty-second president, 25 percent of the eligible workforce was unemployed. The Depression's impact would be felt in the heavyweight division, too. Though both Sharkey–Schmeling fights drew well, attendance and receipts dwindled over the next few years, making the million-dollar gates of the Dempsey years seem like a dream.

★

Boxing had not seen his like since Jess Willard: he stood six foot six, weighed over 250 pounds, and wore a size 22 shoe. He was considered a giant, even a freak—and he was expected to be not just powerful but fierce. But Primo Carnera had little ferocity in him.

He was born in Sequals, Italy, in the foothills of the Alps near Slovenia, in 1906, the first son—hence the name—of a stonemason and his wife. Folklore would later have it that he weighed 22 pounds at birth. His childhood was desperately poor. For years, he worked in France as a laborer, toiling in backbreaking physical jobs. At seventeen, he came upon a traveling circus in Paris and was soon starring as a strongman and as a wrestler.

When the circus broke up in 1928, the twenty-two-year-old Carnera met Leon See, a French fight promoter and manager who took one look at him and sensed his drawing power. See launched Carnera's career in Paris against the most unthreatening opposition he could arrange and then took him back to Italy and Germany, where he compiled an impressive record of victories against undistinguished opposition. In time, Carnera learned some basic boxing skills. His size alone made him someone to reckon with, and his courage was boundless. But against fighters of real ability, he was usually outmatched.

As Carnera's fame on the Continent grew, he drew the interest of American backers—in his case, gangsters. Racketeers had always dabbled in boxing, but in the 1930s, they stepped up their involvement. Mob elements soon coalesced around Carnera and See. They were led by notorious underworld figures Broadway Bill Duffy—a prominent Prohibition figure who had done time in Sing Sing for robbery—and Owney Madden, who had made a fortune in bootlegging before taking over the Club Deluxe in Harlem from none other than Jack Johnson and reopening it as the Cotton Club.

Madden and Duffy elbowed See aside, buying out most of his interest in Carnera. Their eyes were on the American market, where they stood to make tidy sums, so long as they could keep Carnera winning. The way to do that was to pick fighters so inept that they posed no threat or to intimidate or pay off fighters he couldn't beat honestly. The Carnera team eventually arranged a series of setups, with the goal of propelling the Italian into a match for the heavyweight title.

A gentle and disingenuous man, Carnera was a mismatch for his body, which suggested destructive power; but the destructive power resided in the forces gathered around him. His halting knowledge of English and general innocence made him a plaything in the mob's hands. While he generated a steady flow of income—his first tour of America brought in $700,000—he saw almost none of it. They told him that his money was being invested; they could have told him anything. Even See, an archangel compared with the Americans, gulled him financially.

In an era when Americans whom sociologists later dubbed the "white ethnics"—immigrants and their descendants from southern and eastern Europe—flocked to boxing, Carnera's Italian heritage provided a new locus of excitement in the sport's premier division. Carnera was even more marketable than Schmeling, who drew support from German fans but was too complex to be packaged neatly. Carnera's size—he was often photographed towering over much smaller men, like a museum curiosity—made him a good sell, and he was an easy target for caricaturists in a less sensitive time. (It was discovered years later that he suffered from acromegaly, a pituitary disorder that often produces gigantism.) Sportswriters dubbed him the Ambling Alp, Il Ponderoso, and Satchel Feet—or, more affectionately, Da Preem. He endured endless puns about his size and intelligence. At one point, he boxed a kangaroo.

Some sportswriters pointed out the fraudulent nature of the Carnera buildup, but nothing could be definitively proved. The Italian's progress to a title shot became inexorable after he knocked out respected contender Ernie Schaaf in New York in February 1933. Many at ringside yelled, "Fake!" when Schaaf, who was being managed by his friend Jack Sharkey, went down from a light punch in the thirteenth round. But Schaaf was rushed to the hospital and died a few days later of a brain hemorrhage. The incident prompted calls for the abolition of boxing.

An autopsy revealed that Schaaf had come into the Carnera fight a damaged man: doctors found that his brain showed inflammation from recent bouts with influenza and meningitis. These facts were soon forgotten, however. While some sportswriters pinned Schaaf's death on the punishment he had suffered in earlier fights, especially against a rising California heavyweight named Max Baer, the Carnera syndicate exploited the Schaaf tragedy to tout Primo's "killer" punch.

Thus Carnera found himself in the Madison Square Garden Bowl in Long Island City, on June 29, 1933, challenging Sharkey for the title. The massive bowl was barely half-filled, with forty thousand fans paying a paltry $200,000. Though outweighed by nearly sixty pounds, Sharkey controlled the action for five rounds. Then in the sixth, Primo came out more aggressively, trying to use his superior bulk to dominate the smaller man. He drove Sharkey to the ropes, and a retreating Sharkey lost his balance and slipped just as Carnera was throwing a right uppercut. Sharkey jumped back up and the fighting resumed, but he seemed suddenly weary and flustered by Carnera's pressure. Carnera backed him to the ropes and threw another right uppercut. Sharkey's head shot up, and he collapsed. Referee Arthur Donovan counted him out. Primo Carnera had become the first Italian to win the heavyweight title.

"Nothing will ever convince me that that was an honest prizefight," wrote novelist Paul Gallico, who covered sports until the late 1930s.[6] *Ring* magazine's Nat Fleischer agreed, saying that Carnera had won with an "invisible punch."[7] Boxing historian Mike Silver believes that "Sharkey threw that fight for a huge amount of money," but no evidence has ever surfaced.[8]

Both boxers insisted that the result was legitimate. Near the end of his life, though, Sharkey told boxing historian Mike DeLisa that "Carnera couldn't have hit me in the ass with a handful of tacks if I didn't let him."[9]

Was that a confession that he threw the fight, or did it reflect Sharkey's frustration at losing the title?

Whatever the truth, Sharkey found himself a thirty-one-year-old ex-champion with a robust bank account but a tarnished reputation. He could hear the petunias calling. Carnera's situation was the opposite. His win made him heavyweight champion, but he woke the next morning with barely $300 to his name. A month later, he declared bankruptcy.

★

Despite the dubious nature of Carnera's victories, some felt that Da Preem's massive bulk would be too much for challengers to overcome—much as earlier observers had felt about Jess Willard. Others saw the division's future in a twenty-four-year-old slugger from California whose right-hand punch was as devastating as his personality was infectious. His name was Max Baer—Maximilian Adelbert Baer, to be precise. Three weeks before Carnera lifted the crown from Sharkey, Baer had burst into national prominence in a dramatic battle against Max Schmeling. The fight, on a sweltering early June evening, drew sixty thousand fans to Yankee Stadium. Schmeling, the more experienced fighter, was trying to position himself for a third battle with Sharkey for the title. He was a 2–1 betting favorite, and early on, while taking a pasting from Baer, he hurt the younger man with his trademark right. But Baer, six foot two and 203 pounds, with shoulders like a lumberjack's and back and chest muscles like a weightlifter's, shook the punch off—with the help, as the story goes, of Jack Dempsey, who had promoted the fight and would work closely with Baer.

"I see three of him," Baer was purported to have said between rounds. Dempsey was unfazed. "Hit the one in the middle," he told his young charge.[10]

The fight was close, with several momentum shifts. Baer was a free swinger, looping long punches and leaving himself wide-open. When he pressed his advantage, his punching power gave him the edge. When Baer tried to box with Schmeling, he was undone by the German's superior skills.

In the tenth round, Baer landed a crushing right, and Schmeling sagged. He wobbled backward as Baer followed him, throwing the right hand again and again—along with numerous illegal backhand punches. Finally, he sent Schmeling to the canvas in a heap with another right. The German made it to his feet at nine. Baer moved in; the German tottered under the assault, turning his back to Baer and clinging to the ropes. Referee Arthur Donovan jumped in and stopped the fight.

If Baer–Schmeling was free of any concerns about foul play, it was shad-owed by something darker: international politics. That January, Adolf Hitler had come to power in Germany, and the climate for German Jews quickly worsened. Within months, the Nazis had imposed economic sanctions on Jewish businesses, barred Jews from certain jobs, and organized the burn-ing of more than twenty thousand volumes of books, including works by Thomas Mann, Karl Marx, and Erich Maria Remarque, Germans all. Most ominously, the SS had already established Dachau, the first concentration camp in Germany.

Looking for representatives for their ideological and racial claims, the Nazis adopted Schmeling as a champion of Aryan achievement, even though Schmeling moved in heavily Jewish circles, from the boxing world to the cultural scene. The Nazis were captivated by the German fighter, just as the Weimar intellectuals—many of them now on the run—had been. Though the two groups admired Schmeling for different reasons, both saw him, in their own ways, as a symbol of German vitality. Now, just as Alfred Flechtheim had done, Hitler invited Schmeling to receptions and lunches, and, as Schmeling headed to the states to take on Baer, the Führer urged him to put in a good word for the new Germany.

Arriving in New York, Schmeling did as Hitler asked. He made no pro-nouncements in favor of Nazi theories but told reporters that he had seen no mistreatment of Jews—and, subtly contradicting himself, suggested that Jews had brought their troubles upon themselves with their harsh criti-cisms of the Nazis. This early in Hitler's tenure, it was possible for many to believe him, and perhaps Schmeling believed it himself. But American Jews, especially in New York, tried to organize a boycott of the Baer fight. Their efforts only heightened public interest. Baer–Schmeling was the first politically themed fight of a decade that would see more.

Baer had been swept up into the political currents, too. The young Californian wore the Jewish religious symbol on his trunks for the first time against Schmeling, though his Jewish heritage consisted of a paternal grandfather and no tradition of religious observance. "Every punch in the eye I give Schmeling is one for Adolf Hitler," the normally easygoing Baer said.[11] Some dismissed Baer's eleventh-hour Jewishness as opportunism, but he never looked more focused in a boxing ring.

Baer's conquest of Schmeling was a star-making performance and posi-tioned the young fighter for a shot at the winner of the Carnera–Sharkey fight. It also set him up for lucrative opportunities outside the ring because Max Baer was a personality first and a fighter second. In fact, he didn't like boxing.

He was born in 1909 in Omaha, Nebraska, the son of a butcher who eventually relocated the family to Livermore, California, on the eastern end of the San Francisco Bay Area. Young Max did lots of physical labor, building his remarkable physique; but unlike many of his predecessors, he grew up in relative comfort. From the start, he had a gift for making people laugh. He didn't throw a punch in anger until his teenage years, when he laid out a brawny lumberjack at a local dance. The power in his right hand made a boxing career seem fated. The young Adonis won twenty-three of his first twenty-six fights, most by knockout. He was just twenty-one, a crowd-pleasing slugger and a free spender, woman chaser, and fancy dresser outside the ring. He signed up with Ancil Hoffman, a Sacramento-based manager, and the two looked to take Baer east for big-money fights.

Their ambitious plans went off course in August 1930, when Baer fought a tough heavyweight named Frankie Campbell in San Francisco. The fight was an all-action battle while it lasted. In the fifth round, Baer trapped Campbell on the ropes and assaulted him with one blow after another. Campbell was losing consciousness, but the ropes held him up, so Baer kept hitting him. One punch sent Campbell's head crashing against the metal turnbuckle connecting the ropes and the ring posts. Finally, the referee stopped the fight; many felt that it should have been stopped much sooner. Baer was rushed out of the ring to celebrate and knew nothing of Campbell's condition until he got a phone call the following morning: Campbell was in the hospital and not expected to survive. He died later that day.

Those who knew him best said that Baer was never the same fighter afterward. "After Frankie Campbell," said Buddy Baer, Max's brother, who would also fight as a heavyweight, "the clowning started. It was something to do instead of fighting."[12] Several later opponents said that Baer hurt them and then let them off the hook. Yet Baer's performance against Schmeling showed that he was still capable of ferocity, and it wouldn't be the last time that he seemed to enjoy his work in the ring.

If Primo Carnera made good copy, Max Baer could fill a newspaper on his own. He was a wit and a ham, a vaudevillian trapped in a boxer's body. Before he met Hoffman, he sold well over 100 percent of himself to investors, under the mistaken impression that there was 1,000 percent to sell. "I've got a million-dollar body but a ten-cent brain," he said.[13] When he said that his full name was Max Adelbert Baer, a reporter asked: "Not Maximilian, is it?"

Baer replied, "I still have the million to get."[14]

Baer would often joke about his lax training methods—he sometimes stamped on the feet of sparring partners instead of punching them—leading John Kieran of the *New York Times* to call him Max Addled-a-Bit Baer. He saved his most strenuous efforts for the pursuit of Hollywood starlets. Despite his great physical talent, he could never apply himself seriously to the work of being a boxer, especially the hard months of training and self-denial. So he became the clown of the ring. He was dubbed the Livermore Larruper for his punching power, but sportswriters also called him the Magnificent Screwball, Madcap Maxie, the Larruping Lothario of Pugilism, the Playboy of Pugilism, the Clouting Clown, and the Fistic Harlequin—as many nicknames as any fighter ever enjoyed.

Baer really wanted to be on stage, telling jokes and singing songs. He had some success in this ambition later in 1933, when he costarred with Myrna Loy in *The Prizefighter and the Lady*, an MGM musical comedy in which he played Steve Morgan, the boxer of the title who falls in love with Loy's nightclub singer. The film, which doubled as a former champions' reunion—it featured Dempsey in a bit part and cameos by Jess Willard and Jim Jeffries—had considerable charm, thanks to Baer. He was a plausible leading man and even pulled off a long musical sequence, singing an original number written for him, "Lucky Fella." The *New York Times* called Baer "easily the outstanding thespianic graduate of the squared ring," and lest that sound like a backhanded compliment, the paper added that he "sings and dances a good deal better than some of those who consider themselves experts."[15]

One other notable participated in *The Prizefighter and the Lady*: Primo Carnera, who, billed as himself, shared the ring with Baer in the climactic fight scene. Carnera may have regretted doing the movie at all. From the moment he ran into Baer, he was off balance. He had no answer for Baer's needling and teasing, which went on throughout the filming. Worse, the script had the big fight ending in a draw, with "Steve Morgan" knocking Carnera down twice. What heavyweight champion would consent to playing himself in a film, against a prospective challenger no less, and let the challenger batter him around? It was another example of the thoughtlessness of Carnera's handlers: they didn't care about their man's psyche, so long as they got paid. With his mocking of Carnera off camera and his dress rehearsal with him in the boxing ring, Baer was setting up the big man psychologically for their eventual showdown.

When Carnera and Baer met for the title on June 14, 1934, at the Madison Square Garden Bowl in Long Island City, their real-life battle proved even more absurd than the celluloid version. Near the end of the first round, Baer dropped Carnera with a clean right to the jaw, and Carnera rose on wobbly legs. Baer went after him, clouting him into the ropes, and

Carnera fell backward without quite going down to the canvas. He then rose and staggered away from Baer, who followed close behind, unloading wild roundhouse rights. Carnera fell again into the ropes. He kept falling and rising before the referee, Arthur Donovan, could start a count and thus kept putting himself in the way of more mayhem from Baer.

In the second round, Baer's assaults sent Carnera down three more times. Each time, Carnera, trying to keep himself upright, held on to Baer, pulling him down with him as he fell. And so the crowd was treated to the absurdity of two men falling together to the canvas, as if part of a comedy routine. "Last one up is a sissy!" Max shouted at one point.[16] Some at ringside laughed; others shook their heads in disgust. This was a heavyweight championship fight?

Carnera had been mocked for his fighting skills and shady connections; ridiculed for his hulking size; and denigrated for his mental capacities, halting English, and Italian heritage. But no one watching now could fail to recognize his fighting heart. After enduring another knockdown in the third round, he started working his left jab and using his bulk to get himself back into the fight. Amazed that Carnera had survived, Baer paced himself—and mugged for the crowd. He made faces, dropped his hands to his sides, hitched up his trunks, and laughed. Between his punching and his clowning, which had an edge of cruelty, he didn't seem like a man haunted by Frankie Campbell.

Finally, in the tenth round, one of Baer's well-placed rights found the champion's jaw. Down went Primo, and the sequence mimicked that of the opening round: he rose, he staggered; Baer followed, punching him at will as he fell and rose; and Donovan raced after the two men, trying to keep up. After Baer dropped Carnera twice more in the eleventh round, Primo motioned to Donovan, seemingly seeking intervention. Donovan waved the fight over, leading Baer away and declaring him the new heavyweight champion.

Meeting the press afterward, Carnera denied that he had wanted Donovan to stop the fight. He would never quit, he insisted. Then he burst into tears. Carnera's exploitation is one of boxing's darkest chapters, analogized by Budd Schulberg in his novel *The Harder They Fall*, which became Humphrey Bogart's last film. Some would see later parallels in Rod Serling's *Requiem for a Heavyweight* and in Fellini's *La Strada*.

Max Baer had attained the prize, though his performance had been anything but artful. Still, with his talent, it seemed that he might be a legitimate heir to Dempsey. He was only twenty-five and figured to wring massive wealth out of the title. Baer got busy with the usual promotional work of a heavyweight champion and landed the starring role as a detective in a radio series, *Lucky Smith*, sponsored by Gillette, which ran multiple promotional contests to keep the audience tuned in. One campaign asked listeners to choose a name for Baer's dog.

★

For all his efforts, FDR couldn't get Americans to shake the sense that they were living through a national curse. If they doubted it, they could look at the dust in the air of eastern cities in May 1934, a month before Baer fought Carnera—a 350-million-ton onslaught that traveled from the Great Plains to Chicago, New York, Boston, Atlanta, and Washington, leaving a few grains in the Oval Office and forcing some cities to halt business and turn street lamps on during the daytime. The storm was part of a broader catastrophe of drought and dust storms torturing the West and portions of the South for most of the decade. Meanwhile, though FDR's programs put millions back to work in public-works jobs, countless others remained idle.

One of them was James J. Braddock, a once-promising light heavyweight contender whose boxing career hit the skids not long after the stock market crash. Braddock had lost sixteen of his last twenty-six fights, breaking his good punching hand, the right, several times along the way. He was considered more or less retired in spring 1934, when the dust came east. A father of three living in North Bergen, New Jersey, Braddock worked whenever he could as a longshoreman, but shifts weren't steady. He had once earned four-figure purses for fights in Madison Square Garden, played in the stock market, and invested in a taxicab company. Now, as with millions of others, his savings had vaporized and he could not pay his bills. When the gas and electric utilities shut off his service, he sent his kids to live for a time with their grandparents—and applied for public assistance, the final indignity. Bringing home the $6 per week to his young family, he exemplified what the Depression did to men's dreams.

Born in 1905 to Irish immigrant parents in the Hell's Kitchen neighborhood of New York City, Braddock was drawn to boxing in 1919, when, outside the offices of the *Hudson Dispatch*, he listened to a blow-by-blow account over megaphone of the Dempsey–Willard fight in Toledo. A few years later, he had become a talented amateur, winning several championships in New Jersey. Tall and rangy at six foot two, Braddock weighed barely 180, but his powerful right hand brought him many victories against bigger men.

In his early pro career, Braddock moved from triumph to triumph, and he found himself in Yankee Stadium in July 1929, fighting for the light heavyweight championship of the world against Tommy Loughran, perhaps the most brilliant defensive fighter who ever lived. (Two years later, baffled by Loughran's skill and hearing boos from the crowd, Max Baer turned to a ringsider and said: "I'd like to see you try and hit this guy."[17]) Moving away from Braddock's right while using his powerful and accurate jab, Loughran frustrated his challenger's timing and confounded him with his defense, winning nearly all fifteen rounds.

The Loughran setback inaugurated a long and torturous slide. One bad break after another bedeviled Braddock: he lost some close fights; he hurt his hand repeatedly; he saw his purses cut; he lost more fights; and his money ran out. Soon Braddock's name had dropped well out of the conversation of legitimate contenders or even journeyman opponents. Though he always had plenty of Irish in him—a genuine belief that he could beat anyone—the cascade of negation wore him down. "I think I should quit," he said to his loyal manager, Joe Gould. "I don't want to embarrass myself."[18]

Gould, however, never gave up on Braddock, not only because the two men were good friends but also because Gould didn't have a better alternative. He kept pressing Jimmy Johnston, the Madison Square Garden matchmaker, to give Braddock another fight. Johnston liked Braddock—everybody did—but had grown weary of Gould's pleas. But in June 1934, Johnston found himself in need of an opponent for John "Corn" Griffin, a young contender fighting in the preliminaries to the Baer–Carnera title bout. When Griffin's original opponent dropped out, Gould happened to be standing in Johnston's office. Reluctantly, Johnston conceded, and Gould hopped a ferry across the Hudson to find his fighter, who was working a shift on the docks. Braddock would get $250 to serve as Griffin's stepping-stone.

With people still filing in to the Bowl, Griffin charged out of his corner, looking for an early knockout. He hurt Braddock with one of the first punches he threw and gave him a thorough going-over. In the second round, he dropped Braddock with a right. But Braddock was in another place mentally. "It meant so much to me to win this fight," he later remembered. "My wife and kids depended on me. I had to win."[19]

Getting to his feet at the count of nine, Braddock thought: he's going to come at me with a left hook. As Griffin tried to deliver the finisher, Braddock stepped inside the left and nailed the young prospect with a perfect right cross. Griffin crashed to the canvas, to the astonishment of the crowd. He got up and fought back gamely until the bell. In the third round, Braddock swarmed Griffin with a fusillade of punches, until the referee stopped the fight. Corn Griffin's brief career as a contender was over.

Braddock and Gould celebrated modestly; they didn't have much to celebrate on. But Braddock's old confidence was back. "I did that on hash," he told Gould. "Get me a couple of steaks and there's no telling what I'll do."[20] Then he and Gould watched from the wings as Baer destroyed Carnera in the main event.

Most observers regarded Braddock's upset win over Griffin as a fluke. But near the end of 1934, he beat John Henry Lewis, a gifted light heavyweight and a top fighter of the 1930s. In March 1935, Braddock was matched with Art Lasky, a Minnesota-born heavyweight rated near the top of the division, at Madison Square Garden. Looking better than he ever had, Braddock outboxed Lasky over fifteen rounds to win a clear decision. He had won three fights in a row, all against highly rated contenders who had been prohibitive favorites, and positioned himself for a shot at Baer.

Baer agreed to put his title on the line against Braddock in June, at the Madison Square Garden Bowl in Long Island City. Oddsmakers made Braddock a 7–1, 10–1, or even 15–1 underdog. Baer agreed, treating Braddock's challenge as a joke, and the champion knew something about that: for the past year, he had been doing more joking than fighting.

He trained for the Braddock fight with indifference, joking with sparring partners and drinking beer after workouts. By contrast, Braddock set up a training camp in the Catskills so grueling that observers called it Homicide Hall. Stronger and fitter than he had been in years, Braddock believed he would win.

As the fight approached, reporters, digging for angles on the challenger, ran stories about Braddock's recent experience on the relief rolls. In 1935, public assistance was a new concept; its recipients often felt shame for taking it, though there were millions of others in their predicament. Despite widespread support for Roosevelt's efforts to use government power to help the unemployed, many viewed "the dole" with dread or scorn. Braddock certainly did. So did his wife, Mae, who was mortified when the family's struggle became public news.

But Braddock was unbowed. He had done what he had to do for his family. Besides, after he earned $4,000 for the Lasky fight, he paid back his local welfare agency all the relief money he had been given. "I gave $300 to the Relief Fund of Union City," he told a reporter. "That covered the $240 I got all told when we were on relief. It was the only fair thing to do. I couldn't let the kids go hungry. I'm not ashamed."[21]

His story and his candor made Braddock a hero to millions. Public support for him against Baer, already considerable, now overflowed. Sportswriters understood that Braddock's story resonated among Americans in 1935 like almost nothing else. "In all the history of the boxing game," Damon Runyon wrote, "you'll find no human interest story to compare with the life narrative of James J. Braddock."[22] And then he hung on Braddock the name with which history would remember him: the Cinderella Man.

But for all that, the odds didn't change much, and one sportswriter warned that, if the referee didn't watch closely, Baer might kill Braddock.

★

On Thursday night, June 13, 1935, Jim Braddock climbed into the ring at the Madison Square Garden Bowl. He had beefed himself up to 194 pounds and was in the best shape of his life, though he would be out-

With Jack Dempsey looking on, the Cinderella Man, James J. Braddock (left), strikes a pose with champion Max Baer (right) a few months before their 1935 title fight.
Associated Press

weighed by the 210-pound champion. The Bowl was not even half-filled, with just thirty thousand fans paying a total of only $200,000—a measure not only of the Depression's suffocating effects but also of the general sense that Braddock had no chance.

But from the moment the bout began, Braddock was in charge. He put his fight plan into effect immediately: circle and move to stay away from Baer's right, keep his left jab in the champion's face, and throw his own right when the openings came. It was a disciplined, strategic plan for taking Baer's title away. The unpolished champion struggled to find a rhythm against the steady jabbing and moving of his challenger. It didn't help, either, that Baer wasn't taking the fight seriously and that he was following after Braddock like a man forced to walk around the block for exercise. As he had against Carnera, Baer mocked his opponent, pulling faces when a punch got through his guard, looking as though he wanted to be anywhere else.

"Is that Myrna Loy?" Baer, gazing out into the crowd, asked one of his cornermen between rounds.[23] They warned him that he was giving away rounds; Braddock was pitching a shutout after six. But in the seventh, Baer wound up his big right and found Braddock's jaw, and the Cinderella Man buckled at the knees. Baer went after him, though with no great urgency. Braddock pumped his jab, tucked his chin into his chest, and rode out the storm. In the eighth, when Braddock landed a light punch, Baer did a mock stagger and laughed.

The fight was getting away from Baer, and the crowd sensed it. They kept cheering for Braddock, but more than anything they wanted to see a good fight and weren't getting it. It wasn't Braddock's fault. At least he was trying, though his yeoman efforts weren't exactly thrilling to watch. As the rounds passed, Baer grew more frustrated. "Hey, Max, you better get going," Braddock told him. "You're way behind."

In Baer's corner, Ancil Hoffman gave him the same advice. "What's wrong with you, Max? You've got to knock him out!" Baer tried to put over the right that could end it, but Braddock stood firm. Most discouraging for the champion, the crowd in the Bowl was rooting overwhelmingly for Braddock. Baer the showman had lost the audience.

After fifteen rounds, the ring announcer stepped to the microphone and only got as far as saying, "The winner and new champion" before the crowd drowned him out.[24] And for the fourth time in four title fights, a heavyweight champion had lost his title at the Madison Square Garden Bowl. No champion at any weight, in fact, had retained his title fighting at the Bowl, which became known, for the rest of its brief life, as the Graveyard of Champions.

Braddock–Baer hadn't been much of a fight—the *New York Times* corre-spondent, James P. Dawson, called it "one of the worst heavyweight cham-pionship contests in all the long history of the ring"[25]—but its outcome was hugely popular, sealing the happy ending to the incredible Braddock story. "It just goes to show you how far a stout heart will take a fellow, provided he has a good left hand to go with it," Frank Graham wrote.[26]

Even Baer graciously credited his conqueror. "I have no alibis to of-fer. Jimmy won, and no better fellow deserves a break."[27] Later, speaking over the radio, he demonstrated the casualness that had doomed him as champion and the personality that made him hard to forget. "I'm glad and really happy to see Jimmy happy. . . . He'll appreciate it more than I did, I guess, and he needs it more. After all, he's got a family and he's married. Of course, I might have a family around the country, too, but I don't know it!"[28] The off-color outburst, shocking to many ears in 1935, cost Baer his radio show and probably other endorsement deals. All in all, June 13, 1935, had to be the most expensive night of Max Baer's life.

Braddock's grit and courage were timeless qualities that took on added meaning in the Depression years. As W. C. Heinz wrote of him: "In no list that you will ever see will he be listed among the ten greatest, but that is as it should be. . . . He may, however, in the sense that others see themselves in him and read their own struggles into his, have belonged to more people than any other champion who ever lived. . . . What happened to him . . . happened to a whole country, and that is why I believe that no other fighter was ever as representative of his time."[29]

★

The heavyweight championship had never changed hands so often as it did between 1930 and 1935: five men, each lacking in some crucial respect, had claimed the title. Some may not have deserved to be champion; others could not seem to fill the role once they stepped into it. One historian called the era the Dark Ages of heavyweight boxing. But if the quality had dropped off, the human interest had never been higher. Max Schmeling and Primo Carnera were international champions—from Germany and Italy, no less—in a decade when those nations haunted the minds of millions. Jack Sharkey was a tor-mented diva, Max Baer a sad clown, Jim Braddock an inspirational working-man. Whether undistinguished or underachieving, they all shone as individual characters. And they would all have one more starring—or costarring—role to play in the heavyweight drama. Even as Jim Braddock's hand was raised in Long Island City, the future of boxing had arrived in New York.

BLACK MOSES

He had "sloping shoulders, powerful arms with sinews as tough as whip-cords and dynamite in his fists," wrote James Dawson, the *New York Times*'s boxing reporter, in 1935. His "inscrutable, serious face" revealed "no plan of his battle" and offered "no sign whether he is stung or unhurt." His punches were precisely thrown and accurate, helping him launch "the most savage, two-fisted attack of any fighter of modern times."[1]

Dawson had sat in the rain in Philadelphia in 1926 and watched Tunney outbox Dempsey. He'd been in Chicago the following year, when Dempsey exploded out of his crouch in the seventh round and put Tunney down, dead to rights, or so it seemed. And he had been ringside for most of the nine dreary title fights that had taken place since the Long Count. In none had he seen what he was witnessing now: June 25, 1935, in Yankee Stadium, when the former heavyweight champion, Primo Carnera, faced a twenty-one-year-old black fighter from Detroit named Joe Louis.

Though they were fighting just ten days after the Braddock–Baer championship bout, Louis and Carnera had aroused much more public interest. The Madison Square Garden Bowl in Long Island City was less than half full on the night that Baer frittered his title away. In Yankee Stadium, sixty thousand people paid nearly double that fight's gate, $375,000, to see Carnera and Louis. Part of the interest was racial: it had been twenty years, back to Jack Johnson and Jess Willard in Havana, since a black man had faced a white man in a heavyweight match of such consequence. Part of the interest was political: Carnera, an ex-champion only a year removed from his crown, was a son of Italy and a hero of Benito Mussolini. Now Mussolini was making plans to invade Abyssinia (Ethiopia), whose emperor, Haile Se-lassie, was a hero to blacks around the world. Thus the young heavyweight, Joe Louis, found himself for the first time—but not the last—cast in the role of representative of his race. The Carnera–Louis fight, like Max Baer's battle against Max Schmeling in 1933, took on the trappings of war.

Fighting mostly in Chicago and Detroit, Louis was unbeaten in nineteen fights, with fifteen knockouts, most inside three rounds. *Ring* magazine already rated him among its top ten heavyweights. The Carnera fight was Louis's first appearance on boxing's big stage. Blacks drove east from De-troit in one-hundred-car caravans. Others boarded special trains to New York from cities around the country. Louis had already become the most famous black man in America.

Though Carnera outweighed Louis by more than sixty pounds, Louis attacked the giant without fear. One of his first punches, a left hook, split Carnera's lip open. The former champion's eyes opened wide. Carnera tried to use his left jab, a decent weapon, to keep Louis off him, but Louis worked his body, pounding the midsection to bring his hands down. Then he resumed rearranging Carnera's face. Even Carnera's attempt to muscle his foe backfired; Louis pushed him back into the ropes. "I should be doing this to you," the big man said.[2]

The fight was no contest, though somehow Carnera withstood the pun-ishment until the sixth round, when Louis sent him to the canvas three times. Carnera kept getting up, just as he had against Max Baer. But his face was covered in blood, and he hung on to the ropes to steady himself. Referee Arthur Donovan stopped the fight. Blacks in Harlem celebrated in the streets, and people began talking seriously about Louis fighting for the heavyweight title.

"He punches like Dempsey," Dawson wrote of Louis. Those were magic words in 1935, but soon Dempsey and others would seem less like Louis's peers than preparers for his arrival.

★

"Red clay. You would have thought the whole world was red clay," Louis wrote in his autobiography, describing the soil of his native Lafayette, Alabama, where he was born, the seventh of eight children to Lillie and Munroe Barrow and the grandson of slaves.[3] Worn out by the strain of supporting his family, Munroe Barrow broke down and was put away in the Searcy Hospital for the Negro Insane in Mount Vernon, Alabama. He periodically escaped and came back home, once staying for over two years—during which time, on May 13, 1914, Joe Louis Barrow was born. But Joe never knew his father. Munroe returned to Searcy, and not long afterward, Lillie Barrow was told that her husband was dead (he wasn't). She remarried a widower, Pat Brooks, himself with eight children, and the combined Brooks-Barrow household of sixteen kids tried to make a go of it in a rural world without electricity and plumbing.

Joe learned to speak late, with a slight speech impediment. He was soon several grade levels behind in school. Quiet and deferent from the start, he cultivated silence. For the rest of his life, others would read into that silence what they wished.

When Joe was twelve, the family moved north, to Detroit, where Pat and his older sons would seek work in the Ford plants. Even in rural Alabama, Henry Ford's legend was pervasive: everyone knew that he paid five dollars a day. Joe enrolled in vocational school.

Looking for constructive activities for her son, Lillie Barrow signed Joe up for violin lessons, but he had no feel for the instrument. A friend, Thurston McKinney, a promising boxer, asked Joe to come along to the Brewster Recreational Center, where he trained. Joe fell in love with boxing from his first visit—hitting the bag, skipping rope, shadowboxing. One day, Thurston asked Joe to spar. Joe took a pasting, until he landed a right that buckled Thurston's knees and made his eyes glaze over. Neither could believe it because McKinney was the Golden Gloves welterweight champion of Detroit.

"Man, throw that violin away," McKinney said.[4]

When he began boxing, Joe billed himself as simply "Joe Louis," hoping that by dropping "Barrow" he could keep his mother from finding out how he was spending his time. But she supported him when she learned that he had become a fighter. His talent as an amateur was apparent right away; he won most of his fights. Joe had always worked part-time, delivering ice, coal, or vegetables, and later, he worked full-time, pushing truck bodies onto conveyor belts at Ford's famous River Rouge plant. But by his nineteenth birthday, in 1933, his working days were over. Devoting himself full-time to boxing, he won the 1934 Detroit Golden Gloves and the National Amateur Athletic Union title in the light heavyweight division.

Louis attracted the attention of John Roxborough, one of black Detroit's power brokers. Roxborough was lord of the Motor City's thriving numbers industry—an illegal lottery system. With his wealth and influence, Roxborough helped young black kids get educations, sometimes right up to college. He was, Louis later wrote, "well encased in dignity and legitimacy."[5]

Roxborough bought Louis new boxing equipment and new clothes, even putting him up at his family home. He soon got Joe's consent to a managerial copartnership with Julian Black, Chicago's black numbers king.

The final piece of the puzzle was a trainer: Jack Blackburn, a black contemporary of Jack Johnson's who had been one of the best lightweights of the early twentieth century. Blackburn never got a title shot, though, which embittered him—not that he needed prodding to bitterness. After an altercation involving his common-law wife in 1909, he served five years in prison for the murder of another man. Along the way, he also became a sworn enemy of Johnson's, the result, some said, of his outboxing Johnson once in a gym. Blackburn was profane and hostile, terrifying when drunk—he would escape another murder conviction in 1936—but ingenious, principled, and even lovable to his friends.

"You've got to be a killer; otherwise I'm getting too old to waste any time on you," Blackburn told Louis.

"I ain't gonna waste any of your time."[6]

The two men quickly became close, calling each other "Chappie." Besides teaching Louis the ins and outs of boxing, Blackburn gave him an education in how to carry himself. The most important thing, he said, was to avoid arousing the anger or suspicion of whites. Jack Johnson's shadow continued to hang over heavyweight boxing. "If you really ain't gonna be another Jack Johnson," Blackburn said, "you got some hope. White man hasn't forgotten that fool nigger with his white women, acting like he owned the world."[7]

Blackburn, Roxborough, and Black devised a code of behavior that essentially stripped Louis of any public show of personality or ego, thus renouncing—implicitly, if not explicitly—everything that Johnson had represented. The rules included admonitions never to enter a nightclub alone; never to be photographed with a white woman; never to gloat over fallen opponents, which usually meant white opponents; and to "live and fight clean." Combined with Louis's own natural reticence, the rules made him as unobjectionable—and as unknowable—as a public figure could be. Never in his long career would he let the mask slip. (In private, he had plenty of fun, and not all the women whose beds he shared were black.) Where Johnson's gold-toothed smile shaped his public image, Louis's stoic expression would identify him to millions of Americans.

Five uninspiring heavyweight champions plus Depression economics made the boxing public more receptive to breaking the color line. And Louis's arrival on the scene was about to remake boxing's power structure. After Madison Square Garden kingpin Jimmy Johnston spurned his overtures, Roxborough found a willing suitor in Mike Jacobs, a ticket seller and scalper extraordinaire who had helped Tex Rickard finance some of his million-dollar promotions in the 1920s. Jacobs had started a rival organization, the Twentieth Century Sporting Club, that he hoped would contend with the Garden as boxing's key matchmaker. He saw his chance with Louis, signing the young fighter to a long-term contract. Jacobs, who would become famous for his unswerving devotion to profit and his clattering false teeth, would be to Louis what Rickard had been to Dempsey.

Boxing fans had heard about the "next Dempsey" from the moment the original had retired, but Louis would prove the real thing, possessing the singular ability of the knockout artist to end any fight with one punch. Like all such fighters, Louis was a gate attraction. Blacks and whites put their money down to see him. His talent created an irresistible momentum.

★

In the Sugar Hill section of Harlem, Louis spent the afternoon and early evening of September 24, 1935, relaxing at an apartment that would later become the property of Duke Ellington. His management team had introduced him to a beautiful nineteen-year-old Chicago stenographer, Marva Trotter, and she and Louis planned to marry soon. But now, Louis decided that there was no point waiting. He and Marva took their vows in a brief ceremony, with her brother presiding, and then Louis and his crew piled into a limousine for Yankee Stadium, where he had a date of a different kind: with former champion Max Baer.

The prospect of the two heavy punchers squaring off—one white, one black—had brought boxing excitement not seen in New York since Dempsey and Firpo. Even with a ring pitched over second base and thousands of additional field seats, Mike Jacobs could not meet the demand for tickets. A crowd of ninety-five thousand came out, nearly producing the first million-dollar gate since the Long Count. Though the Cinderella Man, Jim Braddock, was the heavyweight champion, it seemed to many that Baer and Louis were fighting for the real title.

Watching from ringside as Baer entered the ring, Braddock saw no sign of Madcap Maxie, the ring's great clown, or of the slugging Livermore Larruper. Instead, he thought, Max looked like a man going to the electric chair. Worried about pain in his right hand, Baer told his trainer, Jack Dempsey—working with Max in a futile quest to make him a serious fighter—that he didn't want to go through with the bout. As the story goes, Dempsey told him that he could fight Louis in the ring or him, Dempsey, in the dressing room. Baer took his chances with Louis.

Baer came out for the first round pawing with his long left and trying a few feeble rights that left him standing wide open before Louis. Louis jabbed and then opened up with combinations, the speed and power of which many at ringside had never seen from a heavyweight. By the end of the first round, Baer's face was red, his eyes cut. It got worse in the second, when Louis pummeled him and the huge crowd roared, waiting to see Baer fall. But Baer fought back furiously, and the two men even traded punches after the bell. Encouraged, Dempsey exhorted Baer between rounds.

"He hasn't hit you yet, kid," the Manassa Mauler told him.

"Then you better keep an eye on [referee] Arthur Donovan," Baer said, "because somebody in there is beating hell out of me."[8]

In the third, Louis put Baer down for the first time in his career, with a right, and then again with a savage left hook. Baer seemed finished, but the bell saved him. Late in the fourth, Louis landed a pile-driving right. Baer raised his left arm as if in surrender and fell to his knees. He took the ten-count on one knee and then walked to his corner as some in the crowd booed. Afterward, reporters asked him why he didn't get up. Baer's response: "When I get executed, people are going to have to pay more than twenty-five dollars a seat to watch."[9]

The violence of Louis's work against Carnera and Baer, two former champions, stunned many. Boxing writers outdid themselves trying to come up with alliterative nicknames, all referring to the color of his skin: the Sepia Slugger, the Dark Destroyer, the Chocolate Chopper, the Mahogany Mauler, and finally the one that endured: the Brown Bomber. White sportswriters, straining for metaphors, often fell back on racist caricature. They repeatedly referred to Louis as a wild and savage beast operating on instinct. Watching Louis destroy Carnera from behind that blank expression, Grantland Rice wrote that Louis "seems to be the type [of jungle animal] that accepts and inflicts pain without a change of expression." Before the Baer fight, Paul Gallico described Louis as "the magnificent animal" and wondered whether Louis was "all instinct, all animal? Or have a hundred million years left a fold upon his brain?"

When they weren't portraying Louis as a primitive beast, many white writers reverted to the flip side of the racial stereotype—depicting the young fighter as simpleminded and lazy. "He's a big, superbly built Negro youth who was born to listen to jazz music, eat a lot of fried chicken, play ball with the gang on the corner, and never do a lick of heavy work he could escape," wrote Bill Corum in the New York Journal. "The chances are he came by all those inclinations quite naturally."[10]

Many whites still saw Louis as something less than human, but for blacks, Louis was something more. He was becoming a figure out of folklore, a John Henry–type hero who took on massive impersonal forces and triumphed. In Louis's case, that force was American racism. He was a physical hero whose deeds had moral force: they provided uplift to a demoralized people. The

Joe Louis, a stoic champion for a stoic time

Depression years were hard on all Americans economically but worse for blacks. In the South, lynchings continued, but little was done to prevent them. Civil rights advocates pushed the Roosevelt administration for an antilynching law, but Roosevelt, leery of opposition from Southern Democrats, demurred. Louis's wins over Carnera and Baer were like a mass spiritual tonic; they set off mad celebrations in black communities around the United States. When Louis fought, American blacks gathered around radios—by now, the national mass medium—and listened as if the world were riding on the outcome. Assessing Louis's effect on blacks, novelist Richard Wright wrote: "From the symbol of Joe's strength they took strength, and in that moment all fear, all obstacles were wiped out, drowned."

It was not only the black "masses" who loved him. "No one else in the United States has ever had such an effect on Negro emotions—or mine," wrote Langston Hughes.[11] Years later, in his book *Why We Can't Wait*, Martin Luther King Jr. repeated a popular folktale that illustrated the stature that Louis enjoyed in black America. In the 1930s, in a Southern state, as a condemned black prisoner drew his last breaths in the gas chamber, he was supposedly heard to plead: "Save me, Joe Louis! Save me, Joe Louis!"[12]

In 1936, Edward Van Every, a white writer, published *Joe Louis, Man and Super-Fighter*, in which he described the fighter as a "Black Moses" whom God had called for a special mission. A decade earlier, Van Every had written a biography of Gene Tunney, whom he had exalted for his Christian virtues, so he was well rehearsed in this kind of thing. But in linking Louis with Moses, he was only recording what millions of blacks already felt.

★

Louis hoped to fight Jim Braddock soon for the title, but in the meantime, Louis's team wanted to keep the momentum building. So they signed for a bout in June 1936 against another member of the former champions club: thirty-one-year-old Max Schmeling.

By the time he squared off with Louis in June 1936 in Yankee Stadium, Schmeling had become increasingly entwined with Adolf Hitler's Nazi regime—an irony, considering not only his Weimar past, in which he was friendly with many Jewish artists and intellectuals, but also his career struggles. After losing the title to Jack Sharkey in 1932, Schmeling had suffered another huge setback the following year, when Max Baer knocked him out in New York, and still another in 1934, when he lost to Steve Hamas. Boxing observers wrote him off, but then he rallied, beating Hamas in a rematch and besting his fellow German Walter Neusel, both before huge

Hamburg crowds. Despite his ups and downs, he never lost his standing as Germany's top boxer—and the Nazis were solicitous. Hitler had lauded the virtues of boxing in *Mein Kampf* and saw the sport as a vital discipline for the nation's youth; he even instituted compulsory boxing training. In Schmeling, the Führer saw a representative of Nazi skill, intelligence, and might. Schmeling welcomed Hitler's regard, and Max and his blond actress wife, Anny Ondra, became Germany's glamour couple. Still, many in the American sporting press absolved Schmeling of Nazi sympathies; he had, after all, refused to join the Nazi Party. They liked Max—he was intelligent, articulate, and ingratiating.

Though he was given almost no chance to beat Louis, Schmeling had studied fight films and spotted a flaw: that Louis dropped his left hand after jabbing, leaving himself open to a right—which happened to be Schmeling's specialty. He trained vigorously in the Hudson Valley hamlet of Napanoch, New York, determined to prepare his body and mind for what he knew would be his hardest fight. Louis, meanwhile, put himself through desultory preparations in Pompton Lakes, New Jersey. Much to Jack Blackburn's dismay, Louis brought Marva with him to the training camp and spent a good deal of his energies in conjugal pursuits. Blackburn ordered Marva out, but other women flocked into the camp. And Louis often cut short training sessions to pursue his new obsession: golf.

After rain forced several days of postponements, a smaller than expected crowd—only about forty-five thousand—came out to Yankee Stadium. The weather wasn't the only problem: Jewish groups were urging a boycott, just as they had three years earlier, when Schmeling fought Baer. But the fight went forward. At the weigh-in, Schmeling surprised reporters with his good cheer. Seeing Louis, he smiled, shook hands, and said: "Good luck tonight, Joe."[13]

Schmeling came out for the first round showing great caution, sticking out his left mostly to paw at Louis but holding his right in reserve. Louis went after the German with his piston-like jab. After three rounds, Schmeling's lips were split and his eyes discolored. But this was what Schmeling had trained himself so diligently for: to maintain his presence of mind while under assault, to keep himself together until the time came when he could act.

In the fourth, he saw his chance. Louis jabbed and paused, dropping his left—and Schmeling fired the right, timing it perfectly. The punch changed both men's lives. Louis wobbled, his legs stuttering underneath him, his face suddenly gone blank. Schmeling moved closer and landed two more rights, and Louis dropped backward, landing on his backside to gasps across the stadium. He popped back up almost immediately, but his eyes had lost focus. Now fighting on instinct, he remained dangerous. In the fifth, Louis gave as good as he got, but hearing the bell, he dropped his hands, and Schmeling—perhaps not hearing it—nailed him with another right that sent Louis back to his corner in desperate shape. Yet he fought back bravely, rallying in the seventh and eighth rounds.

Both men were heavily marked by now—Schmeling's face was cut and puffed, while the left side of Louis's face was swelling up like a balloon from Schmeling's rights, which landed for the rest of the fight with the persistence of a judgment. Continually stung by the punch, a dazed Louis threw numerous low blows, for which he was warned. He draped his arms around Schmeling's neck and bowed his head in apology. He had lost all his considerable self-possession in the ring.

In the twelfth round, Schmeling flashed over another series of rights and Louis backpedaled, his hands down, no longer able to disguise his condition. He stood helpless for a pregnant second before Schmeling threw one last right. Louis fell to the canvas in a praying position against the ropes. Then he rolled over onto his back, shaking his head like a man trying to get water out of his ears. Attempting to rise, he turned over prone, putting his head on his arm as the referee counted him out. Blackburn and others carried Louis to his corner; a crew of New York City policemen bore the semiconscious fighter to his dressing room.

It was the greatest victory of Schmeling's career. Arno Hellmis, the German-language ringside announcer, called out the final moments to the audience in Germany, where millions listened in the middle of the night: *Aus! Aus! Aus!* Those gathering in Nazi propaganda minister Joseph Goebbels's living room exulted—especially Anny Ondra, a special guest of the Goebbelses. They heard Max's voice as he spoke over American radio, asking if Hitler had been listening and signing off with "Heil Hitler!" Goebbels and Hitler wired Schmeling congratulatory telegrams, and Germany planned a hero's welcome, sending its famous airship, the *Hindenburg*, to fly him home.

In the black community, meanwhile, the result was devastation. Langston Hughes described walking down Seventh Avenue in Harlem and seeing "grown men weeping like children, and women sitting on the curbs with their heads in their hands." Several men died of heart attacks listening to the radio broadcast. In Cincinnati, nineteen-year-old Lena Horne, performing with Noble Sissle's band at the Moonlite Gardens, listened along with the other band members to the radio broadcast of the fight during breaks. Some of the male members began crying as Louis's predicament became clear. Finally, Horne herself broke down. Her mother chided her for this unprofessionalism. "You don't even know the man," she told her daughter.

"I don't care!" Horne retorted. "He belongs to all of us."[14]

With his shocking victory, Schmeling had halted the march of boxing's new star and raised questions about his legitimacy. Some writers, having attributed Louis's victories to animalism, saw in his demise proof of black inferiority—especially since Louis had fallen to Schmeling, the Aryan. Others, abstaining from racial conclusions, wrote Louis off as a fighter. Even Jack Dempsey, who knew something about adversity, predicted in *Ring* magazine that Louis would never improve and that he would be an easy mark for future opponents.

"I let a whole race of people down," Louis wrote later, "because I thought I was some kind of hot shit."[15] Indeed, Louis had fallen prey to overconfidence as much as to Schmeling. At twenty-three, Louis was young enough to absorb the fight's lessons, which were technical and philosophical: correct the flaw of dropping the left that Schmeling had exposed and never again take an opponent for granted. While Schmeling was feted by Hitler and Goebbels and while sportswriters praised his Teutonic analytical mind, Louis and Jack Blackburn got back to work. The first thing that Blackburn noticed was that Louis was listening to him again. The loss to Schmeling would probably turn out to be a blessing, the old trainer decided.

★

Beating the supposedly invincible Louis put Schmeling first in line for a shot at Jim Braddock. It seemed a good bet that Schmeling would become the first man to regain the heavyweight championship, bucking the old boxing truism, "They never come back."[16] Schmeling, who had won and lost the title dubiously, could etch his name into history.

He didn't count on politics getting in the way. Returning home on the *Hindenburg*, Schmeling was greeted by adoring crowds in Frankfurt and then in Berlin, where he had dinner with Goebbels and watched a film of the fight with Hitler. The Führer decreed that the film—with an added voice-over narration celebrating Aryan virtues and denigrating Louis—be shown around Germany with the title *Schmeling's Victory: A German Victory*. Schmeling reveled in the attention, though some resisted similar enticements. Marlene Dietrich, for instance, spurned lucrative Nazi offers to return home as Germany's foremost film star, applying instead for American citizenship. But Schmeling stayed in Germany, accepting the regime's endorsement.

Hitler's embrace finally changed Schmeling's image in the United States. Until then, criticism of him had come mostly from Jewish groups. But Schmeling's win over Louis and the Nazis' eagerness to celebrate him coincided with events that made Hitler's intentions clear. In 1935, the Nazis passed the Nuremberg Laws, depriving non-Aryans of German citizenship and forbidding marriages or sexual relations between Germans and non-Aryans. And Hitler was remilitarizing Germany, in violation of the Treaty of Versailles. In March 1936, German troops reoccupied the Rhineland in western Germany, nervously awaiting French reprisals. None came.

Two months after the Schmeling–Louis fight, Germany welcomed the world to the Summer Olympics in Berlin. The Nazis covered up anti-Jewish notices and put on a grand show, a spectacle that Leni Riefenstahl captured in her landmark documentary, *Olympia*. But Nazi racial theories were trumped by the black American sprinter Jesse Owens, who won the gold medal in the 100-meter, 200-meter, and long-jump events—beating German athletes, among others—and another in the relay with his American teammates, becoming the first man to win four gold medals. Owens and his teammates nearly missed the competition; under pressure from Jewish groups, the American Olympic Committee, chaired by Avery Brundage, came within a few votes of a boycott. While the boycott resolution was being debated, Schmeling, on a trip to New York, carried a letter from the German Olympic committee promising fair treatment for black and Jewish athletes. What role the letter played in persuading the Americans to participate is debatable. But Schmeling had gone to bat for Hitler again—and the Americans had come to Berlin.

Watching as Schmeling moved into the Nazi orbit, Mike Jacobs, a Jew himself, had a sinking feeling. If Schmeling won back the heavyweight title, Hitler could insist that he fight only in Germany and dictate which challengers he would face. The title, unofficially an American prize, would be held hostage by the Third Reich.

Jacobs resolved to prevent a Schmeling–Braddock fight, and he found a willing partner in Braddock's manager, Joe Gould. Braddock hadn't fought since beating Baer in June 1935; he'd been doing testimonial dinners and enjoying the public acclaim. He knew that he stood to make a big payday when he finally put his title on the line, provided he picked the right challenger—and that challenger was not Schmeling but Louis, who soon returned to his winning ways, knocking out thirty-four-year-old Jack Sharkey in three rounds and ending the former champion's halfhearted comeback attempt. A Braddock fight with Louis would command the best box office, especially since Jewish groups would try to block a fight with Schmeling.

Defying the New York Athletic Commission, which insisted that Braddock fight the German next, Gould announced that his champion would take on Louis instead—in Chicago, an independent boxing jurisdiction. The champ's $350,000 payday would have been impressive in the 1920s but was positively kingly in Depression-mired 1937. And thanks to Gould's negotiating skill, Braddock got 10 percent of the gate receipts for all Jacobs's heavyweight title promotions for the next ten years. The deal helped ensure that the Cinderella Man would never stand inside a relief office again.

In the first heavyweight title fight in Chicago since the Long Count between Dempsey and Tunney, Braddock and Louis fought on June 22, 1937, before a crowd of sixty thousand in Comiskey Park. As many as twenty thousand black fans came out, most sitting in bleacher seats, to see if Louis could follow in Jack Johnson's footsteps and win American sports' richest prize. "This is it, Chappie," said Blackburn before the bell. "You come home a champ tonight."[17]

It didn't look that way in the first round, when Braddock came out swinging. Surprised by Braddock's aggression and drawn into the brawl, Louis got sloppy, winding up punches and leaving himself open. The champion stepped inside a Louis jab and landed a right on his chin, dropping him to the canvas. Louis scrambled to his feet before the referee could begin a count, and Braddock went after him. But he did not meet the damaged fighter Schmeling had; instead, the knockdown energized Louis. He pumped his jab and whipped his left hook into Braddock's body and head. At the end of the first round, Braddock's face and mouth were already cut.

Louis punished Braddock brutally in the second round, his punches stunning for their speed and power. Braddock's mouth swelled and filled with blood. Grimly determined, he fought it out with Louis in every round. Louis maintained his methodical style, obeying Blackburn's counsel to bide his time. In the sixth, he opened up on Braddock with left hooks. His face a crimson mess, Braddock looked wobbly heading back to his corner. There, Joe Gould, who had been agonizing with each passing round, told Braddock: "I'm going to stop the fight." Some of the punches that Louis was landing looked as though they could kill a man.

"If you do," Braddock said through bloody lips, "I'll never speak to you again." Gould knew his friend too well to take the chance. Grinder, hero, refunder of welfare offices, Jim Braddock was the kind of man who made good on such threats. "I'm the champion," he said. "If I'm going to lose, I'll lose it on the deck."[18] Gould sent him back out.

In the eighth, Louis hooked a left to the body and then came over the top with a right that drove Braddock's mouthpiece through his lip. The punch, which some at ringside described as the most awful they had ever seen, seemed to stop time. Braddock froze for a moment and then, in a motion that resembled a man trying to sit down on a low chair, dropped to the canvas, rolled onto his face, and lay motionless as the referee tolled the ten-count. A puddle of blood accumulated on the canvas near his head. He was carried to his corner, and it took at least ten minutes before he could leave the ring under his own power.

A black man was heavyweight champion, twenty-two years after Johnson lost the title in Havana. Even now, as the referee raised his arm and the Comiskey Park crowd heard his name announced as the new heavyweight champion, Louis betrayed no emotion. He was observing the code of behavior, but his reserve also suggested unfinished business. "I don't want nobody to call me champ until I beat that Schmeling," he told reporters.[19] The impending battle would become the most politically charged sports event in American history.

★

Never were two athletes more freighted with symbolism than Joe Louis and Max Schmeling in 1938. Outside Hitler, Schmeling seemed to be the man of the hour in Germany. His identification with the regime, whatever his private feelings might have been, grew ever closer. He was regularly celebrated in the German press, including the magazine of the SS and *Der Angriff*, Goebbels's Nazi Party newspaper. He attended Nazi Party rallies at Nuremberg and participated in public celebrations of the Führer's birthday. He encouraged Germans to vote *ja* in the phony referendum that Hitler set up to ratify the *Anschluss*—the Nazi annexation of Austria—and was photographed doing so himself. He attended preview screenings of Leni Riefenstahl's *Olympia* documentary, along with other favored insiders.

But it was Louis who bore a national burden that few would have imagined. By 1938, his stature in black culture had reached new dimensions, as reflected in black popular music. At least forty-three songs about Louis have been documented or recovered, more tributes by far than any other athlete has ever inspired. The songs ranged widely across blues, jazz, and gospel, from performers as well-known as Cab Calloway and Count Basie, as legendary as Memphis Minnie, and as forgotten as Lil Johnson. Some were straightforward celebrations of Louis's fighting skill, such as Johnson's "Winner Joe (the Knockout King)," which described Louis's victory over Primo Carnera. Others praised his good deeds outside the ring, such as buying his mother a house (and, just as Braddock had done in New Jersey,

Louis paid back the Detroit welfare agency that had helped his family). Songs portrayed him as a source of power, like something out of Genesis, as in "King Joe," recorded with Count Basie's band and sung by Paul Robeson. Or Louis's feats might be likened to Joshua fighting the battle of Jericho— as in the Dixieaires' infectious tribute, "Joe Louis Is a Fightin' Man."

As adored as Louis was in black America, though, the Schmeling fight hovered over his future. Would he prove equal to the test? Blacks and Jews agonized over the answer.

Many whites, too—perhaps even most—wanted Louis to win. Here was one of history's surprises, perhaps the first harbinger of the civil rights revolution that would galvanize the United States a quarter-century later. White Americans en masse had never rooted for a black man to do *anything*—let alone to prevail in a contest of physical supremacy against another white man. Though some whites rooted for Schmeling, many others saw Louis as an American standard-bearer against Hitler and Nazi Germany. The second Schmeling fight would prove the turning point of Louis's career, when he became a figure deeply tied to the country: a symbol of American democracy. That he was the representative of a people that had been denied the full benefits of democracy made the identification more haunting and profound. Louis, wrote *Detroit Times* sports editor Bud Shaver, was "far more than a superbly competent fighter. He is a challenge to tolerance in an intolerant world."[20] Thus did Joe Louis became a vital figure in the history of American race relations—and thus did boxing, so often derided for its tribalist impulses, become, for a moment, an instrument of national unity.

A long-told story, debunked but immune to fact-checkers, illustrates the transition in Louis's public image. Franklin Roosevelt beckons Louis to the White House for a private meeting not long before the second Schmeling fight. Squeezing Louis's biceps, FDR says, "Joe, we need muscles like yours to beat Germany"—though the United States was not yet at war with Germany. The 1938 meeting never happened—Louis did have a friendly visit with FDR a few years earlier—but the tale captures the sense that many had that the Louis–Schmeling fight carried global implications.

Whatever their rooting interests, though, some sportswriters weren't convinced that Louis could learn the lessons of the first fight or recover psychologically from what Schmeling had done to him. Schmeling himself, arriving in America in April 1938 to begin training, suggested to reporters that after the two were back in the ring, a few right hands would send Joe down to defeat again. His victory in the first fight, Max suggested, gave him a psychological advantage, especially over "a man of Joe's race."[21]

The experts did not account for Louis's competitive fire. Their view of him as an easygoing and not terribly bright Negro blinded them to the rage he felt at his 1936 defeat, his anger at Schmeling's later accusations that Louis had deliberately fouled him, and his resentment, to the extent that he followed the news, of the Nazis and their "master race" talk. How wholeheartedly Schmeling endorsed the Nazis, Louis didn't know and didn't care; he only knew that he wanted to win this fight more than he'd ever wanted anything. And beating Schmeling wasn't enough. He needed to destroy him.

On the day before the fight, Louis sat at his training camp with the young sportswriter Jimmy Cannon, who had just filed his prefight column.

"You make a pick?" Louis asked.

"Yes."

"Knockout?"

"Six rounds."

"No," Louis said, "One." Cannon stared. Then Louis held up a finger. "It go one."[22]

★

"Wars, involving the fate of nations, rage elsewhere on this globe," the *New York Mirror* editorialized on Wednesday morning, June 22, 1938, "but the eyes of the world will be focused tonight on a two-man battle in a ribbon of light stabbing the darkness of the Yankee Stadium." The bout's centrality was captured in several variations of a cartoon showing a globe with a human face, looking down anxiously at the Yankee Stadium ring where Louis and Schmeling clashed, waiting to learn the outcome. More than seventy thousand people crowded into Yankee Stadium on a cool summer night, paying $1,015,012, the first million-dollar gate since the Dempsey–Tunney Long Count. An estimated sixty million people—nearly half the nation's population—tuned in to hear the radio broadcast, then the largest audience to listen to any program, even FDR's fireside chats. In cities and towns across America, friends and neighbors gathered around radios to listen. Movie houses stopped films so that the fight could be patched in over the intercom. Even Eleanor Roosevelt, no student of pugilism, consented to listen—she had heard so much about the fight in recent days that she couldn't ignore it. Another forty million people listened around the world, including in Germany, where it was 3 a.m. Early in the day, Hitler cabled a telegram to Schmeling: "To the next world's champion, Max Schmeling," the Führer wrote. "Wishing you every success."[23]

Jack Blackburn had long worried that Louis might be too kind to make a great fighter. "You just gotta throw away your heart when you put on those boxing gloves," he would tell Joe, "or the other fella'll knock it out of you." But watching Louis warm up in his dressing room, working himself into a lather of sweat, Blackburn sensed his intensity. Others in the crowd felt it, too. When both fighters were in the ring, someone yelled out near ringside, "Kill that Nazi, Joe! Kill him!"[24]

At 10 p.m., the bell rang, and Louis advanced on Schmeling with cold purpose. Everything about his movements, from the way he held his hands to the whipsaw power of his punches, was a world away from 1936. He wore his classic blank expression, and he walked Schmeling into smaller and smaller parts of the ring.

Schmeling held his left out, trying to keep a distance between himself and Louis, waiting for his opening. Then Louis seemed to leap at the German, firing punches—every one thrown with knockout power. The punches were short and precise, not the untrammeled assault of Dempsey against Willard or Firpo but calculated, controlled ferocity.

Schmeling had taken several stiff jabs to the face when he backed along the ropes, still holding out his left. Louis broke through it, landing a clean right to his jaw. Schmeling's knees buckled, and he almost went down. Louis let go with a fusillade as Schmeling reached out to grasp the ropes with his right hand—but the hand would have been better used protecting himself, especially in the belly, where Louis pounded him. As Louis fired a savage right hook to the body, Schmeling, turning his torso slightly in defense, wound up absorbing it in his left side. The punch shattered Schmeling's third lumbar vertebra and drove it into his kidney. He screamed, the sound echoing out into the Yankee Stadium air and striking fear into some at ringside. Louis, his mind churning, thought that it was a woman in the crowd. "How's that, Mr. Super-Race?" he remembered thinking.[25]

Manning the radio controls for NBC was Clem McCarthy, normally a horse-racing announcer—he would call the famous Seabiscuit–War Admiral match race later in 1938. A man accustomed to talking quickly, McCarthy struggled to follow Louis's onslaught and reproduce it for his listeners. He didn't get it nearly right. But his gravelly voice suited the occasion: it sounded as though he was narrating a street crime from a third-floor window. "Louis with the old one two! First a left and then the right. . . . Schmeling is going down. But he held to his feet, held to the ropes, looked to his corner in helplessness."[26]

Schmeling had begun to go down; his left knee bent to the canvas but then straightened up. It was close enough that the referee, Arthur

Donovan, stepped between the fighters to start a count. Seeing that Schmeling was already upright, Donovan waved Louis in. Louis landed a clean right to Schmeling's jaw—the punch could have come out of a boxing manual—and the German tumbled down. He was up quickly, just in time to absorb another volley of punches. Everything Louis threw landed—jabs, left hooks to the body, rights to the head. The German started to the canvas again, with both gloves touching the mat, and then straightened himself up. Again, Donovan moved in to count and then motioned Louis back in.

"Donovan is watching carefully!" McCarthy intoned. Donovan was; he wanted to give Schmeling every chance while also protecting him from serious injury. In Schmeling's corner, too, the urge to rescue Max was mounting. Everything was happening too fast. Across the Atlantic, over static-ridden radio connections, Germans listened in silence and confusion.

Donovan wiped Schmeling's gloves off and made way for Louis again. The champion landed a right and a left hook to Schmeling's body, and then, stepping away slightly to give himself room, he placed a crushing right to Schmeling's downturned jaw. Schmeling crumbled to the canvas and Louis retreated again, almost skipping to avoid getting tangled in Schmeling's feet. As Louis leaped away, a white towel floated into the ring from Schmeling's corner, signifying surrender. Donovan tossed it away—American rules stipulated that only a referee could stop the fight—and it landed on the top rope, where it hung like a ghostly talisman. Donovan moved to start counting over Schmeling, but Schmeling's men had had enough of the rules; they rushed into the ring to save him. Louis had won in 2:04 of the first round, just as he had promised Jimmy Cannon.

The fight was so brief that some people hadn't made it to their seats before it was over, and some late arrivals rushed into the stadium against a torrent of people filing out. Others had simply missed it. Count Basie dropped his hat behind some seats after the bell rang and was rummaging for it when "everybody started jumping to their feet, hollering, and I looked up and the goddamn fight was all over." But Roy Wilkins of the NAACP, who had managed to catch the end, had no complaints. It was, he said, "the shortest, sweetest minute of the entire thirties."[27]

In Harlem and elsewhere, the celebrations were like nothing ever seen in black America. One writer compared it with the Fourth of July, New Year's Eve, and Christmas Day all rolled into one. Nonblacks were happy, too. In Tampa, ten-year-old Ferdie Pacheco, later the physician for Muhammad Ali, remembered his mother giving him a nickel for an ice cream cone—a surpassingly rare gesture in his house in those Depression years. Perhaps

Joe Louis blitzes Max Schmeling in the first round, Yankee Stadium, June 22, 1938.
Associated Press

even happier than blacks were American Jews, for whom Louis's victory came as a temporary deliverance.

Schmeling was taken to Polyclinic Hospital in Manhattan—he was driven there in a circuitous route to avoid Harlem—where he recuperated for ten days before boarding the *Bremen* and sailing for home, where no rapturous crowds waited. Contrary to Schmeling's later claims, the Nazis did not disown him. He remained a national hero, if a diminished one. Schmeling would surely have lost his remaining stature, though, and perhaps his life, if the Nazis had found out that, in November 1938, during Kristallnacht, he had sheltered two Jewish teenagers in his Berlin hotel suite, probably saving their lives—an act of heroism not revealed until fifty years later. Yet the degree of responsibility that Germany's greatest boxer bears for his affiliation with the Third Reich remains a subject of some debate.[28]

Joe Louis's performance on June 22, 1938, joined a select company: John L. Sullivan in Richburg, 1889; James J. Corbett in New Orleans, 1892; Jack Johnson in Reno, 1910; and Jack Dempsey in Toledo, 1919. Yet none of these feats had been achieved under the same pressure that Louis faced in

1938—pressure magnified by international politics and mass media. Louis's victory over Schmeling remains the supreme example of an athlete's ability to execute under pressure. And "execute" was the word.

★

With the cloud of Schmeling removed from his worthiness, Louis settled in to the most dominant championship reign in boxing history. Sportswriters resumed writing of him as the invincible juggernaut of the ring, the Brown Bomber and Dark Destroyer against whose fists no one could stand for long. Some already considered him the greatest heavyweight, and he set out to defend his title with a frequency that no previous champion had ever attempted. He took on every contender available, several of whom he would fight twice. "Some fellows put up better fights than others and are invited back again," the *New York Times*'s John Kieran wryly noted.[29] For the most part, Louis's opponents gave him little serious opposition.

Louis's busy schedule was just a warm-up for 1941, when he would defend the title six times in the first six months of the year. Sportswriters called Louis's challengers the Bum of the Month Club, but his opposition was mostly drawn from top-ranking heavyweight contenders. The problem was that he often made good fighters look like bums.

For Louis, 1941 would be remembered for one fight: his June battle with light heavyweight champion Billy Conn. An Irishman from the fighting city of Pittsburgh, Conn was brash, cocky, movie-star handsome, and enormously popular. Conn's appeal made a match with Louis attractive to Mike Jacobs, who booked them into New York's Polo Grounds on June 18, 1941. Outside Pittsburgh, few gave Conn a chance. Louis outweighed him by at least thirty pounds, though Jacobs tried to fudge the difference by announcing Conn's weight as 174 (more than he was) and Louis's as 199 (less). A crowd of fifty-four thousand came out for a bout that most thought would be a curiosity.

Instead, they saw one of the great heavyweight fights. The first few rounds were familiar to experienced Louis watchers. The champion came out in his deliberate way, taking his time. When he got close to Conn, the power of his punches was evident. But Conn soon discovered that he could hit Louis and evade him with considerable success. He was much quicker afoot, and he moved from side to side, circling, landing combinations before Louis could get set. The fight was even through the first five or six rounds, but then Conn surged into the lead.

Never had Louis looked so slow with his hands or so unimaginative with his feet. He could not keep up with Conn, and after eleven rounds, it was clear that his title was at risk. He had faced down murderous hitters like Max Baer, hulking men like Primo Carnera, and skilled boxer-punchers like Max Schmeling. Conn was something different: a feather that Louis could not pull down from the air.

"You've got a fight on your hands tonight, Joe," Conn told the champion. "I know it."

In the twelfth round, Conn buckled Louis's knees with a left hook to the jaw and then swarmed him with punches as Louis, looking disoriented and getting tangled in Conn's feet, grabbed on to the challenger to steady himself. With three rounds to go, Conn led on two of the three scorecards, seven rounds to five and seven rounds to four, with one even; the other card had the fight deadlocked, six rounds to six. He could win the title by decision if he won one of the last three rounds or if he knocked out Louis. And knocking out Louis was what Conn had in mind.

"This is easy," the hyped-up challenger said in his corner before the thirteenth round. "I can take this son of a bitch out this round."[30] Forty-one years earlier, on Coney Island, Jim Corbett had thought much the same thing, and his corner had begged him not to stand and trade with Jim Jeffries. Now Conn's corner made the same vain pleas to their man.

In the champion's corner, Jack Blackburn told Louis that he was in trouble. "You're gonna lose that title if you don't knock him out, Chappie," he said.

"Guess I'll have to knock him out, then, Chappie."[31]

Conn came out in the thirteenth ready to go after Louis, putting himself in the champion's punching range. Louis scored with body punches and then a series of blows to Conn's head. The choreography changed, with Louis advancing, cuffing Conn about the ring, landing clean shots. A right buckled Billy's knees, but instead of backing off, he kept trading with Louis. A right uppercut snapped his head up. Conn refused to back down, but his feather would no longer float; Louis had the wisp at his fingertips.

The round was nearly over when Louis unleashed yet another combination—a left and right to the body—finishing with a hammering right to the side of the head. Conn's body sagged, and he crashed to the canvas as flashbulbs popped at ringside. The referee, Eddie Joseph, moved in to count over him. Conn got to his haunches and stared ahead with glazed eyes. He was working his way up as Joseph tolled the fatal ten. Walking to his corner, Louis passed Conn without acknowledgment, like a man moving by a stranger on the street.

"I lost my head and a million bucks," Conn sobbed afterward. "What's the sense of being Irish if you can't be dumb?"[32] Conn's epic failure did more for his stature than winning a fifteen-round decision would have. He was "dumb" but also heroic.

The twenty-seven-year-old Louis had experienced what Theodore Roosevelt once described as a "crowded hour," and his heart-stopping win over Conn added another page to his legend. He had awed crowds for years with his power and speed; he had awed opponents, too. Against Schmeling, he had avenged his only loss under conditions that no athlete had ever faced. Three years later, he had managed a different feat: the comeback, an art requiring not overwhelming power but steely nerves. It was Louis's eighteenth defense of the title he had won from Braddock four years earlier. His dominance was unparalleled. In fact, the part of his boxing career that really mattered was over. But his impact on American social history was just beginning.

★

On December 7, 1941, Japanese warplanes bombed Pearl Harbor, and the United States was finally brought into World War II. The attack shocked the country, though the event seemed inevitable in retrospect. War, in Asia and in Europe, had been on Franklin Roosevelt's mind for years. Now the fight was on for real.

Louis knew that he would be in the army soon; he had been classified 1-A, eligible for service, and had a low lottery number. The army offered him a commission, but he turned it down, feeling that he lacked the education to be an officer. He enlisted as a private, though he wouldn't see combat. The army wanted him to visit bases, box exhibitions to entertain troops, serve as a liaison to black soldiers, and act as a spokesman for the war effort, especially for blacks. All this, Louis would do.

Before he left stateside, though, he defended his title two more times—for free. In January 1942, he fought for the Navy Relief Fund, raising money for families of naval personnel injured or killed at Pearl Harbor. And in March, he fought for the Army Relief Fund. These were not exhibitions: they were genuine contests in which the heavyweight championship of the world was on the line. If Louis were beaten, he would lose the title without a penny in compensation. Moreover, the men he chose to fight—Buddy Baer (Max's six-foot-six kid brother) and 260-pound Abe Simon—were serious contenders. He had beaten both the previous year in tough matches. Baer had knocked Louis through the ropes and onto the ring apron—he landed on his head—before Louis cut him down in six rounds. Simon had shown great resilience in lasting into the thirteenth round. But in true Louis fashion, he beat both more convincingly the second time around. Simon went out in the sixth round; Baer didn't make it through the first. No one could think of another instance in which a heavyweight champion had voluntarily fought for nothing.

"You don't see a shipyard owner risking his entire business," Jimmy Powers wrote in the *New York Daily News*. "If the government wants a battleship, the government doesn't ask him to donate it. The government pays him a fat profit. . . . The more I think of it, the greater a guy I see in this Joe Louis." When a reporter asked Louis if it worried him that he was fighting for nothing, Louis replied: "Ain't fighting for nothing. I'm fighting for my country."[33]

He'd already gotten most of the writers past the watermelon-and-jungle-cat imagery, and his quiet dignity had won praise not just from the press but from millions of white Americans, who admired him as they had never admired a black person before. Jimmy Cannon wrote that Louis was "a credit to his race. Naturally, I mean the human race."[34] The line seems condescending now, but it was a testament to the barriers, physical and mental, that Louis had broken down.

The armed forces were segregated during World War II, and the nation's racial situation was generally poor. In fact, during the summer of 1941, as Louis prepared to meet Conn, President Roosevelt fended off a planned civil rights march on Washington led by A. Philip Randolph, president of the Brotherhood of Sleeping Car Porters. (The march that Randolph envisioned would eventually take place in 1963, when it was led by Martin Luther King Jr.) Some blacks questioned why they should fight for the United States in a war to uphold democracy and equality when they often saw little of either at home.

The army knew that Louis could help rally African American support, and he did his part with public appearances and public-service announcements. In March 1942, Louis attended a war rally at Madison Square Garden, and he was called to the stage to make some remarks. Wearing his army uniform, he told the crowd: "I'm only doin' what any red-blooded American would do." The crowd cheered, and then Louis said: "We're gonna do our part and we'll win 'cause we are on God's side."[35] The army used the motto in posters, etching the heroic Louis image deeper.

Not all blacks appreciated this. Some would have liked to see Louis speak out more forcefully for civil rights. In the 1960s, these criticisms would resurface as many younger blacks viewed Louis as a relic of an era when blacks were obedient and silent.

What his critics didn't see was that Louis was much more than an Uncle Sam public-relations tool. He agreed to box exhibitions for the army only before integrated audiences of white and black troops. And Louis used his influence to improve conditions. He often called Truman Gibson, a lawyer and member of FDR's so-called black cabinet, to complain about what he saw—Jim Crow arrangements in barracks and in transportation, poor supplies, and racist treatment by commanding officers, military police, and other superiors. He intervened to help qualified blacks, including Jackie Robinson, then a young private, get admitted to Officer Candidate School. And he showed that his own forbearance had limits.

All told, Louis flew some seventy thousand miles visiting American GIs and boxed almost one hundred exhibitions before nearly two million troops. His presence was often a powerful morale boost. When he heard that Louis was making the rounds, one GI, being treated for serious eye injuries, asked to have his bandages removed. "Let me have just one look at him," he said. "I'll take my chance with my eyesight."[36] When the war ended, Louis was awarded the Legion of Merit.

But he was broke. He had earned enormous sums but had spent money as fast as it came in, and he never got a handle on his tax obligations. For years, he had borrowed against future fight purses from Mike Jacobs, driving himself further into debt. Jacobs deducted whatever Louis owed from his purse for the next fight and prepared all of Louis's tax returns. Jacobs kept lending Louis money to support the champion's lavish spending and arranged for Louis always to pay him back before he paid a dime to the IRS. Louis's irresponsibility and Jacobs's machinations ensured the accrual of a tax bill that the Brown Bomber could never pay.

★

Louis pegged his financial hopes on the long-anticipated rematch with Billy Conn, held in June 1946 at Yankee Stadium. Now thirty-two, the champion hadn't had a real fight in four and a half years. His body was thicker, and the back of his head showed the beginnings of a bald spot. But so much interest rode on the rematch—along with the 1946 baseball season, the bout marked the return to peacetime life in America—that fans paid $1.9 million, making it the second-richest live gate, behind only Dempsey–Tunney in Chicago. Conn–Louis II was also the first boxing match broadcast on television, though there were fewer than ten thousand sets in the nation at the time. Most heard the fight over radio, as usual. They waited to learn

Joe Louis was a key figure in encouraging blacks to enlist in the armed forces, which used his famous words in recruitment.
National Archives and Records Administration

what Louis had left and whether Conn could top his brave performance of five years earlier. Not likely, Louis suggested before the match. "He can run but he can't hide," he said of Conn.[37]

Unfortunately for fans, Louis's assessment was on target, and the second fight was a pale imitation of the original. Conn, eager to avoid his mistakes in the first fight, stayed away from Louis, and Louis plodded after the smaller man without much success. The crowd booed the lack of action until the eighth, when Louis caught up with his rival and knocked him out.

When a reporter asked Louis afterward if he was as good as ever, Louis said: "Seems as if I am, don't it?"[38]

In truth, Louis was near the end of the line. His personal physician had noticed his diminished reflexes in Ping-Pong games. His main weakness in the ring—slowness of foot—grew more pronounced. His weight ticked up. And like all aging fighters, he lost the drive to train and sacrifice. He looked for other moneymaking ventures to clear his exit from boxing.

On April 15, 1947, Louis watched as Jackie Robinson took the field for the Brooklyn Dodgers—the first black man to play modern major league baseball. Robinson's entry represented a breakthrough in American life, and more than half a century later, his name remains iconic, while Louis's has faded. But Robinson knew whom to thank (besides Dodgers owner Branch Rickey) for his chance: "I'm sure if it wasn't for Joe Louis," he said, "the color line in baseball would not have been broken for another ten years."[39]

Louis hadn't fought in over a year in December 1947, when he stepped into the Madison Square Garden ring to face Jersey Joe Walcott, a God-fearing, hard-luck black fighter with a crafty boxing style. The thirty-three-year-old Walcott was a prohibitive underdog but had been around the block in boxing and knew how to fight. And unlike Louis, he was light on his feet.

The unheralded challenger gave Louis a boxing lesson. He moved at angles, throwing punches from directions that Louis didn't recognize, and he used his footwork to throw off Louis's rhythm. In the first and fourth rounds, he dropped Louis briefly with rights after he had seemed to turn away from the champion. Louis was thoroughly frustrated, though he kept stalking Walcott. Convinced that he was ahead on points, Walcott danced the final rounds away. Louis was so disgusted with his performance that he tried to leave the ring before the decision was announced. But two judges awarded the fight to Louis—the referee, Ruby Goldstein, scored it for Walcott—and he retained his title. For the first time in his long career, Louis left the ring hearing boos.

Anyone who knew Louis knew that he would want to fight Walcott again. They met on June 25, 1948, at Yankee Stadium, nearly ten years to the day since Louis had beaten Max Schmeling. Louis looked older than his thirty-four years; the bald spot and the thickening body and fleshier face bore little resemblance to the lean warrior who had demolished the Nazi idol. Louis fought old, too. Walcott dropped him in the third round with yet another right, and the challenger led on the scorecards going into the eleventh. Overconfident, Walcott went into his routine of stutter-step moves, twisting and turning and juking. But in one of these performative intervals, Walcott lingered too long in front of Louis, and the champion caught him at last with a right carrying the old power. The punch took Walcott's legs away and put an end to his prancing. Presented at last with a stationary target, Louis opened up with a combination from years gone by, and Walcott sank to the canvas. He struggled up but could not beat the count.

It was Louis's twenty-fifth and final title defense. He'd held the crown eleven years, and by the time he'd sorted out his plans and announced, in March 1949, that he was retiring, it had been nearly twelve. Joining forces with Jim Norris, son of the owner of the Detroit Red Wings, in a new venture called the International Boxing Club (IBC), Louis hoped to become a promoter, in direct competition with Mike Jacobs's Twentieth Century Sporting Club. Jacobs, whose health had begun to fail, saw his iron grip on the sport give way, especially after the IBC announced that it had signed contracts with Walcott and Ezzard Charles to fight for Louis's vacated heavyweight title. The match was set for June 1949 in Chicago.

Nearly seventy years after Louis relinquished the title, many still regard him as the greatest heavyweight. The historians of the International Boxing Research Organization (IBRO) put Louis at the top in their 2005 poll. He did, after all, beat the five preceding heavyweight champions and one (Walcott) who followed. No one held the title so long or defended it so many times. And Louis was a near-perfect technical fighter, throwing punches with textbook precision and rarely being caught off balance. Men like Eddie Futch, who worked with Louis in the gym and went on to become one of the sport's greatest trainers, thought that Louis would have beaten Muhammad Ali. Others, noting the trouble that Louis had with fleet-footed boxers like Walcott and Billy Conn, find this notion farfetched.

Whatever one's view, to watch Louis at his peak, against Schmeling in 1938, is to see a fighter combining grace with fury. Everything from his deliberate advance on an opponent to his absence of emotion in celebrating victories suggests mastery and control over circumstances—enviable attainments in any time, but especially for blacks in those years. Louis was a light in black America's darkness, and a generation would never forget him for it.

As Louis announced his retirement in 1949, the U.S. economy was poised for a long, generational boom that would transform the country, create a vast new middle class, and anoint America as the defender of the free world. The world of the 1930s was already graying into memory. Like Franklin Roosevelt, who had been president for much of his title reign, Louis had redefined his office and ruled for so long that many could not remember his predecessors.

Unfortunately, Louis's career as a boxing promoter proved short-lived. Just a year into his retirement, the IRS sent him a back-tax bill for $246,056—about $2.4 million in today's dollars. The tax men had pursued him for years, and they were just getting warmed up. His tax debt was already beyond reach, especially with compounding interest. The IRS even assessed taxes on the fight purses he had donated to the armed forces in 1942. Only by boxing again could Louis hope to make even a dent in the bill.

And so, in summer 1950, Louis announced that he would return to the ring and try to win back his old title. There was a new champion now, new contenders coming up, and new circumstances—a postwar boxing audience with spending money, a shakeup in boxing governance, and the emerging technology of television. All promised good paydays, Louis felt—just what he needed. But he was thirty-six years old.

THE LAST WHITE KING

In June 1948, the same month as the Louis–Walcott rematch in New York, Rocco Marchegiano stepped into Manhattan's CYO gym on West Seventeenth Street. Squat and powerful, he looked more like a baseball catcher, his original ambition, than a heavyweight prospect, but he had made the trip from his hometown of Brockton, Massachusetts, to work out—to audition, really, for Al Weill, one of boxing's most influential managers, and Charley Goldman, one of the sport's best trainers.

Putting the novice in the ring to spar with a big heavyweight named Wade Chancey, Weill and Goldman couldn't believe how bad he was: his punches were crude, he had no defense, and his feet kept getting tangled up. "We stood there and laughed," Goldman remembered.[1] They stopped laughing when Marchegiano laid Chancey out cold with a right.

"He's no boxer," Goldman told Weill later, "but the kid can punch. That's the most important thing."[2] Weill agreed to give the twenty-five-year-old "kid" a chance, and the following month, Marchegiano—now fighting as Rocky Marciano—made his pro debut with a first-round knockout. Starting out, Marciano stayed in Brockton and fought out of nearby Providence, coming down to New York for periodic instruction from Goldman. If there was a diamond hidden in this rough stone, it would take all of Goldman's skill to find it. Taking notes as he watched the fighter work, he wrote: "Wild punches, no balance, legs too far apart, stride too long, no defense, stands up too straight, needs to get more body into punches, not enough leverage, doesn't know how to use combinations, relies too much on the right, no left hook." But Goldman saw other things, too: not just Rocky's natural punching power but also his iron determination and work ethic and a relentless quest to improve.

Still, Goldman couldn't have known that Marciano's first day in the gym was nothing less than boxing prophecy—or that the short-armed, crude-swinging fighter could, by force of will, climb to the very summit of the sport. More than anything, what Goldman saw in 1948 was all the work that had to be done. Even as his eager charge built an unbeaten record in Providence, the venerable trainer told him: "You've got so much to learn it ain't funny."[3]

★

While Marciano took boxing lessons with Charley Goldman, the heavy-weight title stood vacant after Joe Louis's retirement in March 1949. On June 22, 1949, two talented but enigmatic contenders squared off in Chicago Stadium to determine a new champion. They were Jersey Joe Walcott, thirty-five, two-time loser to Louis, and Ezzard Charles, twenty-eight, who held victories over several top-rated heavyweights but who, at 184 pounds, was barely more than a light heavyweight.

The fight drew a respectable crowd of twenty-five thousand to Comiskey Park, but few, if asked, would have agreed to watch the fight a second time. For fifteen desultory rounds, Walcott and Charles circled each other, flicked out jabs, kept their gloves high, and clinched whenever they got close. Each waited on the other, communicating with motions of their shoulders, elbows, or eyes. No information that passed between them could produce what the spectators had come to see: action. By the ninth round, the fans were booing, and they kept booing until the end of the fight. Not even the onset of the fifteenth and final round could rouse the combatants. It put some in mind of an old sportswriter's crack about two lackluster baseball teams playing in the World Series: "I don't see how either of them can win."[4]

But when the judges' scorecards were tabulated, Ezzard Charles was the winner by a unanimous decision, making him, by the dictates of the National Boxing Association—the governing body in forty-six states but not in New York, Massachusetts, or Great Britain—the new heavyweight champion of the world. Few champions had won the crown in a less resounding manner. Charles was highly skilled, excellent on defense, and an all-around boxer, but he had fought like a forensic analyst. Heavyweight champions were supposed to be demolition men. Charles would prove to be a spectral champion, coming into focus only when people wanted to point out what wasn't there.

He was born Ezzard Mack Charles in Lawrenceville, Georgia, in 1921, the son of a truck driver for a cotton mill. His parents split up, and young Ezzard was raised in Cincinnati by a God-fearing great-grandmother, a former slave. He was introspective from the start, and boxing would never hold the key to his self-definition as it did for many other champions—yet he excelled at it. He won numerous amateur titles and was moving along as a pro when World War II intervened. He spent nearly three years in the army, mostly in Italy, before resuming his boxing career. By the late 1940s, Charles, known as the Cincinnati Cobra for his speed and slashing punches, was a top-ranked light heavyweight and a genuinely great fighter. In February 1948, his career was changed forever after he knocked out Sam Baroudi in the tenth round of a bout in Chicago Stadium. Baroudi lost consciousness and died the next day. The deeply religious Charles wanted to quit boxing but was persuaded to return to the ring, though he never showed the same aggression. Boxing critics always felt that he was capable of more. W. C. Heinz likened him in the ring to Ferdinand, the reluctant bull from the children's story.

Yet there he was the following year, back in Chicago, beating Walcott for Louis's vacated throne. Not long after leaving the ring, Charles and his friend and traveling secretary, Richard Christmas, went out to hear some music at a Chicago nightclub. But where other champions would have soaked up the notoriety, Charles donned dark glasses to disguise his identity.[5]

If he spurned the attention that other champions enjoyed, Charles did crave recognition for his achievements. His problem was that boxing fans still considered Louis the real champion. The only way to settle things was for Charles to fight Louis—and, as it happened, this was precisely what Louis had in mind. The Brown Bomber's tax problems had worsened, and by summer 1950, he had gone back into training. On September 28, 1950, a 218-pound Louis (the heaviest of his career) stepped into the ring at Yankee Stadium to face Charles.

Louis might have known how things would go. He had always had trouble with boxers and movers; Charles was both. Charles kept the action in the center of the ring, where he dictated the tempo with crisp jabs and combinations. After a few rounds, Louis's eyes began to swell up. He plodded after Charles in his usual way but slower than ever before and less effectively. Only in the tenth round did Louis show a flash of the old Bomber magic, when he got a left hook across that stunned Charles. The Yankee Stadium crowd urged Louis on, but they were cheering for the memory of a champion, not the weary-looking shell fighting under his name. Louis couldn't follow up. By now his eyes were slits, his face an immobile mask. After fifteen rounds, no one in the stadium had any doubt about the verdict, which was unanimous. New York extended its recognition to Ezzard Charles as the heavyweight champion of the world.

"I'll never fight again," Louis said.[6] He probably meant it when he said it.

★

In March 1951, Charles fought Walcott a second time, in Detroit. It was another tactical boxing battle, the chess match interrupted only in the ninth round, when Charles caught the challenger with a left hook and sent him to the canvas for a count of nine. After fifteen tactical rounds, Charles won the decision by a wide margin. Many were puzzled when Charles chose to fight Walcott yet again, in Pittsburgh, just a few months later—Jersey Joe's fifth crack at the heavyweight title!—but the division was thin on marketable challengers.

The champion's limited drawing power was one reason why only one of his nine title defenses took place in New York; the changing economics of boxing was another. When Charles won the title in 1949, the International Boxing Club, under the direction of James D. Norris, had just come onto the scene. Norris and his partner, sports entrepreneur Arthur Wirtz, moved quickly to consolidate control of the sport. The IBC supplanted the ailing Mike Jacobs as the decision maker at Madison Square Garden and gained the promotional rights to other key New York arenas and outdoor stadiums. Norris and Wirtz already controlled major arenas in other cities, and they soon locked up most leading fighters to binding contracts. In short order, the IBC became the nearly all-controlling authority in boxing and was known as the Octopus, for its many-tentacled connections.

One of these connections was to organized crime, particularly to Frankie Carbo, a gangster whose career dated back to the Prohibition beer wars. By the early 1950s, Carbo had gained financial and managerial control of most leading fighters through a set of managers under his employ—including Al Weill. Carbo-connected managers muscled others into signing up with the syndicate or forced them out of the picture. They got little resistance. Some called Carbo the Underworld Commissioner of Boxing.

A crucial aspect of the IBC business model was the rapid expansion of television into American homes. Attending fights in person became less important, and major sites—like Yankee Stadium and Madison Square Garden in New York—would not be as vital, since a match could be seen nationally no matter where it was held. Television revenues mitigated declining attendance receipts. The days of New York's primacy in boxing were numbered. Already the new medium was having an effect: when Charles fought Louis in Yankee Stadium, only twenty-two thousand fans came out, paying just $205,000. But the TV broadcast rights fetched another $140,000, as the fight was shown over fifty-eight CBS stations.

So there was Charles in the ring again with Walcott, this time at Pittsburgh's Forbes Field. A modest crowd of twenty-eight thousand came out, paying just $245,000—but television and radio revenues raised the take by another $100,000, as millions watched the fight at home. They saw a more aggressive Walcott, who had to know that this chance would be his last. His physical assertiveness rattled Charles and gave Walcott the edge on the scorecards after six rounds. About a minute into the seventh, Walcott walked toward the champion in what looked something like a strut. Then he stopped and whipped a left hook with everything he had behind it—and it caught Charles coming in. Charles crumbled to the canvas face-first, a position from which few fighters rise. Somehow he struggled up, only to collapse backward, falling into the ropes as the referee halted the fight. With one punch, thirty-seven-year-old Jersey Joe Walcott had become the oldest man to win the heavyweight championship.

It was a popular victory. Walcott was a devoted husband and father of six children who had been fighting since 1930 and had been denied the title in 1947, when many felt that he had beaten Louis. He enjoyed the goodwill of nearly everyone in boxing, and his hard-luck story resembled that of his fellow New Jerseyan Jim Braddock. He was born with the unpugilistic name Arnold Raymond Cream in 1914, in Pennsauken, near Camden, where, as a youngster, he saw great boxers like Sam Langford train. He turned pro in 1930 as a teenager, taking the fighting name of Joe Walcott after a turn-of-the century battler who had been a Cream family friend. "Jersey" was appended later. In 1934, Walcott was training in Philadelphia when he caught the attention of Jack Blackburn, who saw his ability. But Blackburn was soon tapped to work with a young prospect in Chicago—Joe Louis—while Walcott came down with typhoid fever and was sidelined for a year. It wasn't until 1936 that Blackburn sent for Walcott, asking him to work as a sparring partner for Louis. Walcott bedeviled the future champion in sparring sessions, hitting him repeatedly with right hands and, according to some accounts, knocking Louis down. His services were not retained.

Circumstances were difficult for Walcott and his family, and at one point he went on relief. In 1940, he gave up boxing and during the war years he landed a good-paying shipyard job. Like Braddock and Louis before him, he repaid the welfare agency that had helped his family in time of need.

He may not have put the gloves on again if he hadn't run into Felix Bocchicchio, a boxing manager with a checkered past—could boxing managers have another kind?—who offered him a loan. Under Bocchicchio's guidance, Walcott surged in the heavyweight ranks and earned a shot at Louis in December 1947. At least on the scorecards, Louis wasn't beaten, but he was embarrassed by Walcott's quickness and craft. For the judges, though, Walcott was too "cute" for his own good; he didn't rout Louis in the decisive fashion needed to take a champion's title away. Louis knocked him out in their 1948 rematch.

Since then, Walcott had been everyone's sentimental favorite, but after so many failed attempts, he arrived in Pittsburgh a 12–5 underdog. Those shifty feet and unique moves came through for him when he needed them most, along with help from another quarter. "If you keep putting your faith in God," Walcott said afterward, "he will hear your prayers."[7] Walcott was as hard to dislike as Charles was to know. But likability and star power were different things.

★

In the 1950s, American consumerism took off like the rockets that Americans would soon send into space. Middle-class consumers wanted it all: cars, washing machines, vacuum cleaners, automobiles—and televisions. By the early 1950s, Americans were buying five million sets a year; by decade's end, nearly nine in ten homes would have one. The mass availability of televisions fueled greater demand for programming, including sports—and the most popular sport on TV was boxing. Just when Americans were bringing their first televisions home, the fighter who had won his countrymen's hearts over the radio was still in the game: Joe Louis.

In debt half a million dollars to the federal government, Louis started another comeback in late 1950, winning eight fights against mid-grade heavyweights, looking slow and ragged but building momentum for another title shot against Ezzard Charles. Walcott's surprise victory upset those plans because the new champion was contractually obligated to give Charles a rematch—but not before he took a long vacation. That left Louis looking for other opponents, and the logical choice was the rising contender from Brockton, Massachusetts: Rocky Marciano. The Louis–Marciano fight would be shown nationwide on forty-two NBC stations; perhaps fifty million Americans would watch Louis, now thirty-seven, try to keep his career alive against the younger slugger.

The twenty-eight-year-old Marciano had come to boxing late. Born in Brockton on September 1, 1923, Rocco Marchegiano had devoted his youthful athletic dreams to football and baseball. He showed up at Al Weill's doorstep in 1948 only after his baseball hopes had finally been dashed, when he failed in a tryout with a Chicago Cubs minor league team in Fayetteville, North Carolina. Heading back home to Brockton, determined to find another path to the success he craved, he decided on boxing.

He didn't want to follow his father into the shoe factories for which Brockton was famous. Pierino Marchegiano had come to the United States in the 1910s, a time of peak Italian immigration. Pierino, a slight man made sickly after he was gassed in the Argonne Forest while fighting for the United States in World War I, went off to work every day in a suit and tie; his children didn't see him in his workingman's clothes. "He never made any money and he never had any fun," his eldest son, Rocco, lamented years later.[8]

Anything but the factory, Rocco thought. Dropping out of high school to earn money, he worked construction, on ice- and coal-delivery trucks, and for the Brockton gas company. He got his first taste of boxing in the army during the war, when he worked on ships ferrying supplies across the English Channel to Normandy. Fighting in army tournaments, he knocked his opponents stiff.

Rocco's physical limitations, however, made success as a heavyweight unlikely. He stood only five foot ten and a half inches tall, weighed just 185 pounds in fighting trim, and his reach measured only sixty-eight inches. (By comparison, Joe Louis stood six foot two and weighed near 200 during his fighting prime, with a reach of seventy-six inches; Jack Dempsey was six foot one and weighed about 190, with a seventy-seven-inch reach.) The "reach" refers to a fighter's total wingspan, determined by measuring the distance from middle finger of the left hand across the shoulders to the middle finger of the right hand. A reach advantage lets a boxer hit his opponent from a greater distance than his opponent can hit him. Short arms meant that Marchegiano would have to get close to his opponents to land punches—and be willing to take punches himself.

Had Marchegiano not landed that fateful right hand on Wade Chancey in the CYO gym, Al Weill and Charley Goldman probably would have sent him on his way. Instead, with one punch, the late-blooming novice fighter had won himself a managerial team second to none. Goldman remains legendary among boxing trainers today; in his own time, he was not only respected for his work but also revered personally. Barely five feet tall, with the cauliflower ears of an ex-boxer who had had hundreds of fights, he shared the proclivity of great boxing characters for homespun sayings, such as "Never buy anything on the street, especially diamonds."[9] The affection that boxing people felt for Goldman contrasted with the fear and contempt with which they regarded Weill, a man with close ties to Jim Norris and Frankie Carbo. Weill insisted on total control over his fighters' careers—and their earnings. The first bit of authority he wielded over the Brockton prospect was to insist that he change his name from "Marchegiano." Okay, the fighter said, but "it's got to sound Italian." They removed the *h-e-g* and came up with the somehow more palatable "Marciano."

His savvy and well-connected team guided Rocky carefully. Marciano knocked out twenty of his first twenty-two opponents, but nothing came easy. In one fight, he nearly killed an opponent, knocking him into a coma from which he emerged days later, partially paralyzed; in another, he won a hotly disputed decision over a promising contender, Roland LaStarza. (A few years later, in their second fight, Marciano would pound LaStarza into submission.) Goldman kept working with Marciano to improve his balance, to make him a smaller target by accentuating his crouch, and to develop a left hook to go with his lethal right, which the Marciano men called the Suzy Q.

"The kid always listened," Goldman later said. "You never had to tell Rocky anything twice. The thing I liked best besides his right hand was that he was always trying to improve."[10]

Marciano arrived as a serious contender in summer 1951, when he knocked out Rex Layne at the Garden, and he followed that up with a knockout of Freddie Beshore. It was with a mix of excitement and sorrow that he saw that the man blocking his way was Joe Louis. As a boy, Marciano had listened to Louis's fights on the radio. Though Louis was black and Marciano white, they shared a certain outsider status. The Brown Bomber's success inspired many nonblacks because Louis suggested possibility—a broadening of awareness, an expansion of opportunity. And racial and ethnic loyalties were getting more complicated. Louis was so admired by 1951 that thousands of whites in Madison Square Garden came out to root for him against Marciano.

★

Though he outweighed Rocky by nearly thirty pounds—212 to 184—Louis was forced onto the defensive from the opening bell. Showing no deference, Marciano crowded him, letting his fists fly to the body and the head and mauling Louis in clinches. Louis preferred to work at medium range, where his advantages in hand speed and boxing technique could be brought to bear; fighting Marciano was like scuffling with an angry janitor inside a broom closet. Near the end of the first round, Marciano landed a heavy right to Louis's jaw. The old champion's knees buckled, and he returned to his corner on shaky legs.

Louis stood his ground in the second and third rounds, taking shots but trading back and scoring with left hooks as Marciano tore in. But he couldn't keep his brawling opponent off him. Marciano often looped his right hand—it almost looked like a lasso, sailing through the air and descending—but Louis could not get out of its way. Still, the old Bomber gave his backers hope by winning the fourth and fifth rounds behind his left jab, which Marciano later compared to getting hit with a hammer. Halfway through the scheduled ten-rounder, the fight was about even.

In the next two rounds, Louis's thirty-seven-year-old legs began to fail. More than ever, he was a stationary target, and Marciano's relentless pace was wearing him down. The looping right hand got shorter, and Louis's punches resembled slaps. Marciano pulled ahead on the scorecards.

In the eighth, Marciano knocked Louis down with his improved left hook. Louis got to one knee, gripping a strand of the ropes and listening to referee Ruby Goldstein's count. He rose as Goldstein reached nine.

Marciano was on him right away. Louis traded gamely but moved like a sleepwalker; he wasn't really there. Backed up to the ropes, he took a pulverizing left hook and dropped both arms to his sides—he was finished, the savior ready for the sacrifice. Marciano brought over the right, and Louis fell backward through the ropes, his head nearly colliding with the cameras of the ringside photographers. Goldstein moved in to count and then thought better of it. He waved his arms to signal that the fight was over.

"I knocked him out!" Marciano exclaimed, as his handlers rushed to congratulate him. But when he saw Louis being helped to his feet, he felt a pang of regret. In his dressing room, he wrote a condolence note to Louis, and some say that he wept. "Rocky worshipped the guy," said a business associate of Marciano's years later. "He hated to knock him out."[11]

Many at ringside were in tears, too, including some reporters. For Red Smith, writing for the *New York Herald Tribune*, the fight was a melancholy exercise in stubborn realities. "An old man's dream ended. A young man's vision of the future opened wide," Smith wrote. "Young men have visions, old men have dreams. But the place for old men to dream is beside the fire."[12]

Louis would do his share of dreaming beside the fire in the remaining thirty years of his life, and he would have one more shining moment: in 1952, he became the first black golfer to compete in a PGA event, creating such bad publicity for the organization that it agreed to change its whites-only rules. If inspiring people could coin money, Louis would never have gone broke, but the problem that had sent him back into the ring against Marciano and Ezzard Charles—his terrible debt to the Internal Revenue Service—hadn't been solved. In the mid-1950s, much to the chagrin of his admirers, Louis joined the pro wrestling circuit, but he had to leave the ring for good after a 300-pound opponent stood on his chest, dislocating his ribs. His future looked bleak: an unpayable debt, an expensive personal life—he had been divorced twice and owed child support for two kids he barely knew—and the aimlessness common to ex-athletes. Fortunately, his third wife, Martha Jefferson, the first black female attorney in the state of Nevada, stepped in to manage his affairs. The IRS eventually conceded that Louis could not repay all that he owed.

In the late 1960s, as Black Power took hold, Louis seemed increasingly marooned in the past, a feeble symbol for younger, more assertive black athletes. And he had bigger problems. Some years earlier, he had gotten into cocaine and possibly heroin, and the drugs, plus the stresses of his IRS situation and perhaps some head trauma from fighting, made him paranoid and even delusional. Martha committed him to a psychiatric ward in 1970. He emerged relatively stable, and his final years were spent working as a "greeter" at Caesars Palace for $50,000 a year. Though frail and confined to a wheelchair after a stroke, he often showed up at big fights at Caesars. Some of his generation couldn't seem to look upon him without feeling sorrow and guilt. Maybe they saw in his infirmity a reminder of their common fate; he might almost have convinced them that it could never happen to him.

On April 11, 1981, Louis was wheeled into Caesars to watch Larry Holmes defend his heavyweight championship. The next morning, he was dead of a heart attack. Invoking his authority as commander in chief, President Ronald Reagan waived restrictions that barred noncombatant soldiers from burial in Arlington National Cemetery, opening the national military shrine to the most consequential athlete in American history. And so Joe Louis won again.

Beating Louis made Marciano a national name and, for some, an heir apparent to the title. Others doubted that he was really championship caliber.

Either way, Marciano would have to wait before he could get Jersey Joe Walcott into the ring. First, the champ had to get through the last of his four fights with Ezzard Charles, a series that could be called the Sleepy Quartet: four movements barely distinguishable from one another except in brief changes of tempo. The final installment, in Philadelphia, exemplified the quartet's defining quality: indeterminacy. After fifteen rounds, Walcott prevailed by the slimmest of margins on the judges' scorecards; at ringside, twenty-one writers had Charles winning, while eighteen scored it for Walcott and two had it even. But Walcott's win set up a heavyweight title fight that captured public imagination for the first time in years.

Walcott–Marciano offered the contrasts that boxing has always thrived on: it pitted a boxer (Walcott) against a slugger (Marciano) and an older man (Walcott, thirty-eight) against a comparatively young one (Marciano, twenty-nine). And if Marciano won, he would become the first white man to hold the crown since Jim Braddock. In years past, this prospect might have been the fight's main storyline. By 1952, however, the racial obsessions that had long gripped many sportswriters and fans were muted. Millions of whites had become comfortable with (or, at least, indifferent about) a black man holding the title, owing largely to changes in consciousness that had come with the war and to the influence of Joe Louis.

The fight was set for Philadelphia's huge Municipal Stadium, known as the Sesquicentennial Stadium when it opened in September 1926. There, in a steady downpour, Gene Tunney had beaten Jack Dempsey and won the title before 120,000 soaking-wet spectators. A quarter-century later, only 40,000 fans came out on a cool and damp night, but national interest ran high: in dozens of cities, fans flocked to movie theaters to watch the live broadcast on "closed-circuit" television.

The 196-pound Walcott had built a career on evasive, often perplexing ring tactics; sportswriters called him a "prince of prudence."[13] In Philadelphia, to everyone's surprise, he came out swinging. A minute into the fight, Walcott caught Marciano with his dangerous left hook and dropped him for the first time in his career. Marciano, who weighed 184, got to one knee quickly and waded back into the action, scoring a few blows but taking a pasting from the keyed-up champion. The second round wasn't much better for Rocky.

Over the next four rounds, the men traded freely, fighting at close range and giving spectators a bruising, stirring show. Marciano's youth and strength began to tell, as he won the third and fourth rounds. If Walcott was worried about Marciano's power, he didn't let on. The aged champion repeatedly traded with Rocky at close range, avoiding serious damage from the Marciano right. Often, the Suzy Q swept past Walcott, hitting only air.

The battle changed in the sixth, when the two fighters clashed heads. Walcott emerged with a cut over his left eye, Marciano with a gash on the crown of his forehead. Both corners got busy stanching the flow of blood between rounds. But after the seventh round, Marciano came back to his corner blinking. "There's something in my eyes; they're burning," he said to Charley Goldman. "Do something. I can't see."[14]

A burning, astringent solution had gotten into Marciano's eyes and effectively blinded him. Marciano always felt that Felix Bocchicchio, in Walcott's corner, had deliberately put the substance on Walcott's gloves or body—without Jersey Joe's knowledge—in an effort to hinder the challenger. Others believe that Marciano's corner inadvertently got solution that was used to control his cut into the fighter's eyes. Whatever happened, Marciano's corner was in a near-panic. Al Weill and Charley Goldman were chattering anxiously when cut man Freddie Brown, a short, grizzled boxing lifer whom Weill had hired to work that night for fifty dollars, knelt down close to Marciano and said: "Now, listen, you don't have to see. Don't worry about it. Just get your hands on the guy's body so you know where he is and then fucking pound."[15] Brown's instructions and calm tone put the fighter at ease.

Marciano fought on even terms with Walcott in the eighth and ninth. These rounds, like others, were hard to score; both men took and gave punishment. By the tenth, Marciano's vision problems had cleared, and he seemed poised to win the title, rocking Walcott with rights, always pressing forward.

Then the tide turned again. Walcott came out for the eleventh and began picking Marciano apart. He caught Rocky leaning in with his left hook, hurting Marciano worse than he had in the first round. In the twelfth, Walcott dominated the exchanges. He had put the fight out of reach on the three scorecards, leading eight rounds to four, seven rounds to five, and seven rounds to four, with one even. Walcott could lose the last three rounds and still retain his title on a draw. In Marciano's corner, Goldman told Rocky that he needed a knockout.

"Here comes Round 13," said ringside commentator Bill Corum. "The unlucky round. Maybe." Champion and challenger circled for half a minute. As he had throughout the fight, Marciano moved forward and backed Walcott to the ropes. The champion planted his feet and let his right go, but Marciano, fighting from a deep crouch, fired his own. The Suzy Q got there first. It exploded on Walcott's jaw with a bone-crunching sound that those at ringside would always remember. The force of the blow, with the strength of Marciano's squat legs behind it, sent Walcott's head back as if on a swivel, after which it snapped back to its normal position, like a car passenger getting whiplash. The champion pitched forward, his left arm hooking a strand of rope. Facedown, Walcott lay there like a sculpture that becomes more venerable with observation, not moving a muscle as referee Charley Daggert ticked off the seconds of his improbable championship reign. One of boxing's oldest clichés—"they could have counted to 100"— was never more apt. The battered new champion raised his arms in victory.

Many at ringside began cheering, sounding their approval for a battle rarely equaled in the history of the crown. Rocky's Brockton rooters came rushing down the aisles of Municipal Stadium toward the ring. The stampede began far up in the cheap seats, where people usually watched football. As the fans got closer to ringside, they overwhelmed cops, climbed over reporters, and trampled on typewriters, telegraphs, and movie cameras, mobbing the new champion in his corner. It took fifteen minutes for the ring to be cleared and for a phalanx of police to bear the new champion to his dressing room. It was the most intense crowd reaction to a new champion since 1919, when sunbaked Toledo fans hoisted Dempsey onto their shoulders.

Rocky Marciano had won the heavyweight title fighting from behind. He had won despite possible dirty work by the opposition. And he had won in the most dramatic fashion, with a punch that was, as A. J. Liebling put it, "about as hard as anybody ever hit anybody."[16]

★

The epic battle in Philadelphia took place on the same night that sixty million Americans listened on radio or watched on television as Republican vice presidential candidate Richard Nixon gave his famous Checkers speech. Facing expulsion from the ticket because of a controversial expense account, Nixon laid bare his family's modest finances and insisted that he had not profited from the arrangement. But he did receive one gift: a black-and-white cocker spaniel that one of his daughters had named "Checkers." Harnessing all the melodrama he had in him, Nixon said: "The kids, like all kids, love the dog and I just want to say this right now, that regardless of what they say about it, we're gonna keep it."[17] Telegrams supporting Nixon flooded in to the Republican National Committee. The GOP presidential nominee, Dwight D. Eisenhower, kept the senator on the ticket and went on to win the White House in a November landslide.

Eisenhower's entry into the White House marked the real beginning of the 1950s, commonly derided today as an era of blandness and conformity.

For the people living then, however, the 1950s—marked by constant change, technological innovation, and rising living standards—were anything but dull. Gross national product was growing at rates far exceeding inflation and the rate of population growth. Average family incomes nearly tripled in the quarter-century from 1940 to 1965. For the most part, people felt assured that the American way of life was blessed.

Rocky Marciano fit into this cultural outlook about as neatly as Joe Louis had fit earlier, more embattled moods. Marciano's impact was less dramatic, but his virtues were timeless: modesty, family devotion, and, most of all, grit. Marciano's entire success as a fighter owed to his surpassing determination to make it. No heavyweight champion worked harder. His training camps became legendary for the extreme discipline with which he prepared. He separated himself from his wife and family, he did not read newspapers, and he would not take phone calls. The idea was to enter the ring in mental and physical condition that no opponent could match. Purists found fault with his crude ring style, but for the average fan, Marciano's bruising approach to fighting—in which, like Jack Dempsey before him, he did not always honor every rule—had considerable appeal. Rocky's victories seemed as mental as they were physical, a testament to his will. He was an embodiment of American striving.

He also exemplified Italian American struggles and successes. Only one heavyweight champion before him, Primo Carnera, had been of Italian descent. Marciano remembered the bonfires that happy Italians lit in Brockton on the night that Da Preem won the title in 1933. But Carnera was not an American, and questions of legitimacy undermined his stature. In Carnera's day, prejudice against sons of Italy ran deep in American culture. Marciano came to prominence in a more tolerant postwar world, in which second- and third-generation Italian Americans were absorbed into the American melting pot, joined the middle class, and saw some of their own represented prominently in politics, business, and entertainment. The Brockton Blockbuster, as Marciano was called, served as proof that the American dream was not a lie. Even today, his photo hangs in Italian American establishments.

Americans connected with Marciano's regular-guy persona, which extended to his physical dimensions. "So you're the heavyweight champion of the world," President Eisenhower said when he met Marciano at a White House event. "Somehow I thought you'd be bigger." Rocky smiled. "No, sir."[18] Modesty and lack of guile were Marciano trademarks. He exemplified a code of civility and stoicism that would soon become passé. He was fond of an Italian expression, *Fa i fatte e no parole*: "Do it. Don't talk about it."[19] The morning after he beat Walcott, he vowed to himself that he would never do anything to disgrace the heavyweight championship.

Since Joe Louis's retirement, the title had existed in a kind of limbo. Neither Charles nor Walcott captured the public mind or inhabited the title in the distinctive ways that its great occupants had done. From the moment the Suzy Q landed on Walcott's jaw in Philadelphia, Marciano served notice that the American crown once again had a king.

★

The king's first order of business was a rematch with Walcott. The Philadelphia battle, the most dramatic heavyweight fight since Louis and Conn, had elevated the stature of both men. Unfortunately, the rematch, in Chicago Stadium, turned out to be a bitter disappointment. After two minutes of light sparring, Marciano landed a left hook and what looked like a modest right uppercut as Walcott backed up along the ropes. Walcott collapsed to the canvas in a heap, heels flying up into the air. Then, as he sat on the canvas, holding a strand of rope with one glove, Walcott listened as the referee, Frank Sikora, tolled seven, eight, nine, and ten. He rose just after "ten." The crowd moaned. For a few seconds, Walcott seemed unperturbed, but as boos descended, he turned to the referee, protesting that he had gotten up in time. Felix Bocchicchio protested with him. But Sikora raised Marciano's arm. Rocky was the winner by knockout at 2:25 of the first round.

The bout left a sour taste, and some suspected in the aftermath that Walcott, fighting for his richest purse—$250,000—took a dive. No evidence has emerged to corroborate that argument. Walcott and Bocchicchio blamed the referee, claiming that Sikora had given Walcott a short count—in a boxing city best known for its long count—but the film didn't support their charges. Perhaps Walcott was legitimately knocked out. Or maybe, as the film strongly suggests, he quit on the floor. Walcott's body language as the count tolled was not that of a man separated from his senses but of one trying to make a decision. No experienced boxer—and Walcott had experience enough for several careers—waits until the count of nine to begin rising from a sitting position. If Walcott really did want to keep fighting, his change of heart came too late.

"He should have gotten up," Marciano said later. "I would have."[20]

"Walcott was guaranteed a quarter of a million dollars for this night's work," the normally mild-mannered Red Smith wrote in the *New York Herald Tribune*. "If its finish guarantees his departure from boxing, the price was not too great."[21]

It was a shameful way for Walcott to end his career, but he retained most of the public affection that he had won. In time, Walcott's stature as a peculiar master of pugilism was recognized as well. He died in 1994.

★

By the early 1950s, the heavyweight title had come to be known as "the richest prize in sports." In a young nation, anything with over half a century of documented history qualified as venerable—and, in the title's case, lucrative, too. Like his predecessors, Marciano found that the chances for making money—through personal appearances, speaking engagements, and business and franchising deals—were virtually unlimited, especially for a popular champion. He found, too, as others had, that the title gave him a standing in the world not attainable otherwise. It was a long way from Brockton.

"Do you realize what you are, Rock?" actor Jerry Lewis asked him. "You are the boss of the world—the whole world."[22]

One way to prove that you were boss was to tie up loose ends. When Joe Louis beat all five champions of the early 1930s, he ascribed to himself command of the era that followed Gene Tunney's retirement in 1928. In 1910, when Jack Johnson beat Jim Jeffries in Reno, he vanquished the man who boasted victories over Bob Fitzsimmons and Jim Corbett. It was Corbett who had dethroned John L. Sullivan—and that took things back to the beginning. With his wins over Louis and Walcott, Marciano had a chance for a similar kind of consolidation, but there was one missing link in the chain: Ezzard Charles. If Marciano could get past the aging Cincinnati Cobra, then he would hold wins over all the heavyweight champions dating back to 1937. Now thirty-three, Ezzard was on the downside of his career; he had started losing to men who couldn't have touched him years earlier. But as a former champion, he made a compelling opponent, and 47,585 fans came out to Yankee Stadium on June 17, 1954, to see if Charles could become the first man to regain the title.

Over the first four rounds, Charles used his masterful boxing skills to punch Marciano silly. He was more offensively daring than usual, landing right-hand leads—a right not set up with a left jab and thus more risky, as it resembles a go-for-broke maneuver. Marciano ate one right hand after another, but he kept coming forward. Charles kept the battle within a tight perimeter around the ring, refusing to let Marciano pin him on the ropes. His punches bloodied the champ's nose and opened up a large cut over his left eye.

"You've got to punch your way out of this fight," Charley Goldman told Rocky, and Marciano began breaking through Charles's defense in the fifth round.[23] In the sixth, he attacked Charles with an unrelenting barrage of punches, barely pausing, it seemed, to breathe. Near the end of the round, Marciano showed that he was mortal: he stopped punching for a moment. Charles punished him for the lapse, nailing him with a left hook to the jaw that would have knocked out anyone else.

Marciano had turned the tide. In the eighth, he hit Charles with a left hook to the Adam's apple, and it took Ezzard two rounds to get his breathing back to normal. The challenger kept working on Rocky's left eye; the cut bothered Marciano throughout. But Marciano's corner savior, Freddie Brown, kept the bleeding under control. Charles was hardly unmarked himself. His right eye was closing, and his lips were swelling. On the left side of his face rose a lump larger than a golf ball. It turned out to be a blood clot.

The fifteenth and final round was like a clinic in everything that made Marciano special as a fighter: he threw punches the entire way, not stopping even when he missed four, five, or six in a row. This was the Marciano approach to fighting, boiled down, and no man yet had been able to cope with it. When the bell sounded, the fighters embraced, and Marciano smiled through his mouthpiece at his noble adversary. The decision was unanimous: by rounds, the scores were 8–6–1, 8–5–2, and 9–5–1, all for Marciano, but the postfight glory belonged to Charles. Like Walcott, he hadn't won the fight crowd's affection until he went to war with Rocky Marciano.

"Charles unquestionably offered the greatest fight of his long career," Wilfrid Smith wrote in the *Chicago Tribune*. "Charles was the man who rose to greater heights."[24] If Charles had "fought all his fights the way he did against the rock-ribbed, rock-jawed and rock-fisted Rocky," Arthur Daley wrote in the *New York Times*, "he would have been heavyweight champion of the world for a much longer time."[25] The battle had been so gripping that a rematch was quickly ordered for September in Yankee Stadium.

Charles talked bravely about his confidence that he would beat Marciano this time, but when the bell rang, he didn't fight as though he thought he could win. Instead, Charles let Marciano dictate the pace. He initiated fewer exchanges and showed less willingness to fight. Marciano sensed the difference early on. In the second round, he did what he couldn't do over fifteen rounds the previous June—he knocked Charles down. Over the next several rounds, he battered the former champion around the ring. A knockout seemed imminent.

In the sixth round, Marciano pulled away from a clinch, with blood spurting from his nose. In fact, the nose was split, with a harrowing line running more than halfway up the bridge. It looked as though someone had held Marciano's nose between two fingers and snipped with a scissors. The split nose put the champion in imminent danger. If the referee, Al Berl, chose to stop the fight, Charles would win the title.

In Marciano's corner, no one, not even nerveless Freddie Brown, had ever seen such a wound. Brown tried his best to stop the blood flow. Some say he applied Monsel's solution—a coagulant that, according to one modern trainer, "sears blood vessels shut and creates knots of black scar tissue." Others say he used Negatan, a formaldehyde-containing embalming fluid that "turns skin to leather in a matter of seconds."[26] Whatever it was, it went on as orange-yellow, making Marciano look, in the words of radio announcer Russ Hodges, "like a Halloween character" as he came out for the seventh round. Charles quickly punched off the protectant, and the blood cascaded. Rocky won the round, but the scorecards seemed irrelevant.

"Go after him now or you'll bleed to death," Goldman told Rocky in the corner.[27] A few jabs from Charles in the eighth, and the blood was gushing again. But Charles had no legs under him and could not keep Rocky away. Marciano crossed a right over Ezzard's jab, and the former champion went down. He popped up quickly, only to face more clubbing blows from the desperate Marciano. A final right, thrown like a hammer chop, sent him to the canvas again on his haunches, where he stayed. Marciano was the winner by an eighth-round knockout.

The accolades that Charles earned from his first gallant effort were now withdrawn. He stayed in boxing five more years as a journeyman, fighting for money and losing often, another champion with no savings to show for his long years in the ring. Things got worse: in the mid-1960s, he was diagnosed with ALS, Lou Gehrig's disease. He died at age fifty-three in Chicago, barely noted, in 1975—a fittingly quiet end for a gifted but lonely champion.

★

As much as any heavyweight champion since Dempsey, Marciano cherished the title, but he could feel himself wearing down. Top challengers were in short supply. In May 1955, Marciano fought the British champion, Don Cockell, in San Francisco. Few outside the British press thought that Cockell had a chance, but he proved dead game, taking an incredible battering over nine rounds before the referee stopped the fight.

Marciano's win over Cockell didn't excite anyone, but his next challenger did: light heavyweight champion Archie Moore, another of those

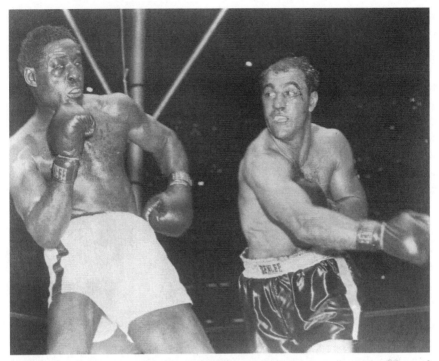

Rocky Marciano swings his Suzy Q (the right) at former champion Ezzard Charles in the first of their two brutal battles in 1954.
Peter Newark Historical Pictures / Bridgeman Images

self-creating figures that boxing provides with such uncanny regularity. Moore disputed his official age, which was at least thirty-eight in 1955 but more likely forty-one. His boxing skills and guile had earned him the nickname the Old Mongoose, and he had also developed a reputation as a sage. He read widely, was involved in African American political causes, and developed a lingo of expressions about life and boxing that made him a press favorite. A boxer who avoided getting hit—as he did—Moore said, was practicing "escapology."

Marciano and Moore signed to fight for the title at Yankee Stadium on September 21, 1955. Not since he had faced Walcott in Philadelphia had Marciano been involved in a promotion that aroused more interest. Television had cut into live gates for years, but sixty-one thousand fans came out to Yankee Stadium, paying $940,000, the closest that a bout had come to a million-dollar gate since Louis–Conn II in 1946. Another one hundred thousand people in thirty-six cities watched in theaters over closed-circuit television.

After a quiet first round, Moore caught Marciano with a flash right on the chin in the second round, dropping Rocky to the canvas on one knee—only the second time in his career that he had been down. He was up at two, and he caught a break. Referee Harry Kessler had a momentary brain freeze: he thought that the mandatory eight-count—in which a referee counts to eight, even if a knocked-down fighter has already gained his feet, in order to give him extra time to recover—was in effect. In fact, the "standing eight" had never been used in a heavyweight title fight up to this time. Kessler reached five and then, remembering, halted his count and waved the two combatants together. Moore would later claim that those extra seconds cost him dearly.

Marciano came out refreshed in the third round and pounded Moore in his usual way, not worrying about aesthetics. In the fourth, Marciano pinned him on the ropes, but Moore put on a virtuoso defensive display. He swiveled his shoulders, darted his head, and used elbows and crossed arms to evade most of Marciano's punches.

The Yankee Stadium crowd maintained a steady roar throughout, and the battle kept giving them reason to roar. Marciano battered Moore without letup in the sixth, dropping him with a right for a count of four. Rocky followed up with a breathtaking display of continuous punching. His stamina seemed extra-human, as if he had an internal motor that could break down oxygen on demand. His ceaseless punching—like an airplane propeller constantly whirring in your ear, Moore later said—wore the older man down. Moore hit the deck a second time from a cavalcade of Marciano blows. But he got up again and was fighting back at the bell.

Signs of the end were now apparent, but Moore went out and won the seventh round, stunning Marciano with the right again. He could still sharpshoot Marciano coming in, but he couldn't hurt him. Marciano had him down twice in the eighth, and Archie's men hurried him back to his stool. Kessler approached and asked if he should stop the fight.

"I'll go down fighting," Moore told him.[28]

In the ninth, after another fusillade from the Marciano armory, Moore collapsed in his own corner, arms resting on the ropes. He made a move to rise, but his legs buckled, and he slumped back down as Kessler counted him out. Like some men before him, he had fought and lost against Marciano but burnished his reputation.

Writing in *Sports Illustrated*, Time-Life's weekly sports magazine that had launched a year earlier, Budd Schulberg placed Marciano in the lineage of the best heavyweights. "The old-timers talk of Sullivan and Jeffries and

Dempsey. We may have another such immortal slugger in our midst. Are we too close to his shortcomings to recognize his incomparable virtues?"[29]

★

Marciano might have kept fighting had it not been for his disgust at sharing so much money with Al Weill. The only way out of Weill's clutches was to leave boxing. On April 27, 1956, at Manhattan's Hotel Shelton, Marciano told reporters that he was hanging up the gloves. He would retire from the ring with a perfect record of 49–0, including forty-three knockouts.

"Retirement," though, doesn't do justice to the life he led for the next decade and a half. Admired for being a down-to-earth, ordinary guy, Marciano was in reality far from ordinary—like most high-achievers. He was forever on the move, from one speaking engagement or business deal to another, slowing down only long enough to keep a running tally of his thoughts. He once scratched on a hotel address book, "If you want to live a full life, live dangerously," and then on the facing page, in capital letters, he wrote, "INSECURE."

Marciano was more insecure about money than anything else. He often carted around a brown shopping bag filled with thousands of dollars in cash. He distrusted banks and turned down checks as payment for public appearances, insisting on "green stuff." He hoarded cash wherever he could, stuffing it into electrical sockets, pipe fittings, curtain rods, and toilet-bowl tanks around the United States.

This miser-like behavior had little to do with greed. Marciano lavished little money on himself. His real motivation was fear, a fear rooted in his past: it was all about the shoe factory and his father's life, which haunted him to the end of his days. "It was rough for me when I was a kid, Willie," he told his friend the great featherweight champion (and fellow Italian) Willie Pep. "It's never gonna be like that again. I'm never gonna be broke now, Willie. Never."[30]

Even Marciano might have stopped worrying about poverty had he accepted any of the lucrative comeback offers that came his way for years. The tradition of heavyweight champions breaking their retirement vows was a rich one. Even as late as 1966, when Marciano was in his early forties, people hadn't given up on seeing him return to the ring. For many, especially whites, Rocky was a symbol of a better time, of an America they remembered longingly and wished to get back. Yet Marciano wisely refused these temptations. He took his reputation, his earnings, and his perfect

49–0 record with him into permanent retirement—the only heavyweight champion never to lose a fight.

In 1969, a radio producer, Murray Woroner, devised an ingenious series, the All-Time Heavyweight Tournament, a fantasy competition between the great champions of the past. Using a National Cash Register 315 computer, Woroner produced readouts of punches and movements and translated these into blow-by-blow radio broadcasts of imaginary fights that proved immensely popular, attracting twelve million listeners. In the final bout, Marciano knocked out Jack Dempsey to become the all-time heavyweight king—at least, according to the computer.

One man was dissatisfied: Muhammad Ali, the undefeated heavyweight champion, then exiled from boxing and facing a jail term for refusing induction into the armed forces. In Woroner's tournament, Ali had lost to Jim Jeffries, an outcome he found ludicrous. He filed a $1 million suit against Woroner for defamation. Woroner settled with Ali by offering him $10,000 to act out, on film, a fantasy match with Marciano, based on computer simulations. The final product would be marketed as the "Super Fight," and both champs would share in the profits.

Marciano lost at least forty pounds, put on a ponderous toupee, and met Ali in a Miami warehouse, where the two moved around the ring over several days, filming seventy-five one-minute rounds. They acted out multiple scenarios and rehearsed seven different endings: Ali winning on cuts; Marciano winning by decision; Ali by decision; Marciano by knockout; and so on. They were faking it, but competitiveness broke out. Ali knocked Marciano's hairpiece off with a jab; Marciano, enraged, demanded that the cameras be stopped while Ali and his men suppressed laughter. Then he punished Ali to the body.

"Ask him about his ribs," Rocky told a friend later, referring to Ali.

"That guy's crazy," Ali said. He lifted up his shirt to show a ribcage red with welts.[31]

The fighters' camps had worried that the get-together would be tense. Marciano was no Ali fan; he felt that Ali dishonored the heavyweight title. Others thought that Ali might be dismissive of the conservative old champion. But they got on well from the outset, calling each other "Champ." They even talked about making a national tour to promote racial harmony.

On August 31, 1969, a few weeks after he had wrapped up the Super Fight filming and the day before his forty-sixth birthday, Marciano's hustling lifestyle—he called it "bouncing"—caught up with him. Accepting a last-minute request to help out at a fund-raiser in Des Moines, Rocky phoned home with news of his delay and climbed into a rickety Cessna plane. In a mounting storm, the inexperienced pilot became disoriented, crashing the plane in a Newton, Iowa, cornfield. Marciano's body was found inside, cut in two. Unfortunately for his wife and daughter, whose lives after 1969 were difficult, not a dollar of the loot that Marciano stashed around the country was ever found.

Boxing felt the loss. Marciano had become one of the sport's regal champions, remembered not only for his indomitable will but also for that astounding symbol of perfection: 49–0. "Rocky couldn't box like [Gene] Tunney, and probably couldn't hit like [Joe] Louis, but in one respect he had no challenger," Red Smith wrote. "He was the toughest, strongest, most completely dedicated fighter who ever wore gloves. . . . Fear wasn't in his vocabulary and pain had no meaning."[32] The most eloquent tribute came from the man who seemed so often to have just the right words: Joe Louis. Told of Marciano's death, the old Bomber said: "This is the saddest news I've ever heard."[33]

In Brockton, about two thousand people crowded into Saint Colman's Catholic Church to pay tribute to Marciano. At least one thousand more stood outside. Boxing royalty came out: Willie Pep, Tony Zale, Paul Pender, and others. In a tender scene, Louis bent down to kiss Rocky's casket.

Muhammad Ali rushed through traffic to make it to Rocky's funeral on time. The world didn't know yet about the Super Fight. It wouldn't be released until January 1970, when it was shown in movie theaters in the United States, Canada, and Europe. The filmmakers edited out the last alternative ending and sealed the film up in steel canisters, to be opened by projectionists just before showtime. Finally, the ending was revealed: Marciano was the winner by a thirteenth-round knockout. Ali joked that the "computer was made in Alabama" but called Rocky his "buddy" and spoke of how happy he would have been to have seen the final show.[34]

Years later, Ali sat beside a fireplace at his Deer Lake, Pennsylvania, training camp with Howard Cosell, taping a segment for ABC's *Wide World of Sports* in which he watched film of past heavyweight champions and discussed how he would have fared against them. For much of the program, Ali was dismissive of his predecessors. Then Cosell got to Marciano.

"Marciano!" Ali said, shaking his head. "Ooh, he hit hard!" Cosell asked him how an Ali–Marciano fight would have gone. "I don't know if I would have beaten him," Ali said. "His style and my style, he could have out-pointed me, he could have knocked me down. . . . I did a computer fight with him, when he was an old man just pretending, and my arms are sore just from joking with him. In his heyday, he may have won, he probably would—it's up for the imagination."[35] Rarely in his long public career had Muhammad Ali sounded so uncertain.

★

The heavyweight championship rose to world prominence as a white American property, but Rocky Marciano would be the last white American to hold it. As the years passed, he stood not only as a symbol of whites' lost prominence in boxing but also of the last era in American life in which whiteness held unquestioned cultural dominance. A famous shot showing Marciano standing with Joe DiMaggio at the White House, both flanking a beaming Eisenhower, is a representative image of the time. With Marciano's departure, blacks came to dominate the championship picture as never before, though white contenders occasionally emerged, inspiring talk of White Hopes but with little of the passion of earlier times. Other passions were boiling, however. The United States was about to embark on a generation of change and strife, and the heavyweight title would be right in the middle of it.

FREUDIAN FLOYD,
THE SWEDE, AND SONNY

"I don't like that boy!" the child said, holding the black-and-white photograph of a family gathered together—father and mother and three young sons. He meant the two-year-old in the photo, who wore a shy smile. Floyd Patterson was pointing to himself. He was so repulsed by his own image that he etched an X across his face.

Born in Waco, North Carolina, in 1935, Floyd had moved with his family to the Bedford-Stuyvesant neighborhood of Brooklyn a year later as his father sought work and opportunity in the North. Thomas Patterson found lots of labor—as a longshoreman and in construction and sanitation—but little opportunity. He left the house early and didn't return until past dinnertime and sometimes the middle of the night. He sat with his head bowed at the supper table, where young Floyd, pitying him, cleaned his feet. Then Thomas would rise, enter the bedroom, and collapse into bed, sometimes in his work clothes.

Self-hatred seized Floyd early on. His mother, Annabelle, who worked as a domestic, watched with mounting distress as her son's antisocial behavior increased. He woke screaming in the middle of the night. He sleepwalked, sometimes out on the street. He became a truant and a petty thief. He craved solitude and found refuge in a tool room above the High Street subway station in Brooklyn Heights. Floyd took the A train to that stop, climbed a ladder, and sat or lay down in the dark. He seemed always to be slinking away into the shadows.

Another boy spent his life in the shadows, even after he had become a man. "He went through alleys all the time," one associate remembered. "He always went around things. I can still see him, either coming out of an alley or walking into one."[1] Born to desperate poverty in rural Arkansas, one of twenty-five children, Charles "Sonny" Liston lacked everything: food, clothing, affection, and instruction. He didn't even have his own birthday. The date, he said years later, had been carved onto a tree, but the tree was chopped down. His father whipped him daily. Sonny became a man early, a hulking bruiser by the time he was thirteen, illiterate and unmoored.

The motif of darkness defined him: the darkness of the streets and alleys in which he committed his first crimes, the darkness of the prison walls, the darkness of his connections with criminal elements, the darkness of his unknowability. After he discovered boxing, he worked out every day to the tune of the same slow, grinding blues: "Night Train." For many opponents, facing Sonny Liston was like taking a journey downward into a lightless space of fear and pain.

Sonny and Floyd, two men who often sought to conceal themselves, would find their destinies in the public spectacle of boxing, testifying again to the capacity of this beleaguered sport to absorb such varieties of human character. They would become contrasting symbols of black identity and possibility, not quite a yin and yang but close enough for most observers. Together—along with an improbable Swedish interloper—they defined the heavyweight championship in an era remembered as tranquil but in which everything, from race relations to technological advancements to the governance of boxing, seemed in flux.

★

"When I was small," Patterson told W. C. Heinz, "I could never look people in the eye. When I tried to look them in the eye, it always seemed that they could read my mind. . . . Then one day I woke up and I could look people in the eye. It had kind of sneaked its way in."[2]

That happy day was a long time coming. Ten-year-old Floyd Patterson was eventually picked up for truancy and became a familiar figure in juvenile courts. The authorities finally assigned him to Wiltwyck, a school for emotionally disturbed boys, in Esopus, in New York's Hudson Valley. The school's bucolic setting was a revelation to a city kid who had never seen cows or chickens or so much green. At Wiltwyck, he turned his life around, learning to read and write and finding mentors who helped him overcome his crippling shyness. Eleanor Roosevelt, who bankrolled the school, hosted groups of Wiltwyck boys at Valkill, her Hyde Park estate, for Christmas. His transformative experience at Wiltwyck cultivated in Patterson a lifelong passion for helping the downtrodden, particularly troubled kids.

It was at Wiltwyck that he first put on boxing gloves, winning the school's annual tournament. From that moment on, Patterson thought of little but boxing. After enrolling in Brooklyn's P.S. 614, a specialized public school, Floyd, now fourteen, joined his older brothers at the Gramercy Gym on East Fourteenth Street in Manhattan. There, he drew the attention of Cus D'Amato, the Gramercy's head man, who would become his boxing guru.

A strange, haunted man, intensely paranoid—he wouldn't ride the subway, lest he be pushed onto the tracks by nameless enemies—D'Amato had a gift for grudges and a vast capacity for philosophizing. He believed that boxing came down to individual character. "Skill will prevail," he taught, "only when it is so superior to the other man's skill that the will is not tested."[3] Fear could be crippling or empowering. "Fear is like fire," he taught. "It can cook for you. It can heat your house. Or it can burn it down."[4] D'Amato sought to mold his fighters not only into warriors but also into active psychologists.

D'Amato was embroiled in a long-running feud with Jim Norris's International Boxing Club, which still controlled professional boxing. Cus had once worked closely with the IBC, but he now dreamed of grooming a fighter who could win the heavyweight title and remain free of the Octopus—and thus break the organization's stranglehold on boxing. D'Amato lived like an angry monk. He didn't care about money; he had no family; he did not drink or dabble in drugs, women, or gambling; and he didn't care what people thought about him. He understood that the world's standard inducements were so effective because most people were weak.

D'Amato's war on convention extended to boxing fundamentals. Convinced that the standard boxing stance for a right-hander—left foot forward, right foot trailing behind, left hand raised to eye level, right hand below the chin—confined fighters to a predictable style, D'Amato devised a different approach. He told his charges to stand squared up, with both gloves pressed against the cheeks, almost as if the boxer was hiding behind them. He had them bob their heads, swiveling their torsos from side to side to avoid punches. From this "peekaboo" stance, Cus felt, fighters could throw explosive punches, though the style expended enormous energy and required top conditioning to execute.

Patterson embarked on a hugely successful amateur career, winning back-to-back New York Golden Gloves titles, and then, in 1952, at just seventeen, winning the gold medal in the 165-pound class at the Summer

Olympics in Helsinki, Finland. From the beginning, his youth, speed, and boxing skills hailed him as a coming star in the professional ranks. D'Amato had big plans for Floyd: though the kid was still straining to reach 170 pounds, the trainer believed that he could become the heavyweight champion. After all, the current champ, Rocky Marciano, weighed barely 185. Jack Dempsey had never weighed 200 for a fight, and Joe Louis was best at right about 200. Patterson had time and the frame to add the pounds. He won his first thirteen fights before losing a disputed decision to former light heavyweight champion Joey Maxim. Interviewed afterward, he gave reporters an early glimpse of his modesty.

"Don't you think you beat him?" one asked.

"The officials could see it better than I could," Floyd replied. "I was too busy fighting."[5] In another match, Floyd knocked an opponent's mouthpiece out but paused and helped him retrieve it. No one could recall seeing a boxer do that before.

Patterson rattled off sixteen more victories after the Maxim loss, to bring his record to 29–1 in April 1956. Late that month, Marciano announced his retirement. Patterson, twenty-one, with a chance to become the youngest heavyweight champion in history, was matched against "Ancient" Archie Moore, thirty-nine (or forty-two, or whatever), who could become the oldest. The fight was set for November 30, 1956, in Chicago.

★

It's easy to see, more than half a century later, the tensions that lay beneath 1950s America's seemingly placid exterior. Flush as they were economically, Americans were unsettled by Cold War fears. By the late 1950s, the Eisenhower administration was promoting family fallout shelters. Days before the U.S. presidential election in November 1956, Soviet tanks rolled into Budapest to crush the Hungarian revolution. Watching *The Ed Sullivan Show* a few months later, in January 1957, Americans responded eagerly to calls for donations to Hungarian relief efforts made by the show's young guest star, Elvis Presley. The twenty-one-year-old from Tupelo, Mississippi, began 1956 as a barely known singer and ended it as the top-selling recording star in the United States. Leonard Bernstein would later call Elvis "the greatest cultural force in the twentieth century."[6] If Bernstein was right, it was in good part because Presley, who was mistaken for black when many listeners first heard him on the radio, blurred racial lines—a revolutionary if unintentional achievement in 1956, when America's racial torment was becoming harder to ignore.

In 1954, the Supreme Court had ruled, in *Brown v. Board of Education*, that "separate but equal" arrangements in American schools were unconstitutional and ordered the nation's schools desegregated. In the South, though, states and localities resisted. The following year, a fourteen-year-old Chicago boy, Emmett Till, was murdered in Mississippi, after a white woman told her husband that he had gotten fresh with her. The viciousness of the crime shocked the country. Later in 1955, in Montgomery, Alabama, a black citizens' boycott of segregated buses began, led by the young Baptist preacher Martin Luther King Jr.

When American blacks sought encouragement, they often looked to sports. It had been nine years since Jackie Robinson integrated baseball, and most teams had at least one black player. Most pro football teams had black players by the early 1950s, and the National Basketball Association had begun integrating in 1950. But no sport had been friendlier to blacks than boxing. In Helsinki, all five gold-medal-winning American boxers were black. In the pro ranks, blacks were among the top contenders in most divisions, and two blacks had followed Joe Louis as heavyweight champion: Ezzard Charles and Joe Walcott. With Marciano's retirement, the vacant title would be claimed by Archie Moore or Floyd Patterson—both black men.

The oddsmakers made Moore a 2–1 favorite, but from the opening bell, Archie looked tentative and slow, and he was beaten to the punch repeatedly by Patterson, who never looked faster. Nor did Patterson ever give a better exhibition of the peekaboo style and the way it enabled him to explode suddenly on opponents, especially with his best punch, the left hook. With his gloves pressed close to his cheeks, his shoulders squared, his torso bobbing left and right, Patterson looked as though he might set off in any direction. At times, he left his feet in throwing the left hook, in violation of boxing fundamentals. But the leaping hook, which some called Patterson's "kangaroo punch," often found its target. The Old Mongoose never had a chance. In the fifth round, Patterson's left hooks sent the veteran down to the canvas. A short right put him down again, and Archie took the ten-count. At twenty-one years, ten months, Floyd Patterson—born four days before Elvis Presley—was the youngest heavyweight champion in history. By beating the IBC-controlled Moore, he had also become, as *Sports Illustrated* would later describe him, "the first free heavyweight champion since the IBC was formed."[7]

No one knew quite what to make of the boy king. His gentle personality didn't fit the role that he had assumed: the toughest man in the world, a symbol of American might. But his talents were clear.

In April 1957, Patterson embarked on an exhibition tour, boxing short bouts before paying audiences. What he saw in his travels left a lasting impression on him. In Fort Smith, Arkansas, Patterson was greeted by an all-white crowd that blocked his exit from the train station. (Arkansas was about to take center stage in the civil rights movement: later that year, after Governor Orval Faubus used his state guard to prevent black students from integrating Central High School in Little Rock, President Eisenhower called out the 101st Airborne division to usher the black students to school.) Things might have turned ugly if not for the intervention of a white Catholic priest, Samuel J. Delaney, pastor of Saint John the Baptist Church, who escorted Patterson and his traveling group through the crowd. Patterson performed in Fort Smith before what he thought was an all-white audience, but a few rounds into the exhibition, he heard cheers coming from the rafters, in the black section. Looking up at the black faces, Patterson promised himself that he would never again perform before a segregated crowd. After returning home, he sent Father Delaney's parish a $3,000 donation and joined the NAACP.

Patterson's natural talent suggested the potential for a long reign, but D'Amato's careful selection of opponents frustrated fans and critics. The manager ruled out fights against other top heavyweights because of their IBC connections, instead putting Patterson in the ring against overmatched opponents—including a former Olympic champion, Pete Rademacher, fighting for the first time professionally. Patterson won, as expected, but his underdog challengers managed to embarrass him with knockdowns, exposing a weakness that would plague him throughout his career. Sportswriters like Jimmy Cannon also noticed his unwillingness to go for the kill. After Patterson confessed that he had eased off a hurt opponent, Cannon told him: "Compassion is a defect in a fighter."[8] Two years after winning the title, Patterson remained an enigma. Then in September 1958, a new face emerged, one untainted by the defects of American boxing.

★

Eddie Machen, a top-ranked heavyweight, couldn't get Patterson into the ring, so he journeyed to Göteborg, Sweden, hometown of the European heavyweight champion, Ingemar Johansson. Machen went into the ring a heavy favorite; he left it as damaged goods. Johansson knocked Machen down with the first right he threw. Getting up on wobbly legs, Machen was clouted around the ring and knocked through the ropes. The fight was over in one round. Johansson's upset win vaulted the twenty-six-year-old Swede into position as the top contender.

Few boxers in history have been so defined by a punch. Johansson's right hand was about to propel him to fame and riches he had barely dreamed of growing up in Göteborg, where he was born in 1932, the son of working-class parents. Sweden had never been a haven for boxing; the sport was banned there for many years. But Johansson made a connection with the country's leading boxing figure, Edwin Ahlquist, a sports magazine publisher and owner of a dockside company for which the teenage Johansson worked as a laborer. Ahlquist managed Johansson through a successful amateur career, steering him to a spot on Sweden's 1952 Olympic boxing team. In the Olympic heavyweight finals, however, Johansson was ignominiously disqualified. He started his pro career under a cloud, but as he piled up wins, Swedish fans forgave him. The knockout over Machen made Ingo, as he was often called, a national hero.

Johansson traveled to the United States in early 1959 to arrange a match with Patterson. The American press was drawn to the outgoing, handsome, stylish European, who dressed in classy suits and spoke several languages. Reporters were also intrigued by the Swede's big punch, which earned several nicknames: Thunder and Lightning, or just "Toonder," in mimicry of Johansson's English pronunciation; the Hammer of Thor, tapping into his Scandinavian heritage; or, most popularly, Ingo's Bingo.

Still, American sportswriters weren't convinced that Johansson could beat Patterson, and the Swede was made a prohibitive 5–1 underdog. But Johansson was supremely confident, and his confidence showed in the way he prepared for the fight at Grossinger's, in New York's Catskills. The Swede went easy on his sparring partners, never unveiling the right for eager American reporters; some concluded that the punch was just hype. While Patterson worked out in Spartan solitude, Ingo brought in a Swedish chef, invited his parents and siblings to join him in camp, and broke boxing's oldest taboo by taking along his fiancée, Birgit Lundgren, who joined him upstairs in a private suite. The two made frequent trips into Manhattan for evenings out. It was a training camp to make Max Baer proud.

★

It rained in New York most of that Friday, June 26, 1959. The bout's promoters had already postponed the fight once, and the weather kept people away from Yankee Stadium: only thirty thousand fans showed up, paying a live gate of less than $500,000. But the pay-television promotion brought a generous windfall. The closed-circuit company, TelePrompTer, broadcast the bout to half a million paying fans in theaters around the United States.

Listening to the referee's instructions before the opening bell, the 196-pound Johansson looked much larger than the 182-pound Patterson. In the first two rounds, though, the size difference seemed incidental. Johansson was cautious, flicking out his left jab, refusing to let the right go except once, near the end of the first round, when it landed short. Fighting in his peekaboo style, Patterson held the edge but seemed distracted, as if he lacked a fight plan.

The Swede had a plan, and in the third round, he unveiled it. Boxing at ring center, Johansson jabbed and then let the right go, connecting with Floyd's chin. Just as Machen had, Floyd collapsed to the canvas. He barely beat the count, and as Ingo moved in for the kill, Patterson turned his back and walked away, like a man who had just gotten out of bed in the dark. He was on "queer street," as the old-timers called it—out on his feet.

Johansson didn't wait for Patterson to turn around, clubbing him from behind. The champion dropped again. It was a brutal move from Ingo, legal but not terribly sporting. Patterson somehow got up, again barely beating the count. Ingo attacked with both hands and soon had Floyd on the floor for a third time. He kept getting up—even after being knocked down a fourth, fifth, sixth, and seventh time. He was rising again when referee Ruby Goldstein stopped the fight.

No champion since Jess Willard in 1919 had lost his title in such bludgeoning fashion. Ingemar Johansson, the first Swede to win the heavyweight title, was also the first non-American to do so since Primo Carnera in 1933. In Göteborg, Stockholm, and around Sweden, where three million people had listened to the broadcast on Radio Luxembourg, Johansson's countrymen danced in the streets, downed shots of Aquavit, and drove around honking their horns. Even Sweden's state-owned radio network, which had refused to carry the fight, broadcast enthusiastic reports of Ingo's victory. The nation prepared an extravagant welcome home.

Though he had taken the crown from an American, Johansson was a popular victor in the United States. He had a taste for the finer things, suffered no ambivalence about fame or success, and exuded self-assurance such as Patterson had never shown. And yes, he was white, to boot—that still counted for something, even though Ingo was not an American. "We have a fair-haired champion!" one radio announcer had exclaimed.[9] Some suggested that Johansson was a new Jack Dempsey.

Ingo wasted no time capitalizing on the title. He embarked on a dizzying round of honors, appearances, and profiteering. He became a familiar guest star on American television programs, appearing with Ed Sullivan, Steve Allen, Jackie Gleason, and especially with Dinah Shore on her show, where he showed off his considerable vocal talents, crooning Swedish songs so affectingly that hundreds of letters poured in; Shore brought him back. He got acting roles in film and on television. The UN enlisted him to do goodwill work on the Gaza Strip. In 1959 and 1960, Ingemar Johansson was everywhere.

The Swede's effortless success in the public eye was a special kind of torture for Patterson, who spent months in seclusion, trying to shake off the depression that had set in after his humiliating defeat and get his mind right for the rematch with Johansson, which had already been signed. For most boxing observers, Floyd's "glass jaw" seemed to be the fatal strike against him—hadn't Johansson proved it? Ingo was too big and hit too hard, and Floyd was barely even a heavyweight, anyway: he weighed only 182 pounds for the first fight, just seven pounds over the light heavyweight limit. And when one factored in Floyd's complexes—some called him Freud Patterson or Freudian Floyd—and set them against the Swede's self-confidence, it seemed to many that a second match would go the same way. Oddsmakers made Ingo an 8–5 favorite.

Patterson secluded himself in an abandoned roadhouse in then-remote Newtown, Connecticut, preparing with the grimmest determination he had ever shown. He and D'Amato had grown apart, professionally and strategically. His new trainer, Dan Florio, felt that Floyd should abandon the peekaboo style, or at least modify it, so that he wasn't so off-balance. They mapped out a different fight plan, in which Patterson would attack Johansson more actively, keeping him from throwing the right. Patterson got reinforcement from a surprise visitor: Joe Louis.

"The only way to beat a puncher," the Brown Bomber told Floyd, "is to crowd him. If you give him punching room, he'll beat your brains out."[10] They studied films of the first fight together. Though he tried to tune out the news, Patterson couldn't help but notice the Swede's boastful confidence. "When I hit [Patterson] square with my right," Ingo said a week before the rematch, "the referee can count to a thousand."[11] Floyd felt his mind hardening as it never had against an opponent.

"Somebody is going to be carried out of that ring," he told his wife, Sandra, "and I don't think it'll be me."[12]

★

They fought again on June 20, 1960, in New York's Polo Grounds, the last major fight held at the old home of New York's baseball Giants, who had relocated to San Francisco three years earlier. Patterson weighed in at 190 pounds, eight pounds heavier than the first fight, and he looked it; his body rippled with muscle. Though he had trained again in leisurely fashion, Johansson came in slightly lighter, at 194.75. But the Swede's mind was unfocused. He was so confident that on the eve of the match, he made an encore appearance on *What's My Line?*, the long-running program in which blindfolded celebrities guessed the identities of special guests. Ingo's cover was quickly blown, and then regular panelist Arlene Francis asked the question that must have been on the minds of others watching at home: "Why aren't you home in bed?"[13]

Floyd came out with a fury in the first round, attacking Johansson and crowding him, as Louis had advised. At times, Floyd resorted to his leaping style with the hooks. Johansson looked rattled. Floyd had quickly sent a message to the champion that he could expect rude treatment. But in the second round, Ingo landed the right—and, for a moment, it looked as though all of Floyd's preparations would be in vain. The challenger backed off and Ingo pursued, but the Swede, curiously tentative, could not follow up. In the third and fourth rounds, Floyd kept a busy left jab in Ingo's face and hurt the champion with a "kangaroo" hook. Ingo kept trying to set himself to throw the right, but Floyd's activity and speed upset his fighting rhythm.

In the fifth, Floyd went after Ingo again, double-hooking to the body and then, with another leaping hook, knocking Ingo to the canvas. The champ got himself to one knee, and as he listened to the count, he looked up at Floyd with an expression of lost innocence. Johansson, 22–0, had never really been tested as a professional. Now he was learning what most heavyweight champions realized before winning the title: that at its highest level, boxing was war. He got up at nine.

On this one night, Floyd had no mercy. His hands flying, Patterson attacked, making the big man gasp with body punches and then coming up to the head with hooks. Ingo tried to smother Patterson, but Floyd prodded Ingo out of a clinch and moved him over to where he was hittable, like a photographer positioning someone for a shot. Then Floyd let go a parabolic left hook that crashed onto Ingo's jaw with the force of a sock full of heavy coins, and the Swede dropped to the canvas on his back. Blood pouring from his mouth, Ingo lay motionless but for a quivering of his left leg as he was counted out. Floyd turned to look over the ropes to the writers, who had made him the underdog. Grinning, removing his mouthpiece, he could barely contain his joy. This most fragile of boxers had done what Corbett, Fitzsimmons, Jeffries, Dempsey, Schmeling, Louis, Charles, and Walcott had failed to do: regain the heavyweight title.

It took nearly ten minutes for Ingo to get to his feet. He had been knocked out in the most decisive manner and exposed as a fighter with limitations that some had identified before he won the title: a right-hand puncher with not much else. Floyd, meanwhile, had showed that he could adapt and prevail. It was the shining moment of his career and, as he told reporters afterward, the happiest night of his life.

★

Both Patterson–Johansson fights had resulted in historic outcomes, but they also represented a new business order outside the ring. In 1952, the Justice Department charged the IBC with violation of the Sherman Antitrust Act. The government's case was simple: the IBC owned or managed the sport's major arenas, forced top fighters and their managers to operate under IBC auspices, and presided over the matchmaking for the sport's lucrative television programming. In short, the IBC was a monopoly. Litigation ensued, with the IBC pursuing a claim that boxing, like baseball, should be exempt from antitrust laws. But in 1955, the Supreme Court ruled that boxing was subject to normal interstate commerce and came under the Sherman Act.

The monopoly case against the IBC was proceeding in federal court when Patterson beat Archie Moore for the title in 1956. Then, the following year, federal judge Sylvester Ryan handed down the death sentence: he found the IBC guilty as charged, and he ordered the organization dissolved. The Supreme Court upheld the ruling on appeal. Stripped of their power over fighters and managers, Jim Norris and his partner, Arthur Wirtz, also lost their hold on television programming. Boxing's golden age on the small screen had already begun to wane. In 1952, with programming still relatively thin, boxing attracted nearly one-third of TV viewers. By 1959, as the IBC met its demise, boxing viewership had plummeted to 10 percent. The following year, NBC dropped its boxing coverage. The era of one organization's control of the sport—and, alas, of boxing's dominance on television—was over.

The years to come would see many promoters and groups put together heavyweight championship fights. In this sense, at least, the breakup of the IBC could be called successful. But boxing would remain, in Jimmy Cannon's words, "the red light district of sports."[14]

★

Never before had two men fought three times for the heavyweight title, let alone in consecutive matches. Patterson and Johansson met again in March 1961, this time in Miami Beach. Though both matches between the rivals had been action-packed, Patterson's victory in the second fight seemed so definitive that he was installed as the prohibitive 4–1 favorite. The only hint of drama leading up to the fight was Patterson's insistence on integrated seating in the Miami Beach Convention Center, a condition that the promoters met without incident.

Johansson seemed out of sorts as the climactic battle approached. Visitors to his camp observed behavior that suggested despair about his chances. "He was, I had heard, on an eating jag," A. J. Liebling wrote of the Swede, "creamed chicken, strawberry shortcake, cherry cheesecake. It sounded compulsive to me, the prisoner stuffing before the execution."[15] Ingo weighed in at a pudgy 206.5, ten pounds heavier than he had been for the first fight. Patterson, too, would be his heaviest, at 194.75, but he carried the weight well.

The first round sounded the themes of the series. After some light sparring, Ingo's Bingo came over the transom again. Down went Floyd. The champ was up fast, a decision that didn't cost him here because, for the first time in heavyweight title fights, the mandatory eight-count was in effect. Stunned but alert, Floyd stood as referee Bill Regan tolled the seconds. Ingo landed more clubbing rights and Floyd again went down, this time with his arms outstretched, as if trying to hug a reluctant relative. Again he rose quickly and took the eight-count. But just as a replay of the first fight seemed to be unfolding, Floyd uncorked a left hook that dropped Ingo on the seat of his pants. Now it was Ingo's turn to take the eight-count and go back to it. The two flailed at each other until the bell.

"Flail" was the word for the next several rounds. Johansson looked both desperate and timid; he would wind up the right and then pull it back. Floyd showed little of the art of his second-fight performance. Even his footwork was bad, as he slipped to the canvas twice.

Ingo was breathing heavily in his corner between the fifth and sixth rounds. His extra heft figured to do him no good, but he was still fighting, and in the sixth, he got the right over yet again. Patterson retreated but stayed on his feet, and with the round nearly over, he landed a glancing left hook and two rights to the side of Ingo's head. The challenger tumbled forward, gloves outstretched, his face meeting the canvas. He got himself to one knee but fell backward; he was just rising as Regan reached ten. Some thought that Ingo had made it up in time—as did the Swede himself—but the fight was over.

The Patterson–Johansson trilogy had brought great excitement to boxing, but it was clear that neither man fit the bill of a definitive champion. Johansson looked more and more like an accidental titleholder, and Patterson's weaknesses were well-known—from his fragile psyche to his "glass" jaw. Johansson had sent him to the canvas nine times, and lesser men had also put him down. Though gifted with great natural talent, Floyd seemed more vulnerable than ever. And looming on the horizon was a contender who looked vastly superior to Patterson or Johansson—and had offered to knock them both out in the same evening.

★

Even as Patterson and Johansson squared off in Miami Beach, many considered Charles "Sonny" Liston "the uncrowned heavyweight champion." Liston stood six foot one, weighed between 210 and 215, and punched heavy bags off their hinges. During the late 1950s and early 1960s, Liston mowed down the top heavyweights, including men whom Patterson had beaten (like Roy Harris) and others he had avoided (Eddie Machen, Zora Folley, Nino Valdes). Most dramatically, he had twice destroyed hard-punching Cleveland "Big Cat" Williams, a six-foot-three bomber who hit Liston with shots that made ringsiders gasp. But Liston kept moving forward, showing subtle footwork and extraordinary composure. He knocked Williams out in three rounds in their first fight and two rounds in the rematch. It didn't require much boxing acumen to imagine what might happen if Sonny Liston hit Floyd Patterson.

Liston's fighting prowess was reinforced by his persona: his icy gaze; his moods, which ranged, as one critic put it, from neutral to ugly; his violent past and his ties to organized crime—all made Liston something like a gremlin from one of Patterson's nightmares. He was the most fearsome presence that the heavyweight division had ever seen. He stuffed his robe with towels to make himself look more massive, and he stared his opponents down during prefight instructions. Boxers had been coming face-to-face for generations, but the Liston stare brought overt psychological intimidation to sports.

Frightening people was nothing new to Sonny. His life had been brutal and directionless, the classic apprenticeship for budding criminals. Its main constant, though, was loneliness. He was born the twenty-fourth of tenant farmer Tobe Liston's twenty-five children (with two women) in a clapboard shack near Forrest City, in St. Francis County, Arkansas, some years before Floyd Patterson's birth—how many, it has never been determined. He gave different answers during his life, finally settling on May 8, 1932, as his official birthdate, though it is almost certainly false. Recently available census data strongly suggest that 1930 is the correct date, but during Liston's lifetime, it was widely assumed that he was much older.[16]

Whatever his age, a cold wind blew throughout his life. "We grew up like heathens," he remembered. "We hardly had enough food to keep from starving, no shoes, only a few clothes, and nobody to help us escape from the horrible life we lived."[17] Tobe Liston beat him so viciously that it left scarring. Years later, when boxing trainer Johnny Tocco asked about the tracks on his back, Liston said plainly, "I had bad dealings with my father."[18]

In the early 1940s, Tobe Liston's wife, Helen, had had enough. She left for St. Louis, where one day she had a surprising visitor: Charles, then about twelve years old. The boy had thrashed pecans from his brother-in-law's tree, sold the nuts in town, and bought a bus ticket to St. Louis with the proceeds. To think of this abused, deprived, and illiterate child traveling the three hundred miles alone is to realize that by the time he showed up at his mother's door, Charles Liston was already a young man. Hopelessly unlettered, he was soon a creature of the St. Louis streets.

When the police caught up with him in 1950, for armed robbery and larceny, they sent him to the Missouri State Penitentiary in Jefferson City. It was in prison that Liston took up boxing. None of his fellow inmates could handle him, in the ring or out: he once left several white gang members on the floor after a prison fistfight.

Released in 1952, Liston started a brief amateur career, establishing himself as a fighter of great talent. His fists measured fifteen inches around, and special gloves had to be made to fit them. Though not unusually tall for a heavyweight, he was blessed with a freakishly long eighty-four-inch reach, behind which he unleashed the most pulverizing jab in history. After he turned professional, his original managers, looking for outside financing, turned to John Vitale, the mafia kingpin in St. Louis, who managed various front businesses while engaging in labor racketeering and dabbling in boxing. Vitale got Liston a job at the Union Electric Plant, but mostly he used him as a labor goon, calling on Sonny to break heads when his unionized workforce got out of line.

Sonny's boxing career was humming along in May 1956 when he got into trouble again, this time for assaulting a police officer with intent to kill, the cops alleged. Liston claimed that the patrolman had instigated the trouble between him and his friend, a fellow ex-con. In the struggle that ensued, Sonny got the officer's gun away and beat him over the head with it. The two left the cop battered in an alley. It took a small battalion of St. Louis's finest to bring Sonny in.

Liston got nine months in the St. Louis workhouse, but he was soon facing off with the law again. In one incident, he was said to have deposited a cop headfirst into a garbage can. Finally, the cops told Sonny to get the hell out of St. Louis if he wanted to stay alive. Liston left for Philadelphia.

It wasn't until early 1958 that Sonny was back in the ring. Mobsters from the East had taken interest in this formidable new heavyweight, especially Frank "Blinky" Palermo, who worked out of Philly, and Frankie Carbo, the big man himself, still running things in New York. Banned from fighting in Philly—and in New York and California—but not in Chicago or Miami Beach or Pittsburgh or even St. Louis, Liston raced up the heavyweight ranks.

Using his remaining influence with Patterson, Cus D'Amato tried to persuade the champion not to fight Liston—at least until Liston could find a clean management team. Some charged that D'Amato didn't want Patterson to fight Liston under any circumstances, which was true. D'Amato saw no way that Patterson could win. But D'Amato, while widely disliked, had allies in this cause, since many state officials and leading voices in the sporting press dreaded the idea of Liston on the heavyweight throne. They claimed that Sonny's criminal record and underworld associations should bar him from challenging for the title.

Liston didn't help his cause by continuing to run afoul of the law. In June 1961, he was arrested in Philadelphia's Fairmount Park for pulling over a female motorist late at night and allegedly impersonating a police officer. The charges were eventually dropped, but Sonny was a marked man in the city, just as he had been in St. Louis. It was said that all Philly cops kept a photo of him pinned up in their cruisers. The cops' view of Liston as a menace to society likely became, at least to some degree, self-fulfilling, and police forces of half a century ago did not excel at racial sensitivity. But Liston's long record of trouble makes it hard to accept the characterization, popular today, that his problems were mostly generated by others.

Sonny's glowering public image made it easier for the sporting press, almost entirely white, to view him as a nearly subhuman monster. They missed his native intelligence, to which prison guards had testified in their reports. Those who found a way into his company saw an alert, if wary, mind. José Torres, the light heavyweight boxing champion and Cus D'Amato protégé, said that he had never met a more intelligent athlete. Geraldine Clark, who became Liston's wife in 1957, painstakingly set out to teach him how to read, at least well enough so that he could sign his name to autographs. From listening to Geraldine read newspaper articles to him, Sonny understood how he was regarded by most reporters, and he would always be reticent in their presence.

To the few journalists he did trust, like Jack McKinney of the *Philadelphia Daily News*, Liston spoke more expansively. It was to McKinney that Liston offered the evocative words by which he is best remembered: "Someday they'll write a blues song just for fighters. It'll be for a slow guitar, soft trumpet and a bell."[19] And no one ever offered a more poetic metaphor for what happens to fighters when they get hit in the head. "See, the different parts of the brain set in little cups like this," he said once, pressing together his knuckles. "When you get hit a terrible shot—pop!—the brain flops out of them cups and you're knocked out. Then the brain settles back in the cups and you come to. But after this happens enough times, or sometimes even once if the shot's hard enough, the brain don't settle back right in them cups, and that's when you start needing other people to help you get around."[20]

By late 1961, Liston's merits as the best heavyweight in the world were clear. The demise of the sport's most notorious organized-crime figures helped his cause as well. In 1958, Frankie Carbo was convicted of illegal matchmaking; he served a two-year sentence on Rikers Island. Then in May 1961, Carbo and Blinky Palermo were convicted of conspiracy and extortion. Carbo was sentenced to twenty-five years in the McNeil Island Federal Penitentiary in Washington. Palermo went to Leavenworth. With Palermo and Carbo prison-bound but underworld influence still hanging over his career, Liston took on George Katz, a man without known mob ties, as his official manager. The move was met with skepticism, especially when it was revealed that Katz would take only a 10 percent cut instead of the usual one-third share—leading to questions about who was getting the rest. Sitting in court with Katz, waiting for a resolution on the Fairmount Park incident, Liston leaned over and told the manager, "If I get time, you're entitled to ten percent of it."[21]

★

Since regaining the title, Patterson had been determined to wear the crown with more confidence and bearing, though he could never hide his conflicted nature. "My feelings are rather delicate," he told the young *New York Times* reporter Gay Talese. "You can hit me and I won't think much of it. But you can say something and hurt me very much."[22] Patterson's complex inner life, so evident in his behavior in and out of the ring, made him a puzzle to more traditional journalists. For others, like W. C. Heinz and especially Talese, Patterson was fascinating.

The nation's racial tensions kept building, and a black heavyweight champion had once again become an important symbol. In early 1960, as Patterson geared up for his comeback try against Johansson, black college students in Greensboro, North Carolina, conducted sit-ins at Woolworth's lunch counters, refusing to leave when told that they could not be served. The demonstration soon spread to other Southern cities. The following spring, a few months after Patterson had won the third Johansson fight, James Farmer and activists from the Congress of Racial Equality began the Freedom Rides, protesting segregated seating in public transportation in the South. Though white mobs attacked the activists, the Freedom Rides went on for months.

Patterson watched all this with growing passion. He was crushed to discover the depths of racial resistance—even in the North, where his family met a cold reception in upscale Scarsdale, New York. Patterson clung to his Catholic faith, though it wasn't easy.

"I used to think Jesus was a white man," he told Talese. "All the pictures I've ever seen of Him showed Him white. But I no longer can accept Him as a white man. He either is a Jesus of no color, or a Jesus with skin that is all colors."[23]

The NAACP welcomed Patterson's support and cheered his example, but the organization, along with other civil rights groups, did not want him to take on Sonny Liston. Even President John F. Kennedy, an avid sports fan, had an opinion. Depending on what account you believe, Kennedy, meeting Patterson at the White House, urged Patterson either to fight and beat Liston or to avoid him.

In any case, Patterson's pride finally got the better of him. It wasn't right to deny a man an opportunity he had earned. And Patterson even identified with Liston. After all, he had been a youthful troublemaker, too—albeit one who shrank away to brood, not toss police officers headfirst into trash cans. Didn't Sonny deserve a chance? The two men signed to fight for the title in Chicago's Comiskey Park, on September 25, 1962.

★

Black men had fought each other for the heavyweight title before, but no heavyweight fight between two blacks had aroused such public interest. The fascination had to do with the civil rights movement and the country's dawning confrontation with its racial legacy, and it had to do with the different visions that the fighters seemed to represent. Patterson was boxing's nonviolent analogue to Martin Luther King, another example of the heavyweight title's tendency to produce champions evocative of their times. Just as the great American prophet of nonviolence had come along, so, too, had come a champion determined not to hurt his foes. A conflicted man, Patterson had been champion of a deeply conflicted society. Liston, meanwhile,

Floyd Patterson (left) greets his fearsome challenger, Sonny Liston, as they sign for their 1962 title fight.
Associated Press

was the black criminal of stereotype and lore, the white man's nightmare, as disturbing as Jack Johnson in his way.

These contrasts attracted writers like James Baldwin, the black essayist and novelist. Covering the fight for *Nugget*, a men's magazine, Baldwin visited the fighters at their training camps. Though he was no boxing fan, Baldwin saw the Liston–Patterson fight as an enactment of "our terrible American dilemma" and the two attitudes for overcoming it: "the disciplined sweetness of Floyd, or the outspoken intransigence of Liston."

Like Talese, Baldwin found Patterson sympathetic. Floyd was a man "more complex than he was yet equipped to know," Baldwin wrote, "a hero for many children who were still trapped where he had been, who might not have survived without the ring, and who yet, oddly, did not really seem to belong there." He considered that Floyd, "quite probably the least likely fighter in the history of the sport," had done well in life despite his scars.

The man Patterson would face, meanwhile, was seen by almost all as the villain and by many as a dumb thug. But Baldwin found Liston neither menacing nor unintelligent. Liston's toughness reminded him of the hard exterior that many black men showed "in order to conceal the fact that they weren't hard." He saw the sadness in Liston's eyes, which suggested that he had "a long tale to tell which no one wants to hear." What had hurt Liston most was his rejection by the civil rights crowd. "Colored people say they don't want their children to look up to me," Liston told the writer. "Well, they ain't teaching their children to look up to Martin Luther King, either. . . . I wouldn't be no bad example if I was up there." Baldwin, humbled by this massive, lonely man, told Liston: "I am here to wish you well."[24]

In a rare instance of a challenger heading into a heavyweight title fight as the favorite, Las Vegas oddsmakers installed Liston as the 7–5 betting choice. Some thought those odds were too close. One of them was Bud Shrake, then a young journalist and later novelist and screenplay writer, who visited with Liston one day and asked the challenger about Patterson's hand speed. Liston said nothing for a moment and then shot a hand into the air and brought it back to his body, slowly opening it. He had caught a fly, and the insect lay dead in his palm. "Do you think that will be fast enough to take care of that skinny-assed son of a bitch?" Liston asked.[25]

The promoters touted Liston–Patterson as the fight of the decade and estimated a $5 million gross, combined, of the live gate with the closed-circuit broadcast. The closed-circuit haul, nearly $4 million, accounted for most of the revenue. All who watched the closed-circuit broadcast in theaters and arenas nationwide saw it from the same central feed—with two exceptions: separate lines were patched in to the White House and to the home of Frank Sinatra in Hollywood.

★

It was all over in two minutes and six seconds. Patterson, at 189 pounds, strangely opted to go straight at Liston, trying to mix it up with the 214-pound challenger. Liston pounded Floyd to the body. From long range, Liston landed a jolting right uppercut, and Floyd clinched, his legs rubbery. Sonny backed Patterson to the ropes, and the two men hooked each other's arms. Then Patterson seemed to lose his footing and gripped the rope, holding on. Liston stepped in with a right to the belly, and, as Patterson's body twisted, already seeming to seek the floor, Liston nailed him with a left hook to the jaw. Patterson crumbled to the canvas and lay still for several seconds before raising himself to his haunches and getting to his feet, too late. Never had the title changed hands so quickly. It was the most abject performance that any heavyweight champion had ever given. Floyd's rapid demise prompted familiar questions about his state of mind.

The critics were merciless. The young heavyweight contender Cassius Clay said that the fight was "an embarrassment to boxing. The champion of the world should be able to take a beating longer than that."[26] Gene Tunney uttered the thought that others had avoided: that Patterson had been scared. "He was so frightened he didn't even box," Tunney said. The fight, he said, was "a terrible hoax," and "the people who paid were burglarized."[27] Jimmy Cannon, never a Patterson fan, took the knives out. Patterson, he wrote, was a bigger fraud than Primo Carnera—and, he added, somewhat puzzlingly, an "ungrateful and egotistical parody of a pug."[28]

Floyd's analysts in the media had more to pick over when reports circulated that he had left Comiskey Park wearing a disguise, which he had brought with him—a fake beard, glasses, and cap that made him look, Talese wrote, like "a Beatnik." (In fact, Floyd had come equipped with disguises before the second and third Johansson fights, too.) Floyd donned his makeover and then, with his brother-in-law driving, began the twenty-two-hour-long trip back east to New York. He had left Chicago so abruptly that even his wife did not know where he was.

Meanwhile, Sonny Liston soaked in his new status. "Hold it now," one of his aides said to reporters. "This is the heavyweight champion of the world. This is Mr. Liston. Let's treat him as you would the President of the United States."[29] Liston said that he wanted to emulate Joe Louis, his idol. On the flight home, Liston sat with Jack McKinney, imagining what he would do with the title. "I want to go to a lot of places—like orphan homes and reform schools," he said. "I'll be able to say, 'Kid, I know it's tough for you and it might get even tougher. But don't give up on the world. Good things can happen if you let them.'"[30] Philadelphia mayor James Hugh Joseph Tate sent a congratulatory telegram, leading Sonny to believe that a crowd would be waiting. But when the new champ's plane arrived, the tarmac was empty.

The Philadelphia snub resonated with Sonny's experience of life. "In some part of my mind," he once said, "I always felt like a chicken in a bag full of cats."[31] Being heavyweight champion wouldn't change that.

In April 1963, Martin Luther King and civil rights activists from the Southern Christian Leadership Conference began a sustained effort to protest segregated conditions in Birmingham, Alabama. They set about in their familiar way, with marches, pickets, and boycotts, but after a few days, a judge handed down an injunction barring their activities. The activists went forward anyway, and on Good Friday, April 12, 1963, King and others were arrested, roughed up, and brought to Birmingham City Jail. An aide smuggled in a newspaper, where King read a letter written by white clergymen disavowing his methods and calling on other leaders to withdraw support for his efforts. King began scribbling a rebuttal in the margins of the paper. In what would become his famous "Letter from Birmingham Jail," King wrote: "Oppressed people cannot remain oppressed forever. The yearning for freedom eventually manifests itself, and that is what has happened to the American Negro. Something within has reminded him of his birthright of freedom, and something without has reminded him that it can be gained."[32]

Inspired, Patterson resolved to go down to Alabama to show solidarity with the movement. On May 13, 1963, Patterson and Jackie Robinson entered Birmingham's jam-packed Sixth Avenue Baptist Church. Patterson spoke haltingly to the throng. "And I've got my training camp, and I felt very guilty . . . that here I was sitting in camp watching you people, my people, go through this. . . . And I would like to thank you from the bottom of my heart."[33]

Liston didn't publicly share these civil rights passions. "I ain't got no dog-proof ass," he said.[34] But later in 1963, when four young girls were killed in the bombing of a Birmingham church, he cut short a British tour and was heard to say that he was ashamed to be an American. And Liston won praise for stipulating no segregated seating in his closed-circuit TV contracts.

When it came to boxing, Liston's coarser approach, along with his heavy hands and bruising strength, had it all over Patterson. Sonny was made the 4–1 favorite in the rematch, held in Las Vegas in July 1963. Floyd tried to convince the press of his confidence but spent as much time discussing hypothetical defeat. He came out once again with no apparent strategy, standing in front of Sonny, easy to find, stoic in his pending doom. Sonny simply stalked Floyd down, pole-axing him with his left jab and clubbing him to the body. A left hook dropped Patterson. He rose at the count of three. Liston was on him again, and Patterson tried a right-hand haymaker that grazed Liston's head. Sonny walked through it and landed a right to the jaw, and down Floyd went. Again Liston came at Patterson, hammering a left hook to the body and a right-left combination to the head. Patterson fell backward. He was counted out at two minutes, ten seconds of the first round. He had lasted four seconds longer than in the first fight.

Liston's performance suggested that he would be champion for a long time—a depressing prospect for most commentators. Jim Murray compared having Liston as champion to "finding a live bat on a string under your Christmas tree." Conjuring its own Christmas imagery, in December 1963, *Esquire* put Liston on its cover—dressed as Santa Claus and wearing his usual doleful expression. Letters poured in from irate readers, canceling their subscriptions. Advertisers fled, too, costing the magazine $750,000 in lost revenue.

As champion, Liston had tried in vain to change his image. Those who knew Liston best said that being in Geraldine's company kept him straight, but even when she was around, Sonny wasn't always a bargain. People in Vegas spoke of his nastiness to busboys, bellhops, and wait staff; similar tales circulated about his behavior in England. He got into more scrapes with the Philadelphia police. Finally, the Listons left the City of Brotherly Love and moved to Denver.

"I'd rather be a lamppost in Denver than mayor of Philadelphia," Sonny said.[35]

★

Esquire's "Sonny Claus" cover hit the stands just before the country withstood the shock of shocks: John F. Kennedy's assassination in Dallas. The trauma would later mark, for many, the true beginning of the epochal decade known as "the sixties." In time, controversies about black men on magazine covers would seem quaint.

But shock, or even surprise, was alien to the heavyweight division in late 1963. Liston seemed to have few viable challengers. Only Cassius Clay, the twenty-one-year-old Kentuckian, offered any interest. Clay was unbeaten in nineteen fights, a 1960 Olympic gold medalist, and a natural showman who had done everything in his power to bring excitement back to boxing. He boasted, he recited poetry predicting the outcomes of his fights, and he fought in a style reminiscent of Sugar Ray Robinson: floating around the ring, relying on his hand speed and fast feet. Clay stalked Liston around the country, demanding a title fight. Some were delighted by his antics, others embarrassed. Almost all agreed that the youngster stood no chance against Liston.

After the fight was signed, for February 1964, Clay stepped up his badgering of the champion. Sonny's rage at the loudmouthed young brat—who, he suggested, might be homosexual—was building. Finally, one night in Las Vegas, Liston came across Clay playing in a casino and tapped him on the shoulder. When Clay turned around, Liston slapped him across the face with the back of his hand. Cassius was frightened.

"What did you do that for?" he asked, his voice rising.

"Because you're too fuckin' fresh," Liston replied and stalked off. On his way out, he turned to a companion and said, "I got the punk's heart now."[36]

But he didn't.

THE BUTTERFLY

The weigh-in for the Sonny Liston–Cassius Clay heavyweight champion-ship fight was scheduled for 10:30 a.m. on February 25, 1964, in the Miami Beach Convention Hall's Cypress Room. Most had given it little thought. For fighters in the lower weights, struggling to make a 135- or 147- or 160-pound limit, weigh-ins could hold some drama. For heavyweights, who tipped the scales at whatever they liked, these were ceremonial occasions, mostly for the benefit of the media. Reporters could watch the fighters step onto the scales, record their weights, and note physical differences as they had their chests, fists, waists, and necks measured and then spread their arms out to have their reach recorded. And they could watch as the fight-ers stood side by side, polite in a way they would not be later, and look for clues. Once in a while, a character—such as Max Baer—might disrupt the harmony. Maxie once pulled some chest hair off an opponent and, separat-ing the strands, intoned, "She loves me, she loves me not." More often, the fighters offered little to interpret. Expressions were stoical, thoughts unreadable. Decorum reigned.

It reigned in other sports, too. In baseball, hitters weren't welcomed into the batter's box with personally selected theme songs. They didn't walk up the baseline admiring home runs or point to the sky when they crossed home plate. Pitchers didn't pump their fists after strikeouts. In football, when a player reached the end zone, he flipped the ball to the referee or tossed it over his shoulder. His teammates rushed over to . . . shake his hand. There were no end-zone celebrations, chest thumpings, or demonstrations after routine tackles. In basketball, even the biggest shot in the biggest game brought celebrations that were joyous but restrained.

Boxing had been this way, too. In the old days, even the fiercest competitors, like Jack Dempsey, would help opponents off the canvas after a knockout. Joe Louis celebrated his two most dramatic victories—over Max Schmeling and Billy Conn—by accepting the congratulations of his cornermen, his expression unchanging. Rocky Marciano said that he didn't feel right celebrating his win over Jersey Joe Walcott when Walcott was still on the canvas. The outliers—Baer with his clowning, Jack Johnson with his taunting—only underscored the code, for which the weigh-in was a preliminary staging ground.

The television age had more or less done away with the ritual's stagier elements—especially the posed picture, in which both men assumed fighters' stances. Viewers would soon see the combatants in action, and these images, relics of an era when images were harder to come by, now seemed old-fashioned. But the weigh-in itself remained old-fashioned, a venerable component of a tradition-minded sports world. Then Cassius Clay burst through the door to the Cypress Room, and that world was gone forever.

★

He was born Cassius Marcellus Clay Jr. in Louisville, Kentucky, on January 17, 1942, the first son to a mural and sign painter and his wife, Odessa Clay. Those who knew the parents would see traces of both in the son: the ego-driven, racially conscious father and the warm and charming mother. Cassius Sr. was named for the nineteenth-century abolitionist Cassius Marcellus Clay, the Lion of White Hall, a Kentucky planter and Unionist whom Abraham Lincoln appointed minister to Russia. Though they lived in Louisville's mostly black West End, the Clays were comfortably middle class by black standards of the time. When Cassius was twelve, his father bought him a gleaming red Schwinn bicycle.

The bicycle would be the propellant toward a boxing career. After spending time at a county fair with a friend, Cassius discovered that the bike had been stolen. Distraught, he went to the police department to report the theft. Barely holding back tears, he told Officer Joseph Martin that he would "beat up" the boys who took the bike. "Do you know how to fight?" Martin asked. Cassius conceded that he did not. Martin, who ran a youth boxing program, suggested that Cassius come down to the gymnasium and learn some basics.

Clay took to boxing like a natural prodigy. He was unusually fast and physically gifted, and his work ethic exceeded everyone else's, though he was resistant, for the most part, to instruction. "Boxing made me feel like somebody different," he remembered. "I used to sit in school before I won the Golden Gloves and just draw the back of a jacket and write 'National Golden Gloves Champ' on it, and then I would write 'World Olympic Gold Medal Winner' on it, and then I would sign my autograph: 'Cassius Clay, World Heavyweight Champion.' I used to do all that, just wishing one day that I could do it for real."[1]

True to his vision, Clay won a host of amateur titles, and in 1960, just eighteen, he earned a spot on the U.S. Olympic Boxing Team for the games in Rome. He went on to win the gold medal in the light heavyweight class, and his eyes welled up as he heard the national anthem played. He wore the medal around for weeks, sleeping with it at night.

Turning pro, Clay got the financial backing that most boxers only dream about. A group of Louisville civic leaders and businessmen, individuals with ties to Brown-Forman and Churchill Downs and U.S. Steel, formed the all-white Louisville Sponsoring Group (LSG) to bankroll his career. The terms included a generous monthly salary so that he could train full-time and regular deposits to a pension fund that he couldn't touch until he was thirty-five. The LSG also secured the services of trainer Angelo Dundee, who had learned his trade working with men like Charley Goldman (Rocky Marciano) and Whitey Bimstein (Ingemar Johansson). Clay moved to Miami Beach, where Dundee had his headquarters in the famously seedy, unventilated Fifth Street Gym.

Clay's early pro career made clear that he was a boxer of uncommon athletic gifts. He barely scaled 190 pounds when he started out, and he was lanky at six foot three. He fought in a style never seen before in men of his size, winning fights not with heavy punching power but with the speed of his hands and the balletic grace of his feet. He could deliver a jab in 4/100 of a second, and he was so quick that he rarely bothered with the traditional rudiments of defense. An extraordinarily keen judge of distance, he kept his hands low, leaning away from opponents' punches instead of blocking them. He didn't even retreat in the approved fashion. Where the boxing book said that a right-handed fighter should move backward right foot first, left foot following, Clay preferred to backpedal on his toes. No wonder, then, that as a young fighter, he told a reporter, "Who made me is *me*."[2]

Some trainers would have balked at such independence. Dundee, a student of boxing fundamentals but also a good psychologist, let Clay do his thing. Instead of urging Clay to try something in the ring, Dundee would praise him for having done it. The next day, Clay was doing it for real.

Clay had never lacked confidence, but his natural inclinations received a fateful boost one night in 1961, when he was in Las Vegas for his seventh professional fight and shared a radio interview with the wrestler Gorgeous George. Clay listened as George derided his next opponent and boasted that he was the greatest wrestler in the world. Then, at the arena, Clay watched as George, dressed in sequins, entered to the strains of "Pomp and Circumstance" and sprayed himself with perfume. There wasn't an empty seat. "I saw fifteen thousand people coming to see this man get beat," Clay remembered. "And his talking did it. I said, this is a *gooood* idea!" Afterward, the forty-six-year-old grappler told him: "A lot of people will pay to see someone shut your mouth. So keep on bragging, keep on sassing, and always be outrageous."[3]

And so Cassius Clay adopted his persona. He declared himself "the Greatest" boxer of all time. He boasted about his looks: "I'm as pretty as a girl."[4] He predicted the rounds in which he would knock out opponents—a sporting feat roughly equivalent to Babe Ruth's pointing to the fences and hitting a home run in the designated spot. He said that he'd get Alex Miteff in six and Willie Besmanoff in seven, and out they went as ordered. Sonny Banks, he said, would go in four, and Banks did. "They all must fall in the round I call," said Clay, who took to giving his predictions in verse. Before his sixteenth pro fight, against Archie Moore—who was nearing fifty, by whatever calendar one used—Clay prophesied: "Archie had been living off the fat of the land / I'm here to give him his pension plan. / When you come to the fight don't block aisle or door, / 'Cause ya all going home after round four."[5] Clay stopped Moore in the fourth. The fight was sold out.

Cassius Clay brought a rare quality to prizefighting: joy. The years 1962 and 1963 were gloomy, marred by deaths in the ring and renewed calls for the abolition of the sport. Sonny Liston's annihilation of Floyd Patterson in September 1962 turned over boxing's marquee role to an ex-con who could not surmount his past. After Liston wiped out Patterson again in their July 1963 rematch, the intimidating champion was seen as unbeatable by many, including Joe Louis. More gloom.

The only star on the horizon was Cassius Clay. He spent 1963 campaigning for a bout against Liston, whom he had begun calling the "big, ugly bear." Charming, handsome, and audacious, Clay made himself impossible to ignore. Even some traditionalists cheered his arrival. "I don't care if this kid can't fight a lick," Jack Dempsey said. "I'm for him. Things are live again."[6] His magnetism drew in others, like Sam Cooke, who recorded a song with him. Clay also recorded an album of poems, *I Am the Greatest* (though some were penned by television writer Gary Belkin). He made his first cover of *Sports Illustrated*. He bought his parents a new home.

But his ring performances in 1963 sowed doubts. In March, he rallied to win a ten-round decision over Doug Jones in New York that some felt should have gone the other way. Against Henry Cooper in England, where Clay arrived as a conquering hero and entered the ring in a king's robe and crown, he was knocked down in the fourth round by Cooper's bread-and-butter punch, the left hook. Luckily for Clay, the bell sounded to end the round. He walked back to his corner on unsteady legs. Dundee, seeing a tear in Clay's left glove, put his thumb into the hole and tore it further and then alerted the referee about the damaged glove—buying Cassius a few extra seconds. In the fifth, Clay poked at a wicked gash over Cooper's left eye, and the blood cascaded down the Englishman's face. The fight was stopped.

Clay's performances against these ranked contenders made people fear for his safety against Sonny Liston. Still, with his gift for promotion, he had made himself the most marketable opponent. "I'm the hottest attraction to come along since talking pictures," he said. "Pick up any magazine, there's Cassius Clay on the cover."[7] It was true. Clay had tapped into an audience beyond boxing, and Liston, like all heavyweight champions, was a businessman. As Sonny saw it, the kid was doing him a favor—building up the gate for an easy payday.

★

As the Liston–Clay fight approached in February 1964, the United States was still recovering from the Kennedy assassination. The tragedy in Dallas had the effect of separating recent history into before and after, but the fight had a foot in both worlds: the buildup had been going on for months, most of it instigated by Cassius Clay. Clay's hype had progressed to outright harassment of the champion, especially in one of Liston's favorite spots, the Thunderbird casino in Las Vegas. Then, in the predawn hours of November 5, 1963, Clay showed up outside Liston's Denver home, honking the horn of his large touring bus and calling for the champion to come out. Liston shouted back and waved a gold-headed cane, but he stayed put and called, of all people, the police, who for once intervened on his behalf. Later that day, the two men signed articles for the fight. "If Sonny Liston whups me," Clay said, "I'll kiss his feet in the ring, crawl out of the ring on my knees, tell him he's the greatest, and catch the next jet out of the country."[8]

All this had occurred before the events in Dallas, and sports-loving Jack Kennedy would have been aware of it. But the fight would belong to a post-Kennedy world, one in which charisma and youth—as if in compensation for the lost president—would take center stage. As Cassius trained in Miami Beach, four avatars of youth paid him a visit.

The Beatles had just landed in the United States for their first American appearances. They were in Miami to play *The Ed Sullivan Show*, the same venue that Elvis Presley had used to vault himself to national stardom. Many in the American media were as dismissive of the British group as they were of Clay's chances against Liston. But the Beatles' lighthearted public image, like Clay's, obscured steely self-assurance and intuitive gifts for managing the media.

Clay and the musicians staged a famous photo in which the four Beatles stood on the receiving end of a Clay punch and another in which Clay stood over their sprawled forms. "As they pose for the photographers, I watch this Summit meeting—the Beatles and Cassius Clay—the two hottest names in the news, worldwide," publicist Harold Conrad wrote. "They are all about the same age. I wonder how posterity will treat them."[9] After the Beatles departed, Clay asked an aide, "Who were those little sissies?"[10]

The Beatles had wanted to visit the champion, not the long-shot challenger, but Liston had no interest. Sonny's tastes ran to blues and Dave Brubeck; the Brit lads were pure bubblegum. "Is this what all the people are screaming about?" he asked. "My dog plays drums better than that kid with the big nose."[11] (Years later, on the cover of *Sgt. Pepper's Lonely Hearts Club Band*, the Beatles included one boxer in their gallery of notables: Sonny Liston.)

Disdain was a familiar feeling for Liston in February 1964. He didn't take Clay seriously, to put it mildly; at one point he suggested that Clay should be arrested for impersonating a fighter. He went through the motions in training. He indulged himself with hot dogs, beer, and prostitutes. Forty-three of forty-six writers picked Sonny to win; oddsmakers made him a 7–1 favorite. The outcome was not seriously debated, and many wondered if Clay could last a round.

Clay saw things differently. "I'm gonna put that ugly bear on the floor," he told reporters, "and after the fight I'm gonna build myself a pretty home and use him as a bear-skin rug. . . . This will be the easiest fight of my life."[12] To dramatize the event, he recited his (or Belkin's) most accomplished poem yet, "Will the Real Sonny Liston Please Fall Down," which envisioned Clay knocking Liston into the heavens, ending with these inspired lines: "Who would have thought / When they came to the fight / That they'd witness the launching / Of a human satellite? / Yes, the crowd did not dream / When they laid down their money / That they would see / A total eclipse of the Sonny!"[13]

On Tuesday morning, February 25, 1964, the fighters arrived for the weigh-in. "I'm the champ!" Clay bellowed as he came through the door, dressed in a blue denim jacket with the words "Bear Huntin'" stitched on the back. He was flanked by Sugar Ray Robinson, the middleweight boxing master and Clay's ring idol, and Drew "Bundini" Brown, a former aide to Sugar Ray, now listed as Clay's "assistant trainer." His real job was to exhort, inspire, and glorify Clay—and at this, he had no peer. Most of the time, Bundini seemed at least one-quarter mad. Picking up on imagery that A. J. Liebling had used in *The New Yorker*—Clay floated, Liebling wrote, like a butterfly, and his hands stung like bees—Bundini devised a mantra. In the crowded and stuffy space, he and Cassius got busy.

"Float like a butterfly, sting like a bee, aahh!" they bellowed, their faces close together. "Rumble, young man, rumble! Aahh!" It was as if two wild men had disturbed the tranquility of the neighborhood bar. Then Clay approached the microphones, his body swaying, his eyes popping.

"You tell Joe Louis and Sonny Liston that I'm here with Sugar Ray!" he shouted. "Joe Louis was flat-footed, and Sonny Liston is flat-footed. Sugar Ray and I are two pretty dancers. We can't be beat!" Then he turned to go, yelling out, "I'm the champ! I'm ready to rumble!"[14]

A half-hour later, he reemerged in a terry-cloth robe and mounted the scales. The room was packed with hundreds of press from the states and around the world, along with boxing authorities and public officials. Clay weighed in at 210.5, lighter than expected. The door opened and Liston entered, his bulk accentuated by the towels he always wore under his robe, determined to give the kid his practiced glare. Screaming and pointing, Clay kept moving toward him; Sugar Ray and Bundini tried to hold him back.

"Hey sucker," Clay called out. "You a chump. Are you scared?"

"Don't let anybody know," Liston said. "Don't tell the world."[15] He weighed 218, heavier than expected.

While the commission doctor, Alexander Robbins, listened to his heart, Clay, his mouth open wide, held up eight fingers: he'd knock out Liston in the eighth round. Robbins recorded Clay's pulse at 120 beats a minute. His normal resting rate was fifty-four. His blood pressure was out of sight, too. He was scared to death, most assumed. If Clay's vital signs didn't stabilize, Robbins said, the fight was off. Finally, Clay was hauled away by his handlers. "I predict someone will die at ringside from shock!"

Through it all, Liston's expression barely changed. But the scene rattled him in ways not visible to the naked eye. Perhaps Clay really was crazy. Sonny's life had been filled with lots of what normal people called madness—armed robbery, police assault, public drunkenness—but those things all had their reasons. Madmen didn't need reasons, and they didn't have problems. Madmen were your problem. Within an hour, Clay's vital signs were back to normal.

★

The weigh-in chaos was only the latest obstacle to what had been a bumpy promotion. The tickets were overpriced, and few sold; the overwhelming odds against Clay didn't help. And hovering over everything were the rumors that Clay had joined the Nation of Islam—the Black Nationalist group led by its "Messenger," Elijah Muhammad—which rejected integration and taught that whites were "blue-eyed devils." Clay had addressed a Nation of Islam rally, and in Miami he was seen frequently in the company of Malcolm X, the Nation's best-known leader, a mesmerizing public speaker who struck fear into whites and who had once cheered news of a plane crash in which whites had perished. In February 1964, though, Malcolm X was on the ropes. He was still reeling from the backlash to his comments after Kennedy's assassination, when he said that the president's death signified America's "chickens coming home to roost." That was too much even for Muhammad, who suspended Malcolm from public speaking, and a rift widened between the two men. But Malcolm hoped that a Clay victory—in which he was certain—might somehow help smooth things over.

Worried about the live gate, the promoters tried to force Clay to renounce the Nation, but Clay called their bluff: he started packing his bags for home. Finally, a compromise was reached. The fight would go on, but Malcolm agreed to leave Miami until just before the opening bell.

It didn't help much. With 8,294 in attendance, the Convention Hall was filled to about half its capacity. But Liston–Clay broke records on closed-circuit television, showing to seven hundred thousand fans nationwide and generating $4.5 million in revenue. (Those numbers sound small today, but in 1964, major league baseball's entire television package, running from April to October, was worth $13.6 million.) The closed-circuit telecast was anchored by Steve Ellis, a popular former broadcaster of the New York baseball Giants, with analysis from Joe Louis.

When the two fighters met at the center of the ring, observers were surprised to see how Clay, at six foot three, towered over Liston. Sonny wore the same look of disaffected malevolence that had sent others to dark corners of the mind. Not Clay. He met Liston's stare, and as the men touched gloves and separated, he hissed, "I've got you now, sucker!"[16]

The bell rang.

Liston came after Clay immediately and missed a lunging right to the body. Clay was on his "bicycle," as boxing men say, using his legs to move out of range, fighting on the retreat. The only chance that Clay had, most reasoned, was to stay away from Liston long enough to tire him out. Liston backed Clay to the ropes, but the challenger bent his left shoulder down, lowering the target of his head, and moved left, off the ropes and back to center ring. The crowd cheered. Clay opened up with a few jabs and then a combination, rights and lefts, all to Liston's face, most getting through. Liston missed a right by several feet. He threw a left hook and swept air. He missed jabs, too, as Cassius darted his head away. Then Cassius opened up again, this time mixing a left hook and a right cross, and Sonny backed up. In the waning seconds, Clay scored with six straight left jabs. Already, it seemed that Liston's eyes looked puffy. In his corner between rounds, Clay opened his mouth wide, looking down to the press at ringside.

Louis called it one of the best rounds he'd ever seen a man fight, but the Bomber, who had become close to Liston, figured that his friend would rally in the second round, and Liston did, getting closer to Clay and clubbing him around the midsection. In the third, Clay dazzled Liston with a two-fisted assault, and Sonny wobbled for the first time in living memory. The champ was cut now, too, under the left eye, and his battered face made him look years older than whatever age he was. It wasn't just the speed of Clay's punches, but their variety; not just the classic left jab–right cross combo, but right uppercuts and a slippery left hook that materialized only when it was three-quarters of the way to the target. "He's getting hit with all the punches in the book!" said Ellis at ringside. Then Liston awoke. Enraged, he pounded away at Clay's belly and nailed him with a left hook, the punch that was supposed to end things. Clay took it and tied Liston up. The champ's late rally had ringside abuzz.

After a quieter fourth round, Clay came back to his corner blinking. He had gotten something into his eyes—perhaps some of the coagulant that Liston's men were using to control the cut around the champ's left eye or the liniment that they had been rubbing onto his sore left shoulder, which had begun bothering him after the first round. (Sonny had been receiving treatment for bursitis.) The liniment could have gotten into Clay's eyes when the two were at close quarters. The final possibility involved conspiracy: the Liston corner, sensing that the title was slipping away, deliberately set out to blind Clay. So they rubbed a caustic solution onto Liston's gloves, the boxing equivalent of chemical warfare. No one knows for sure.

His eyes burning, Clay panicked. "Cut the gloves off!" he begged Dundee—meaning, stop the fight. "Cut 'em off me; I'm blind!" Dundee was having none of it. "Forget the bullshit. This is for the championship. Sit down." He washed out the fighter's eyes with water and a sponge, but the burning sensation remained. At the warning buzzer for the fifth round, Clay stood up and made a futile gesture with his arms. The no-nonsense referee, Barney Felix, thought that Clay might be quitting. "Dammit, Clay, get out here!" he barked.

"This is the big one, Daddy!" Dundee said, pushing Clay out. "Stay away from him—run!"[17]

And Clay did. He held Liston, slipped around him when he could find a path, and used his remarkable reflexes to pull his head away from punches. Liston threw everything in his dwindling arsenal. Those who wondered if Clay could take a punch had their answer now—he was ripped to the body and took several Liston hooks to the head. Clay put his left jab out, trying to block Liston's way in. Many in the Convention Hall were on their feet. Some, suspicious about Clay's change of tactics, yelled, "Fix!" But Liston's haymaker punches kept missing, and the winded champ was losing heart. As the round wore on, Cassius got bolder. Holding out his left, he did a pinball routine on Sonny's head, mocking the champion. His eyes were clearing. At the bell, Liston's shoulders slumped as he walked back to his corner.

The sixth round was all Clay, his jab rarely missing.

In Liston's corner between the sixth and seventh rounds, another disputed scene unfolded. The pain in his left shoulder had rendered his best punch impotent. Against Liston's wishes—"I can beat that bastard one-handed"—his men stopped the fight. Another version: Liston sat down on his stool after the sixth, hissed, "That's it," and spat out his mouthpiece. Either way, like only Jess Willard before him, Sonny Liston had conceded the heavyweight championship while sitting on his stool. But Willard had been butchered. Liston just gave up.

"I don't think the shoulder made him quit," Joe Louis said. "A guy as tough as Liston, I don't figure it hurt him that much."[18] A Liston cornerman said, years later: "We cooked up that shoulder thing on the spot."[19] Not true: eight doctors confirmed a torn tendon. But champions go down fighting. Didn't Liston still have one good arm?

Across the way, seeing the mouthpiece lying on the canvas—an unambiguous sign of surrender—Clay went into a shuffle, gliding to the center of the ring with his arms aloft as Bundini and Dundee rushed to embrace him. But where champions before had shared their moment of victory with a close circle of supporters, Clay's attention was fixed on the media at ringside, especially the boxing writers. Almost all had picked him to lose.

"Eat your words!" he yelled. "I'm the greatest! I'm the king of the world!"[20]

The reporters sat like a losing legal team, listening to a jury announce a shocking verdict. Steve Ellis, with Joe Louis by his side, got to Clay for a brief interview, though it was more of a monologue.

"I shook up the world!" Clay said, sweat pouring down his face. "I shook up the world! I'm the greatest! I'm a bad man." Ellis, laughing, tapped Louis in the chest, as if to say, "Ain't this fun?" but Louis remained expressionless, perhaps shocked over the outcome—he had suggested that Liston

Cassius Clay has just beaten Sonny Liston and is about to inaugurate the modern era of sports, too—Miami Beach, February 25, 1964.
Associated Press

was the greatest heavyweight of all time—but also bemused by this loud-mouthed young kid, who broke every rule in the Louis book of stoicism. "I'm so great, I don't have a mark on my face, I upset Sonny Liston, and I just turned twenty-two years old. I must be the greatest!" Clay exulted. He had acted like a madman, but now he seemed more like a medium, trying to harmonize the voices in his head.

It was the biggest upset in heavyweight history. "It's still almost impossible to believe," Arthur Daley wrote in the *New York Times*, "but Cassius Marcellus Clay is the heavyweight champion of the world."[21]

★

There was much to sort out in the aftermath. Many speculated—and some still do—that the fight was fixed. But then why had Liston worked so hard trying to knock Clay out, especially in the fifth? No one could explain why Sonny and the men who owned him would voluntarily relinquish the heavy-weight title. Logic and evidence pointed to a different conclusion: mastered physically, Liston, the bully who relied on intimidation, came apart mentally. So he quit.

The Miami miracle was soon upstaged by developments outside the ring. When a reporter asked Clay if he was a Black Muslim, he did not deny it. "I don't have to be what you want me to be. I'm free to be who I want."[22] The next day, he made it official. "They call it the Black Muslims," he said. "This is a press word. It is not a legitimate name. But Islam is a religion and there are 750 million people all over the world who believe in it, and I am one of them."[23]

Only Malcolm X, who announced his break with the Nation of Islam shortly after the Clay–Liston fight, had seen the possibilities in Clay's public identification with the group. "One day this kid is going to be heavyweight champion of the world," he told an associate, "and he's going to embrace the Nation of Islam. Do you understand what that could mean?" A week after the fight, Malcolm and Clay visited the United Nations and met with delegates from African and Asian countries. Clay, Malcolm thought, would "mean more to his people than any athlete before him." Elijah Muhammad watched nervously; he had been convinced that Clay would be destroyed by Liston, that he would embarrass the Nation, but now he saw that Malcolm had been right, not only about the outcome but also about Clay's potential stature. So, on the same day that Clay and Malcolm went to the UN, the Messenger gave Clay a "completed" Muslim name, an honor denied even long-serving Nation loyalists. He would be known as Muhammad Ali.

"That's a political move!" Malcolm thundered in his car, listening to the news over the radio. "He did it to prevent him from coming with me."

He was right. Malcolm was now considered a traitor in the Nation's ranks, described as a man deserving of death. The same day that he renamed Clay, Muhammad warned him to cut off contact with Malcolm. Clay took any warning from the Messenger seriously; he had already seen how Nation dissidents tended to vanish. Just twenty-two and far out of his depth, he resolved his loyalties quickly. He stopped returning Malcolm's calls. He and Malcolm had planned an African tour; now Clay/Ali made the trip alone. Observers felt that Clay's African journey, in which he rode in open-top cars greeting legions of admirers, was the moment that he became, in his own mind, Muhammad Ali—a *world* champion, a figure bigger than boxing and sports.

Fearless to the end, Malcolm X called out the Nation's hypocrisy and corruption and worked with scant resources to start alternative organizations. On February 21, 1965, after months of cat and mouse with Nation goons, Malcolm was gunned down at the Audubon Ballroom in the Washington Heights area of Manhattan. The night that Malcolm died, a fire broke out in Ali's Chicago apartment. "Somebody started it on purpose," Ali said privately, though it was probably accidental.[24] Ali remained a Nation acolyte but would live to regret the depths to which his devotion, or his fear, took him.

★

From the moment the guns stopped firing in the Audubon Ballroom, the police and the FBI had been on alert for reprisals. Some of their concern focused on Muhammad Ali, now the best-known member of the Nation of Islam. Aubrey Barnette, a former Nation member, warned that Ali's life might be in danger from Malcolm's loyalists—or, for that matter, from Elijah Muhammad's, who might suspect the young fighter for his friendship with Malcolm.

And where better to make such a hit than in out-of-the way, under-resourced Lewiston, Maine, where the Ali–Liston rematch would be held? Originally scheduled for November 1964 in Boston, the bout had to be rescheduled to May 1965, when Ali suffered a hernia. Then, three weeks before the May 25 bout, Boston pulled out. The official reason was that Liston's company, Intercontinental Promotions, lacked a license to promote bouts in Boston—somehow this hadn't been noticed until now—but the city was more worried by the rumors, ranging from mob-engineered fixes to murder plots. Braving these concerns, Lewiston, a city of about forty thousand, most of French Canadian extraction, accepted the fight, to be held at the Central Maine Youth Center, usually home to youth hockey games. Lewiston had a rich local boxing tradition but had never managed anything like this before.

Talk of trouble was everywhere. One report had Malcolm's men on their way by car to Maine, heavily armed. "They're after Clay, aren't they?" Liston asked, spooked by the whole assassination business. "Not me." The promoters announced that all ticket holders would be searched upon entry into the arena. Ali might become "the first heavyweight champion to lose his title by assassination," mused sportswriter Jim Murray. He signed off his prefight column with: "And may the better man live."[25] Ali remained unperturbed, perhaps because he had FBI agents standing twenty-four-hour watch over his training quarters.

Only 2,434 people came out to the arena, the smallest modern crowd to watch a heavyweight championship bout. Jersey Joe Walcott, the popular former champion, would serve as referee, though he had never officiated at a title fight. With so much on the line—the title, a resolution to the first match, and the safety of the two fighters in this tense environment—the Maine boxing commission had essentially chosen an amateur referee.

About halfway through the first round, Liston backed Ali toward the ropes, and the champion, moving backward, threw a right so short and quick that few saw it. The punch caught Liston coming in, and he dropped to the canvas. The small crowd gasped. What had happened?

Ali wondered, too, and his perplexity took the form of rage: Neil Leifer's famous photo shows an infuriated Ali, his right fist cocked, standing over Liston, looking down with disgust and beckoning him to get up as referee Walcott tries to steer him away, to a neutral corner, as the rules dictated. Ali wouldn't cooperate; he kept rushing back to the scene of the crime, berating Liston, jogging around the ring in a kind of war dance, even once jumping into the air. Walcott tried in vain to restrain him.

Liston remained on the floor. He had gone down with his gloves touching the canvas, then flopped onto his back, then righted himself to one knee, then flopped over again. A groan sounded through the house when Liston rolled over the second time. Finally, Sonny got to his feet. The beleaguered Walcott had not had any chance to count over him.

Walcott brought the men together, and Ali opened up with a barrage. Then, hearing his name called by the timekeeper, Francis McDonough, and *Ring* magazine's Nat Fleischer, Walcott walked to the other side of the ring, abdicating his fundamental job: to control the action. McDonough and

Fleischer told him that Liston had been down for more than ten seconds. Walcott rushed back to the two fighters and raised Ali's hand, declaring him the winner by a first-round knockout. Boos echoed throughout the arena.

All was confusion. No one could understand what had happened when Liston was down or why Walcott had stopped the fight. Ever since the Dempsey–Tunney Long Count in Chicago in 1927, it had been understood that when a fighter scores a knockdown, he must retreat to a neutral corner—and that the count over the fallen fighter will not proceed until he does. Yet Ali had made a mockery of the rule. It was the referee's job to count over a fallen fighter, and it was his authority alone that determined whether a fight was over, not timekeepers or magazine editors. How could Liston be "counted out" if Walcott never gave him a count?

Those were only the procedural questions. Few people in the arena or viewing on closed-circuit TV saw the punch that had dropped Liston—at least, not while watching the fight in real time. Replays showed that Ali had, in fact, connected with a short right that landed on the side of Liston's jaw. But replay was in its infancy in 1965; the broadcast had to play back the entire round to show the punch again, and not everyone stuck around to watch. Besides, Ali wasn't known for his knockout punching power, and he had hit Liston with dozens of blows in the first fight. How could Liston, who had never been knocked off his feet, whose head had shattered nightsticks, be felled by a "phantom" punch?

Thus the conspiracy theories that surround the Lewiston fight to this day: that the fight was fixed, either at the behest of the Muslims or the mob or both, and that Liston "took a dive" because someone either threatened him harm or promised him lavish compensation (or both). Some said that a member of the Nation of Islam had visited Liston, warning him about dire consequences if he beat Ali. That was easy to believe. But wouldn't the mob protect Sonny?

Nothing tangible has surfaced to substantiate a fix, leaving only more conventional explanations. Maybe Ali legitimately knocked out Liston with a punch so fast that it could be understood only on slow-motion film. Milt Bailey, one of Liston's seconds, said that Sonny asked for smelling salts in the dressing room afterward. Whatever his real age, Liston was an old man by boxing standards in May 1965. Everyone close to him said that the postponement hurt him terribly. He looked bad in training. One good punch is sometimes enough against a diminished fighter.

The likeliest explanation for what happened in the ring in Lewiston, though, is not a conspiracy or Ali's sudden discovery of knockout punching power, but Liston's state of mind. Sonny went into the ring in bad spirits, whether feeling doubtful about his chances or frightened by the climate. Maybe's Ali's right hand stunned him enough to drop him, and maybe, as he fumbled on the canvas—waiting for the sound of gunshots?—he thought: the hell with this. As he had quit on his stool in Miami, he quit on the canvas in Lewiston. Ali himself believed this, at least in the moments after the fight ended, when he told his brother, Rahman: "He laid down."[26] (Only later did Ali mythologize his victory, attributing it to a special "anchor punch.") Yet even Sonny's surrender was confusing, since, in his defense, he had finally gotten up—even if he'd been down for more than fifteen seconds—and started fighting again. In short, Liston didn't know what he was doing in the ring at any moment. He reacted spontaneously, and his reactions were hard to interpret, like much of the rest of his public life.

All in all, the Lewiston fight should be remembered as the strangest sports event ever held on American soil. It took place in the unlikeliest setting and under the most adverse circumstances, and it ended with the most mysterious sequence in all of sports, a series of images that devotees have gone over with the intensity that others would bring to analyzing the Zapruder film. No wonder boxing historian Don Majeski considers Ali–Liston II the Kennedy assassination of boxing.

The Lewiston debacle finished off Sonny Liston as a serious heavyweight contender. Though Sonny started winning fights again, the stigma of the Ali losses or his bad reputation or both kept him from another chance at the big prize, and age finally caught up with him in the ring. Living in Las Vegas, he drifted into bad circles, and he may have gotten mixed up in the drug trade. In January 1971, his wife, Geraldine, returning home from out of town, found his body, dead several days and riddled with needle marks. Heroin was found in his bloodstream.

"I think he died the day he was born," publicist Harold Conrad said.[27] His unsolved death added the final dark chapter to Sonny's story. Conspiracy theories persist to this day about his death—a drug hit, a mob vendetta— but the simplest conclusion is that he accidentally overdosed. His life's final indignity was that, just as he had no official birth date, he had no official death date, either. Meanwhile, the losses to Ali compromised his standing with historians, who have never reached consensus on where he ranks. In the ring and out, Sonny Liston leaves a legacy of shadows.

★

The newspapers still called him Cassius Clay. Sometimes they would add, "aka Muhammad Ali," and more rarely they would refer to him as Muhammad Ali, "aka Cassius Clay." Senior *New York Times* editors frequently clashed with a young reporter, Robert Lipsyte, who insisted on calling him Ali. The name dispute became symbolic of a generational divide in the sporting press. Lipsyte and other younger newspaper writers, like Jerry Izenberg and Jack Newfield, saw Ali as part of a generation that was forging its own path. Older writers, like the *Times*'s Arthur Daley, the *New York Herald Tribune*'s Red Smith, and Jimmy Cannon of the *New York Journal-American*, were alienated by Ali's boastfulness and especially by his racial and political views, symbolized in the adoption of his Islamic name.

Divides were opening up in the country now—social, cultural, and political. In the black community, fissures developed between those who wanted to stay with Martin Luther King's peaceful approach and others, more militant and usually younger—many inspired by Malcolm X—who chafed at the nonviolent gospel. This tension was dramatized in the November 1965 fight between Ali and former champion Floyd Patterson, who had fought his way back into contention. "I am a Roman Catholic," Patterson told *Sports Illustrated*. "I do not believe God put us here to hate one another. I believe the Muslim preaching of segregation, hatred, rebellion and violence is wrong. . . . No decent person can look up to a champion whose credo is 'hate whites.' I have nothing but contempt for the Black Muslims and that for which they stand."

Ali responded to Patterson's critique with a blistering counterattack. He was especially offended by Patterson's suggestion that he wanted to win the title back for America. "Patterson says he's gonna bring the title back to America. If you don't believe the title already is in America, just see who I pay taxes to. I'm American. But he's a deaf dumb so-called Negro who needs a spanking. I plan to punish him for the things he's said. . . . This is going to be a beautiful fight. . . . This little old dumb pork-chop eater don't have a chance."[28] He dubbed Patterson "the Rabbit" because he was "scared like a rabbit" and also for his peekaboo style of fighting. And, showing that not all the buildup was so deadly serious, Ali took a page from his younger, breezier self: he brought lettuce and carrots to Patterson's training camp.

Still, with the war of words, the atmosphere for Ali–Patterson, in Las Vegas, was nearly as charged as that for the second Liston fight. And it was held on November 22, 1965, two years to the day since Kennedy's assassination. It was hard not to see metaphors in the Las Vegas ring. Floyd Patterson was a noble advocate of racial brotherhood, or he was a white man's dupe. Cassius Clay—no, Muhammad Ali—was a bold racial rebel, or he was a charismatic front man for demagogues. But a boxing match could only resolve which man was the better fighter.

Ali spent the first round dancing around the ring, making play-punch motions, while Floyd plodded after him, gloves up in his familiar peekaboo style. Ali's physical gestures suggested scorn. He even raised his arms above his head and taunted Floyd, like a child playing king of the hill. The crowd booed. In the second round, Ali started fighting, pumping out his left jab at Patterson in a steady rhythm. When Floyd tried one of his leaping left hooks, Ali tied him up or evaded him.

The pattern of the fight was established. Round after round, Ali gave Patterson a shellacking, led by his rhythmic, punishing jab and following up with rights to the head, right uppercuts, left hooks—often in unconventional sequences. Had any heavyweight ever thrown punches like this, moved like this? After the fourth round, British boxing commentator Reg Gutteridge compared Ali with Jack Johnson. "No contest," Ali shouted to ringside between rounds. "Get me a contender." Others heard him call out to Floyd during the fight: "C'mon, American! C'mon, white American!"[29]

After a few rounds, most at ringside could see that Patterson had no chance, and he seemed barely able to get himself around. He had slipped a disk in his back during training, but his camp kept the injury a secret. He felt his back go out on him early in the fight; as the rounds passed, the pain became excruciating. Increasingly immobile, he was a fixed target for Ali's assaults. The bout was a relentless beat-down, sometimes heartbreaking to watch but for the revelation of Ali's brilliance. It was not Patterson's best moment in the ring, but it was his bravest. And with Patterson, one always had to ask subterranean questions: Was he enacting some kind of penance? Was he conceding not just the fight to Ali, but the argument?

Finally, in the twelfth, after another Ali barrage, referee Harry Krause stopped the fight. Ali's verbal taunting led many to believe that he had deliberately carried Patterson, to punish him. The normally sympathetic Robert Lipsyte compared Ali's performance to that of a boy pulling the wings off a butterfly. Yet the evidence from the film is that Ali did his best to knock out Patterson but couldn't; Ali said afterward that Patterson had taken his best punches.

From almost the moment the bout was halted, the hostility between the two men dissolved, and they rarely had another unkind word to say about each other. Patterson fought until 1972 and hovered around the heavyweight title picture for much of that time, winning grudging respect from critics and building a warm relationship with Ali, who, as young Cassius Clay, had looked up to him. "I came to love Ali," Patterson said, some years before his death in 2008. "I came to see that I was a fighter and he was history."[30]

That wasn't how most Americans saw Ali in the mid-1960s, however. Ali's membership in the Black Muslims had already driven a wedge between him and fans, mostly white fans, who might otherwise have embraced him. And any hopes of accommodation came to an end when another issue intervened: Vietnam.

In 1964, Ali had scored a dismal sixteen on the armed forces aptitude exam and was classified 1-Y, ineligible. (The test required a minimum score of thirty.) "I said I was the greatest, not the smartest," he quipped, but he was embarrassed when the results were made public. The Johnson administration's escalation of U.S. involvement in the Vietnam War in 1965 caused the military to reexamine its eligibility standards. The qualifying score was lowered from thirty to fifteen—making Ali eligible. On February 14, 1966, Ali's phone rang with the news: he had been reclassified from 1-Y to 1-A and could expect to hear from his induction center. Reporters came flooding to Ali's doorstep in North Miami. Lipsyte watched as Ali struggled to field their questions. Ali floundered, and he responded at first like a spoiled celebrity.

"Why me?" he asked. "I can't understand it. How did they do this to me—the heavyweight champion of the world?"[31] The reporters kept at him. Finally, in response to another battery of questions, Ali said it: "I ain't got nothing against them Vietcong."[32] His lawyers, citing his Muslim faith, would seek to get him classified as a conscientious objector.

Ali's admirers would always see his "Vietcong" statement as an example of his unlearned gift for articulation. Ali's critics say that the line was fed to him by his Black Muslim keepers. Regardless, the reaction was swift and harsh.

"Squealing over the possibility that the military may call him up, Cassius makes himself as sorry a spectacle as those unwashed punks who picket and demonstrate against the war," Red Smith wrote.[33] "As a fighter, Cassius is good," wrote Milton Gross in the New York Post. "As a man, he cannot compare to some of the kids slogging through the rice paddies where the names are stranger than Muhammad Ali." Jimmy Cannon faulted Ali for his insolence and entitlement and linked him with a tectonic generational transition. The champion was "part of the Beatle movement," Cannon wrote, "the whole pampered style-making cult of the bored young."[34]

Ali's Vietcong comment scuttled a planned fight in Chicago against Ernie Terrell, when Illinois officials demanded that he apologize. He refused. The outcry against him grew so intense that the bout's promoters couldn't find an American site. Ali wound up journeying to Toronto to fight the rugged Canadian heavyweight champion, George Chuvalo.

Ali dubbed the Canadian "the washerwoman," for what he considered his flailing, wild, messy style of fighting. Chuvalo, playing along, paid a visit to Ali's training camp dressed like an old maid. He and Ali had been jawing at each other for some time—Chuvalo had leaped into the ring in Lewiston after Liston was counted out, all but accusing Ali of taking part in a fix—but there was no genuine ill will between them. Chuvalo and Ali went on to fight fifteen bruising and sometimes stirring rounds in Toronto's Maple Leaf Gardens. For six rounds, the fight was competitive, but Ali dominated the rest of the way, doling out astounding punishment to Chuvalo, hitting the challenger with hundreds of jabs and power punches—but none even wobbled the Canadian brawler, who had never been off his feet. For his part, Chuvalo focused on pounding Ali's midsection—and his attack included as many as one hundred low blows, for which the referee never penalized him. The champion retained his title by a wide margin on the scorecards, but he visited Wellesley Hospital afterward, his midsection bruised from the pounding.

It was only Ali's third defense of his title since winning it two years earlier, but now he became the busiest champion since Joe Louis, defending his title five times in 1966—mostly outside the United States. In the spring and summer, he fought twice in England, returning first for a long-awaited rematch with Henry Cooper. The second Ali–Cooper fight, seen by more than forty thousand in Arsenal Stadium, a British soccer venue, had none of the fireworks of the first, but it ended the same way: with the referee halting matters after an Ali right ripped open scar tissue around Cooper's left eye. A few months later, indoors at Earls Court in London, Ali knocked out Brian London in the third round with a combination so fast that only replays could do it justice.

From there, it was off to Frankfurt, West Germany, where Ali faced European champion Karl Mildenberger, the first Teuton to get a crack at the title since Max Schmeling. Mildenberger was a "southpaw," or lefty, standing in a mirror image of a righty—right foot forward instead of left, right hand leading with the jab instead of the left. He caught Ali with left hooks to the body often in the early rounds, chasing the champion around the ring as forty-five thousand fans in Wald Stadium urged him on, but the twenty-four-year-old Ali's combination-punching genius carried the day. Mildenberger took a lacing over twelve rounds before the referee stopped the fight.

Ali closed out 1966 by returning home to fight Cleveland "Big Cat" Williams in the Astrodome in Houston. The crowd booed the champion and cheered the once-promising challenger, who had twice gone toe-to-toe with Liston. Now the Big Cat was thirty-three, his youthful potency a memory, especially since he was carrying a .357 slug in his belly as a result of a run-in with a cop in the previous year. Some still figured that he might give Ali a go.

Perhaps the boos spurred Ali because he put on what many consider his ring masterpiece, a three-round demolition in which his talents were fully on display: his unequaled hand speed; his creativity in combinations; his graceful movement, weaving away from danger while floating back inside to throw punches; and his showmanship. In the second round, Ali dropped Williams three times with punches so fast and accurate that they seemed to be fired from a gun. In the third round, Ali unveiled his "Ali Shuffle"—a quick motion of both feet while standing in place—before dropping Williams again with another combination. The referee, Harry Kessler, stopped the fight.

Even Ali's detractors could not withhold praise. "The Clay who fought tonight was a revelation," wrote Daley in the *Times*. "There was no way this performance could be faulted." Others were realizing that Ali—or Clay, as many still called him—was taking his place in the heavyweight lineage. "On what I saw, I'd have to rate Cassius with the top heavyweights of any generation," said Teddy Brenner, matchmaker at Madison Square Garden.[35] A year that began with the Vietcong imbroglio ended with a celebration of Ali's talents. But the vise was tightening: Ali's attorneys had no luck in appealing his draft classification.

★

The Vietnam War was closing in on thousands of young American lives in early 1967. By the end of the year, American troop levels in Southeast Asia stood at nearly half a million men. Antiwar passions exploded. Draft resistance spiked; young men burned their draft cards or fled to Canada. The generational split was profound. Parents were baffled by their children's open rebellion against the federal government. In rising to the forefront of American life, the antiwar movement displaced civil rights. Martin Luther King was pursuing open housing campaigns in northern cities like Chicago and meeting furious resistance. King's struggles seemed to justify, at least to younger militants, a less peaceful, less accommodating approach. American cities went to the torch in 1967 and 1968. Newark and Detroit destroyed themselves with frenzies of murder, arson, and looting. Neither city ever recovered.

Ali's struggle with the draft board resonated with the Black Power militants as well as the white antiwar advocates, though he stood apart from both. No black man was more prominently engaged in a battle with Washington, but while Ali was well practiced in parroting Nation of Islam rhetoric on race, he sometimes threw out the talking points. He admitted to a reporter in 1964 that it wasn't skin color that made men evil but their deeds. He didn't advocate or condone violence. Antiwar activists admired him, but the feeling wasn't entirely reciprocal. He blanched at the burning of draft cards—he still had his—and allowed that some wars were necessary. If Elijah Muhammad declared that Vietnam was such a war, he said, he would go.

But such distinctions between Ali and those who sided with him were not as easy to see in the fevered climate of the late 1960s, and Ali didn't always make them easier to see—especially when, inside the ring, he showed himself capable of viciousness that would make any conscientious-objector candidate feel sheepish.

In February 1967, after a year's postponement, Ali finally faced off against Ernie Terrell—not in Chicago but in Houston's new Astrodome. A record indoor crowd of thirty-seven thousand turned out to see the fight, which was promoted as a contest to reunify the heavyweight title. The World Boxing Association had stripped Ali of recognition after he signed for a second fight with Sonny Liston, saying that such rematches violated its rules. Terrell then won the WBA's vacant title. But the most sacred boxing rule was unwritten: champions can lose their title only in the ring, not in office buildings. Everyone knew that Ali was the real champion, but the WBA's move made a fight against Terrell more marketable. A Chicago-based boxer, wooden in style but with a formidable left jab, Terrell stood six foot six, making him one of the few Ali opponents with a height advantage.

In promoting the fight, Terrell called Ali "Cassius Clay," the name he had always used for a man he had known for years. "Why don't you call me by my name, man?" Ali asked. "Are you going to be one of those Uncle Tom Negroes?" Terrell had meant nothing derogatory, but after he saw Ali's reaction, he kept saying "Clay." Ali promised to humiliate Terrell as he had Patterson. "I want to torture him," he said of Terrell. "A clean knockout is too good for him."[36]

The fight itself was a monotonous exhibition of Ali's superiority. Terrell spent fifteen rounds following Ali around the Astrodome ring in robotic fashion, his gloves held up so high and tight that it almost seemed he could not see through them. His vaunted left jab had little effect. By the middle rounds, Terrell's eyes were puffing up from the steady rat-a-tat of Ali's jabs and combinations. By the end of the fight, his eyes had walnut-size swellings, along with cuts. Some at ringside blamed the referee, Harry Kessler, for permitting the drubbing to continue.

But most blamed Ali for the ugly spectacle. Terrell claimed that the champion had rubbed his eye against the ropes in the second round, blurring his vision for the rest of the fight (an infraction not apparent on the film). Many believed that Ali intentionally prolonged Terrell's agony, refusing to knock him out because of the bad feeling between them. Their main exhibit was Ali's behavior in the eighth round, when he shouted to Terrell, "What's my name?" several times after delivering combinations.

"What's my name?" became another Ali mantra, along with his Vietcong declaration, remembered to history as "Ain't got no quarrel with them Vietcong." Both statements epitomized the sixties' elevation of self, and both are celebrated today in a culture that often equates self-assertion with wisdom. If "Ain't got no quarrel" was citizenship as subjective judgment, "What's my name?" was aggression justified by petty grievance; no slight to the ego could go unpunished.

A month after the Terrell fight, Ali was back in the ring, this time in Madison Square Garden, for the first heavyweight title fight in New York since 1960. His opponent was thirty-four-year-old Zora Folley. A veteran of eighty-six fights, Folley was a clever boxer and a consummate pro who had never gotten a shot at the title.

Battling Folley reacquainted Ali with his better angels. With Folley's wife and eight children looking on, Ali fought almost gently, letting his challenger—his bald spot visible in the ring lights—lead and win a few rounds. Ali dropped Folley with a right in the fourth. In the seventh, he snuck the right through again and Folley fell to his face before struggling up, a second or two too late. He had done well, landing numerous right hands, and made $100,000. If the Terrell fight was Ali at his ugliest, the Folley bout showed him at his kindest.

"This guy has a style all his own," Folley said. "It's far ahead of any fighter's today. How could Dempsey, Tunney, or any of them keep up? Louis wouldn't have a chance; he was too slow. . . . There's just no way to train yourself for what he does. . . . He could write the book on boxing, and anyone that fights him should be made to read it."[37]

Ali's long dance with the draft board was coming to an end. He received notification to report for induction to Local Board No. 61, on San Jacinto Street in Houston, on April 28, 1967. He stood in line with others, waiting to be called. When he heard his name, he did not step forward. A navy lieutenant informed him of the seriousness of refusing induction, and he was given a chance to reconsider. He declined.

Within an hour, the New York State Athletic Commission and most other state commissions revoked Ali's boxing license. The NYSAC and the WBA also stripped Ali of the heavyweight title, which was now vacant as far as they were concerned. Ali faced felony charges of draft evasion but hadn't been convicted or even arraigned. Spurning due process, state commissions took away his ability to earn a living. Like Jack Johnson, Ali was estranged from his government and country, but Ali's circumstances were the reverse of Johnson's—he stayed in America but couldn't fight. On June 20, 1967, Ali was convicted of draft evasion and sentenced to five years' imprisonment and a $10,000 fine. He remained free on appeal.

★

The WBA set up an eight-man elimination tournament to determine a new heavyweight champion. Some of these fighters—Ernie Terrell and Floyd Patterson—had lost to Ali already, but the tournament's biggest weakness was the absence of Joe Frazier, a top contender regarded by many as the best of the lot. Frazier's manager determined that he would gain more by staying out of the round robin and fighting the winner. In June 1968, Jimmy Ellis—a former Ali sparring partner—beat Jerry Quarry to become the new heavyweight champion, if one chose to accept him. If one didn't, there was always Frazier, who had won recognition in the meantime as heavyweight champion in New York and five other states. An Ellis–Frazier match would unify the title—unless you recognized neither man and insisted that the one and only heavyweight champion was Muhammad Ali.

While his legal appeals ran their course, Ali needed money. High taxes, lavish spending, and the Nation of Islam's claim on his revenue drained him of resources quickly. (His contract with the Louisville Sponsorship Group expired in 1966; he would be managed for the rest of his career by Elijah Muhammad's son Herbert.) In 1968, he found a new source of income as a college speaker. His statements about American racism drew wide applause on many campuses, but he was most admired among students for his stance on the war. "Whatever the punishment, whatever the persecution is, for standing up for my religious beliefs, even if it means facing machine-gun fire that day, I will face it before denouncing Elijah Muhammad and the religion of Islam," he said. "I'm ready to die."[38]

The mention of Elijah illustrated a crucial distinction between Ali and his college audiences: in a culture beginning to see individual choice as transcendent, his antiwar stance was determined not by conscience but by dictate. On other topics, too, he bucked the counterculture line: he condemned interracial romance, homosexuality, drug and alcohol use, and radical politics. Before one appearance in Buffalo, he insisted that signs reading "LBJ, how many kids did you kill today?" be taken down before he would speak.

Among blacks, Ali's stature grew to martyr's proportions. Following his example, black athletes spoke out with new defiance, and Ali was their guiding spirit. Eldridge Cleaver called Ali "the first 'free' black champion ever to confront white America," the "Fidel Castro of boxing."[39]

Ali also won support from mainstream voices. *Esquire* pictured him on its cover as Saint Sebastian, with arrows piercing his chest. Martin Luther King came to admire Ali as well. Initially, King had been another critic, lamenting Cassius Clay's allegiance with the Nation of Islam. But as Ali faced off with the government over the draft, King, who was moving toward explicit opposition to the war, celebrated Ali's stand. "No matter what you think about Mr. Muhammad Ali's religion," King said, "you certainly have to admire his courage."[40]

Yet Ali's stance had mostly to do with fear of disobeying Elijah Muhammad. The army almost certainly wouldn't have sent him into combat; he would have played a ceremonial role, as Joe Louis had. But the Nation of Islam's position was absolute. Ali was trapped. In March 1967, the night before Ali fought Folley in New York, his boxing idol, Sugar Ray Robinson, visited him. Ali told Robinson that Muhammad had ordered him not to join the army. Robinson warned Ali that he was jeopardizing his career, but he was brought up short by Ali's response.

"I'm afraid, Ray. I'm really afraid." He had tears in his eyes.

"Afraid of what? Of the Muslims if you don't do what they told you?"

Robinson said years later, "He never answered. . . . If you ask me, he wasn't afraid of jail. He was scared of being killed by the Muslims. But I don't know for sure."[41]

Throughout the tumultuous years of Ali's exile—1967 through 1970—efforts persisted to get him reinstated and arrange a fight. One effort after another ran aground. On February 3, 1970, Ali announced his retirement from boxing. Two weeks later in New York, Joe Frazier knocked out Jimmy Ellis to win the undisputed—well, you know—heavyweight title. *Ring* magazine made it official: Joe Frazier was the one and only heavyweight champion. Muhammad Ali was out of the picture.

★

Ali's formal departure from boxing came just as the culture moved in his direction on Vietnam. A 1965 Gallup poll found that 24 percent of Americans thought the war was a mistake; by 1971, 60 percent did. Ali's travels around the country had acquainted him with people from all walks of life, many of them whites who disagreed with him but liked him anyway. Newsmen missed his showmanship and artistry. Recognition grew that he had been hounded out of boxing before his legal case could be resolved.

The case wasn't going well. A federal appeals court ruled against Ali in May 1968. The Supreme Court was about to reject the case—thus upholding the lower-court rulings and sending Ali to jail—when revelations surfaced about government wiretapping of militant figures, including Ali. The justices delayed so that they could investigate what effect, if any, the wiretaps had had on Ali's case. Eventually, they agreed to hear it, and Ali had another reprieve.

Then in August 1970, a federal judge ruled that New York's ban of Ali represented an "arbitrary and unreasonable departure" from the state commission's usual practice of giving boxing licenses to those convicted of other felonies. The way was cleared for Ali to fight in New York, but something even more remarkable was happening in Georgia, where a group of civic leaders—led by the state's first black state senator—secured a bout for Ali in Atlanta against top contender Jerry Quarry, on October 26, 1970. Tickets sold briskly.

The event, held in Atlanta's City Auditorium, turned into a coming-out party for black America: Sidney Poitier, Harry Belafonte, Diana Ross, Julian Bond, Coretta Scott King, Ralph Abernathy, and many others turned out. Jesse Jackson walked with Ali to the ring. Ali had been watching films of Jack Johnson, projected on a bedsheet; when he stepped into the Atlanta ring, Bundini exhorted him by invoking the outlaw black champion. "Ghost in the house! Jack Johnson's here!"[42] Ali had not seen real ring action in forty-three months. Only Joe Louis had gone longer between fights, during World War II. But at twenty-eight, Ali still looked sleek—and for three rounds, he glided around the ring, stuck the jab, and threw combinations while evading Quarry's rushes. In the third, he opened a gaping cut over Quarry's left eye. At the end of the round, the referee, Tony Perez, inspected the cut and stopped the fight.

Referring to Joe Frazier, Ali said that he hoped "something can soon be worked out where we can solve this whole heavyweight mess." Frazier hoped so, too, as did Madison Square Garden and a host of competing promoters, along with the sporting press and public, all sensing that Ali–Frazier could be the greatest sports event of all time. What Frazier and Ali didn't know was that they were about to forge a rivalry unequaled in sports, one grounded in conflicts of politics, religion, temperament, and ethics and filtered through some of the most divisive times that America had ever endured. But overhanging it all was the fundamental dispute that drew John L. Sullivan and Jake Kilrain to a green field in Mississippi some eighty years earlier: Who's best? Who's the real champ?

It was not true, as more than one writer had alleged, that Ali scorned the heavyweight title. On the contrary: Ali loved that title more than he loved anything else, and he was willing to endure just about anything to get it back. In the years to come, Americans would learn just how important the heavyweight championship was to Muhammad Ali—and to a few other men.

THE GREATEST AND
A GOLDEN ERA

With Ali back in the game, all energies turned to getting him into the ring against Joe Frazier—and quickly. Ali's Supreme Court appeal was pending, and time was short, but he needed more work to get himself ready. So in December 1970, he was matched against the rugged Argentinean Oscar Bonavena—known as Ringo, for his Beatles haircut. Held in Madison Square Garden and marking Ali's return to boxing in New York, the bout was a bruising affair. Though Ali outpunched Bonavena and led on the scorecards, he looked ragged, missing punches and lacking his once-fluid movement. Then, in the fifteenth and final round, Ali threw his most underrated punch—the left hook—and caught Bonavena charging in, putting him down. The Garden crowd erupted. Ali battered a reeling Bonavena to the canvas twice more, forcing stoppage of the fight under New York's three-knockdown rule. Ali had knocked out two Top Ten contenders in six weeks. What he needed now was some rest and then one more good, hard fight.

He would get neither—there wasn't time. On December 30, 1970, the agreements were signed in New York: Ali and Joe Frazier would meet in Madison Square Garden on March 8, 1971. Both would earn guaranteed purses of $2.5 million—more money, by far, than any fighter had ever made for one bout. In 1971, athletes didn't make $2.5 million for a whole career. On financial terms alone, Ali–Frazier was a sporting event set apart.

The bout was aptly dubbed not the Fight of the Century but simply The Fight. Its sporting fascination owed to its classic matchup of a master boxer versus a bruising slugger, both near their physical prime and close in age (Ali was twenty-nine, Frazier twenty-seven). The historic element was compelling, too: Ali, the undefeated (31–0) yet deposed champion, against Frazier, also undefeated (26–0) and now the official champion. Two unbeaten fighters had never met for the heavyweight title before, let alone two men with valid claims to that title.

In the brief months of buildup that followed, public interest grew to obsessive levels. The event would be seen in fifty nations, via satellite, with the closed-circuit broadcast reaching three hundred million people—more than had seen the 1969 moon landing. In America, fight talk filled newspaper columns, radio and TV reports, and magazine pages. Ali and Frazier appeared on the covers of *Time* and *Life*, still significant cultural barometers. "I don't know how you could have been in America and not have cared about that fight," said Larry Merchant, then a *New York Post* columnist and later an HBO commentator.[1]

For the most part, the fascination concerned Ali. He was a world figure now, more popular overseas than at home and, with the possible exception of Pelé, the first truly global sports star. Even in the United States, he was becoming more accepted. It didn't matter whether his stance on the war constituted that of a legitimate conscientious objector or whether he had taken the position by his own choice or had it forced on him. Millions of blacks saw him as a champion of racial pride and political courage; millions of Muslims around the world revered him. Liberals admired his antiwar stand. The war itself was winding down, at least for Americans. Polls showed that majorities now opposed U.S. involvement, and President Richard Nixon was bringing more troops home each month.

Ali had transcended sports. He was black power and black pride, antiwar and antiestablishment. And he was the greatest fighter many people had ever seen—the best-looking and most articulate, too. He would undermine forever the ideal of the modest and quiescent athlete. His charisma was like a force field.

Baked in the embers of the 1960s, The Fight suggested to many a looming verdict on the era's political battles. In any other time, Joe Frazier might have been adopted as a black sports hero. Not now. Instead, Frazier saw himself portrayed—by Ali, especially—as a symbol of white conservatism and the repression of blacks. Ali's supporters had ignored the finer points of their man's stance against the draft; they just as easily bought the caricature that Ali drew of Frazier.

Only Jack Johnson and Jim Jeffries, Joe Louis and Max Schmeling, had ever come down the aisle bearing more freight than Ali and Frazier would carry—Ali almost entirely by choice, Frazier almost entirely against his will. But Joe Frazier may as well have been born to take up arms against a sea of troubles.

★

He was born January 12, 1944, in Beaufort, South Carolina, the eleventh child to Rubin Frazier, a sharecropper, and his wife, Dolly. Beaufort was then known as the poverty capital of the United States. Blacks lived in conditions that, two decades later, would inspire the War on Poverty: shacks with no running water or electricity, lack of access to doctors and medical facilities, ill-educated children with not enough food in their stomachs but too many parasites in their blood. Frazier's schooling was mostly lost to truancy. By the age of ten, he was driving a tractor, and he worked alongside Rubin on a white-owned farm near Beaufort. By the light of the moon, Joe helped Rubin run a liquor bootlegging operation, often making midnight deliveries.

"I was never little, or played little," he remembered. "I ran with my father."[2]

He headed north when he was all of fifteen. In Philadelphia, he found work in Cross Brothers slaughterhouse, where he swept blood down the drain. It was grim business, though once in a while, passing through the meat locker, Joe would pound slabs of frozen beef, practicing combinations. (Sylvester Stallone borrowed this motif for *Rocky*.) Always short and thick, Joe found himself putting on weight, and he showed up one evening at the Police Athletic League gym, telling its director, a man named Duke Dugent, that he wanted to learn to box. "He had more fortitude than any man I've ever known," Dugent remembered.[3] Frazier would arrive at the gym each evening after an eight- or ten-hour shift at the slaughterhouse and make his way past the fighters on the gym floor to his locker, his clothes spotted with animal blood. Dugent mentioned the young prospect to Yancey "Yank" Durham, a friend and boxing trainer, who agreed to take him on. Theirs would become one of boxing's great partnerships.

Shorn of flab, Frazier became a tireless hard-body who punctuated his roadwork by running up the steps of the Philadelphia Museum of Art (Stallone borrowed that image, too). His left hook powered a successful amateur career. He and Durham eyed a spot on the 1964 U.S. Olympic team, but Frazier lost in the Olympic trials to Buster Mathis, a 300-pounder who fought like a dancing bear. When Mathis injured his hand in Tokyo, Joe, accompanying the team as an alternate, took his place. Fighting with his own broken thumb, Frazier won the gold medal in the heavyweight class—the first American ever to do so.

His pro career started modestly, in August 1965, with small purses and low expectations. He stood only five foot eleven, short for a heavyweight, and his seventy-one-inch reach meant that he would have to be an inside fighter, willing to wade through jabs and uppercuts to get close enough to do damage. Durham helped Frazier develop a style that compensated for these limitations: he became Smokin' Joe, a workhorse who emerged from his corner for every round throwing punches, always moving forward, digging his left hook to the body and head. Durham got Frazier to move his head and swivel his upper body, a "bobbing and weaving" style associated with Jack Dempsey but given new life by the Philly fighter. Frazier's pressure-cooker style relied on bottomless determination and conditioning that most boxers wouldn't attempt. And Frazier and Durham kept honing the fighter's meal ticket, the left hook.

Durham's stewardship proved nearly flawless. He moved Frazier slowly at first, ignored criticism, and, as the stakes got higher, played his hand with shrewdness and guile. By July 1967, when Frazier butchered George Chuvalo and forced a fourth-round stoppage of their battle in New York, Ali had been suspended from boxing. A heavyweight elimination tournament loomed, but Durham held Frazier out, reasoning that he could fight the winner for more money. In 1968, Frazier won partial recognition when he knocked out his old Olympic rival, Mathis, in New York. By the time Frazier caught up with the tournament winner, Jimmy Ellis, in February 1970, he was broadly regarded as the best active heavyweight. His destruction of Ellis in four rounds confirmed that judgment. But his relatively simple life then became consumed by an American fever that would scar him forever.

Ali was coming back. A fight against Frazier, the once and future champion promised his supporters, would be no contest. Ali assured them of something else: if they cared about the progress of black people, they would root for him, not Frazier, the backwoods South Carolinian whose skin was several shades darker and whose life experience was far more typical of ordinary blacks' than Ali's. Never mind: Frazier was a white man's dupe, Ali said. "Anybody black who thinks Frazier can whup me is an Uncle Tom."[4] Ali ridiculed Frazier's intelligence, impersonating him as a slow, mumbling pug, even pressing down his nose to mock his Negroid features. It was racial caricature that might have been expected in Jack Johnson's era—from whites. But now one black man was ridiculing another.

A man of immense pride, with well-developed notions of loyalty and honor—and their opposites—Frazier was infuriated by Ali's slanders, which worked a spell on white liberals and legions of blacks. As buildup for The Fight reached a peak, Frazier involuntarily took on the role of hero of the conservative white establishment. And when Frazier, livid at the Uncle Tom smear, retaliated by calling Ali "Clay," the stakes were upped further. The black and white elite of media, show business, and sports aligned itself with Ali; civil rights leaders, whose cause Ali had scorned, rallied to him, too. Frazier felt friendless, estranged from the black community by what *Sports Illustrated's* Mark Kram called Ali's "thermopolitical combustions."

Talking wasn't Frazier's thing, but he roused himself to respond to Ali's charges. "What he ever do for people but give 'em a lot of silly words?" he asked, speaking of Ali. "He's no martyr. The heroes are them kids with their pieces of body all over Vietnam, a lot of poor blacks. . . . He stop the war? How do people buy his shit?"[5]

He trained with monkish commitment. To stay away from Ali's sharp-shooting and fast hands, Frazier would have to move his head and upper body as never before. Durham and co-trainer Eddie Futch stretched a rope from corner to corner and made Joe bob over and under it ceaselessly. Frazier brought himself to an unrepeatable peak of physical condition, but the tension had him weary before the fight, when he was secretly diagnosed with high blood pressure. Shots of Vitamins E and C kept him going. He had his mind on war.

Ali had already made the contest a morality play, neatly splitting the country along lines familiar today: between liberals and conservatives, doves and hawks, black and white. In less divisive fashion, he did his showman's part as well, offering some verse: "Joe's gonna come out smokin', / And I ain't gonna be jokin', / I'll be peckin' and pokin' / Pouring water on his smokin' / This might shock and amaze ya, / But I'll destroy Joe Fray-shuh."[6] And he promised to deliver his prediction, live on closed circuit, before the opening bell. About 350 venues would show the fight around the country.

Outside Madison Square Garden, on Monday, March 8, 1971, fans dressed in high fashion and outrageous outfits, as if they were going to a movie premiere—or to a midnight screening at a whorehouse. The literati were out: Norman Mailer was covering the fight for *Life*, Budd Schulberg for *Playboy*, William Saroyan for *True*. Star power extended to the closed-circuit broadcast team. Boxing stalwart Don Dunphy anchored the telecast; joining him for commentary were ring legend Archie Moore and Burt Lancaster, whose only boxing experience came from the movies. Lancaster wasn't the only headliner serving in an unusual capacity: Frank Sinatra sat near ringside, taking photographs for *Life*.

At about 10:15, the fighters came down the aisle: Ali first, then Frazier. Ali's last act before emerging to the throngs was to read his prediction to the millions watching worldwide: "Frazier Falls in 6." He was as confident as ever—perhaps too confident, some worried.

"Don't underestimate this Frazier," Odessa Clay had told him. "Work hard. I'm too nervous."

"Don't worry, Mom," Ali said. "I'll be in top shape. He's a bum."

"Sonny, he's no bum."[7]

★

From the opening bell, it was the most bitterly contested, brilliantly fought of all heavyweight fights. Up on his toes, working from mid-range, Ali found Frazier's head repeatedly in the first round with stinging left jabs and right hands as Frazier bore in, bobbing and weaving up and down and side to side. When Joe got close enough, he let the left hook go, usually missing or grazing Ali, who shook his head, as if to say, "That didn't do anything to me."

Those who had watched Ali for years were struck by the heaviness of his punches in the early rounds. They landed on Frazier's face with a thudding sound, and, thrown by a 215-pound man who was setting himself when he fired, they had the power to send an ordinary man home early. Frazier, who weighed 205.5, was spitting blood minutes into the action. "Goddamnit, roll that head!" Yank Durham shouted, concerned that Frazier was standing up too straight.

"You gonna get us both killed the way you goin'," Durham told Joe after the third round.[8] But Frazier was finding the pathway inside. Ali had unloaded heavy artillery on Frazier for three rounds to little effect. By the fourth and fifth, Ali was spending more time on the ropes, where Frazier whipped left hooks to his midsection, kidneys, and hips. His punches came with their own bell tones—a thick, liquid sound, like that of a man plunging a clogged drain—often punctuated with grunts.

In the sixth, Frazier made a mockery of Ali's knockout prediction as he stalked the man he called "Clay" around the ring. The sound of his body punches grew louder. When Ali pulled his head back now, Frazier's left hook was finding him. He kept moving forward, forcing Ali around the ring, swiveling, swaying, bobbing, and punching, a "motorized Marciano," as *Time* had described him. No matter how much punishment he took—and Ali kept doling it out—Frazier would not let himself lose heart, his whole being focused on the job.

Ali's energies were flagging. He spent the seventh and eighth rounds lodged against the ropes, trying to turn the fight into a burlesque. Covering up, he pinballed Frazier's head with his glove and mugged for the crowd. Frazier scored with a few hooks, but he took Ali's cue, in the silent pact fighters sometimes make to take a breather. The Garden crowd booed.

"Stop playing," Angelo Dundee scolded Ali. "Do you want to blow this fight? Do you want to blow everything?"[9] In the ninth, Ali rediscovered his pot-shotting marksmanship, and he laid an onslaught on Frazier—a one-two, a right, a left hook, another one-two, two left hooks, a right—that backed the champion up and left ringsiders breathless. He followed up in the tenth, lashing Frazier's face, which was becoming lumpen, especially around the eyes. It was Ali's round, but he paid dearly, taking another body beating. For the first time in his life, he could not physically control what was happening in a ring.

The fight hung in the balance. After ten rounds, referee Arthur Mercante had Ali ahead, six rounds to four, while judges Artie Aidala and Bill Recht had Frazier in the lead, 6–4 and 7–3. Five rounds remained—the "championship rounds," as boxing people called them.

In the eleventh, Ali waved Joe in from a corner, disdain written on his face. He set himself to throw uppercuts, but he missed the bobbing target, and Frazier caught him with a hook that wobbled him against the ropes, his eyes going wide. As the din rose in the Garden, Frazier threw the left again and again. Digging into his bag of tricks, Ali playacted a hurt fighter, lolling his head like a drunk—a convincing simulation of reality. The bell rang. Bundini Brown shook a wet rag into Ali's face, but it didn't help. He took another shellacking in the twelfth.

In the thirteenth, Ali found another gear. Dancing briefly, he caught Frazier with one-twos that resembled his punches in the early rounds. Clear-eyed men had trouble seeing Ali's punches; Frazier's puffed eyes were closing down his lines of vision. But he pinned Ali in the corner, crucifying him against the turnbuckle with a hook and working him over. Ali summoned his remaining strength to fight a strong fourteenth, leaving one round to go.

Few had guessed that the battle would come down to the judges' cards. Ali had landed more punches, but Frazier's were heavier, and he had controlled the manner in which the battle was waged. Frazier's corner was confident of victory; Ali's sensed that their man needed a rally.

Ali came out for the fifteenth firing the jab. Barely twenty seconds into the round, the two came together, Ali setting to throw a right uppercut—his shoulder dropping—and Frazier, from a deep crouch, emerging in a swiveling motion with a left hook that crashed onto Ali's jaw. Down he went, his legs shooting up high. The Garden vibrated with sound, as flashbulbs popped.

Though he had taken a punch that would slay a mortal, Ali forced himself up; the count only reached four. He looked more shocked than hurt, his eyes betraying a look of defeat that no one had seen there before. The right side of his jaw was billowing, as if he had a small melon lodged in his cheek. He retreated on leaden legs, and Frazier nailed him with another deadly hook. Joe stepped away to let Ali fall, but Ali stood.

The fight neared its end. Neither man would give in, and the crowd applauded them both. "Frazier is tired!" Dunphy said from ringside, as if noticing for the first time. "And his eyes are closing!" They clinched. Mercante moved in to separate them, but sensing that they might collapse if he forced it, he backed off. "The way they were hitting," the referee said, "I was surprised that it went fifteen. They threw some of the best punches I've ever seen."

Finally, the bell. "I beat your ass!" Frazier spit through his mouthpiece, cuffing Ali on the head. Mobs descended on the ring.

Ring announcer Johnny Addie gathered the scorecards and announced the tallies, using New York State's system of scoring by rounds. "Referee Arthur Mercante scores it eight-six, one even, for Frazier," he began. "[Judge] Artie Aidala, nine to six for Frazier. Bill Recht, eleven rounds for Frazier, four Ali—eleven to four. The winner by unanimous decision and still heavyweight champion of the world—Joe Frazier!"

His jaw swelling up, Ali skipped the postfight press conference and headed for Manhattan's Flower Fifth Avenue hospital. When X-rays on his jaw came back negative, he declined to stay overnight. His arms draped around his physician, Ferdie Pacheco, and trainer Angelo Dundee, he headed back to his hotel. "I got to get to bed," he kept saying.[10]

Frazier answered reporters' questions with cold packs pressed to his ruined face. "That man can sure take some punches," he said of Ali. "I went to the country, back home, for some of the shots I hit him with."[11] Then he went to his dressing room and soaked his head in ice before making a brief showing at his victory party.

By the next morning, Ali was his old self—and he even claimed that he had won. "I think I won nine rounds," Ali said. "I hit him more punches, three to one, without exaggeration." Then, contradicting himself, he said: "I didn't give the fight to him, he earned it."[12] And, remembering the Frazier left hook, he muttered: "Damn evil thing. Underestimated it."[13]

For Frazier, the victory brought relief but little joy, especially as he realized that the outcome changed nothing in the public's perception of the two men. Not long after the fight, Frazier checked himself into a Philadelphia hospital for observation. He was suffering from mental and physical exhaustion and a kidney infection; his blood pressure skyrocketed. At one point, doctors put him on a sheet of ice to stabilize him. A rumor spread that he had died; he didn't miss by much. Finally, he rallied and went home, but he was in no hurry to fight again.

His low profile, along with Ali's postfight spin-doctoring, stole the public glory of Frazier's victory. He had won the best heavyweight fight ever waged, but beyond financial riches—after paying nearly half the $2.5 million purse in state and federal tax, that is—his triumph netted him little. Only when he was invited to address the South Carolina legislature—the first black man to do so since Reconstruction—did Frazier wear the mantle of the heavyweight champion's office. Even this tribute was criticized by those who saw symbolism in Frazier's speaking to a legislature that flew the Confederate flag. Hadn't Ali said that he was an Uncle Tom? For the media, liberals, and most blacks, the wrong man had won.

★

On June 28, 1971, by an 8–0 vote, the Supreme Court acquitted Ali of draft evasion. He would never understand how close he had come to jail.

After he was reclassified 1-A in 1966, Ali appealed to the Selective Service board, claiming that, as a Black Muslim, he was a conscientious objector to the Vietnam War. The board denied his appeal on guidance from the Justice Department, which argued that Ali didn't meet all three qualifying criteria: that his objection was sincere, that he was opposed to all wars, and that his opposition to military service was based in religious belief. After Ali's case reached oral arguments in the Supreme Court, however, the government conceded that he was sincere and that his position was grounded in religious conviction. Solicitor General Erwin Griswold questioned only whether Ali was truly opposed to all wars, arguing that he would fight in a war that concerned Muslims. (Ali had said as much himself.) By yielding on two of the three grounds, the government gave the Court an out—because the appeal board, in rejecting Ali's plea, did not specify the basis for its decision. Thus it may have been ruling on grounds that the government had since conceded. The Court acquitted Ali on a technicality. "Insofar as precedent is concerned," said a clerk to Justice John Marshall Harlan, "it is so thin that if you turn it sideways, it doesn't even cast a shadow."[14] But Ali was free.

Scraping away the remaining rust from his exile, Ali got back in the ring for three more fights in 1971 and six in 1972, fighting often in strange,

The best heavyweight fight of them all: Joe Frazier drops Muhammad Ali in the fifteenth round on his way to victory, New York, March 8, 1971.

Ali-like places: Zurich, Switzerland; Budokan, Japan; Vancouver, British Columbia; and Dublin. He rattled off wins against familiar names: Jimmy Ellis, Buster Mathis, Jerry Quarry, and thirty-seven-year-old Floyd Patterson, in his last fight. Ali called himself the People's Champion. Elvis Presley gave him a rhinestone-bedecked robe. He made the rounds of the talk-show circuit, from Dick Cavett to Johnny Carson.

When it came to interviews, though, Ali's most memorable interlocutor was ABC's Howard Cosell, whose rise to prominence in the 1960s, on radio and then on television, had been propelled by his rapport with Ali. The Brooklyn-raised, NYU-educated Jewish lawyer and the Louisville-born, semiliterate black boxing savant became one of television's most durable odd couples: part comedy team—Ali liked to pretend that he wanted to remove Cosell's toupee—and part cultural touchstone. Cosell didn't hide his affection for Ali, but he also put more challenging questions to him than most other reporters did.

Ali liked to tease Cosell that the broadcaster owed his career to him, but by 1970, Cosell had become a fifty-something national sensation as the star of *Monday Night Football*, a sports and television landmark. The era of total sports absorption—24/7 cable channels, rabid adult fans wearing team jerseys like children, and fantasy leagues—was years away, but *Monday Night*

Ali with Howard Cosell in 1972
Associated Press

planted the seed. Football was now king, with baseball hearing whispers—as it still does—that it was too slow for an accelerated age. As for boxing, the 1970s proved robust, at least on television, with matches showing regularly on all three major networks. Old-timers saw a sport in crisis, but younger fans would remember it as a golden age.

Hovering over it all was Ali, never out of the news for long. In 1972, he bought a six-acre training camp in Deer Lake, Pennsylvania, overlooking the Poconos, and outfitted it in archaic, Old West–style motifs—with coal stoves, "rope" beds, and hand-pumped water. The most memorable pieces of design were the enormous boulders that lined the camp, all painted with the names of his predecessors and peers. Joe Louis, Jack Johnson, Rocky Marciano, Floyd Patterson, Jersey Joe Walcott, Sonny Liston, even Joe Frazier—the lineage, in physical form, surrounded Ali as he worked. And Ali invited the world to Deer Lake; a more accessible and generous celebrity has never lived. He did not distinguish between reporters from high school newspapers and beat writers from New York dailies, and he entertained a constant wave of children, sick and well, among legions of others making the pilgrimage. When one of his camp followers erected a rope barrier to keep visitors at a distance, Ali told him never to do it again. His entourage grew Shakespearean in character and scale. He employed people to call "time" after rounds or read him entries from the *Guinness Book of World Records*. As in Shakespeare's day, you could get on the payroll if you could entertain the king.

But the king had no title. After each fight, Ali was asked about a rematch with Frazier, the invisible champion. Frazier's long layoff, which stretched into early 1972, lent credence to an observation that Ali had made about him on the morning after their battle. "He's strong, he's good at his style. . . . But a man with his style won't be in boxing long."[15]

★

Monday, January 22, 1973, was a big news day. In Washington, D.C., Hamaas Abdul Khaalis, a former Nation of Islam member who now called Elijah Muhammad a "lying deceiver," blamed the Nation for the massacre of his family days earlier at a residence owned by basketball star Kareem Abdul Jabaar, where several NOI men had murdered everyone in the home, including a newborn. The massacre was a dramatic reminder of the Nation's deadly character. Also in Washington that day, the Supreme Court, in a 7–2 vote in *Roe* v. *Wade*, struck down state laws barring abortions in the first trimester of pregnancy. The *Roe* decision and the Nation of

Islam's treachery would have headlined most news broadcasts, but not that day: at his ranch in Texas, former president Lyndon Johnson succumbed to a heart attack.

And the day had one other major event: a heavyweight championship fight, in Kingston, Jamaica, where Joe Frazier would take on the second-ranked contender, George Foreman. It marked the first serious heavyweight action since Ali–Frazier nearly two years earlier. In that span of time, Frazier had fought only twice, both against unranked boxers. The public wanted to see him against Ali again, but a rematch deal kept breaking down over money. And insiders in the Frazier camp whispered that Joe was not the same fighter he had been.

With shadows of decline descending, Frazier overruled Yank Durham and agreed to fight Foreman, owner of a 37–0 pro record, with thirty-four knockouts, most against nonentities. It was a strange decision financially: Joe would get $850,000, but he could have made several times that amount in an Ali rematch. Then again, Frazier didn't see Foreman, a 3–1 underdog, as a serious risk. The way Joe had it figured, he'd knock out Foreman and quiet the whispers, then destroy Clay once and for all—and take to the road to sing with his band, The Knockouts.

George Foreman made his way to the ring in Jamaica just hours after the passing of LBJ, a man he held in high esteem. It was Johnson's Great Society that had created the Job Corps, the program that had helped Foreman turn his life around. Born in Marshall, Texas, on January 10, 1949, Foreman grew up in a large and poor family. His father, J. D. Foreman, worked for the railroad but drank too much; his mother, Nancy Ree Foreman, supported the family on meager wages as a cook. George grew up in Houston's infamous Fifth Ward, where crime and vice ran rampant. His mother worked long hours, and he grew up with little supervision. He'd leave the house in the morning for school and then climb back up the window to his room when his mother had gone. One day, he was surprised to see another relative, a cousin, standing there. Foreman stammered for an excuse, but she waved him off. "Don't worry about it," she told him. "You're nothing. You're never gonna be nothing. Go to sleep."[16]

Her words haunted Foreman. Why was he being told that his life didn't matter—didn't it matter? He briefly graduated to mugging and thievery, but restlessness and shame made him renounce a life of crime. One day, listening to the radio, he heard Jim Brown, the retired pro football great, talking about the Job Corps, where young men could learn trades. Foreman became a dedicated trainee, and through the program he found boxing. From the beginning, Foreman was known for his punch and his size: he stood six foot four, had a seventy-eight-inch reach, and owned a punishing left jab and a wrecking-ball right. Under trainer Doc Broadus's guidance, Foreman would represent the United States in the heavyweight division at the 1968 Summer Olympics, in Mexico City.

Tensions ran high on the American team. A group of black athletes had joined up with the Olympic Project for Human Rights, founded by the black sociologist Harry Edwards to bring attention to the plight of blacks in America and around the world. After American sprinters Tommie Smith and John Carlos finished first and third in the 200 meters, they stood on the medal stand in bare feet, signifying black poverty, and raised their black-gloved fists to signify Black Power. Foreman wasn't asked to join the activist athletes, though he might have declined, anyway. He didn't like "being called or set apart as a 'Black Athlete.' I was an American athlete."[17] He remembered keenly that many of the people in his life who had written him off were black, too, and throughout his public career, he would resist every enticement to sort people and events through the American racial lens. A few days later, when Foreman won the heavyweight gold medal, he paraded around the ring holding a small American flag. The gesture endeared him to millions.

As a novice pro, Foreman sparred briefly with Sonny Liston and was astounded by Sonny's still-powerful left jab. When he learned to handle it, he was on his way. He absorbed something else from Liston: the art of intimidation. By the time Foreman arrived in Kingston, he had perfected his own version of the Liston stare. He used it on Frazier when the two men met in the ring in Jamaica before the opening bell.

For a minute and a half, Foreman, at 217 pounds, manhandled Frazier, popping him with jabs and rights and pushing him away rudely whenever he tried to charge. Then he sent the champion sprawling with a right uppercut. "Down goes Frazier! Down goes Frazier!" exclaimed Howard Cosell at ringside. Frazier, looking thick at 214 pounds, got up, but Foreman pinned him on the ropes and landed another right uppercut, and Joe dropped like a tent whose supporting pole has been removed. He got up, tottering around the ring. Foreman nailed him with another right and Frazier crashed down again as the bell rang to end the first round. Filled to its thirty-six-thousand-seat capacity, Kingston's National Stadium was a madhouse. The events were too unexpected to assimilate in the sixty seconds between rounds.

Any thought that Frazier might regroup was dashed immediately in the second round. He had never fought defensively; his whole career was a conspiracy against physical distance, and now proximity was killing him. The Foreman blitz became expressionistic, rich in exaggeration, almost comic. Assaulting Frazier along the ropes, Foreman sent him skipping away, Joe's legs doing a windup as if he were pedaling a bicycle, before he hit the canvas again. Four times he had been down. He tried a left hook but was crushed by Foreman's left instead. Five times. From across the ring, Foreman eyed Yank Durham in the Frazier corner.

"I'm going to kill him," he shouted.[18]

On the broadcast, Cosell sounded hysterical. "It's target practice for George Foreman!"

Frazier was pinned on the ropes again, taking one monster shot after another. Foreman's right crashed home, the punch carrying a delayed neurological charge. Frazier sagged, then was lifted off his feet by the force of the blow before hitting the deck again. Six times. The choreography defied imagination. Referee Arthur Mercante waved his arms, stopping the fight.

Frazier's courage—he had finished on his feet—was beyond question, but the visuals suggested a man being bounced around the ring like a toy, and Cosell's hyperactive audio made it worse. "Down goes Frazier!" would later become a popular chorus on ESPN Classic reels, an easy belly laugh for sports fans lacking insight or empathy—never a small faction. Smokin' Joe left the ring not only an ex-champion but also a diminished one.

The Frazier–Ali rematch was now off the market, the long-awaited bout like a stock whose fundamentals had plunged. Ali had long claimed that Frazier hadn't recovered from their battle, and Jamaica seemed to prove it. But he couldn't gloat for long. On the last day of March 1973, in San Diego, the thirty-one-year-old Ali was shocked by Ken Norton, a tough ex-Marine who beat him on a twelve-round decision and broke his jaw. Now Frazier and Ali looked like has-beens and the twenty-four-year-old Foreman like boxing's new king.

★

Facing an existential threat to his career, Ali trained furiously for the Norton rematch, another twelve-rounder, in Los Angeles in September 1973. He came in lean, at 212 pounds, and dominated the bout's first half, using his jab. As Ali tired, Norton came on, closing the gap. But Ali won a desperate twelfth round, taking a split decision by the narrowest of margins. Norton could plausibly claim that he had won both fights, and he was rewarded with a shot at the title.

That left Ali and Frazier marking time. With their downgraded status, they needed big wins to reposition themselves. The obstacles to a rematch dissolved, and they met again in Madison Square Garden, on January 28, 1974, two faded ex-champs fighting for $850,000 each.

Frazier's continuing anger at Ali—who had branded him "ignorant" in the prefight buildup, causing a near-brawl in ABC's studios—didn't translate as well to the ring, where he came after Ali with diminished energies. In the second round, Ali, at 212, hurt Frazier with a right; the referee, Tony Perez, thought he heard the bell and separated them, giving Frazier an accidental breather. It was the only break that Joe, at 209, got all night. Ali scored light combinations and clinched Frazier at every turn, holding him behind the head, an illegal tactic that Perez did nothing to stop. The battle was waged on Ali's terms: he picked off Frazier from long range and smothered him when Joe got close. He won a twelve-round unanimous decision—a sensible, but far from definitive, verdict.

Thus Ali avenged the two losses of his career, but the victories were hardly smashing. Two months later, in Caracas, Venezuela, Foreman did the smashing: he rendered Ken Norton senseless in the second round. Foreman had vaporized Ali's conquerors—Frazier and Norton—in two rounds apiece. At ringside, Ali was undaunted. "I'm the onliest man that can whup George Foreman, and I'm going to do it in, of all places, in Africa, in the Congo, where the Lumumba boys are!"[19]

The mention of Patrice Lumumba was as ironic as it was incoherent, since "the Congo" was now known as Zaire, renamed by the nation's strongman president, Joseph Mobutu, who had helped facilitate Lumumba's demise in 1961. But Ali was right about one thing: there would be a heavyweight championship fight in Africa. Ali and Foreman stood to earn $5 million each, double what Ali and Frazier had made for their first battle. The Rumble in the Jungle, Ali called it—the richest prizefight yet.

★

In Zaire, Mobutu ruled with brutal force, and his lust for riches gave rise to a new word: kleptocracy. He chartered his personal airline, Air Zaire, for Paris shopping trips. He kept palaces around the country. His wealth approached $5 billion, most of it looted from the treasury of a nation rich in natural reserves.

Mobutu was not the only demagogue on the scene, however. The rumble would never have come to the jungle if not for Don King, a former Cleveland numbers runner who had twice served prison terms for killing another human being. Yet such was his potent leveraging of mob connections, intimidation, bribes, charm, and sheer will that he was able to get the second conviction—for stomping a man's brains in—pled down from second-degree murder to nonnegligent manslaughter and even managed, years later, to get the governor of Ohio to pardon him for it. King had only recently insinuated himself into the boxing business, but now he went to Ali and Foreman separately, asking them to sign an agreement for a fight—provided that he, King, could secure the funds. Both accepted. Now all King needed was $10 million. That's where Mobutu, and an investment consortium, came in. The dictator saw a title fight as good publicity for Zaire. With his financing in place, Don King, three years removed from Ohio's Marion Correctional Institute, made himself the public face of Ali–Foreman. With his effortless palaver and his soon-to-be-famous electrified hair, King would become one of boxing's great promoters—a man of pulverizing intelligence and cunning, unencumbered by a wisp of scruple.

Once again, Ali found himself at the center of an event richly tuned to the times. In the mid-1970s, after more than a decade of African independence movements and the American civil rights revolution, a heavyweight championship in postcolonial Congo, against the backdrop of Mobutu's tyranny—the dictator kept pens of political prisoners beneath the stadium where the fight would be held—made the Rumble in the Jungle an Ali pageant beyond compare. Major American newspapers sent their correspondents to Zaire, and they were joined by the men of letters who could not resist following Ali's rake's progress around the world, among them Norman Mailer and George Plimpton. Mailer was struck by King's confidence and rap. "You are a genius in tune with the higher consciousness," King told him, "yet an instinctive exponent of the untiring search for aspiration in the warm earth embracing potential of exploited peoples."[20] Plimpton was intrigued by a meeting with Mobutu's *féticheur*, or witch doctor, who told him that a woman with "slightly trembling hands"—a succubus—would put a spell on Foreman.[21] But the novelty of Zaire wore off quickly. The hovering presence of Mobutu's guards made even hardened American fight reporters uneasy. Foreman's training grounds were an armed camp, complete with barbed wire. And the reptiles took getting used to; one might turn on the bathroom light in the hotel and see a lizard in the shower. Even Ali confessed to an aide that he looked forward to getting back home to the United States.

Then Foreman cut his eye in sparring, and the fight had to be postponed six weeks. Most press headed back home, but Mobutu, worried that the event would be relocated to an American venue, forced the fighters to stay put. For Foreman, the delay only prolonged the unpleasantness. He hadn't connected with the people; he wasn't connecting well with anyone. By contrast, Ali used the extra time to deepen his ties to the country, befriending villagers, playing with their children, and becoming Zaire's popular favorite to beat the scowling, intimidating champion. Zaireans developed a chant: *Ali, bomayee,* meaning, Ali, kill him. When sentiment was set aside, though, few liked Ali's chances, and some even feared for his life against this reincarnated Sonny Liston. Foreman was a 3–1 favorite.

On October 30, 1974, more than sixty thousand souls filled Zaire's 20th of May soccer stadium in the predawn hours so that the fight could be seen in the evening in the United States. Most were seated far from the canopied ring. Ali came down the aisle feted by trumpets and cheers. He waited in the ring for nearly ten minutes before Foreman made a running entrance, wearing a bright red robe. When the fighters met in the ring for instructions, Foreman merely glared, but Ali, as he had against Liston a decade earlier, looked his foe in the eyes and spit words through his mouthpiece. Some heard him say: "You have heard of me since you were young. You've been following me since you were a little boy. Now, you must meet me, your master!"[22]

The bell rang and Ali danced, as promised, moving left and right, while Foreman stalked him, looking to cut off the ring. Whenever Foreman came near, Ali let his hands go: the jab and the right hand but also a right lead, thrown across his body, a gambler's punch. Ali landed every right lead he threw in the first round, and the crowd erupted with his every move. His punches had Foreman's face growing puffy already. But George, driving himself into a rage, cornered the former champion and pounded away before the bell.

Sitting in his corner after the first round, with the voices of Angelo Dundee and others in his ears, Ali did what he had often done before: he went somewhere else in his mind. He had fought a brilliant first round, but Foreman's pressure had put mileage on his thirty-two-year-old legs. He had to conserve his strength. That meant moving less and fighting from the ropes—a death warrant against the champion, most believed.

But Ali stood up for Round 2 determined to try it. The shift in strategy was not immediately apparent to most because Ali's speed was having the same effect that he had promised it would. Time and again, his hands flashed out like lasers into Foreman's face, and the big man, pawing, could not land his thunderous salvos. With his back to the ropes in Round 3, a look of fury etched on his face, Ali picked Foreman apart, making it look easy. He was winning, though his posture on the ropes obscured this fact. Over the next several rounds, Foreman pounded Ali's arms and sides but usually missed Ali's jaw with his punches, some of which made massive, sweeping arcs. When Foreman rallied, Ali tied him up, tugging hard on his neck, wearing him down. And he talked.

"That the best you can do, George?"

"You can't punch!"

"Show me something!"

"That's a sissy punch!"[23]

Still, Ali balanced himself on a sword's point. His corner was in anguish, convinced that he was making himself a sitting duck. Dundee tried to get his fighter to heed his advice. "Get back on your toes," he implored. "Move! Don't let Foreman tee off on you like that."

"I know what I'm doing."[24]

He had always had his own ideas about how to fight. You could give him guidance, but he'd only use what he felt he needed. In Zaire, Ali needed only intuition and memory. The intuition had told him to ditch his original fight plan, and memory supplied him with the alternative, one he had learned as a novice fighter, when he had trained with Archie Moore in California: a defensive posture called the Turtle Shell, where the gloves were held tight to the face, elbows in to protect the body. When executed with cunning and courage, the Turtle Shell could protect a good boxer while his opponent flailed away and burned precious energy.

They came out for the fifth. By now, Ali was taking up occupancy on the ropes with the familiarity of a weekend warrior sinking into the family-room couch. Foreman was amped up, clubbing away. Ali kept leaning back when Foreman's big swings came in—like a man sticking his head out the window to look up at something on his roof, Plimpton thought—and talking to George all the while. Foreman's body blows thudded into Ali's sides, making ringsiders wince. The seconds ticked, and Ali wasn't punching back. Was this the end?

From his defensive shell, Ali peered out at Foreman. The big man was throwing bombs, not even trying to hold back. Ali talked some more and probed Foreman with a jab. Then he opened up: the jab and right hand. He found Foreman's head like a marksman, and the champion tottered backward for a moment. Ali sent water spraying from his head with another right and, grabbing Foreman in a clinch, looked down at ringside and stuck his tongue out. The bell rang.

Even the doubters now sensed what Ali might be about, but not Dundee: he scolded Ali again, urging him to stay away from Foreman, and asked the referee, Zack Clayton, to tighten the ropes. The ropes did seem loose; sagging in the humid air, they gave Ali a cushion on which to lean back and absorb Foreman's blows. Dundee always insisted that he had tightened the ropes. Others said that he had loosened them, perhaps at Ali's urging. Debates about the ropes in Zaire would remain lively for decades.

Foreman's energies were flickering like a dying flashlight. Ali stung him with jabs and rights early in the sixth, then spent the rest of the round putting his weight on him. The fight had slowed down after the high drama of the fifth round, its plot meandering. The seventh was slow and the eighth was dreary, punctuated only by Foreman's giant swing and a miss, which nearly carried him through the ropes and out of the ring. With the round nearly over, Ali landed a short right on the pursuing Foreman, who had pinned Ali, as always, on the ropes. Foreman's momentum carried him forward, and Ali spun and nailed him again as Foreman backed off. The hunter at last, Ali put across one more right, this one landing square on Foreman's jaw.

The big man's arms flew up in a flailing gesture, his torso jerking up and down, his legs moving crazily underneath him. He went crashing toward the canvas, resembling a human spinning top. He could not quite haul himself to his feet in time. Seven years after boxing authorities had taken the heavyweight title from him, Ali had won it back.

How he had won would prove as memorable as the achievement itself. Against Foreman, he had employed tactics fundamental to jujitsu: using his opponent's strength against him, getting the foe to assist in his own demise. It turned out that Ali was not getting badly hurt along the ropes by Foreman, whose wide-arcing punches he could block on his arms and gloves. Foreman left Ali punching room up the middle—and his refusal to pace himself in the tropical heat burned him out. The Rumble in the Jungle added another page to the Ali legend, and, naturally, his winning strategy got a name, too: the Rope-a-Dope.

Sitting for an impromptu interview with David Frost in his dressing room, already flooding from the monsoon rains that had begun shortly after the bout concluded, Ali declared himself, again, "the greatest of all time." After what he'd done in the steamy early morning hours in Africa, it was hard to begrudge him. He remembered to celebrate Elijah Muhammad and the Nation of Islam but, in the next breath, sent greetings to *Playboy* impresario Hugh Hefner—a perfectly surrealistic Ali juxtaposition. Finally, he thanked Joe Martin in Louisville, the police officer who had introduced him to boxing. Louisville: it was sometimes hard to remember what American city Ali had come from. He seemed too big for localism. But on the greatest night of any boxer's life, he remembered how and where it had all begun.

★

Perhaps even more surprising than Ali's triumph was the popularity of his victory. *Sports Illustrated* named him Sportsman of the Year—an ironic

Muhammad Ali regains the title by knocking out George Foreman and, in the process, puts his remaining skeptics out of business—Kinshasa, Zaire, October 30, 1974.
Associated Press

honor for an athlete who had violated every traditional precept of sportsmanship. Time and distance had softened opinions. Unlike many sixties
rebels, Ali had paid a genuine price for his convictions, and he had not
complained. The nation was exhausted in the fall of 1974. Two months before the Zaire fight, Americans had watched a president resign for the first
time in history, as Richard Nixon realized that he faced impeachment and
conviction for his role in covering up the Watergate break-in and obstruct-
ing its investigation. Throughout 1973 and 1974, Nixon's presidency did a
slow dissolve, but history didn't pause: U.S. troops were out of Vietnam, but
the war's political and social impact remained profound. The nation faced
an energy crisis, spiraling inflation, and, most of all, the collapse of its long
postwar consensus. A giant groping in the dark, America needed inspiration—or at least some laughter. Ali offered both.

"You made a big mistake letting me come," Ali told President Gerald
Ford in December 1974, "because now I'm going after your job."[25] Ali's
gentle subversion—ribbing the president in his own office—reflected, in
its way, the dispersion of the sixties ethos of nonconformity and rebellion
into mainstream settings. Ali wouldn't have been permitted near the White
House a few years earlier.

Ali could have retired after Zaire, carried off by the fairy dust of his
greatest feat. But getting his title back had proved much harder than he
expected, and he was determined to enjoy it. He got back into action in
March 1975, defending his title in Cleveland against a beer-swilling club
fighter named Chuck Wepner. Wepner surprised Ali by making it into the
fifteenth round and enjoying a checkered moment of glory: in the ninth
round, he half-punched, half-pushed Ali to the canvas. Wepner's brave
stand gave Sylvester Stallone the premise for *Rocky*.

Two months later, Ali stopped Ron Lyle, a rugged contender who had
done time for murder, in the eleventh round in Las Vegas. Ali trailed on
the judges' scorecards before catching the tiring Lyle with a combination
and finishing him off. Then it was off to another inimitable Ali locale—
Kuala Lumpur, Malaysia—where, in muggy conditions in the capital
city's Merdeka Stadium, he won a lopsided fifteen-round decision over
Joe Bugner.

On that broadcast, American viewers heard periodically from Joe Frazier, who was at ringside. Frazier was biding his time, waiting for one more
crack at Ali, and his patience would be rewarded. Ali–Frazier III would
take place in Manila, capital city of the Philippines, where Ferdinand
Marcos, staunch anti-Communist, American ally, and unabashed autocrat,
had declared martial law a few years earlier. As Mobutu had, Marcos saw a

heavyweight title fight as a promotional opportunity and a distraction from his country's troubles.

Ali got the promotion off to a rousing start by dubbing Ali–Frazier III the Thrilla in Manila. He added a few more rhymes: "It will be a killa," Ali said, "a chilla, a thrilla, when I get the gorilla in Manila." He reached into his pocket and pulled out a black rubber ape. "I got his conscience right here," Ali said, pummeling the little doll, to the delighted laughter of Don King behind him. "C'mon gorilla, this is a thrilla," Ali continued. "C'mon gorilla, we in Manila!"[26] Sticking with animal themes, Ali said that Frazier was so ugly his face should be donated to the bureau of wildlife and that his "smell" could be picked up from great distances.[27] Ali got most of his listeners, press and public, to laugh along with him. Did they, at some level, enjoy the license he gave them to mock an unlettered black man?

In Frazier's camp, Eddie Futch, who had taken over after Yank Durham's sudden death in 1973, sensed his man's resolve, though he worried that Frazier's hatred would consume him. Ali's Manila/gorilla routine seemed like the final straw for Joe. "Whatever happens, don't stop the fight," he told Futch. "We got nowhere to go after this. I'm gonna eat this half-breed's heart right out of his chest. I mean it. This is the end of him or me."[28]

★

Ali and Frazier met in the ring for their third battle on October 1, 1975, at 10:30 in the morning, Manila time. The humidity hung heavily in the morning air, resulting in what Ferdie Pacheco called "boiling water for atmosphere."[29] Though the Araneta Coliseum was air-conditioned, the capacity crowd of more than twenty-five thousand, packed in close, plus the hot ring lights made the air thick and steamy. Spectators felt the stifling temperatures before the opening bell.

Ali, looking thick at 224.5, came out with the same goal that he had had for the first fight in 1971: to blitz the slow-starting Frazier and win the fight early. He found Frazier's head with rights throughout the first round, and Joe's legs buckled with thirty seconds to go. Ali swarmed him, eager for the finish. How glorious it would be to take Joe out in the first! But the bell rang.

Frazier looked a bit thick himself, at 215.5—too heavy to have his best chance. He came after Ali with the old purpose, but his upper body was too straight up, his swiveling movements only a hint of 1971. Ali strafed him; the early rounds in Manila were among the most one-sided that the two men fought against each other.

But as Frazier drew closer to Ali, the fundamental tension of their three fights reasserted itself: Ali's desire for the perimeter versus Frazier's quest for the trench. As the rounds passed in the sauna-like coliseum, sweat and water drenched their gloves, which made such a slapping sound, especially on body punches, that Imelda Marcos turned away.

Ali's corner wanted him off the ropes. Zaire meant nothing. You couldn't "rope-a-dope" Frazier because he threw short punches through the gloves and whacked hooks to Ali's kidneys—and his hips, too, illegal punches but highly effective at degrading Ali's mobility. (The Filipino referee, Carlos Padilla, let him get away with it.) In the sixth, Frazier stalked Ali around the ring, landing left hooks that reminded some of the first fight and attacking Ali mercilessly to the body. Ali sat in his corner heavily between rounds. "Lord, that man can punch," he said.[30] After a halfhearted attempt to get up on his toes in the seventh, he abandoned dancing completely. He hadn't the legs to pull it off. He'd have to resolve the trilogy by fighting it out in the pit with a man who hated him.

Battling at close quarters in the eighth, Ali hit Frazier with a concatenation of punches: his right hand was like a magnet to Frazier's face, and his slithering left hook had Joe's head snapping up to the rafters. And yet, an experienced watcher of the three fights could see Joe's bob moving into mid-fight form; he was down and up, down and up, and you knew that the left hook was coming with him on the rise. Ali knew it, too, but he couldn't avoid it any better than he ever had. Frazier backed his man into a corner and pinioned Ali with crushing body blows.

Frazier seemed poised to take back the title. He looked to be the stronger, fresher fighter, if you disregarded his face, which was already swelling up. Returning to his corner after the tenth, Ali doubled over the ropes, head down, gasping for air. This must be what dying is like, he told Dundee. Ali's ever-loyal cheerleader Bundini Brown was in tears, this time for good reason. "Force yourself, champ! Go down to the well once more!"[31] he exhorted. But the eleventh didn't go much better.

In Frazier's corner, Eddie Futch knew that his man had taken a battering, but he sensed that Ali was spent. Thus he watched in amazement as Ali came out for the twelfth and punished Frazier with a renewed assault. His combinations rearranged Frazier's face as if it were moist clay, even as Joe kept charging. But the challenger's pace had slowed.

"What's with his right hand?" Futch asked Frazier in the corner.

"Can't see it," Frazier said.[32] His left eye was closing, and Ali was destroying him on that side. Joe's vision in that eye was suspect, anyway; at minimum, he was developing a cataract, but he would write years later that he was essentially blind in the left eye throughout his career and had passed physicals by playing a trick with the vision chart. (Futch disputed these claims.) In any case, by the thirteenth round in Manila, Joe may as well have been blind.

Only minutes before, Futch had sensed victory; now he knew that the fight was slipping away. He told Frazier to stand up straighter so that he could see the rights better—though this would leave Joe vulnerable to Ali's whole arsenal. Futch was damned in either direction. But perhaps Ali could be destroyed with one more hook?

Instead, Ali turned up the gas higher in the thirteenth, sending Frazier's mouthpiece flying into a ringside row and battering him without letup. Somehow Joe stayed on his feet. The fourteenth was the ugliest round of all. Joe kept moving forward, but he could not defend himself, especially against the rights. His face was bulbous; blood poured from his mouth. At the bell, he needed the referee's guidance to find his corner.

One round remained. Ali's late charge had pushed him into a wide lead on the official scorecards, but no one knew that yet. Reporters at ringside had it scored much closer. In both men's corners, scoring took a backseat to surviving.

The carnage of the fourteenth round made Futch remember young men who had died in the ring, their names and faces imprinted on his mind. He knew what the fight meant to Frazier. Maybe he could survive one more round, but at what cost? He had a wife and five children.

"Joe, I'm going to stop it."

"No, no, Eddie, you can't do that to me!" Frazier tried to stand up.

"You couldn't see in the last two rounds. What makes you think you can see in the fifteenth?"

"I want him, boss."

"Sit down, son," Futch said, pressing down on Frazier's shoulder. "No one will ever forget what you did here today."[33]

If Futch had sent Frazier out for the fifteenth, some wonder whether Ali would have met him there. Those in Ali's corner heard him say to Dundee, "Cut 'em off"—meaning the gloves—after the fourteenth. He was deranged by exhaustion and pain. Yet what Ali said and what Ali did were different things. He had reclaimed control of the fight. He would have stood for the fifteenth—and if he hadn't, Dundee would have pushed him out there.

When word reached Ali's corner that Frazier wouldn't come out, Ali stood up, raised his arm in victory—and collapsed. He was mobbed by his aides as the ring filled with press and officials and nameless souls. Some in his corner wept.

The names Ali and Frazier remain today the lodestar of heavyweight boxing and the hyphenated entry that defines sports rivalries. The Thrilla in Manila is often remembered as "the greatest fight of all time," but like most historical events, its reputation distorts stubborn realities. For boxing artistry and skill, Manila was a pale imitation of Frazier–Ali I, fought when both men were near their peak. In Manila, they were older, heavier, and less mobile, and Ali's physical advantages, especially his hand speed, were more pronounced. With his rally in the late rounds, Ali's wide lead on the official scorecards when the fight ended seems justified.

Still, Joe had made it hell on Ali, had hurt Ali and punished him like no other man, and Ali at last acknowledged Frazier's greatness. He would always remember Manila as a grim ordeal. Years later, when Mark Kram visited him and asked if they could watch his "good rounds" in Manila, Ali demurred. "What good rounds?" he asked.[34]

"I hit him with punches that would have brought down the walls of a city," Frazier told Kram after the fight. "Lawdy, lawdy, he's a great champion."[35]

The truce wouldn't hold. Frazier's bitterness increased as the years passed, especially as he saw Ali rise to the status of American hero. The media didn't acknowledge the toll that Ali's verbal abuse had taken on Frazier until years later. And when Ali finally got around to offering a genuine apology, Frazier couldn't accept it.

Victory in Manila made Ali think again about leaving the ring. "It was insane in there," he told Kram the next morning, as the sun set behind Manila Bay. "Couple of times like I was leaving my body. . . . This is it for me. It's over."[36] He had conjured death during the fight, and Ali still couldn't shake the thought at Ferdinand Marcos's postfight reception, where he moved stiffly, wearing sunglasses. Leaning over to sign a guest book, he wrote: "Death is so near, and time for friendly action is so limited. Love and peace always."[37]

★

Manila gave Ali a glimpse of his boxing mortality, but developments outside the ring opened up fresh possibilities—especially the death of Elijah Muhammad in early 1975. Muhammad's son Wallace took over the Nation of Islam and steered the organization (which he soon renamed) in a new direction, rejecting his father's racial preachments and welcoming whites. No one who knew Ali well believed that he took the white-devil talk to heart, though he was still capable of shocking statements, as in a 1975 interview with *Playboy*, in which he said that black women should be killed for going with white men.

Before Elijah died, Ali revealed how he really felt about the Nation to Dave Kindred, a Louisville sportswriter who had known him for years. Kindred sat talking with Ali one day when a few Fruit of Islam bodyguards tried to get Ali to come with them. He refused, and they left.

"They always got somebody watching," he told Kindred.

"Who are 'they'?"

"I would have gotten out of this a long time ago," Ali said, now whispering, "but you saw what they did to Malcolm X. I ain't gonna end up like Malcolm X."

"You afraid?"

"I can't leave the Muslims," Ali said. "They'd shoot me, too."

With Elijah's death, Ali could rest easy; Wallace demilitarized the organization. But the moment gave Kindred an answer to the riddle of why "the sweetheart son of a Baptist church lady had so long adhered to the tenets of a religious sect teaching race-based hate."[38]

He'd outlasted Elijah, just as he had outlasted other storms. On April 30, 1975, after Congress refused President Ford's pleas to provide military aid to South Vietnam, Saigon fell to the Communist North Vietnamese, bringing a conclusive end to the Vietnam War. The domestic divisions over the war wouldn't heal, but with Americans no longer dying in Southeast Asia, and with the abolition of the draft in 1973, the fevered political energies of the sixties were at last extinguished. Ali had won his own Vietnam War, beating Uncle Sam at the Supreme Court and convincing a younger generation that he was a man of political significance. Promising to become the "black Henry Kissinger" in retirement, he even appeared on *Face the Nation*.

Ali had evolved into a bourgeois taste, a charming if sometimes off-color clown who could reliably entertain millions. At long last, he became a pitchman, making commercials for roach spray and deodorant. He inspired pop songs and comic books. His rebirth as a mainstream-friendly athlete rankled some admirers who preferred the political rebel, but like most of the shifts in his career, it was well timed. In 1976, the United States was preparing for its bicentennial celebrations, an event that would reunite Americans around common values after a decade of division, unrest, and tragedy. The Bicentennial was as much reconciliation as celebration—and Ali was the sixties radical come home, with a smile.

He was frantically busy in 1976, defending his title four times and appearing in a novelty match in Tokyo against Antonio Inoki, a Japanese wrestler. The idea was that Ali would box and Inoki would wrestle, and a set of strange rules was drawn up, but the contest proved a dud, with Inoki spending fifteen rounds on his back, crab-walking and kicking at Ali's legs. It was a bad show, Ali admitted. But it paid $6 million.

Earlier in the year, he had better luck with two hopelessly outclassed challengers, Jean Pierre Coopman and Great Britain's Richard Dunn, both of whom he stopped in five rounds. They were brought in to create show-cases for Ali's talents and cash in on his burgeoning popularity. Both fights ran on prime-time television.

The public adulation made a poignant contrast with his declining skills. After Manila, his timing off and his elusiveness diminished, Ali relied increasingly on clowning and farce. On April 30, 1976, an overweight Ali looked awful against Jimmy Young, a clever but light-hitting counterpuncher. Ali won a unanimous fifteen-round decision, prompting boos throughout the Capital Centre in Landover, Maryland, and angry calls to the ABC switchboard—as if the network could do anything about it. Almost as bad was his final performance of 1976, for another $6 million check: a deciding third match against Ken Norton, in Yankee Stadium in September. Over fifteen muddled rounds, Ali missed often, effective only in short bursts with a flicking jab. He prevailed on a razor-thin unanimous decision that prompted another outcry. Most at ringside thought that Norton had won.

Ali knew that the Norton decision was unpopular; he promised that he would retire after one more fight, a rematch against George Foreman. Defanged, Foreman had been forgotten for long stretches in the two years since Zaire. The loss in Africa had shattered him mentally. Finally, in 1976, he resumed his career with two big wins. He knocked out rugged Ron Lyle in a slugging match that became a modern version of Dempsey–Firpo, with both men visiting the canvas more than once. Then he knocked out Joe Frazier in five rounds, in a reprise of their Jamaica encounter. Fighting at a blubbery 224 pounds and wearing contact lenses, Frazier, just thirty-two, looked ancient in the ring. He announced his retirement.

When a rematch with Ali was slow to materialize, Foreman journeyed to San Juan in March 1977 to fight Jimmy Young. There, he ran into another Zaire-like surprise, in another tropical clime, against another crafty boxer who improvised defenses against his clubbing blows. Peppered by Young's featherweight punches and stymied by his mousetrap defenses, Foreman dropped a twelve-round decision. Exhausted and demoralized, he made it into his steamy dressing room, where he began hearing voices. He felt himself coming in and out of consciousness, sinking into blackness. He smelled the stench of death.

"I don't care if this *is* death," he said aloud, "I still believe there's a God." Who said anything about God? The word roused Foreman, and, suddenly lucid, he proclaimed, "Jesus Christ is coming alive in me!"[39] Heat prostration, his handlers figured. George would sleep it off.

Instead, when Foreman woke, he declared himself born again. Americans had become familiar with such testimonies in the late 1970s: the Jesus Movement, as some called it, would even claim that uber-1960s figure, Bob Dylan. But Dylan kept on making music; Foreman, twenty-eight, announced his retirement from boxing to dedicate his life to Christ. Few took him seriously, but a year passed, and another and another, and George Foreman did not return.

Ali, Frazier, and Foreman made an unequaled heavyweight trio. It was as if Jack Dempsey, Joe Louis, and Rocky Marciano had all competed during the same era. Now Ali had outflanked and outlasted his two great inquisitors, both younger than he.

★

Ali spent 1977 struggling through two more title defenses, including a desperate fifteen-rounder against the murderous-punching Earnie Shavers; promoting the movie version of his life—titled, naturally, *The Greatest*, and starring, naturally, himself; and trying to quiet the clamor for rematches against Norton and Young. The World Boxing Council set up a Norton–Young elimination fight and ordered Ali to fight the winner. Norton prevailed over Young in November 1977, making a fourth bout against Ali look certain. Buying time, Ali scheduled another payday, for $3.5 million, against a novice pro with only seven professional fights—Leon Spinks, a 1976 Olympic gold medalist as part of the famous American boxing team in Montreal.

Unmotivated, training mostly in a rubber suit to cut weight, Ali got down to 224.5 pounds, but his belly was soft. The twenty-four-year-old Spinks, a former Marine, came in at a lean and ready 197. The bout, on February 15, 1978, was held at Caesars Palace in Las Vegas—a harbinger of boxing's future, when most big-money fights would be held there. A crowd of just 5,298 showed up in the indoor pavilion, while millions watched at home on CBS.

A 10–1 underdog, Spinks had grown up idolizing Ali, but he showed no reverence for the great champion once the bell rang. He swarmed Ali, who went to the ropes in his increasingly dreary Rope-a-Dope posture. Ali gave away most of the first eight rounds, with Spinks doing the only real fighting. His plan was to wait for the youngster to tire, but when that didn't happen, Ali tried to make a charge. He had fallen well behind on the scorecards, and he fought furiously to close the gap. He tried to knock out Spinks but couldn't. The two battled toe-to-toe in the fifteenth round, but it was Ali who returned to his corner on wobbly legs.

When ring announcer Chuck Hull announced a split decision, the crowd moaned. Here we go again, some thought—another gift decision for Ali. And sure enough, the first card was for Ali, 143–142. (The fight was scored on the ten-point "must" system, in which the winner of a round gets ten points and the loser nine or less; 143–142 is 8–7 in rounds.) Then Hull read the next two: 145–140, Spinks, and 144–141, Spinks. "And the *new* . . ." Hull said, and the rest of his words were drowned out. Spinks, riding the shoulders of his men, including his brother and fellow gold-medalist Michael, raised his arms in victory and revealed a mouth of missing front teeth. Ali, his face puffy, moved over to congratulate the kid.

★

Leon Spinks freely described himself as a "ghetto nigger."[40] Born in 1953 in St. Louis, he grew up in the city's nightmarish Pruitt-Igoe housing project, in an urban poverty culture where family breakdown, drug use, guns, and teenage pregnancy were endemic. He was wholly unprepared for mass celebrity. Within weeks of winning the title, Leon's constant run-ins with the law made him a figure of ridicule. He was once busted for a quantity of cocaine valued at $1.50. His daily life, guided by a genius for disaster, was made to order for tabloid consumption. Throughout 1978, he made the news, being busted for DUIs or found with grams of coke under his Stetson. He drank in ghetto bars, landed in ghetto hotels with ghetto prostitutes, and woke with ghetto hangovers, a slapstick Sonny Liston. He was never meant to wear a crown, and he knew it.

Leon's lack of clout encouraged the World Boxing Council's decision to strip him of his title when he refused to fight Norton, opting instead for a lucrative rematch with Ali. The WBC named Norton champion, dividing the heavyweight title for the first time since 1965. The other alphabet boxing organization, the World Boxing Association, continued to recognize Leon, as did the American public—and Ali–Spinks II was the fight that people wanted to see. If the first bout was fought in a crowded ballroom and televised on CBS, Ali–Spinks II would need a Roman Coliseum to contain the multitudes, and only ABC's Howard Cosell could present it.

The rematch was set for September 15, 1978, in New Orleans, where, eighty-six years earlier, James J. Corbett had inaugurated the modern gloved era by knocking out John L. Sullivan at the Olympic Club. Ali promised that Spinks II would be his last fight, and he trained like it. "I hate exercisin'," he had confided years earlier. "It's so boring."[41] Now he endured the most sustained regimen of his life. He scaled Deer Lake's steep hills for six-mile runs at dawn, challenging himself always to go farther, and hammered out sit-ups at rates he'd never approached. When he sparred, he used the center of the ring, instead of idling on the ropes. Arriving in New Orleans, the 221-pound Ali was in superlative condition. By contrast, a distressed and distracted Spinks partied often. Not long before fight time in New Orleans, Leon disappeared, and neither his camp nor his bodyguard—the not-yet-famous Mr. T.—could find him. He was finally located in a hotel room, drunk. "He was drunk every night he was here," promoter Bob Arum said.[42]

Ali's broader victory had been won before the opening bell. "I could announce tomorrow that Muhammad Ali will walk across the Hudson River and charge twenty dollars admission," Teddy Brenner, matchmaker at Madison Square Garden, said in 1970. "And there would be twenty thousand down there to see him do it. And half of them would be rooting for him to do it and the other half would be rooting for him to sink."[43] By September 1978, the "sink" contingent had dwindled, and the public, which had long served as part adulator and part foil, increasingly wanted to embrace him. A crowd of seventy thousand packed the city's enormous Superdome, normally the site of New Orleans Saints and college bowl games, paying a record gate of $5 million, shattering the fifty-one-year-old record held by the Dempsey–Tunney Long Count fight of 1927.

How was it possible that Muhammad Ali, a walking carnival, had never fought in New Orleans? People pressed in tightly on him as he moved up the aisle; Cosell, talking at an ambitious clip even by his standards, wondered about security. Bob Arum had asked Louisiana governor Edwin Edwards to call out the National Guard; Edwards shrugged. Ali arrived in the ring stoic and dignified, perhaps realizing that some moments in life don't lend themselves to bluster. As if he were there to underscore this point, Joe Frazier sang the national anthem.

★

Rhetoric aside, Ali had never danced that much, even when young. He moved, yes, but dancing—bouncing on his toes and circling the ring—he did sparingly. For the rematch, he made a familiar promise: to dance all fifteen rounds. Incredibly, except for the ninth round, he did it. But he did not start promisingly. He missed with everything, jabs and following rights, especially when punching down at Spinks. Leon bulled Ali around the ring in the early rounds. Then Ali found the range, especially from the

fifth round on, and his fight plan was simplicity itself—"jab, jab, throw the
right and grab," as Pat Putnam put it in *Sports Illustrated*.[44] Spinks got no
help from his crowded corner, where advisors, including his accountant,
were shouting advice.

The rounds passed, and Ali piled up points. It was hardly artistic. His
jab was a flicker, his right a feather, and he clinched at every chance.
Spinks could do nothing. By the tenth round, all suspense was gone, but
the crowd's din grew ever louder. At ringside, Cosell had abandoned ob-
jectivity, and he couldn't contain his emotions: here was Ali, bringing the
goods once more, before an audience of seventy million people in eighty
countries. "One has the feeling," Cosell said in the fourteenth, "that Bob
Dylan struck the note in his great song, 'Forever Young.'" By the fifteenth,
Cosell was citing Shakespeare—Ali, he said, wanted "to make assurance
double sure."

The drama of the fight's conclusion had more to do with the atmosphere
in the Superdome than with the outcome. "This crowd, pushing in on us!"
Cosell said. "Dangerous crowd conditions!" Ali had barely reached his
corner after the final bell when the ring was mobbed. Somehow Cosell
reached Ali through the scrum, but his mike cord was jostled and cut off,
and scuffles were breaking out. Then, the decision: scoring by rounds, the
tallies were 10–4–1, 10–4–1, and 11–4, all for Ali—he was the first three-
time heavyweight champion.

And when Muhammad Ali, formerly Cassius Clay, winner of fifty-six
fights and loser of three, was lifted onto his supporters' shoulders, in acknowledgment of this final accomplishment, along with all the glories and
ambiguities that had preceded it, he offered an image with which even the
dissenters could not quarrel. In keeping with his tempered approach to
what he promised would be his farewell, he did not open his mouth wide
or roll his eyes or windmill his arms. Looking into the camera, he raised a
hand to his lips and blew a kiss good-bye.

BLOOM IN THE SHADOWS

In summer 1978, as Ali prepared for his rematch with Leon Spinks, boxing remained as organizationally chaotic as ever and as ethically challenged, but by one crucial criterion—public interest—it was thriving. Ali had been a potent ambassador; the sport was all over television. Now, the sport needed a new star to anchor it, a role traditionally played by the man at the top of the heavyweight division. Succeeding a great champion had proved thankless, however. Fans resented James J. Corbett for conquering the great John L. Sullivan. They scorned Gene Tunney as a pallid replacement for Jack Dempsey, and they simply ignored Ezzard Charles, the next champion after Joe Louis. Whoever took the stage after Ali faced an impossible task. As Thomas Jefferson said when he came to relieve Benjamin Franklin as minister to France: "No one can replace him, Sir. I am only his successor."[1]

The man who wound up with the job was, in some ways, uniquely qualified to take it on: he was tough, hardworking, persistent, and, unlike Ali, as practically minded as a blue-collar laborer. But his resentments often squelched whatever goodwill he gained. Thus, he would not only be compared unfavorably with Ali—as anyone would have been—but also become disliked by many fans and some in the press. This hostility would peak when he faced off against a white challenger in boxing's last great race fight.

But in Las Vegas, as Larry Holmes warmed up in the Caesars Palace ring on June 9, 1978, all this lay in the future. The job before him: beat Ken Norton, holder of the World Boxing Council version of the heavyweight championship.

By winning, Holmes could acquire a piece of the title while also answering his critics, who doubted his talents and questioned his fortitude. Holmes burned to silence those he felt had sold him short, in boxing and in life. His efforts were powered by an expansive vision of a world aligned against him, a useful motivational outlook for any fighter—and a renewable energy source for a man who would spend his career boxing a shadow.

★

Larry Holmes was born on November 3, 1949, in Cuthbert, Georgia, where his parents, John Henry and Flossie Holmes, worked in the cotton fields. Holmes's memories of Georgia were not extensive, though he remembered vividly, as Joe Louis did about Alabama, the red clay soil. Mostly he remembered being poor, living in a crowded shack with eleven siblings and no plumbing, and sleeping under a corrugated-metal roof that rattled when it rained. In 1955, the family packed up and moved to Easton, Pennsylvania, fifty miles north of Philadelphia, an important transport hub and industrial center in the Lehigh Valley. John Henry soon left his family behind, and Flossie raised her children alone, relying on welfare and other generosities.

A seventh-grade dropout, Holmes ran with a tough-guy crowd for a time, embarking on a brief career as a thief. Mostly, though, he worked—at factories; at the Ingersoll-Rand foundry in Phillipsburg; at a rug mill, where he sprayed rubber onto the backs of carpets; at a quarry; and finally as a truck driver for Strong Wear Pants, where he earned $3.50 an hour. He considered himself a bad kid, but his mother remembered him as the boy who, whenever she needed money, would go to the flowerpots on the porch and pull out what he had stashed.

Holmes was nearly twenty when he began competing as an amateur boxer, but he compiled a 19–3 record, and he and his mentor, Ernie Butler, a former professional fighter, eyed a chance at making the U.S. Olympic team. In addition to being a good teacher and an honest man, Butler had a remarkable connection: he knew Angelo Dundee. One day, Butler took Holmes up to Deer Lake, where Ali's famous training compound was under construction. It was only about an hour's drive from Easton. "You're gonna be pretty good," Ali told Holmes after a few rounds of sparring, sending him back to Easton proudly sporting a shiner.[2] He outfitted the kid with new boxing equipment and told him to come back.

Holmes's goal of emulating Ali, Frazier, and George Foreman by winning Olympic gold ran aground in the Olympic trials at West Point, where he was beaten by Duane Bobick, a Minnesota fighter touted as boxing's next White Hope. The manner of Holmes's defeat brought him infamy: he was disqualified in the final round for excessive holding. The Bobick loss would haunt Holmes, tagging him as a fighter who lacked heart, especially after someone fabricated a story that he had tried to crawl out of the ring. It circulated for years.

Undaunted, Holmes turned pro in March 1973. Without the financial backing that bankrolled Ali and Frazier, he was a working-class boxer trying to learn his craft and draw attention in an era dominated by not one or two but three all-time great heavyweights. He began working regularly with Ali at Deer Lake, where he was soon recognized as the best among the sparring partners, and fighting on the undercards of Ali promotions. His style mimicked that of his boss: as tall as the champ, at six foot three, and with a slightly longer reach, of eighty-one inches, Holmes developed a punishing left jab nearly the equal of Ali's, and he often held his hands low, as Ali did, convinced that he could get punches off quicker that way. Like Ali, he would prove to be a classic boxer, disassembling opponents rather than overpowering them. His ring nickname, the Easton Assassin, had more to do with his local roots than his style of fighting.

At Deer Lake, Holmes had a close seat at the Ali circus, and he never forgot Ali's generosity. Ali didn't even mind when Holmes briefly went to work for Frazier, whose training camps operated on a different model: all business. Smokin' Joe broke Holmes's ribs in one session. But Frazier, too, was a generous boss. Between the two great rivals, Holmes had a master-class tutorial for succession to the throne.

He left Ali's employ in 1975, determined to build his own name, and he compiled an undefeated record. Butler was soon elbowed aside by Don King, who was collecting young heavyweights, looking for the next big star. King thought little of Holmes, though, and often treated him with contempt. The promoter was a master of creative accounting and routinely cut Holmes's agreed-upon payouts after fights. When Holmes explored fighting for King's promotional rival, Bob Arum, King told him: "If you do, I'll have your legs broke."[3]

But Holmes kept winning, and on March 25, 1978, with his record at 26–0, he finally met up with a real contender: Earnie Shavers, possibly the hardest puncher in heavyweight history, though he never became a champion. Shavers had come within a punch or two of knocking out Ali in 1977. Fighting on national television, Holmes boxed Shavers silly over twelve rounds, making the bald knockout artist look like an amateur.

Holmes's win propelled him to the top of the heavyweight rankings. One week earlier, the World Boxing Council had stripped Leon Spinks of the

heavyweight title that he won from Ali in February and awarded its title to
Ken Norton. The WBC's move marked a turning point in the title's history.
For two decades, the WBC and the WBA had made a mishmash of boxing
governance, muddying the sport's once-distinct weight classes with "junior"
and "super" divisions and recognizing their own titleholders. By the 1970s,
most weight classes had two "champions." Starting in 1978, the heavyweight
title would be split, too, for the most part.

Oddsmakers thought that the thirty-three-year-old Norton's experience
would prove too much for the twenty-eight-year-old Holmes, but, showing
the questionable strategic judgment that characterized his career, Norton
opted to start slowly and wait for the younger man to tire, an approach that
conceded too much to Holmes's boxing skills. Sure enough, Holmes started
fast. With his sharp and accurate left jab, he set the tempo and controlled
the action. Norton plodded after him, not punching enough to make a difference. After seven rounds, Holmes had built a large lead.

Norton came alive in the eighth round, when he began breaking through
Holmes's defenses with his own left jab and then with his money punch,
the left hook. From the eighth round through the eleventh, Norton rallied,
banging a weary-looking Holmes to the body and pinning him on the ropes.
Holmes's critics thought his legs too skinny for a heavyweight, and those
legs seemed to be failing; they warned that he lacked a knockout punch,
and he couldn't keep Norton off him; and they doubted his heart, and now
Holmes found himself in a desperate struggle against a battle-hardened
veteran.

Summoning the inner resources he supposedly lacked, Holmes made an
all-out charge for the title in the thirteenth round, battering Norton with
combinations. Norton looked spent, but somehow, in the fourteenth, he
surged, and now Holmes looked tired again. As both men slumped on their
stools, the crowd in Caesars Palace, whipped into frenzy by the seesaw action, sensed that the fifteenth and final round would decide the fight. They
were right: all three judges had it scored even going into the final frame. If
Holmes wanted to be heavyweight champion, at least by the WBC's lights,
he'd have to win one more round.

At first, the fifteenth looked as though it would belong to Norton, as he
banged Holmes to the head and body with heavy left hooks. But Holmes
traded back, and they fought furiously at close quarters. With a minute left,
Norton pinned Holmes on the ropes with his hook, but Holmes fought him
off again. He was no longer the mobile boxer, using the perimeter of the
ring, but a stationary warrior, slugging it out. Everyone in the pavilion stood
as the two fighters threw whatever they had left. Norton nailed Holmes

with another hook; as the seconds wound down, Holmes scored again and hurt Norton; at the bell, Norton landed one last hook. They tapped each other and tottered to their corners.

It appeared that Norton had the edge in the final frame, but two of the judges saw the round for Holmes, and by that one-point margin—143–142 on their cards, while Norton prevailed by the same margin on the third— Holmes was the winner by split decision. He could now call himself a champion, of sorts. Yet even his most loyal boosters wouldn't have envisioned all that lay ahead.

★

In July 1979, having won his title back from Spinks the past September and sat on it for as long as he could, Ali finally announced his retirement. The World Boxing Association set up a tournament to determine his successor—excluding Holmes, the WBC champion. That was how it worked: if you held the "other" title, you weren't even ranked by the competing organization. By then, Holmes had already been busy, defending his version of the title. His competition looked weak, but then thirty-four-year-old Earnie Shavers scored a first-round knockout over Norton, setting up a September showdown with Holmes in Las Vegas. Holmes was guaranteed a $2 million payday.

To tune up for it, in June 1979, Holmes took a fight in New York with Mike Weaver, a heavily muscled ex-Marine with nine losses on his record. The networks ignored it. For the fire-sale cost of $150,000, the upstart cable TV network, Home Box Office, purchased the rights. HBO was just finding its footing. It had languished for several years, with a small subscriber base, until 1975, when it helped pioneer the use of communications satellites to deliver signals for broadcast. In 1979, when Holmes fought Weaver, only sixteen million American households had access to cable, and only a fraction of those subscribed to HBO.

Coming in at a career-high 215 pounds, Holmes expected an early night, but Weaver turned out to be the challenger of every champion's nightmares: the supposed pushover who can fight. Weaver shocked the Madison Square Garden crowd in the fourth and fifth rounds, hurting Holmes, first with his good left hook and later with a right. Trying to evade the punches, Holmes went down near the ropes. The referee ruled it a slip, but to many, it appeared to be a genuine knockdown. Holmes gathered himself and went back to boxing Weaver, building a wide lead on the scorecards, but the battle was punishing, and he could not find a way to end it. In the tenth round,

Holmes ran into the challenger's left hook again and looked unsteady. The Shavers payday was in jeopardy—and all for a modest purse in a fight that Holmes didn't have to take.

Risking the title needlessly was a gambler's behavior, not a quality that people associated with Holmes. And yet, underneath Holmes's caution lay a desperado. As a teenager in Easton, he had once approached a white man waving a shotgun in a gas station after a racial scuffle had broken out. "Come on, punk, you ain't gonna do a damned thing," Holmes said, walking toward him and snatching the gun out of his hands.[4]

Now, in the eleventh round against Weaver, Holmes gambled again, un-corking a right uppercut with everything he had behind it. The punch left Weaver splayed on the canvas. He beat the count, but in the twelfth, Holmes battered the exhausted challenger until referee Harold Valan stopped the fight. Holmes had passed a champion's test: winning on an off night.

Yet the Weaver fight only emboldened Holmes's critics, and some felt that a resurgent Shavers would beat him. Stung again by criticism, Holmes trained devoutly and came in at a sleek 210 pounds, armed with a fight plan to use his jab and move laterally to avoid Shavers's power. The plan worked flawlessly at the outset. Holmes's rapier jab tore deep cuts over both of Shavers's eyes, and after six rounds, the Ohio slugger looked not only bloody but exhausted.

But in the seventh, Shavers grazed Holmes with a looping right, backing him up, then stepped forward with another right, thrown over Holmes's lowered left. Holmes went down. Shavers had hit him point-blank with his kill shot; it looked like the fight was over.

Another Easton story: the teenage Holmes worked at a Catholic recreation center, where it was his job to close up and shut out the lights. One night, a group of older guys were playing basketball and didn't want to leave. Holmes shut the lights off. One of them decked him and put the lights back on, and the basketball game resumed. Holmes got up and shut the lights off; they decked him again, and the game resumed. They kept knocking him down; finally, they went home because Holmes kept getting up.

He got up against Shavers, too, standing on jellied legs at first and look-ing to clinch and buy time. Shavers swung wildly, missing by several feet. Holmes recuperated second by second, coming to himself and retaking control as the fog in his head cleared. He survived the round and then resumed his dominance of the fight. Shavers's eyes had been sliced like a cutlet, and he was so tired that he could barely keep his arms up. In the eleventh, with Shavers perched helplessly against the ropes, referee David Pearl stopped it.

Coupled with his gritty win over Weaver, Holmes's triumph over Shavers served notice that it would take a mighty effort to unseat him. He had internalized the calculus: keep winning, and the cash keeps flowing; but lose, and everything is up for grabs. Something else was driving Holmes, too: he wanted to win recognition as "one of the great heavyweight champions in the sport's history."[5] First, he had to be accepted as the legitimate champion, and developments soon worked in his favor. In March 1980, six months after Holmes beat Shavers, Weaver won the WBA title. Since Holmes had beaten Weaver in a title fight the year before, *Ring* magazine declared Holmes the true champion. In time, the public came to see him that way, too.

But Holmes soon had another loose end to tie up: Ali wanted to fight again. Don King touted various grand scenarios: Ali–Holmes in the 165,000-seat Maracana Stadium in Rio de Janeiro[6] or in a 100,000-seat soccer stadium in Cairo, in a bout to be attended, King promised, by President Jimmy Carter and Egyptian president Anwar Sadat.[7] Finally, a more conventional arrangement prevailed: Ali and Holmes would meet in Las Vegas, at an outdoor pavilion near Caesars Palace, on October 2, 1980. Ali was promised $8 million; Holmes would earn $4 million. King called it the Last Hurrah.

★

Ali's attempts to revive the old banter could not disguise the fact that his comeback lacked a compelling rationale. He was returning, he said, to become the first four-time heavyweight champion, but he was already the only three-time champion. The most obvious motivation was money.

Ali had little to show for the more than $40 million that he had earned in the ring. Some of it had gone to taxes, some of it to the high toll exacted by the Nation of Islam and the legions of followers on the payroll, and some of it on lavish spending and bad investments. Ali was also coming back because retirement didn't suit him. Inside the ring, he was a creator; outside it, he was subject to the same gravitational laws as ordinary mortals. He dabbled in acting; he boxed exhibitions; he made public appearances. He tried, briefly, to get hold of his finances. And in February 1980, he attempted some amateur diplomacy for the Carter administration as it tried to build international support for an American boycott of the 1980 Summer Olympics in Moscow after the Soviet Union's invasion of Afghanistan. Carter's people got the idea to send Ali on an African tour to persuade reluctant countries to join the boycott. The trip proved disastrous; the targeted countries were unsympathetic, and Ali had no answers when reporters grilled him about American policies.

Ali's glib public ease had deluded many into believing that he could find a second career as a statesman. What good were his post-boxing ambitions if they were not achievable? Within a few weeks, he had put the word out that he was ready to come back, and his words went straight to God's ear— or to Don King's, which was more or less the same thing. The promoter was happy to oblige him.

Longtime observers of Ali, like the *New York Times*'s Dave Anderson, saw the comeback as a cautionary tale of ego and despair: the great athlete, floundering for an encore, seeks to recapture the past. But as the fight neared, Ali began changing minds, tapping into the nostalgia of writers and fans. He had always delivered before. And when, in the final weeks, he showed off a lean body and a youthful face, aided by black hair dye that dabbed away the gray near his temples, he looked like the Ali of 1970. He weighed in at 217, his lightest since Zaire.

It was all cosmetic. Ali's weight was down in good part through the use of Thyrolar, a thyroid medication prescribed for him, with dubious diagnostics, by his manager Herbert Muhammad's personal physician. The drug sapped his energy, accelerated his heartbeat, dehydrated him—and put him in medical danger as the fight approached, especially since Ali, treating the pills like vitamins, tripled the dose.

Ali entered the ring outside Caesars Palace on Thursday night, October 2, 1980, in the old way: exhorting the crowd, looking confident as ever. When Holmes arrived, Ali ramped up his clowning, trying to get to Holmes and being held back by Angelo Dundee. They met in the center of the ring, and Ali kept his chatter going, his eyes wide. Holmes just glared.

At the bell, Holmes charged after Ali, throwing punches as if he wanted to end the fight fast. His jabs and body punches crackled in the desert air. Hands held high, Ali talked to Holmes, but otherwise he threw barely a punch, except for a grazing right at the bell that missed. In the second round, Holmes backed Ali into the ropes, and Ali, talking between his gloves, unleashed a barrage of profanity that stunned the champion, who could scarcely recall his mentor using a curse word. The crowd whooped, remembering the Rope-a-Dope and George Foreman, but Holmes pounded Ali without any depletion of energy.

It took several rounds of this before the reality of the fight set in. By the fourth round, Ali's left eye was blackening. By the fifth and sixth rounds, only the diehards could tell themselves that Ali's performance was part of some grand strategy. Holmes did not "go easy" on Ali, as some believe. He probably could have done more, and he took no pleasure in the drubbing; but by any standard, he battered his old boss, trying to knock him out or make him quit. He could do neither, and he was amazed by Ali's refusal to fall.

In the ninth, Holmes ambushed Ali with a combination, finishing with a right hand, and Ali moaned and covered up on the ropes, turning sideways, as if to hide from the punishment. At ringside, Howard Cosell, his tones growing more mournful with each round, called for the fight to be stopped. But hadn't Ali earned every chance? And if he wanted to go out on his sword, hadn't he earned that, too?

In Ali's corner, Dundee gave his fighter one more round—the tenth. It went like all the others. Then Herbert Muhammad, Ali's longtime manager, gave a signal from ringside. "I'm stopping it," Dundee said. Drew "Bundini" Brown, Ali's longtime court jester, begged him to let the fight go on. "One more round, one more round!"

"Fuck you!" Dundee hollered, pulling away from Brown, as referee Richard Green approached. "I'm the chief second!" Dundee said to Green. "I stopped the fight!" Green raised Holmes's arm in victory. The crowd made little noise. It was as if Holmes had won a fight in a graveyard, before an audience trying to be respectful of the dead.

On his stool, Ali sat with his head bowed. He would not leave boxing with that final, perfect image, from New Orleans. Ali's failure negated nothing that he had accomplished, but it ruined his gift for endings. And worst of all, he wasn't convinced that this was the ending.

Within days, he was talking about fighting again, certain that he could do better. He did have a sliver of excuse: the dangerous Thyrolar regimen had robbed him of any chance to compete. He reasoned that, without the drug and fighting at a more comfortable weight, he would perform better his next time out. But boxing commissions in the United States wouldn't license him, and so Ali's career approached its final irony: the man with the world's most recognized face would go slumming to find a matchmaker and a venue in which to perform.

It took him more than a year, but in December 1981, he had finally found a willing promoter, a mysterious and felonious entrepreneur named James Cornelius; a venue, the decaying sandlot baseball stadium in Nassau, the Bahamas; and an opponent, Canadian heavyweight champion Trevor Berbick, who had gone fifteen rounds with Holmes earlier that year. To make things worse, Ali wasn't alone in his comeback try: Joe Frazier, thirty-seven, was returning to the ring, too, after more than five years away. Joe's fight, in Chicago against a once-and-future convict named Jumbo Cummings, took place eight days before Ali's. Cummings had no trouble hitting Frazier over ten rounds, but the judges generously called it a draw. Joe blustered about fighting again but never did.

Up to the last minute, it looked as though financial problems might nix Ali–Berbick, but it came off as scheduled, on December 11, 1981. Almost everything about the event was a fiasco. The promoters brought only two sets of gloves; each fighter on the card used one pair or the other. There was no timepiece; someone dug up a stopwatch. There was no bell; an engineer found an old cowbell. Its lifeless din suited the proceedings.

A month away from his fortieth birthday, Ali weighed in at 236, his heaviest ever, but he fought much better than he had against Holmes, and after five rounds of the scheduled ten-rounder, the bout looked competitive. But the awkward Berbick overpowered Ali the rest of the way to win the decision. It was, finally, Ali's last fight.

"I know it's the end," Ali said. "I'm not crazy. After Holmes, I had excuses. . . . No excuses this time. I'm happy. I'm still pretty. . . . I think I came out all right for an old man."[8] He hadn't come out all right, but the world didn't know that, not yet.

★

Depressing as it was, Ali–Holmes had set a new record for a live gate—$5.7 million. More importantly to its hosts at Caesars Palace in Las Vegas, in the thirty days prior to the opening bell, the casino made $30 million, its greatest one-month haul ever and more than double its monthly average. Boxing had found its new mecca. Caesars Palace, and eventually other Vegas venues, held a trump card that New York and other old-line fight cities, with their suffocating taxes and other traditional costs, couldn't match: they used championship boxing as a lure to attract high-roller gamblers to the casino. Seemingly limitless gambling revenue gave Vegas the power to bankroll huge site fees and lavish fighters' purses (and promoters' cuts). "New York is all washed up as the boxing capital of the world," said gambler Lem Banker, an old chum of Sonny Liston's. "You got everything here. Gambling, girls and good times."[9]

Yet, while Vegas proved lucrative for promoters and championship-caliber fighters, a casino-driven sport was unstable and vulnerable, more and more reliant on the big event for relevance. The Vegas environment, with its high stakes, magnified boxing's anarcho-capitalist model. As the 1980s launched technologies from the personal computer to portable music to VCRs to cable television, Americans wanted more of everything, from music to movies to home conveniences. They wanted more sports, too—all the time, if possible, and soon, via the cable channel ESPN, they would get it. But they also increasingly expected a level of professionalism, even corporatism, for their sporting dollar. The major sports delivered on these demands; athletes reached new levels of achievement, broadcasting became more sophisticated, and sports merchandising grew into a globally profitable industry. Only in its pioneering role in the development of cable television and, eventually, pay-per-view, did boxing seem in step with this new world. Otherwise, the sport looked anachronistic: based in a desert; surrounded by showgirls, mafiosi, and gamblers; and overseen by almost comically corrupt sanctioning organizations. And when, later in the 1980s, boxing began vanishing from network television, the sport started its long slide to the margins of American life.

It wasn't in Larry Holmes's power—or any fighter's—to do much about this. He just kept winning—even in November 1981, when, facing an unheralded challenger, Renaldo Snipes, he was dropped by a right hand in the seventh round. Holmes got up, but he was so unsteady that he crashed into the corner post. As he had against Earnie Shavers, though, he cleared his head and went on to win. He was an outstanding champion by any measure, but he remained a non-presence in the broader culture. He didn't help his cause with a prickly personality and a tendency to speak beyond the confines of an internal editor. Years of being shortchanged financially by Don King and underestimated by boxing insiders had fed a fierce pride that made it hard for him to hold his tongue. He regularly groused that he didn't get the credit that he deserved, and his manner often suggested bitterness, even as he grew rich.

Holmes had just turned thirty-two, and some saw his struggle against Snipes as a sign that his grip on the title was weakening. And a challenger stood waiting to wrest it from his grasp: Gerry Cooney, a six-foot-six, 225-pound slugger who had marched up the heavyweight rankings with a series of early-round knockouts, in which he showed a pulverizing left hook. It made little difference that his record was built on wins over fighters well past their primes. What mattered was that Cooney, from Huntington, Long Island, could punch and that he possessed one other priceless asset: he was white.

It had been some time since a white heavyweight had been taken seriously. The best white heavyweight of the 1970s was Jerry Quarry, who couldn't get past men like Norton, Frazier, and Ali. The title had long been an all-black possession—and when the champion was not the mercurial Ali but the stolid Holmes, white America's boredom was palpable. Cooney aroused public interest as no Holmes challenger had done. And so the buildup began for boxing's last great race fight—a White Hope against a black champion, seventy-two years after Jim Jeffries had been called from his farm to take on Jack Johnson.

★

The white/black equation turned Holmes–Cooney into a national event, one with an uncomfortable racial undercurrent. The idea that a white fighter might actually win the title—and against a black champion, to boot—made the bout something like a real-life version of Sylvester Stallone's *Rocky* movies. *Rocky III*, in fact, was just hitting theaters, and *Time* put Cooney on its cover with Stallone—minus Holmes. *Sports Illustrated* also led with Cooney on its cover, relegating Holmes to the inside flap. Many whites rallied around Cooney, who had been shrewdly marketed. His managers, Mike Jones and Dennis Rappaport, were dubbed the Wacko Twins for their unorthodox promotional efforts, which included trying to allow one of their fighters to wear a yarmulke in the ring. Rappaport boasted that Cooney would become "the first billion-dollar athlete."[10]

The Wacko Twins had smartly built Cooney's record while risking little, allowing the momentum of his victories to build while his punching power and gentle personality won people over. It worked: the Cooney bandwagon became unstoppable. The twenty-five-year-old stood to become a rich man, win or lose against Holmes, and his appeal—with its undeniable racial component—gave the challenger an almost unheard-of 50–50 money split with the champion. Holmes and Cooney were promised $10 million each, making their showdown the richest fight in history at the time.

Some couldn't resist stoking racial passions. "This is a white and black fight," barked Don King. "Anyway you look at it, you cannot change that. Gerry Cooney: Irish, white, Catholic." Rappaport fanned the flames, too. "I do not respect Larry Holmes as a human being," the manager said. "I don't think he's carried the championship with dignity."[11] Rappaport touted Cooney with a phrase that neatly combined racial appeal with racial deniability: "He's not the white man; he's the right man."[12] Though he mostly tried to stay above the fray, Cooney made his views known, too, saying that Holmes had no class. The two had several unpleasant run-ins.

But no one brought up race more often or more angrily than Holmes himself. To Holmes, the celebration of Cooney was just another slight in a career that, he felt, had been marked by a lack of appreciation. Cooney and his well-greased path to stardom scraped Holmes raw. He called Cooney the Great White Hoax or the Great White Dope. "If Cooney wasn't white, he'd be nothing," he said. "I'm going to cut him, hurt him, open his lip, blacken his eye—for justice's sake. . . . He jumped ahead because he's white."[13] Most people listening to these diatribes didn't know that Holmes moved in integrated circles and generally regarded people, of any color, with the skepticism that had helped him survive. He wasn't wrong that being white had helped Cooney, but his rancor created a plausible, if misleading, impression of a racist.

Even if Holmes had behaved like Joe Louis, white Americans might have rooted for Cooney, anyway. Many identified with Cooney as an Irish American; others may have rooted for the Catholic, the New Yorker, or the knockout puncher. It's never wise to assume that someone of a certain race is rooting for another athlete of the same race for purely racial reasons; a generation earlier, white fans had already proved that they could root for a black fighter (Joe Louis) against white opponents.

Still, some whites clearly *were* rooting for Cooney out of racial animus. Holmes's house was vandalized; his mailbox was blown up, and someone painted racial epithets near the entrance to his house. Bullets smashed windows on his restaurant in Easton. And he began receiving threats, some over his home phone, which included warnings like: "Don't start up your car tomorrow, nigger."[14] All the race talk and symbolism had some worried that an ugly atmosphere was brewing.

The thermometer had hit 100 earlier that day—Friday, June 11, 1982—but by fight time, the temperature in Las Vegas had dropped to 89 degrees. With the lights and cameras, it would be hotter than that for the fighters. Overhead, from the rooftops of every major hotel overlooking Caesars Palace, police snipers kept an eye out for trouble.

★

One of the biggest American sports events of the early 1980s, the Holmes–Cooney fight took place near midnight for the old-media culture—just before the rise of 24/7 sports news and programming. Like all big fights then and now, it would not be shown on free TV. In 1982, pay-per-view was still a few years away. Closed-circuit television—available for the price of a ticket to a movie house, auditorium, or arena—remained the only way to see such fights live, short of going in person. And, in a pre-Internet era, the only source of live news about the fight was radio, which could not broadcast the action but could provide news updates. The signs of change were looming, however: HBO would rebroadcast the fight first, beating out ABC by a week.

Holmes's fight plan was to move laterally, mostly to his left, away from Cooney's left hook; work the left jab to control the tempo, throw off Cooney's rhythm, and set up other punches; and stay off the ropes and out of corners. Cooney walked toward Holmes, trying to cut off the ring and set him up for the knockout blow, the left hook. In the second round, Holmes showed his own punching power. He threw boxing's classic combination, the left jab–right cross—"the old one-two"—and the right landed squarely on Cooney's jaw. The punch stole Cooney's balance. He wobbled weirdly away from Holmes and tumbled to the floor. He got up and did not seem badly hurt, but the knockdown made some wonder if the worst fears about Cooney were about to be proved true—that he was merely a marketing creation.

But Cooney rallied. The big man landed his left hook in Rounds 3 and 4, mostly to Holmes's body, and his left jab, which became an important weapon. Near the end of the fourth, a Cooney hook dug deep into Holmes's right side, and the champion walked slowly back to his corner. In the next round, the men fought evenly. After five rounds, the fight was close, with the knockdown giving a slight edge to Holmes.

In the sixth, Holmes's one-two wobbled Cooney again, and he opened up on Cooney until the challenger, ducking to get away, nearly went through the ropes. Just before the bell, Cooney fired off three straight left hooks at Holmes's body and head, the last one landing on the chin. It was Holmes's round, but Cooney was proving that he was a fighter.

As grimly focused as anyone had ever seen him, Holmes took command, directing the geometry of the fight and maintaining an economy of movement in the punishing heat. He pumped his punishing left jab but also faked it often, moving his arm up and down, never letting Cooney know when the real thing was coming. He was clearly in it for the long haul.

Cooney, too, seemed resigned to a long fight, not coming after Holmes as aggressively as expected. He had never fought beyond the eighth round, and he worried about pacing himself. And he had fought just six rounds in two years. The Wacko Twins had gotten him his pot of gold and his shot at the title, but they hadn't prepared him to win it. Talented but unproven, Cooney was in with a great pro who had passed every test.

As the bout wore on, fatigue and Holmes's tugging efforts to tie him up sent some of Cooney's body punches south of the belt line. In the ninth, he landed a left hook to Holmes's groin that made the champion double over. The referee, Mills Lane, a no-nonsense circuit judge in Nevada, took two points away from Cooney and gave Holmes several minutes to recover. The fight reached its climax in the tenth round, when Holmes and Cooney took turns landing heavy punches. Holmes had stopped circling and seemed willing to trade; he took several Cooney left hooks for his trouble. At the bell, both men tapped each other in acknowledgment.

Cooney had little left after the tenth. His jab was now a flicker, his left hook a weary swivel. Lane penalized him another point in the eleventh for another low blow. In the thirteenth, Holmes, sensing that the end was near, raked Cooney with right hands. The challenger staggered backward along the ropes, beginning to fall, his left glove touching the canvas—constituting a knockdown, under the rules—but hooking the ropes with his other arm and popping back up. Cooney's trainer, Victor Valle, stormed into the ring and embraced him, stopping the fight. Holmes was the winner and still champion.

Postfight discussion centered on Cooney's low blows and the judges' scorecards, which had Holmes ahead after twelve rounds, 113–111, 113–111, and 115–109. Had Cooney not been penalized three points, he would have been leading on two of the three cards in a fight that Holmes had dominated. As with everything else surrounding the bout, the judging controversy prompted speculation about race. To others, weird scoring went with the territory in boxing.

Cooney–Holmes is remembered today less for the fight than for its climate.[15] Since Louis–Schmeling in 1938, no heavyweight fight involving black and white fighters had aroused such interest and generated such tension. Some felt that the racial polarization suggested that America hadn't come very far since 1910, when Johnson faced Jeffries in Reno, a few hundred miles away. But the 1982 event bore little relation to its predecessor. The most obvious difference: there were no race riots and no deaths. Media bias in favor of Cooney paled when compared with the quasi-mystical favoritism shown Jeffries. Holmes's well-earned win prompted no lamentations, as Johnson's did. And most tellingly, those who sought to make racial appeals had to deny that they were doing so. In 1910, no denials were necessary.

In beating Cooney, Holmes had defended his title for the twelfth time and run his record to 40–0. His title reign had been characterized by versatility and resilience. Against Cooney, he had added the missing chapter: victory against a young challenger in a multimillion-dollar super-fight. At thirty-two, Holmes had his crowning victory. But he couldn't let go of his edge.

"I'm sorry I'm not what all you guys want me to be," Holmes told the press. "I'm not Muhammad Ali. I'm not Joe Louis. I'm not Leon Spinks. I can't continue to prove myself again and again. I wasn't born to be those people. I was born to be myself."[16]

Sounding his perpetual theme—that he never got credit—Holmes ignored the fact that he had been getting credit for years. "It is not hyperbole to say that he has proved himself a great fighter," Michael Katz wrote in the *New York Times* in 1981. "It is easy now imagining a Larry Holmes beating a Jack Dempsey."[17] The universally respected trainer Eddie Futch said that Holmes could have beaten Joe Louis. Another revered trainer, Ray Arcel, called Holmes "the most underrated heavyweight champion in history."[18] Holmes confused "credit" with being liked, and his complaint about proving himself sounded an odd note, too, because a champion's job is to prove himself, again and again. When champions get sick of doing that, they can retire.

Now Holmes seemed to be leaning that way. He was financially set. He had established his mother in comfort and built himself a lavish mansion in Easton with a swimming pool shaped like a boxing glove, but he was more sensible about money than most champions. Early on, Holmes had promised himself that with each championship purse, he would buy a piece of property. After some rest, he resolved to keep on fighting. There was still money to be made, and more buying to be done.

★

When Holmes fought Cooney in June 1982, the American economy was still mired in a brutal slump. By November of that year, unemployment crossed 10 percent, and voters punished Ronald Reagan's Republicans in the midterm elections, ousting twenty-six GOP congressmen. But starting in 1983, Reagan's promised recovery began, and over the ensuing "seven fat years," the American economy achieved the greatest expansion in recorded annals up to that time: eighteen million new jobs, $30 trillion worth of new goods and services, a roughly 50 percent rise in net asset values, and an unemployment rate down to just over 5 percent. Consumer spending exploded—including credit-card spending, which Americans would eventually learn to rue. Former sixties radicals, now middle-aged parents, marched up the ladder in the corporate, professional, and academic worlds. A cohort half a generation behind them became known as yuppies—young, upwardly mobile professionals. Like all periods in American history, the 1980s were better for some than for others, but even critics could concede that the country seemed more confident; and even boosters could admit, if they were honest, to being concerned over where this unprecedented rout of mammon and material was tending. When Gordon Gekko, the villain in one of the era's iconic films, *Wall Street*, uttered his famous line—"Greed is good"—millions of viewers cheered.

Toiling forever in Ali's shadow, Larry Holmes enjoyed his crowning moment by beating Gerry Cooney on June 11, 1982.
Associated Press

Fictional characters like Gekko were far more recognizable to the average American than Larry Holmes, who never did break through with the public. But he did reflect his time in some ways. In describing himself as "a boxing executive," in his no-nonsense focus on dollars and cents, and in his concept of the heavyweight title as just an alternative means to upward mobility and wealth accumulation, he was the perfect heavyweight champion for a decade that made heroes out of financiers and CEOs.

But except for his fights with Cooney and Ali, Holmes was a bystander to the decade's biggest promotions—because for much of the 1980s, the lower-weight divisions eclipsed the heavyweights in notoriety and even in purse money. Boxing found an economy-size Ali replacement in Sugar Ray Leonard, who fought like a 147-pound version of Ali—throwing blindingly fast combinations and adding touches of showmanship. Leonard, Thomas Hearns, Marvin Hagler, and Panama's Roberto Durán fought a series of multimillion-dollar bouts during the 1980s. The only member of the quartet to beat all the others, Leonard stood alone as boxing's competitive and commercial king. His special status aroused resentment in his rivals, and it must have grated on Holmes as well, as if Ali were spinning off clones to torment him.

Yet he kept on. In 1983, Holmes defended his title four more times, though only once against a serious challenger—Tim Witherspoon, a twenty-five-year-old Philadelphian with only fifteen pro fights. Holmes looked all of his thirty-three years, and he was lucky that the bout was scheduled only for twelve rounds. (Recent deaths in the ring had prompted calls to eliminate fifteen-round fights, and the WBC was first to do so.) Badly hurt in the ninth round, Holmes fought back, as always. He won a well-deserved decision, but the close call reminded some of Ali's late-career wins against Jimmy Young and Ken Norton.

Ali himself had been circulating around Caesars Palace the week before the Witherspoon fight, not his normal habit. He was being paid $1,200 for two weeks—"walking-around money," as it was known in the trade. Worse than seeing Ali reduced to such a gig was hearing the thickness of his speech. Boxing writers asked Holmes about it.

"Ali's always talked low to me," Holmes said. "His voice is lower than it was in 1971, 1973, 1975. . . . He's hard to understand. But I don't look for him to stumble when he walks and stutter when he talks," he said. He clearly felt protective of Ali.

A year later, Ali revealed that he had Parkinson's syndrome, a disorder technically distinct from Parkinson's disease but manifesting the same symptoms: slurred speech, stiffness of movement, tremors. His symptoms worsened over the years, but he accepted his condition and, with his fourth and final wife, Lonnie, made a go of what life had left for him. Some found his predicament inspiring, others depressing.

Even his toughest critics had to grant him two final triumphs. In 1990, on the eve of the Persian Gulf War, Ali journeyed to Iraq, where Saddam Hussein held fifteen American hostages. The fear was that Saddam might use them as human shields. The idea that Ali might persuade Saddam to release them was not as crazy as it sounded, given Ali's fame in the Muslim world, though his previous stint as a diplomat for President Carter had been a flop. This time, though, Ali scored a knockout, emerging with the fifteen Americans and flying home with them.

Six years later, in Atlanta, site of the 1996 Summer Olympics, Ali, his upper body wracked with tremors, took the torch from the final runner and carried it to the cauldron to light the Olympic flame. His hand shook so badly that it didn't look as though he could get it done, but after a few anxious moments, the fire ignited. It was Ali's last great American stage.

All of this, the suffering and the twilight glory, were far in the future in May 1983, when the press sat around with Holmes, talking with him about his mentor. When Holmes looked at Ali, one reporter asked, did he see a warning to himself?

"Life is a warning," Holmes said.[19]

★

By mid-1985, Holmes had been champion for seven years, and his career-long struggle to get more control of his earnings and act independently of the dictates of Don King and the World Boxing Council was bearing fruit. When a third governing body, the International Boxing Federation, was formed in 1983, Holmes struck out on his own. He relinquished the WBC belt and accepted recognition as heavyweight champion of the new IBF. The WBC quickly moved to determine a new champion; the WBA "title" had changed hands almost fight to fight. Clearly, Holmes was the real champion—but with the advent of the IBF, three men would now claim the honor.

Holmes had become boxing's version of a venture capitalist, viewing each fight as another revenue infusion—though the wins were getting harder and harder. He now owned a restaurant and bar and a string of real-estate properties; Easton had named a boulevard Larry Holmes Way. Holmes's hometown devotion recalled Rocky Marciano's affection for Brockton, Massachusetts. That wasn't the only similarity between the two champs.

Holmes had run his record to 48–0, one win shy of equaling Marciano's unbeaten mark.

On September 22, 1985, Holmes put his unbeaten record and heavyweight title on the line in Las Vegas against Michael Spinks, the unbeaten light heavyweight champion (175 pounds) who was moving up in weight to take him on. Michael had built a career that far surpassed his older brother Leon's, in part because he had what Leon lacked: comparative mental stability. His success puzzled some observers because Spinks, though talented, with a potent right hand, was an awkward and often unimpressive-looking fighter. He threw punches in improvisational spasms, from strange angles, without his feet set, moving backward or sideways, the punches whipping in like horizontal rain. His oddness masked a ferocious competitive will.

To make the move up in weight, Spinks worked with a pioneering sports physiologist, Mackie Shilstone, who would later train tennis great Venus Williams and other stars. Spinks followed a regimen that broke most of the century-old rules of boxing training. He lifted weights—always a pugilistic no-no—and ran sprints, whereas fighters had always focused on distance running. And he followed a 4,500-calorie-a-day diet composed heavily of carbohydrates. Shilstone worked him over physically, nutritionally, and mentally, and Spinks came into the ring in Las Vegas at a muscular 200 pounds.

The usual approach of heavyweight champions, when faced with challenges from the vice presidents of lower divisions, is to assert their superior size and power early. But Holmes came out cautiously against Spinks, using his jab but not following up with his right—perhaps worried about a pinched nerve in his vertebrae that made throwing the punch more difficult. From the outset, he seemed off his game—or just old.

After making it through a few rounds, Spinks grew more confident, venturing inside and letting loose with combinations, then darting back out of Holmes's range. As the rounds passed, Spinks made his sorties, scoring points with judges and with the crowd. His oddness as a fighter was never more evident: he dropped his hands in mid-ring, walked away from Holmes like a man strolling through a park, then spun back around and punched. At one point, with Holmes bearing down on him, Spinks even began arguing with his own corner from mid-ring. After ten rounds, Spinks had pulled in front, but he had a long way to go: the IBF still mandated fifteen-round fights.

Though tiring, Spinks stepped up his game down the stretch, outfighting Holmes. The champion's puffed eyes made him look aged beyond his years. He came out for the final round needing a strong finish. Instead, it was

Spinks who surged, throwing his jazzman combinations and forcing Holmes to come find him. Holmes couldn't.

Chuck Hull, the ring announcer, collected the scorecards and read the verdict: 143–142, 145–142, 145–142—all for Michael Spinks, the winner by unanimous decision and the new heavyweight champion. Spinks was the first light heavyweight champion to win the heavyweight title; he and Leon were the first brothers to win it. And Spinks had denied Holmes—now 48–1—his quest of equaling Marciano.

As he stepped to the podium for the postfight press conference, Holmes had Marciano on his mind—and not just Rocky. Several members of the Marciano family had made the trip to Las Vegas. With the Marciano clan in his line of sight, Holmes felt his simmering resentments come to a boil.

"If you really want to get technical about the whole thing, Rocky couldn't carry my jockstrap," Holmes said. There would "never be a white champion as long as black fighters are fighting the way they are," he declared. He accused Peter Marciano of "freeloading off your brother," telling him, "You can go back to Boston, or wherever you come from . . . and shove Boston up your ass."

Then, as if waking from a dream, Holmes began walking back his words. "Rocky was one of the greatest fighters of all time," he said. "I would have loved to have met him." He didn't want Rocky to be forgotten, he said. "If I hurt anybody's feelings, I'm very sorry for doing that."[20]

The backlash began immediately. "Now, sadly, Larry Holmes will be remembered as much for his diatribe Saturday night against Rocky Marciano as he will for his seven-year reign," wrote Dave Anderson. "When he finally lost, he didn't know how to."[21] The outburst did lasting damage to Holmes's public image.

At first, Holmes said that he would retire—a sensible choice, given such a bitter end. But on reflection, he decided that he wanted another shot at Spinks. The match was arranged for April 19, 1986, in Las Vegas.

Holmes went after Spinks from the opening bell, even throwing Spinks to the canvas in the first round. He walked Spinks around the ring, popping his left jab and unleashing his right. The first five rounds belonged to the former champion. Then Spinks got busy, returning to his hit-and-run tactics. As Holmes tired, Spinks fought his way back into the match. In the fourteenth round, Holmes landed a right that staggered Spinks, but he was too tired—and perhaps, at thirty-six, too old—to follow up. Spinks escaped; the bout went to the scorecards; and once again, the decision, this one a highly contentious split verdict, went against Holmes.

Talking to HBO's Larry Merchant afterward, Holmes made no attempt at conciliation. "The judges, referees and promoters can kiss me where the sun don't shine—and because we're on HBO, that's my big black behind."[22] And with that, Larry Holmes headed back to Easton for good, having driven poverty far from his mother's flowerpots and earned a place as one of the great champions. He was sure now—just about positive—that he could walk away from boxing.

★

By April 1986, when Holmes and Spinks fought again, the 1980s had taken on their distinctive character. The tone was set from Ronald Reagan's White House. If the sixties epitomized transformation and conflict, the eighties were marked by a hunger for achievement and acquisition. Getting ahead was the mantra, much to the chagrin of those who saw the new American optimism as a betrayal of the sixties social conscience.

But there was another side to the eighties: festering social problems, the AIDS crisis, and an epidemic of crack cocaine in America's crime-ridden inner cities, many of which, like Detroit and some portions of New York, had been barely governable for years. Gangs and drug lords became familiar figures to Americans, if only through television programs like *Miami Vice*. If the economy was soaring for most suburbanites, some ghettos had deteriorated beyond even the dire conditions of the sixties, when Lyndon Johnson's social programs had been put into place to alleviate them. That these efforts had failed was clear from the generational poverty, gang violence, and frightening amorality of teen thugs. Worst of all were the stories of children doomed to live in these neighborhoods—children with incarcerated or drug- or alcohol-addicted parents, whose only mentors, it seemed, were older criminal children or gang leaders.

What must it be like, Americans wondered, to be a child in such a world? And what would such a child look like as an adult—if he even made it that far? The sport of boxing would soon supply an answer.

KID DYNAMITE

It's easy to look at the photo of the young boy, knowing whom he would grow up to become, and say that he has a haunted face. It's a good face, with the sweetness of youth and eyes that suggest kindness or at least the capacity to be kind. But already, what he knew of life was contest: inside the walls of his home, out in the streets of Brooklyn, on school playgrounds. He never met the man listed on his birth certificate as his father. The man he knew as his father was a pimp who surfaced occasionally. His mother worked as a prison matron at the Women's House of Detention in Manhattan. When she lost her job and the family moved from Brooklyn's Bedford-Stuyvesant neighborhood to Brownsville, the picture darkened. Bed-Stuy was gritty; Brownsville was a shooting gallery. His mother went on welfare and never worked again. She and her friends sat in the apartment at night, drinking, smoking, and playing cards; some waited for calls from johns. Lorna Mae Tyson's son saw every kind of violent altercation, including ones resolved through the strategic use of boiling water.

The neighborhood toughs called him "little fairy boy."[1] They routinely robbed him for money and food. He stopped going to school, except for breakfast and lunch; no one missed him. One day, he escaped a beating from a gang of older boys by finding a way to be useful: shooing the boys' pet pigeons off the rooftops of adjacent buildings and back to their owners. He soon came to love the birds. One day, when some punk took his pigeon and ripped the bird's head off, the fairy boy exploded, knocking the older kid out cold in the Brownsville streets. Standing over his victim, he noticed how people were magnetized to him.

The stories of most great boxers, like those of superheroes, usually have some version of an origin myth: the moment when the hero discovers his powers. John L. Sullivan at the Boston opera house, Max Baer at the Livermore square dance, Joe Louis playing hooky from his violin lessons in Detroit, Cassius Clay reporting his stolen bicycle to the Louisville police: heavyweight history brims with such moments. And Mike Tyson's epiphany on the mean streets of Brooklyn was as transformative as any that had gone before. It had to be. As it turned out, the boy from Brownsville would become the final towering figure in the American heavyweight lineage. And, as if fate had worked it up that way, he would bear in his gestures and consciousness traces of his predecessors—bringing them all back to life one more time.

★

The January 6, 1986, issue of *Sports Illustrated* arrived in mailboxes in late December 1985, just after Christmas. On the cover, under the headline "Kid Dynamite," it read: "Mike Tyson: The Next Great Heavyweight—And He's Only 19." The feature story, written by William Nack, was the first exposure that most Americans would have to the Tyson saga. It told of a grim upbringing, of a child deprived of childhood. And it told of how the youngster—born Michael Gerard Tyson, on June 30, 1966, in Brooklyn— embarked on a prolific robbing and mugging career. By age twelve, nearly two hundred pounds, imposing and amoral, he would break into cars, burglarize homes, and mug old ladies. Repeatedly picked up by police, he became a familiar figure in youth courts.

His mother watched in despair as he sank into a life of crime. "How can you steal?" she asked him. "I never stole anything in my life."[2] She "never had any hope for me, going back to my infancy," Tyson remembered.[3] His reading skills were judged at third-grade level, and he was put on Thorazine for supposed hyperactivity.

After run-ins with the police, Tyson was often sent to Spofford Juvenile Center, an infamous youth correctional facility in the Hunts Point section of the Bronx. Tyson spent so much time there that he would recognize middle-aged men decades later as alums. But it was at Spofford that destiny first tapped him on the shoulder. One day, the facility arranged for a screening of *The Greatest*. The boys were dumbfounded when the film ended and Muhammad Ali himself walked in, having come on a goodwill

Mike Tyson at about ten years of age
Boxing Hall of Fame

visit. Tyson never forgot seeing Ali that day and the feeling that surged in him: that he wanted to be great, too—at something.

Tyson wound up at the Tryon School for Boys in Perth, in east central New York State. He got into trouble again, and it took more than one adult guard to subdue him. Some of his rage was real and some calculated: he wanted to get transferred to Elmwood cottage, where Bobby Stewart, a former National Golden Gloves champion who worked as a counselor, trained kids in boxing. Teach me to box, Tyson pleaded.

Stewart agreed, on two conditions: that Tyson start behaving and that he commit himself to his schoolwork. Tyson's reading level shot up to seventh grade in a matter of months. In the ring, he learned quickly, and his punching power amazed his tutor. Stewart felt that there was something special about Tyson, something overwhelming, immense. Seeking an expert opinion, he called Cus D'Amato in Catskill, New York, where Floyd Patterson's old trainer, now in his seventies, lived in a fourteen-room farmhouse and trained boxers. Tyson and Stewart made the trip to Catskill to audition for the guru. After D'Amato and his top trainer, a young former fighter named Teddy Atlas, watched the thirteen-year-old Tyson spar two rounds, Stewart asked him what he thought. They were looking at the future heavyweight champion, D'Amato said.

To have another heavyweight champion was D'Amato's dream. He had operated for years as an exile from boxing, every bit as irascible and peculiar as when he had managed Patterson. He retained the scars from his wars with the various boxing powers—and his distinct psychological convictions about character and the uses of fear. Age had diminished none of D'Amato's zeal to prevail over his enemies, real and perceived. The boy, Cus felt, had the potential to be the youngest heavyweight champion in history—and possibly the greatest. He would not only win glory for himself but also redeem Cus and put to shame the whole small-minded, weak-souled world.

By the time Lorna Mae Tyson died in 1982, Tyson, sixteen, had moved into the Catskill home with D'Amato—Cus became his legal guardian—and D'Amato's common-law wife, Camille Ewald. So began years of spartan preparation for an agreed-upon destiny. Tyson stayed up at night shadowboxing, and he sometimes slept with boxing gloves on. Every day, he watched fight films from the largest collection in the world—twenty-six thousand in all—the property of Jim Jacobs, a boxing historian and former world handball champion, and Bill Cayton, a businessman and boxing buff. Jacobs, who also owned the world's largest comic-book collection, was a longtime friend of D'Amato's; he and Cayton had spent years acquiring and restoring archival films, and their holdings comprised a veritable Library of Congress of boxing history. Tyson also read about the lives of old champions, devouring the books in D'Amato's boxing library and exhausting the guru with questions about John L. Sullivan, Jack Johnson, and Jack Dempsey.

In October 1980, D'Amato took Tyson up to Albany to watch the closed-circuit television broadcast of Muhammad Ali's ill-fated comeback fight against Larry Holmes. After the depressing bout, D'Amato placed a call to the fallen champ. He told Ali that he had a kid who wanted to talk to him—and who would someday avenge him by beating Holmes. Tyson got on the phone with the Greatest, already pledged to a mighty task.

D'Amato's distinctive tutelage rebuilt Tyson's psyche. "Cus wanted the meanest fighter that God ever created, someone who scared the life out of people before they even entered the ring," Tyson remembered. D'Amato told Tyson that he would make the world forget his heavyweight predecessors; he would reign with the gods. "I was this useless Thorazined-out nigga who was diagnosed as retarded," Tyson wrote, "and this old white guy gets ahold of me and gives me an ego." But D'Amato skipped lightly over ethics. Character, a D'Amato byword, seemed to matter only insofar as it concerned reaching a goal and obliterating obstacles—including people—standing in the way. After Tyson made advances on the eleven-year-old sister of Teddy Atlas's wife, Atlas held a gun to the fighter's head and threatened to kill him if it happened again. The next day, D'Amato fired Atlas and replaced him with Kevin Rooney, another former fighter and protégé. D'Amato's vision of steering Tyson to the prize trumped all else.

By the early 1980s, Tyson was a prominent star in youth boxing circles, but in the 1984 Olympic trials, he was beaten by Henry Tillman, who went on to win the gold medal in the Los Angeles games. Tyson's aggressive style was better suited to pro boxing, anyway. D'Amato schooled him in his trademark "peekaboo" style, made famous by Patterson, but Tyson was a very different fighter. D'Amato taught him to throw punches with "bad intentions"—not to probe but to hurt.[4] Because of his physical limitations—he was listed at five foot eleven but was probably shorter, and his reach was just seventy-one inches—Tyson was destined to be an attacking fighter, but nature had blessed him with devastating power. His left hook, right cross, and uppercuts in either hand were all knockout punches. What really set Tyson apart was not just power but speed. In boxing, as elsewhere, a Darwinian process balances strengths with weaknesses. Great punchers like George Foreman, Joe Frazier, and Rocky Marciano lacked hand speed. Great boxers like Ali—he had the fastest hands ever—or Jack Johnson or Gene Tunney, with their defensive skills, lacked a big knockout punch.

Some of Tyson's predecessors, especially Joe Louis and Jack Dempsey, combined elements of both. But Tyson's hands were probably faster than those of any heavyweight except for Ali and Patterson. And the quicksilver movement of his head and upper torso, bobbing from side to side as he came forward, made Tyson rare in another way: he was a knockout artist with defense, a puncher who didn't get punched much himself.

On March 6, 1985, Tyson, making his professional debut, knocked out Hector Mercedes in Albany, inaugurating a run of early-round knockouts rivaled only by Dempsey's march to the title in 1918 and 1919. Fighting at least once a month and usually more, Tyson racked up the kills. He would win his first nineteen fights by knockout, twelve in the first round. In his early fights, Tyson wore trunks of different colors, usually white; but by early 1986, he had adopted black as his signature color. He styled himself in the imagery of old-time fighters, especially Dempsey, circa 1919, when the Manassa Mauler had entered the ring in Toledo robe-less, his hair cut in the "hobo" style. Tyson cut his hair the same way and approached the ring in a full sweat, wearing only his trunks and disdaining a robe, sometimes consenting to having a ripped towel thrown over him. The symbolism was gladiatorial: he had come to make war and wanted no embellishments. With each win, Tyson added another video image to his collection: men sent halfway across the ring by his left hook or seemingly decapitated by his uppercuts. Cayton and Jacobs, now Tyson's managers, sent videotapes of these destructive feats to the press and television networks, and word got around quickly about Kid Dynamite.

New blood was needed. In spring 1986, Larry Holmes, who had defined the post-Ali heavyweight era, retired after his second loss to Michael Spinks. Spinks held the IBF title belt, but he still didn't seem like a real heavyweight, and the public saw him as just one champion among three—none particularly inspiring. Then Tyson showed up.

★

On December 4, 1985, Cus D'Amato died, at seventy-seven, of pneumonia. On his deathbed, he warned Tyson that he would haunt him forever if he did not go on with boxing. Though devastated, the nineteen-year-old Tyson was determined to fulfill the old man's dream, which had defined his own adolescence. The show would go on, as Cus had wished, and on a bigger stage: Tyson had signed contracts with ABC and HBO to televise several upcoming fights. These bouts would be the first chance for the American public to get a look at him, and what they saw, initially, was disappointing.

Tyson labored in his first real test, against journeyman heavyweight Jesse Ferguson, in Troy, New York. The referee stopped the one-sided bout in the sixth round, the longest a Tyson fight had gone. Tyson's knockout string was broken in May 1986 by James "Quick" Tillis, another journeyman. Fighting like an old pro, Tillis tied Tyson up and frustrated his efforts to put over a big punch. Showing poise, Tyson rallied, wearing Tillis down with body punches on his way to winning a decision after ten rounds. Against Mitch "Blood" Green, a former Bronx gang leader, Tyson won a more decisive ten-round decision. The public had been promised dynamite, but so far there had been no detonations.

It was easy to forget that Tyson was still a teenager. He soon proved that he was more than just hype. After returning to form with quick knockouts of light opposition, he took on Marvis Frazier, Smokin' Joe's boxing son, in Glens Falls, New York. The deeply religious, soft-spoken Frazier was a fringe contender, a skilled boxer without a heavyweight's punch or chin, and one of the finest people ever associated with the sport. His pink robe and trunks suggested kindliness. In black trunks and sockless boots, Tyson exuded menace, and he entered the ring leering at the crowd, pacing back and forth. At the bell, he forced Marvis to the ropes, threw a right uppercut that wobbled him, and then threw another that sent his head snapping upward. Frazier collapsed in a corner; for a moment, it appeared as if he had been killed. Lasting just thirty seconds and seen by millions on ABC, the knockout helped establish Tyson's image as a destroyer.

Jacobs and Cayton expertly guided Tyson's career, gradually stepping up the quality of his opponents and keeping their eyes on the prize: a title fight. By the time the chance came, against WBC champion Trevor Berbick on November 22, 1986, in Las Vegas, Tyson, as novelist Joyce Carol Oates put it, had "become legendary, in a sense, before there [was] a legend to define him."[5] The legend mandated that he beat the rugged Berbick, who had extended Larry Holmes for fifteen rounds and ended Muhammad Ali's career. Like other top-ranked heavyweights of the 1980s, Berbick alternated impressive performances with dismal ones, but he was no one's idea of an easy night.

At six foot two and 218.5 pounds, Berbick towered over Tyson, and he hoped to exploit his reach advantage by using his jab. But he was under attack from the opening bell as Tyson pounded his midsection. Ignoring his plan to box, Berbick instead traded with Tyson. It did him no good, and he was staggered before the end of the first round. Tyson opened the second by knocking Berbick to the canvas with a right. Berbick got up and assured the referee, Mills Lane, that he was okay, but he looked as if he were ready to cry. Standing at close quarters with Berbick, Tyson ripped a right to the body and snapped a short left hook to the head. Berbick's legs gave out, and he fell to the canvas.

Berbick then enacted a memorable physical sequence. Spinning over, he pushed himself upright and tried to stand, but his legs gave out and he fell into the ropes on the other side of the ring. He rose again, almost making it to his feet, but careened across the ring back to where he had started and fell again. Finally, he forced himself up, but his tortured pirouette—so grandiose it almost looked staged—was enough for referee Lane, who waved his arms and stopped the fight.

"Do you think Cus would have liked that?" Tyson asked Jim Jacobs, when the manager rushed to congratulate him.[6] He had fulfilled D'Amato's goal, becoming, at twenty, the youngest heavyweight champion—by the WBC's lights, anyway. "This kid don't let you do what you want to do," Angelo Dundee, who had worked Berbick's corner, said of Tyson. "He throws combinations I never saw before."[7] Tyson's eradication of Berbick was so absolute that critics were already eager to mark him down in history. "We have a new era in boxing!" Barry Tompkins said on the HBO broadcast. "Tyson is much more than merely the youngest boxer to hold a share of the heavyweight title," Dave Anderson wrote in the *New York Times*. "He's the glow of a new dawn, the heavyweight that the boxing public has been waiting for since Muhammad Ali stumbled into the sunset."[8]

★

Rough and intimidating as he was in the ring, Tyson started out as a good guy, with an image as a clean-living, utterly dedicated athlete (he even studied film of his own training sessions). He won goodwill with his earnest personality, including an incongruous high-pitched voice and slight lisp, both instantly memorable. Emulating old-time fighters, Tyson helped vanquished foes up to their feet after knockouts. Even when he said, after beating Jesse Ferguson, that he had tried to hit Ferguson "on the tip of his nose because I try to punch the bone into his brain"[9] or, after topping Berbick, that his goal in throwing right hands was to "bust his eardrum,"[10] his confidence came off less as boastfulness than as youthful determination. "I'm the youngest heavyweight champion of the world and I'm going to be the oldest," he said on the night he conquered Berbick.[11]

Most of all, Tyson was vivid: his background was Dickensian, updated for Brooklyn. His promise to redeem the hopes of an old man who had seen the greatness in him provided a Hollywood-worthy narrative hook; his love of pigeons reminded some of Terry Malloy, Marlon Brando's character in *On the Waterfront*; and the image of Tyson, student of boxing history, watching the black-and-white films by himself cemented the idea that he was destined to be champion. The lineage seemed embodied in him: he was the bearer of its past and herald of its future. "He eats dinner, watches fight films, goes to bed early and is up at dawn to run the roads," William Nack wrote.[12]

The truth was more complicated. Tyson's dedication was real, but he rebelled against the monkish lifestyle more often than people knew, sneaking out to drink, smoke pot, and chase girls. For years, D'Amato and his men smoothed over the scrapes Tyson got himself into with women in Catskill bars or with salesgirls at shopping malls. "He's learning to control himself quite good in the ring," Teddy Atlas had warned D'Amato, before leaving his employ, "but he's not learning to deal with his emotions outside the ring."[13]

For the time being, staying busy in the ring kept these feelings under control. HBO organized an elimination tournament to determine the one and only heavyweight champion. With Tyson involved, stoking public interest, everyone stood to make good money, and HBO secured the cooperation of the alphabet-soup organizations themselves, which normally would never consent to letting "their" champions fight one another.

The unspoken assumption was that, when the dust cleared, Tyson would be the one champion left standing—and, by late 1987, he was. Already holding the WBC belt, he won the WBA and IBF versions with twelve-round decisions over James "Bonecrusher" Smith and Tony Tucker. Beating Tucker made Tyson the unified champion of all three governing bodies. Afterward, Don King, trying to muscle his way into the Tyson action, threw a "coronation" party, draping Tyson in a chinchilla robe, giving him a jeweled scepter, and placing on his head a crown studded with "baubles, rubies and fabulous doodads."[14] The new king looked sheepish but stood by while his court ogled him.

Though milestones in Tyson's career, the Smith and Tucker fights were unsatisfying for the public. Tyson failed to knock either man out or even down, and both fights exposed a flaw that some earlier opponents had revealed: he was not effective in breaking clinches or fighting at close quarters against men adept at tying him up. Smith, in particular, excelled at doing this, though his resolution to clinch Tyson at every turn made for one of the worst heavyweight title fights in history. The six-foot-five Tucker also showed that Kid Dynamite had trouble with boxers who could stifle his aggression.

Tyson's other two 1987 fights, however, showed him in top form. Against the seasoned pro Pinklon Thomas, himself a former claimant of one of the bouncing-ball heavyweight titles, Tyson overcame frustration in the early rounds to score a blitzing knockout in the sixth. And he capped off his year in the ring with a brutal pounding of former Olympian Tyrell Biggs, who had once mocked Tyson for not making the 1984 team. Showing patience and tenacity in one of his best performances, Tyson made Biggs sorry over seven merciless rounds before putting him away. Afterward, he told an HBO audience that Biggs was "crying in there" and "making woman gestures."[15]

For all its imagery of masculinity, the heavyweight title had rarely seen such raw aggression and power. "When he hits you, man," a sparring partner said of Tyson, "he changes the taste in your mouth."[16] For spectators and television viewers, Tyson was a thrilling presence: whether the thrill inspired or horrified was an individual taste. People *wanted* to see his fights, many of them neither knowing nor caring about boxing otherwise. In a decade that perfected spectacle—from the blockbuster Hollywood film to the global, corporate-sponsored rock tour to *Lifestyles of the Rich and Famous*—Tyson was the most visceral spectacle of all. He managed to satisfy a contemporary appetite for sensation while also evoking an archaic, timeless primitivism.

Like great champions before him, he drew attention beyond the ring. Few analyzed him more compellingly than Joyce Carol Oates, the first woman to write seriously about boxing. "As with the young, pre-champion Dempsey, there is an unsettling air about Tyson," she wrote, "with his impassive death's-head face, his unwavering stare, and his refusal to glamorize himself in the ring—no robe, no socks, only the signature black trunks and shoes—that the violence he unleashes against his opponents is somehow just; that some hurt, some wound, some insult in his past, personal or ancestral, will be redressed in the ring; some mysterious imbalance righted. . . . That old trope, 'the wrath of God,' comes to mind."[17]

★

There was one piece of unfinished business. Tyson held all the official heavyweight title belts, but Michael Spinks still staked a claim to being the real champion—and, based on the sound principle that titles are won and lost in the ring, not in backrooms, he was right. Spinks had held the IBF belt before the organization stripped him of recognition in a dispute over who his next challenger would be. But he remained unbeaten, the conqueror of Holmes, the "lineal" descendant of past champions.

That wasn't how most people saw it. To the masses, Tyson was the champion, Spinks something less. Tyson had been fighting regularly and knocking off the division's top names. By contrast, Spinks had skipped the HBO tournament, opting for better money against handpicked opponents, knowing that he could face the eventual tournament winner and make more money overall. This bet proved astute for Spinks financially, but it did nothing for his public stature.

And when a great former champ—Larry Holmes—sought to make a comeback, it was Tyson whom he challenged. The old lion versus the young tiger: here was a venerable theme. James J. Jeffries had come out of retirement to take on Jack Johnson; Joe Louis to face Ezzard Charles and Rocky Marciano; and Ali to fight Holmes. Now it was Holmes's turn. Sitting at home in Easton, listening to the buzz, the thirty-eight-year-old former champion told himself that Tyson was oversold. So when Don King showed up at his door, promising Holmes $3 million, the ever-pragmatic Easton Assassin went into training.

Though Tyson was a heavy favorite, the matchup caught on commercially. On fight night, A-list stars like Jack Nicholson and Barbra Streisand crowded into Atlantic City's Convention Hall. Real estate high-roller Donald Trump sat at ringside with Muhammad Ali. People may not have loved Larry Holmes, but they respected him. He represented stature such as Tyson had never shared a ring with.

Holmes came out for the first round looking more interested in survival than winning. He circled and stayed away from Tyson, but instead of working his left jab, he focused on tying Tyson up. Tyson had grown frustrated with those tactics in previous fights, but he seemed undaunted by Holmes's retreat, moving after him and landing grazing right hands and left hooks.

In the third round, Holmes went after Tyson more, showing a jab that bore some resemblance to its prime form. It was enough to win him the round on some cards. Holmes came out for the fourth looking confident, and he even went up on his toes, drawing cheers. But he carried his arms extravagantly low, Ali-style. On film, Tyson had noted that Holmes always dropped his left after jabbing. Sure enough, Holmes jabbed again, dropping the left. Tyson flashed over his right and hit the target, and down went Holmes. He got up, as always; Tyson cuffed him back down, and he got up again. It looked as though he might survive the round, but as he tried to escape along the ropes, Tyson grazed him with a right and followed it with another—a sickening direct hit, the kind of punch that ends arguments. Holmes crashed to the floor, and the referee stopped the bout without bothering to count.

Afterward, Tyson told HBO's Larry Merchant that he was proud to have Holmes's name on his record. What Tyson didn't say was that he remembered the night in 1980 that he and Cus had seen Holmes batter Ali. He had kept the promise that he made over the phone to Ali—now sitting stiffly at ringside—that he would get revenge.

Other promises, too: Tyson's devotion to his forebears took unique and subtle forms. As his own fights approached, Tyson covered his walls with pictures of old fighters. He liked one from 1910, showing lightweight champion Battling Nelson standing, hands on hips, watching as the referee counted out his opponent, Eddie Lang. Now, after taking out Holmes, Tyson moved to the center of the ring and stood in the same way. It didn't matter that almost no one, outside his inner circle, noticed these gestures or understood the frame of reference. Tyson knew.

What did get through to everyone was Tyson's presence. He became an enveloping figure of the late 1980s. Shirtless, clad in his trademark black trunks, Tyson threw his head back, laughing demonically, in the television commercial for his Nintendo video game, *Mike Tyson's Punch Out!* He made spots for Diet Pepsi, Toyota, and antidrug campaigns. And his appeal soon extended beyond the United States.

Few heavyweight champions had ever fought abroad. Jack Johnson did so out of necessity. Neither Dempsey nor Louis, neither Marciano nor Larry Holmes, had ever defended their titles overseas. George Foreman was a rare exception, defending in one exotic locale after another, from Tokyo to Caracas to Zaire. The ultimate globe-trotter, of course, was Ali, who always emphasized that he was heavyweight champion of *the world.*

Showing signs that he might possess comparable appeal, Tyson journeyed to Tokyo in March 1988 to defend his title against Tony Tubbs in the opening act of what some called the Mike Tyson World Tour. Japanese fans celebrated Tyson, whose warrior ethos had a natural resonance in their country. The media followed him everywhere. "He is a symbol of the United States," said a Japanese man.[18]

The symbol of America did not disappoint. He came down the aisle of the brand-new Tokyo Dome, an indoor venue seating sixty-five thousand, robe-less and ready. His opponent, Tony Tubbs, was a skilled boxer with deceptive agility, considering his unfortunately apt last name: he battled weight problems throughout his career. Yet even at a fleshy 238 pounds, he fought a strong first round, working his jab and punching with Tyson at close quarters. But in the second round, Tubbs stood too close to Tyson and got nailed with a right that sent him into a drunken-looking stumble across the ring. He dropped to the canvas just as Tyson was winding up with an uppercut. His cornermen stopped the fight.

The Tokyo wipeout, for which he earned $9 million, suggested that Tyson was maturing. Against Biggs, Holmes, and Tubbs, he had been overpowering. But three forces were combining to threaten what he had achieved.

The first was the passing of Jim Jacobs, who, in Cus D'Amato's absence, had retained a close link to Tyson and guided his career skillfully. Jacobs's death from leukemia left the champion distraught. The remaining member of the original troika, businessman Bill Cayton, had a cordial but distant relationship with the young fighter.

The second force was Don King, who had had designs on Tyson all along. Knowing that Tyson had no real affinity for Cayton, King worked on him with his well-honed racial-solidarity pitch and used his leverage with the WBC to give himself a role in promoting his fights. Tyson knew King's reputation, but he was unfazed. "I can handle a snake if I keep the lights on," he said.[19] He wasn't the first or last fighter to think so.

The third element was Tyson's marriage to Robin Givens, a twenty-one-year-old costar of the sitcom *Head of the Class*. Tyson had met Givens the previous year and fallen quickly in love. Saying that she was pregnant, Givens pressed Tyson to marry her, and he agreed in early 1988. Givens had attended elite private schools and graduated from Sarah Lawrence College; she also claimed, falsely, to have attended Harvard Medical School. She was mostly raised by her businesswoman mother, Ruth Roper. Many who knew Givens and Roper distrusted them. Not long after Tyson married Givens, she announced that she had had a miscarriage, but some doubt that she was ever pregnant.

From the moment Tyson said, "I do," Givens and Roper became obsessed with his finances and his managerial situation. They wanted to force Bill Cayton out. Don King had the same goal. The struggle for control of Mike Tyson was on.

★

"The big fight doesn't come along so often anymore," wrote Tom Callahan in *Time*, "defined as the kind that can get in people's stomachs and occasionally have trouble staying there. But here it is again, for twelve rounds or less."[20] The last time Callahan had written of such a fight was in 1982, when Larry Holmes fought Gerry Cooney. But Mike Tyson versus Michael Spinks—set for June 27, 1988, in Atlantic City, and billed as Once and for All—crossed another financial threshold. Tyson's purse set a new benchmark: $22 million, plus a percentage of the profits. Spinks had to settle for a guaranteed flat rate—however, his $13.5 million payout was more than any fighter had ever made but for Tyson. The live gate—with ringside seats going for as much as $1,500—would surpass $12 million. These staggering sums were made possible in part by the blossoming of pay-per-view—through which cable subscribers could watch premium events by paying a one-time fee. For Tyson–Spinks, that came to $34.99 per household. But closed-circuit theaters were as numerous as ever. Taken in tandem, the live gate, closed-circuit, and pay-per-view buys pushed the fight's profits into the stratosphere.

Tyson–Spinks was also a major salvo in Atlantic City's intense but short-lived battle to wrest boxing supremacy from Las Vegas. The effort centered on Donald Trump, who paid a record $11 million to host the bout, essentially becoming its promoter. By then a symbol of high-flying 1980s culture, Trump spoke in a style that Tyson could appreciate. "I just keep pushing and pushing to get what I'm after," the future president said. "I like beating my enemies to the ground."[21]

For the first time since Ali had fought Frazier in 1971, two undefeated fighters, both with legitimate claims to the heavyweight title, would meet in the ring. For boxing's remaining purists, Tyson wasn't the true champion—not yet, anyway. "Spinks has the real title, my old title," said Floyd Patterson, "the one handed down from person to person."[22] When asked by late-night host David Letterman which sanctioning organization's title he held—the WBA, WBC, or IBF version—Spinks said, "I represent T-H-E . . . *the* heavy-weight champion."[23] The fight promised unequivocal resolution.

But for most people, the fascination had to do not with history but with Tyson himself. By June 1988, Tyson's ferocity had earned him comparison with Sonny Liston, George Foreman, and Joe Louis. His life outside the ring, with the conflicts mounting—the squabbling managers, the glamorous wife, the grasping mother-in-law, everyone zeroing in on the money—added drama to his persona. Like many champions and stars before him, he wondered if he had any real friends. Unburdening himself to Jerry Izenberg of the *Newark Star-Ledger*, Tyson buried his head in the sportswriter's chest and sobbed for so long that Izenberg had to change his shirt. Tyson's distress, though, was not enough to convince most experts that he could be taken, even by so resourceful a pro as Michael Spinks.

On fight night, the crowd at the Atlantic City Convention Center—packed with the usual glamor figures, for whom Trump's ringside price was a few bottles of champagne—grew restless as the appointed starting time came and went. A dispute had broken out in Tyson's dressing room, where Spinks's manager, Butch Lewis, had made the customary visit to watch the opponent's hands get wrapped and the gloves put on. Lewis pointed to a lump around the wrist of Tyson's left glove and insisted that it

be removed. It was just the laces, Tyson's people said. Lewis kept object-
ing until Spinks's trainer, the venerable Eddie Futch, told him to desist.
Lewis finally left, but his effort to rattle Tyson had backfired. Tyson had
begun punching the walls.

"You know," Tyson said to Kevin Rooney, "I'm going to hurt this guy."[24]
Rooney himself had stoked Tyson's tensions even further a few hours earlier, when he told the champion that he had bet both their shares of the
purse on a first-round knockout. Rooney had to know that Tyson would
catch the reference: it was a direct lift from Doc Kearns, who had told
Dempsey the same thing before he fought Jess Willard in Toledo in 1919.
But Kearns had been dead serious; Tyson couldn't tell whether Rooney
was joking.

Spinks finally entered the ring, to the strains of "This Is It." He looked
composed but detached. Some felt that he was terrified, though this was
not clear from his expression.

Tyson's entrance was meant to conjure thoughts of execution. Instead
of a rap song to serenade him as he came down the aisle, he opted for a
tuneless, industrial soundtrack, a metallic hum that suggested dread. One
Spinks aide covered his ears. Stripped down, Tyson made a contrast with
Spinks, who, wrapped in his white robe, looked like a mummy by comparison. Worse, when Spinks removed the robe, his body was dry, as if he had
not warmed up properly.

The bell: Tyson skipped out, kicking his legs up, almost playfully. Then
he attacked: a right to the head, a left to the body, a right missing to the
head. He forced Spinks to the ropes, and they tied up. The referee, Frank
Cappuccino, broke them, and, as he did, Tyson threw an elbow. Cappuccino warned him to "knock it off."

Tyson rushed, and Spinks held his hands high, firing out jabs at Tyson's
bobbing head, missing. He threw his right—the Spinks Jinx—and missed.
Tyson bulled him to the ropes and landed a clean left hook to the jaw and
a right to the body, just under the heart. Spinks took a knee—the first time
he had been down in his professional career.

"You okay?" Cappuccino asked, as Spinks stood. Spinks nodded. Tyson
rushed in, and Spinks fired his best punch, the right. It missed. Tyson was
throwing a right of his own. His didn't miss, meeting Spinks's onrushing
jaw. He seemed to catapult backward onto the canvas, where he lay for a
moment, his eyes rolling in his head. As Cappuccino counted over him, he
began crawling to his knees. "He's not going to make it," Larry Merchant
said at ringside, on the HBO broadcast. As if in reaction to these words,
Spinks fell forward, nearly going through the ropes. The fight was over at

ninety-one seconds of the first round, the third-shortest heavyweight title fight in history. Mike Tyson was *the* heavyweight champion.

His destruction of Spinks seemed to elevate Tyson to the status of the heavyweight gods. Tyson was "the nearest thing to Jack Dempsey in his prime," said the eighty-something trainer Ray Arcel, who had seen Dempsey fight and had walked one contender after another into the ring to challenge Joe Louis. "He's young and powerful and fast. His punches have speed and he's always applying pressure. I'd love to have seen him against Dempsey, or Louis, or Marciano. I'd love to have seen him against Ali or Joe Frazier."[25] Holdouts maintained that Tyson had more to do before he took his place in the pantheon, but for others, the only question was whether Tyson would have beaten them all—even Ali. Three days after the Spinks fight, Tyson turned twenty-two.

★

Tyson's world now began unraveling rapidly. Don King proved successful not only in severing Tyson's relationship with Bill Cayton but also in cutting his ties with most of the old Catskill circle, including trainer Kevin Rooney, whom Tyson fired for "disloyalty." Tyson was parting ways with the team that had made him the best-managed fighter in history. A Price Waterhouse audit later revealed that Cayton, whatever his deficits in personality, was above reproach. He had even overpaid Tyson over the life of their contract.

Brick by brick, King pulled Tyson's old world apart. So did Robin Givens and Ruth Roper. Mother and daughter were a "package deal," Givens insisted, and together, they seemed intent on driving Tyson to madness. Givens spent lavishly, and the couple's furious squabbling became a fixture of tabloid headlines. On the grounds of his new mansion in New Jersey, Tyson drove his car into a tree, in what some claimed was a suicide attempt. Stories suggested that he had struck Givens and that he was taking antipsychotic and antidepressant medications.

In late September 1988, the couple sat for an interview with Barbara Walters, whose specialty was getting her celebrity subjects to reveal something about themselves that normal people wouldn't let slip to a close friend, let alone to millions of strangers. With Tyson sitting meekly beside her, Givens said that her marriage had been "pure hell," that Tyson was a "manic-depressive," and that he had hit her. Sitting beside Givens, Tyson said little. Viewers were torn between horror at what Givens revealed—if it was true—and revulsion at what amounted to character assassination of her husband on national television. Soon afterward, police were called out

Tyson made his case for greatness on June 27, 1988, when he wiped out Michael Spinks in ninety-one seconds.

AP Photo / Richard Drew

to the mansion after Tyson began tearing it apart. A few weeks later, the marriage was over.

The personal and managerial chaos kept Tyson out of the ring for eight months. He didn't return until February 1989, when he fought England's Frank Bruno in Las Vegas. The bout began raggedly for Tyson but ended in the usual way, with the champion pounding his foe so violently that the referee stopped it in the fifth round. It was Tyson's first fight without Rooney, whom he had replaced with loyalists who lacked Rooney's expertise. Tyson himself looked sloppy. His keen defensive skills, especially his remarkable head movement, had diminished. To the casual fan, though, he looked—and sounded—like the same Tyson.

"How dare these boxers challenge me with their primitive skills?" he asked afterward.[26]

In Atlantic City in July 1989, he needed just ninety-three seconds of the first round to vaporize Carl "The Truth" Williams, who had gone fifteen rounds with Holmes four years earlier. A Tyson left hook sent Williams rocketing backward onto the seat of his pants. He got up, but the referee called it off, not convinced that he wanted more. The Williams knockout brought Tyson's record to 37–0, with thirty-three knockouts.

One serious challenger loomed: 1984 Olympic bronze medalist Evander Holyfield, undefeated as a pro and working his way up the heavyweight ranks. After knocking out Williams, Tyson glared out at Holyfield, who was sitting at ringside. He'd fight Holyfield for nothing, he boasted—in a basement. "The guy who comes back up with the key will be the champion," Tyson said.[27] It was another inspired borrowing: Jim Jeffries had told Jack Johnson the same thing, eighty-some years earlier.

Holyfield–Tyson needed time to ripen. In the meantime, the aborted Tyson World Tour could start again, and soon the usual grandiose rumors were flying: Tyson would defend his title on the property of the sultan of Brunei, or fight near the just-crumbled Berlin Wall, or perform in Taiwan or South Korea or Beijing. But after another long layoff, the first stop was a return to Tokyo, where he would meet an underachieving journeyman named James "Buster" Douglas.

★

The spartan existence of Tyson's early days in Catskill was by now a distant memory. Once a kid who lived to fight, he had become a champion who lived to party. He saw his return to Tokyo as the next stop on a tour of pleasures, and he spent most of his energies on nightlife. Tyson's new lead trainer, Aaron Snowell, urged him to get serious, but Tyson shrugged. "If I get my butt whipped," he said with an odd fatalism for an undefeated fighter, "I'll take the blame."

James Douglas was a talented athlete whose career had been notable for its squandered potential. The book on Douglas: talent but no heart. But Douglas had deeper reserves than most people realized. Intelligent and articulate, with a wry wit, he carried a son's timeless burden: he could never seem to please his volatile, intense father, a respected former fighter who never left the customers unsatisfied, the way his son often did. Douglas's kindhearted mother inspired him most. Visiting her in the hospital, where she was being treated for hypertension, he noticed that she was reading a Tyson biography. She was terrified for her son. "Mama, I ain't worried about that punk!" Douglas assured her. "I'm a killer!"[28] But when his mother died three weeks before the fight, some thought that Douglas might pull out. Instead, he headed to Tokyo with nothing left to lose.

The Tyson–Douglas fight was held Sunday morning, February 11, 1990, in Tokyo—but seen Saturday night, February 10, in the United States, where it was broadcast live on HBO. Blow-by-blow man Jim Lampley and analyst Larry Merchant had called their share of Tyson fights and were familiar with the story lines and themes—and with confident challengers who crumbled once the bell rang. They were careful to be respectful of Douglas but approached the bout with a sense of resignation, as did the *New York Times* and the *Washington Post*, which refused to fly their boxing writers to Japan for another Tyson wipeout, instead assigning their Tokyo bureau reporters to cover the match.

The first surprise came in the opening round, which Douglas won clearly by working a crackling left jab and managing physical distance so that he was always near ring center. He neither ran from Tyson nor stood in front of him but punched and moved and punched and moved again. Tyson did not come out with his usual fury. He stood straight up, his gloves in front of his face in the old peekaboo style but throwing few punches. He looked bored. In the second round, Douglas used his size and reach to keep Tyson away and tattooed the baffled champion with his left jab and combinations. Angered, Tyson pressed, trying to get inside, but Douglas punished him for his trouble. In the clinches, Douglas mauled Tyson and pushed him off. As the bell rang to end the round, Douglas clipped Tyson with another shot— and Tyson did nothing in return.

"Another good round for Buster Douglas," Merchant said.

"He even dominated the exchange after the bell," said Lampley.

The HBO duo of Lampley and Merchant had taken boxing broadcasting to a new level. A seasoned pro with experience in multiple sports, Lampley was a terrifically articulate narrator who also brought deep passion to his subject, rarely missing the drama of a good fight. Merchant was a shrewd, sometimes caustic analyst whose flights of verbal hyperbole sometimes misfired but were always redeemed by his refusal to sugarcoat reality and his marvelously frank interview questions. The two had seen Tyson struggle in early rounds before. But Douglas's command, and Tyson's lethargy, suggested something more serious.

It was the first time in his professional career that Tyson genuinely needed corner expertise—but in Rooney's absence, there was little on hand. In fact, Tyson's cornermen hadn't even come equipped with the basic tools of the trade, including an enswell—a small piece of flat metal with a handle, kept in an ice bucket, used to ward off swelling around the eyes. Instead, Snowell held a latex glove filled with water against Tyson's puffing eyes. And the corner was lifeless, with Snowell whispering instructions in Tyson's ear, imparting no urgency.

In the fifth, Douglas fired a combination good enough to finish most heavyweights: a crushing right followed by a straight left and then two left jabs and a follow-up right, all landing with a thud on Tyson's face. The shouts from Douglas's corner filled the Tokyo Dome, which was otherwise nearly silent, the Japanese being a more reserved audience than American fans. Tyson, his eyes beginning to close, seemed to be shrinking on the TV screen, round by round.

Then it happened. Taking another going-over from Douglas near the end of the eighth round, Tyson, backed up against the ropes, set himself and landed a thunderous right uppercut that dropped Douglas. What would have been expected, even customary, a half-hour earlier came as a surprise now. One of Tyson's heroes, Joe Louis, had done something like this, in 1941, finding the punches to drop Billy Conn when he needed to. But Conn stayed down; Douglas got up at referee Octavio Meryan's "nine." As Tyson crossed the ring to get at him, the bell sounded.

Tyson stormed out for the ninth, looking to finish Douglas, but after weathering the rush, Douglas fired back. An explosion of punches sent Tyson wobbling backward into the ropes. Douglas snapped his head back with a right and then stuck his elbow into Tyson's throat before the referee could break them. It was a shocking sight: the self-styled Baddest Man on the Planet was being manhandled. At the bell, Tyson walked on unsteady legs to his corner.

By now, television sets across the United States were turning to HBO in huge numbers. In this pre-Internet, pre–social media age, people did what they had always done when something remarkable was happening: they picked up the phone and called family and friends. HBO's ratings increased round by round.

His title hanging by a thread, Tyson charged out again for the tenth round and landed a picture-perfect right to Douglas's jaw. Surely Trevor Berbick or Carl "The Truth" Williams or Frank Bruno or Michael Spinks would have crumbled from it—but Douglas had come too far. He tied Tyson up, pushed him off, and began jabbing him silly again. Then he feinted a left and uncorked a right uppercut that snapped Tyson's head up to the rafters—so forcefully that, in Douglas's corner, trainer John Russell thought for a moment that Tyson's head had been punched off his shoulders. Tyson lurched backward, and Douglas finished him off with a left hook. The champion hit the deck.

As referee Meryan counted, Tyson made it to his hands and knees, but instead of trying to stand, he groped for his mouthpiece like a blind man. When a fighter got "knocked out," Joyce Carol Oates thought, it didn't mean that he was knocked out of consciousness—though that sometimes happened—but that he was "knocked out of Time," severed from his relationship with time.[29] Here was Tyson, fumbling needlessly as the seconds tolled—getting up before "ten" was what mattered, yet he first seemed intent on restoring some kind of rudimentary order: *must find mouthpiece*. He found it, put it back in—backward—and made it to his feet at eight, but he could barely stand. Meryan waved the fight over, and Tyson fell into his embrace.

Only now did the Tokyo Dome sound lively. In America, the sound would have built round by round as the dimensions of the upset took shape, and the ending would have brought bedlam. The quiet atmosphere was somehow fitting, as if the fight had taken place in some bizarro universe, where a superman's powers were null and void.

"This makes Cinderella look like a sad story, what Buster Douglas has done here tonight," Merchant said. "I would be willing to say it's the greatest upset in boxing history."[30] A champion whom some already ranked with the immortals had lost to a 42–1 underdog.

There was hardly time to register the shock before a postfight controversy erupted, courtesy of Don King. The promoter wanted Douglas's victory nullified, since the challenger had been given a "long count" in the eighth round, when Tyson knocked him down. King argued that the referee, Meryan, was two seconds behind the count of the knockdown timekeeper, whose count he was supposed to follow. This was true, but it was not unusual, and the referee's count is the only one that matters in the ring—as Jack Dempsey had discovered in 1927. Douglas, clearly cognizant, had punched the canvas in frustration when he went down. He listened closely to Meryan's count and got up at the referee's "nine," though he certainly cut it close. No matter: King got the WBC and WBA to suspend recognition of the result, pending review. To his surprise, the media ridiculed his efforts to steal the title from Douglas. Seeing that they had no public support, the WBA and WBC announced that they would uphold the outcome. King abandoned his protest, and Tyson himself conceded that he had been beaten fairly.

Just after the fight ended, the phone rang in the New York home of Thomas Hauser, who was writing a biography of Muhammad Ali. It was Ali, calling from Los Angeles. "Do you think folks will now stop asking if I could have beaten Tyson in my prime?" he asked.[31]

Explanations for why Tyson had lost tended to fall into three categories. Maybe Tyson had been overrated all along. He'd always had those physical limitations—the lack of height, the short arms—and fighters before Douglas had made him look ordinary. Faced with his first great test in the ring, he had failed to persevere. Arrogance and overconfidence provided another plausible explanation: clearly, Tyson had not seen Douglas as a serious threat, and he had not prepared himself. Finally, others saw Tyson's downfall as evidence that he had peaked early as a fighter; his high-voltage style was never meant for a long career.

That career was bound to be even shorter when you have earned tens of millions of dollars by twenty-two and attained every dream you've ever aspired to, ten times over. Like Alexander the Great, whom he admired, Tyson wondered what was left to do. Without an answer, he lapsed into apathy and decadence. Would losing humble him and inspire renewed commitment? After his defeat, Tyson figured that he had "become so big that God was jealous of me."[32] These were not the thoughts of a humbled man.

Yet one defeat was not enough to dispel his drawing power or erode his mystique. On the contrary, it added to his fascination. It was easier to believe, as many did, that he would win his title back than to reckon with the likelihood that what had been shattered in Tokyo could never be put back together.

★

A lifetime resident of Columbus, Ohio, Buster Douglas was given a champion's welcome home, getting a key to the city from the mayor, and he waved to cheering crowds. But Douglas soon realized that people considered him a temporary champion; he had caught Tyson on an off night. He found

The greatest upset in boxing history—James "Buster" Douglas knocks out Tyson in Tokyo, February 11, 1990.
AP Photo / Kyodo / Mitsuru Sakai

himself an afterthought not only to Tyson but also to the man who, sitting at ringside in Tokyo, had expected to challenge Tyson next: Evander Holyfield, the number one contender. Though Tyson's people argued that he deserved an immediate rematch with Douglas, the new champion agreed to defend first against Holyfield, on October 25, 1990.

Born in Atmore, Alabama, in 1962, Holyfield grew up in Atlanta, which remained his home base. He first entered the American radar screen in the 1984 Los Angeles Olympics, where he suffered an unjustified disqualification in the semifinals and settled for a bronze medal in the light heavyweight division. Holyfield endeared himself to viewers with his gracious handling of the misfortune. His humility would define his public persona, along with his devout religiosity. Like most fighters, he had grown up poor, but his character was shaped by a devoted mother, who expected upright behavior and pushed her son to find something that he could excel at in life. Fond of reciting Bible verses, Holyfield spurned Tyson's hedonistic lifestyle, but his gentlemanly comportment sometimes obscured what made him special: he would prove the most tenacious heavyweight competitor since Muhammad Ali himself.

He started his professional career as a "cruiserweight," a new classification for 175- to 190-pound fighters created to bridge the growing gap between the 175-pound light heavyweight limit and the typical modern heavyweight, who fought at weights well beyond 200 pounds. After winning a world title at that weight, Holyfield began the process of bulking up for a move into the heavyweight division, where the real opportunities were. (Suspicions of steroid use would trail his career, though he never failed a test.) He had the height (six foot two) and reach (seventy-seven inches) to make the transition. And if he would never be the biggest heavyweight, he was the most dedicated and most determined. He employed a battalion of fitness specialists, and his work with weights, aerobics, and nutrition blazed a new path in boxing. His sculpted physique resembled that of an NFL running back more than a fighter.

With the knowledge that the winner would fight Tyson, fan interest was high in Holyfield–Douglas. But Douglas had sunk into depression, feeling his mother's loss and drained by a bruising battle with Don King for promotional control of his career. By summer, he may have weighed as much as 300 pounds. Even when Steve Wynn, owner of the Mirage Hotel in Las Vegas, where the fight would be held, got him a hotel suite with a sauna, Douglas ordered room service from the sweat chamber. At the weigh-in, he tipped the scales at 246—fifteen pounds heavier than he had been in Tokyo. Holyfield came in at 208, with the body-fat content of a mockingbird.

It was no contest. Holyfield, lean and hungry, peppered Douglas with combinations, rarely missing his endomorphic target. CompuBox, the statistical technology that tallied the number of punches thrown and landed, showed the challenger connecting on sixty-six of one hundred punches over the first two rounds. In the third round, Douglas made an amateur mistake: he threw an uppercut from long range, leaving himself wide open. Holyfield came over the top with a stiletto right hand, and Douglas dropped to the canvas. He lay there, eyes clear, showing no inclination to rise as he was counted out, surrendering the title he had won so valiantly, with barely a whimper. Now the crown had passed to Holyfield, Atlanta's favorite son, the third heavyweight champion of 1990.

★

For most of the public, the term "heavyweight champion" still signified one man: Tyson. As with Ali, his nonpossession of the title seemed incidental, a nettlesome technicality. When he got back into the ring, he looked, at least superficially, like the Tyson of old. In June and December of 1990, he beat two borderline contenders in vintage fashion: by first-round knockout. Both men looked terrified and seemed to take the first opportunity to bow out.

Tyson then tangled with highly ranked contender Donovan "Razor" Ruddock, a big Jamaican with faulty boxing skills but a left uppercut that he called the "Smash" and a defiant ring personality. Tyson–Ruddock became a double feature, in March and June of 1991. The first bout was a rollicking slugfest that went seven rounds before the referee, Richard Steele, made a controversial stoppage, awarding the bout to Tyson, with Ruddock badly hurt but seemingly able to continue. In a grueling rematch, Tyson knocked Ruddock down twice but could not finish him off. He won a twelve-round decision.

The Ruddock bouts revealed, first, that Tyson's critics were right: he was easier to hit now and threw fewer combinations, tending to load up with one or two punches at a time. Second, Tyson had adopted a new public persona: the goon. The rivals engaged in epic trash talk, the highlight, or lowlight, of which came when Tyson told Ruddock before the rematch: "I'm gonna make you my girlfriend. . . . I'm gonna make sure you kiss me with those big lips of yours."[33] Tyson became more profane in public and more contemptuous of opponents. His hostility seemed to increase as his skills declined.

Later in the summer of 1991, contracts were finally signed for Tyson–Holyfield, to be held November 8, 1991, in Las Vegas. But within weeks, news broke that a grand jury in Indiana was investigating a sexual-assault charge against Tyson. In September, Tyson was indicted; he would go on trial for rape. For a time, the promoters insisted that the bout would go on as scheduled, since Tyson's trial wouldn't begin until afterward. But in early October, Tyson pulled out of the fight, citing a rib injury. His legal troubles may have been the real reason.

Tyson went on trial in Indianapolis in January 1992. The charges stemmed from his visit in July 1991 to the Indianapolis Black Expo, an African American extravaganza that included concerts, art, and a beauty pageant. Tyson arrived intent on partying and carousing. On the expo's second day, he visited the pageant contestants. The girls swooned over Tyson, and he locked eyes with nineteen-year-old Desiree Washington, Miss Black Indiana and a freshman at Providence College. Tyson got her number.

Tyson did not call Washington until after one in the morning of the next day, when Washington was ready for bed. She agreed to get dressed and meet him. He picked her up in his limousine and took her back to his hotel. Tyson said that Washington knew why they were going there. Washington said that she thought they were stopping there briefly and then heading back out. She hoped Tyson would introduce her to famous entertainers at the expo. She had even brought her camera with her.

Once inside the room, however, Tyson made his intentions known. In Washington's version, she tried to leave but he would not let her, pinning her on the bed and raping her. When it was over, she rushed back home and, at her parents' urging, reported the crime to the police.

Tyson told a different tale: they had had consensual sex, just as they had planned to do all along. When it was over, Tyson asked Washington if she wanted to stay overnight. She declined, and Tyson did not escort her out or offer a ride back to her hotel. Maybe his rudeness had motivated her accusation, Tyson suggested.

Tyson's defense team, hired by Don King, did him no favors. The lead attorney was Vince Fuller, who had gotten King out of a tax mess some years back and also represented would-be presidential assassin John Hinckley Jr. Fuller's self-defeating closing argument was that Tyson was an out-of-control, sexed-up beast and that Desiree Washington should have known better.

The verdict came on February 10, 1992: guilty. Tyson received a six-year sentence, which could be reduced by half with good behavior. Wearing an oversize suit—he looked at least thirty pounds over his fighting weight—Tyson was escorted out of the courtroom in handcuffs and transported to the Marion County Correctional Institute.

Tyson's conviction prompted varied reactions. Women's advocates hoped that it might be a turning point for women to report "date rape," then a somewhat new term in American life. (A year earlier, William Kennedy Smith had been acquitted in a high-profile "date rape" trial.) Attorney Alan Dershowitz, who handled Tyson's unsuccessful appeal, maintained that his conviction was a travesty of justice, pointing to withheld evidence and exculpatory witnesses not permitted to testify. Years later, some jurors would express second thoughts.

Many in the black community saw Washington as an opportunist who had entrapped a hero. For the most conspiracy-minded, the facts of the case were almost irrelevant: Tyson was the victim of a setup. White America, always frightened by black men's physical prowess, had found a way to get him out of the picture. It was the Jack Johnson story, all over again. Tyson's conviction made him notorious, but it also added a critical dimension to his legend. He was already a hero to the new gods of the black inner city—rappers and hip-hop moguls—the physical embodiment of their musical rage. In the years ahead, his stature would reach new heights in a subculture that celebrated black aggression and mythologized black persecution.

Even by the standards of American celebrity, few had shot into fame and fortune and crashed more ignominiously, in such a short span of time, as

Tyson had. For those who loved boxing, or who just loved watching Tyson, it was hard not to feel cheated. Wasn't he just getting started? The Tyson World Tour, the testing rivalries, the lion growing older, the final crescendos—these chapters had been torn out of the book.

★

"The heavyweight division is reeling without Mike Tyson," *Sports Illustrated* opined shortly after the rape verdict, painting a picture of uninspiring fighters battling over a diminished title.[34] As it turned out, though, the title was poised for its last great run. The characters would include the current champion, Evander Holyfield; a rising contender, Riddick Bowe, who hailed from Tyson's Brownsville neighborhood; Lennox Lewis, a British/Canadian boxer of imposing size and skills; and Tyson himself, when he emerged from the Indiana jail.

One other figure would join them: a former heavyweight champion, a man half-forgotten by the time Tyson came around, who would captivate the country and show, one last time, the power of the lineage in the national imagination. He had once carried a flag around the ring; now it was as if he bore a torch, a living witness to what had gone before and what remained—and what was passing and never to return.

END OF THE LINE

By 1992, when Mike Tyson went off to prison, the heavyweight title was marking one hundred years in the American consciousness. It was in 1892 that James J. Corbett had beaten John L. Sullivan at the Olympic Club in New Orleans, winning the heavyweight championship while wearing five-ounce gloves. Since then, the title had become an institution inextricably bound up with America and Americans. Tyson embodied these identifications: he was both global celebrity and national symbol—whether of America's power or violence, opportunity or poverty, or whatever else, depended on how you saw him.

The new champion, Evander Holyfield, lacked such a hold on the American psyche. But no one doubted his commitment, and a Tyson–Holyfield match had emerged as boxing's next big event even before Tyson lost his title to Buster Douglas. Under normal circumstances, Holyfield's win over Douglas in October 1990 would have cleared the way for the big showdown. Douglas took his $25 million payday into retirement. Tyson was the obvious number one contender; his legal troubles were nearly a year in the future.

But the prerogative of every heavyweight champion since John L. Sullivan has been to take the best-paying opportunities for the smallest amount of risk. When top money could be found for less strenuous endeavors—in the ring or out—those opportunities went to the top of the pile. What if Holyfield could earn as much money fighting a forty-two-year-old grandfather as he could squaring off against Tyson? And what if the American public wanted to see that match? Then Tyson could wait a little longer.

And so it was that Holyfield signed to defend his newly won title against George Foreman. Yes, *that* George Foreman—though the man who would step into the ring against Holyfield bore little resemblance to his former self. By 1991, Big George, as he was now called, had become one of the most popular figures in American life, orchestrating a reinvention that few could have imagined.

★

On March 9, 1987, in Sacramento, California, thirty-eight-year-old George Foreman climbed back into a boxing ring, ten years to the month since his last fight, against Jimmy Young in San Juan. His opponent was a journeyman heavyweight named Steve Zouski, whom Foreman dispatched in the fourth round before a sparse audience. Foreman weighed 267 pounds, nearly fifty pounds over his best fighting weight. The flesh hung off his sides and over the belt line of his trunks. He sported a shaved head that, with the added girth, made him appear like an entirely different person from the one people remembered. His punching power hadn't changed, though; he busted Zouski up with little effort.

Foreman's goal in coming back: to win the heavyweight title again. His return was greeted with skepticism, mockery, and worries for his safety. A new generation of sports fans remembered his name only as it was associated with Ali and Frazier. Beyond that, Foreman was an image: a leaden puncher, a scowling slugger who didn't suffer fools, and—extra credit for those with good memories—the flag-waving boxer with "USA" on his chest who had gone his own way in 1968, celebrating America when other members of the Olympic team had chosen Black Power. But that Foreman had vanished in March 1977. That Foreman had lain on his dressing-room table and felt himself descending into a bottomless pit, before being saved by Jesus Christ himself, who pulled him out. That Foreman had woken from this vision and exclaimed: "Jesus Christ is coming alive in me!"[1] That Foreman announced that he would devote the rest of his life to God and barely made another headline for a decade.

Foreman went back to Houston and preached the word on street corners and eventually at the Church of the Lord Jesus Christ, where he amassed a congregation. More impressive to many than his new mission was the transformation in his personality. Gone was the glowering visage, the sense of menace; replacing it was an avuncular preacher, who smiled easily as his weight ballooned—courtesy of a penchant for cheeseburgers. He'd never forgotten the scant food in the Foreman home when he was a boy; freed from the rigors of training, he cruised southwest Houston's Westheimer Road, one day in a Ford Fiesta, one day in a Rolls-Royce Corniche, hitting McDonald's, Wendy's, and the "Kentucky fellas" whenever he pleased.[2]

By the early 1980s, sportswriters had stopped asking whether Foreman would fight again. In 1984, he started the George Foreman Youth and Community Center in Houston, which included a gymnasium. It was costly to maintain, though, and by 1986, Foreman had tapped his ring earnings heavily to keep it going. He solicited donations and took speaking fees, but then he got a better idea for generating money: boxing.

This, at least, is the story that Foreman told, and it is probably mostly true. No one doubts Foreman's attachment to the youth center. But he likely also felt the itch for action, for glory—and, yes, even for money; most great athletes do. And then there was the long-festering wound—the loss to Ali in Zaire. He had never experienced that defeat as a standard competitive setback; it was more like a personal evisceration, a public exhibition of a man's inner emptiness. Ali had done him a favor, he figured, set him on a new path. But the loss itself, the feeling of shame: that had never healed.

Years of preaching and pressing the flesh had made Foreman into a magnetic personality. He deflated criticism with a kindly demeanor and self-deprecating humor built around being overweight and middle-aged. He fashioned a figure with timeless American appeal: the lone sojourner with the crazy idea that he knows will work, though he's surrounded by small-thinking detractors. Many saw in Big George's new shtick a kind of Ali reprise, retrofitted for a calmer era. Foreman had become an entertainer. The fat jokes obscured how hard he was working in the gym, but he did insist on fighting at weights around 250 pounds, saying that he felt too weak when he was lighter. He was massive and powerful, but his belly suggested the spongy ease of a man not wasting his finite hours counting calories.

By 1989, the Foreman show was picking up momentum, and rumors flew about a mega-million-dollar Foreman–Tyson fight in Beijing. Tyson would be heavily favored, but some weren't so sure, remembering Foreman's demolition of Joe Frazier in Kingston, Jamaica, in 1973—and seeing in Tyson another short-armed fighter whose aggression would force him right into Foreman's power. In any case, the fight never came off. If the stories told by multiple insiders are true—and they are consistent—Tyson wanted no part of tangling with the old man.[3]

Tyson soon had bigger problems to worry about, anyway. In February 1990, he lost his title to Buster Douglas in Tokyo. When Holyfield vaporized Douglas with that picture-perfect right cross in October 1990, he won the Foreman sweepstakes. The new champ would earn more than $20

million to fight Big George, who was guaranteed a purse of $12.5 million—
enough to keep several youth centers going. The bout, held on April 19,
1991, in Atlantic City, was billed as the Battle of the Ages.

★

Foreman's mushrooming popularity gave the event a feel-good vibe almost
unique to heavyweight title fights. Big George inspired people and made
them laugh. He said that he was fighting for "all the senior citizens" and
that he was "closer to sixty than I am to twenty-five," though, at forty-two,
he was equidistant between the two ages. He said that he wanted to prove
that "the age of forty is not a death sentence," but his fellow baby boomers
had dispensed with that idea as soon as the first of the cohort reached that
milestone—after which they reformulated all their pronouncements about
youth, as militant in their refusal to get off stage as they had once been to
storm it. Holyfield was a mere supporting star in this promotion.

Foreman's relentless joshing about weight, food, and age made some
wonder whether he was serious in his effort to win or was simply cashing
in on an ingenious personal makeover. His weight illustrated the paradox.
It wasn't a matter of getting down to 220 pounds; he wasn't twenty-five
anymore. But at 257, his body mocked rigor. No athlete, with the exception
of sumo wrestlers or nose tackles on a goal-line stand, has been served by
weighing too much. Foreman's rear- and side-view portraits in his white
boxing trunks took some getting used to, especially compared with the
sculpted, wasp-waisted Holyfield, who came bouncing out of his corner to
meet him for Round 1.

The champion was determined to follow a conservative fight plan:
to wage battle inside Foreman's perimeter, tattooing the big man with
punches before George could get off his own. Holyfield shot out jabs and
combinations, ripping hooks into the ample Foreman midriff. Foreman
rumbled after him, to little effect. The discrepancies of age, speed, and
fitness seemed glaring. The first round did not bode well for comebacks.

In the second round, however, Foreman reached Holyfield with a few
rights to the side of his head, and the champ looked momentarily stunned.
Briefly, one could imagine that it was 1973 again, in Jamaica, and could
believe that, short of Ali, no one could stand up to George Foreman, even
now. Holyfield was hurt! The miracle was at hand!

It was the briefest of illusions. Holyfield did not retreat but simply got
his hands going again. If he was punching, Foreman could do nothing;
when Holyfield stopped for a breather, Foreman might break through. In

the third and fourth rounds, as if annoyed by Foreman's momentary surge, Holyfield punished him, but Big George competed bravely. In the fifth round, he made another burst; his right grazed Holyfield's head and forced him backward, but the champion fought George off.

Foreman's eyes were swelling up by now, and his chest heaved for air—but he insisted on standing between rounds, as he had throughout his comeback. In the seventh, he made one last charge, coming across with a good right, close to the target area on Holyfield's chin. The champ backed off but got nailed with another. Foreman kept throwing, missing more than he landed, but inspiring the crowd into its greatest chorus of the evening. Holyfield was not really hurt, though, and when Foreman paused, the champion pummeled him with seventeen straight punches. Foreman teetered; he put his big arms out to push Holyfield away. The crowd stayed on its feet at the bell, cheering both men.

Foreman took a going-over the rest of the way, but Holyfield could not finish him. When the bell sounded after twelve rounds, Foreman and Holyfield were locked in an embrace. "Thanks for the opportunity," Foreman told Holyfield and his manager, Lou Duva. "He won."[4] And Holyfield had, retaining his title on a unanimous decision.

Holyfield–Foreman met every financial expectation, becoming, for a time, the richest fight in history. Public feeling for Foreman, and his courageous showing, colored the bout as a near-great contest in which the challenger had given Holyfield a run for his money. Viewed with a colder eye years later, the fight cannot sustain that judgment.

In victory, Holyfield was left facing a skeptical public that didn't see him, somehow, as the real champion. The real champ was in jail, wasn't he? Holyfield didn't help his case when, in his first fight after beating Foreman, he was knocked down by journeyman Bert Cooper before rallying to win. His standing eroded further when he accepted another $20 million offer, to face another forty-two-year-old former champion—Larry Holmes. Foreman's financial killing had gotten Holmes off his fishing boat. A barrier had been broken: Foreman had proved that people would pay to see middle-aged sports heroes. (And not just in boxing: the "seniors" tour in tennis, featuring such comparatively youthful retirees as John McEnroe, Jimmy Connors, and Björn Borg, became big business in the 1990s.) Holmes modeled his comeback campaign on Foreman's: fighting subpar boxers, capitalizing on his name recognition to build momentum. In February 1992, he put on a boxing clinic in beating a top ten contender, Ray Mercer. The win put Holmes in line to face Holyfield on June 19, 1992, for $7.5 million.

Holmes's fight plan against Holyfield was nearly the opposite of Foreman's. Rather than trying to corner the younger man for the big blow, Holmes would fight off the ropes and counterpunch, as he had against Mercer. But Holyfield was able to get in and out against Holmes, beating him to the punch with his superior hand speed. The styles made for a dull match. The bout's only drama came in the sixth round, when a Holmes elbow opened a precarious cut over Holyfield's right eye. Holyfield prevailed easily after twelve rounds, but only his bank account gained.

Had Tyson's implosion delegitimized the division, so that aging legends had to be pressed back into service? Were Ali and Frazier coming back next?

★

As it happened, the Holyfield–Holmes fight would prove to be the last dull moment in the heavyweight division for years. What lay ahead was a frenzy of activity unmatched for variety, confusion, inspiration, and shock.

It started when Holyfield finally met up with one of the division's young, imposing challengers: twenty-four-year-old Riddick Bowe, a bronze medalist at the 1988 Seoul Olympics and a native of Mike Tyson's Brownsville, Brooklyn, neighborhood. But Bowe was nothing like Tyson. Generally sweet and engaging, he loved to laugh and exuded a remarkable cheerfulness, considering the grim circumstances of his upbringing. One of thirteen children, he had come of age as the crack epidemic ravaged Brooklyn. He'd lost a brother to AIDS and a sister to a stabbing. Yet Bowe never fell in with the bad crowd. For years, he walked his mother to and from her job at a plastics factory.

Though Bowe had the physical tools—he stood six foot five and weighed more than 230 pounds—and punching power to compete for the title, more established managers took a pass on him. But "Rock" Newman, a boxing maverick who had been a college baseball star, radio host, college counselor, PR man, and—yes—a car salesman, saw his potential. The mountainous Bowe and the squat, bearded Newman, a light-skinned African American who wore a dashiki and a fez, partly to disabuse perceptions that he was white, made a memorable fighter-manager team. Bowe, whose nickname, Big Daddy, described his personality perfectly, doled out the charm; Newman handled the hard-charging advocacy. Bowe fought his way to a 31–0 record, earning top contender status.

On November 13, 1992, Holyfield and Bowe slugged it out at the Thomas & Mack Center in Las Vegas. Few heavyweight title bouts have seen such a torrid early-round pace. Holyfield, at just 205 pounds, seemed convinced that he could wear Bowe down with activity. He battled Bowe at close quarters, but to his surprise, the big man liked fighting inside, and his uppercuts were crushing. By the halfway point, Holyfield had exerted enormous energy just to stay on relatively even terms with the challenger, whom he couldn't seem to hurt. Bowe wasn't tiring, and after nine rounds, he had forged ahead. Both men bore the marks of heavy battle. Bowe had swelling around both eyes; Holyfield's left eye was cut, his right eye nearly closed.

In the tenth round, Bowe nailed Holyfield with a right uppercut, and the champion, as if losing all his strength at once, staggered halfway across the ring, crashing into a corner post. Bowe rushed in, pounding Holyfield as the crowd stood, sensing that the title was about to change hands. Holyfield moved like a sleepy passenger on a commuter train who has been told to disembark. He stayed upright, though, and Bowe's assault finally stilled. He was out of gas.

It was at this moment that Holyfield's public image began to change from that of an uninspiring heavyweight to that of a warrior king. He pawed with a few jabs, and when Bowe didn't respond, Holyfield, his face a mask of rage, let loose with two-handed combinations, his rally resembling something from a *Rocky* movie. Then Bowe roused himself to trade back, and he and Holyfield stood at center ring, punching away. At the bell, Bowe tapped Holyfield in the belly, as if to say, "You're pretty good."

It was as fierce a three minutes as any that Ali and Frazier had ever contested, but it was the last hurrah for Holyfield, who was running out of rounds to save his title. In the eleventh, Bowe put him down. The twelfth and final round was relatively uneventful. Holyfield seemed to know what was coming, and it came: the judges scored it 115–113, 117–110, and 117–110, all for Bowe, the winner and new heavyweight champion. Just twenty-four, and with a classic heavyweight's body, updated for extra-large 1990s standards, Bowe looked to be positioned for a long reign. But from here on, nothing would go as expected.

Bowe owned the heavyweight belts of all three boxing sanctioning organizations—the WBC, WBA, and IBF. The WBC insisted that Bowe fight its top contender, Britain's Lennox Lewis, in his first title defense, but the fighters' camps could not come to terms, so the WBC stripped Bowe of recognition and awarded its title to Lewis. Bowe publicly pitched the organization's chintzy championship belt into a trash can. He and Newman were confident that people knew who the real champ was.

Newman had big plans: his feverish mind conceived a world tour for Bowe, on the order of Ali's voyages. Bowe visited U.S. troops in Somalia and met Nelson Mandela in South Africa; he toured Europe, and Newman even got him an audience with Pope John Paul II. These events, Newman said, would "validate Riddick's world reign and elevate his status as a world figure."[5] Bowe was a world figure?

By the time he fought Holyfield again, on November 6, 1993, in Las Vegas, Bowe had had a whirlwind year. He'd been working with an architect to build his dream house—with a kitchen in the bedroom, the better to indulge his Foreman-size appetite. By his own admission, he didn't turn down many pieces of cake. He came into the ring at 246, eleven pounds heavier than a year earlier, and he resorted to the trick of overweight boxers: he wore extra-long trunks, letting him hike up the waistband over his belly.

The champion faced a grimly determined foe. Holyfield had made changes, hiring Emanuel Steward, the boxing wizard from Detroit's Kronk Gym, as his new trainer. Steward and Holyfield worked out a battle plan to box Bowe from the outside, to stay more active with combinations, and to avoid brawling with him on the inside. And to reckon with Bowe's superior size, Holyfield came in twelve pounds heavier, at 217. Unlike Bowe's extra weight, Holyfield's was all muscle.

Bowe–Holyfield II proved nearly as memorable as the first battle—and, in at least one respect, more so. Bowe started strong, winning the early rounds, as Holyfield held back in his new boxing posture. The challenger picked up the pace in the fourth round, bouncing side to side and beating Bowe to the punch. At the end of the fourth, as if a fuse had blown, the two abandoned their caution and traded punches for nearly ten seconds after the bell, causing a near-melee in the ring. In the next two rounds, Holyfield took command, outpunching Bowe, whose extra weight seemed to be telling on him.

Then, in the seventh round, a figure appeared in the night sky over the outdoor arena of Caesars Palace: a man in a paraglider, with a motorized pack on his back, was swooping down toward the canopy-covered ring. As James Miller descended, his parachute cords got caught in the overhead lights, and he tangled himself in the ring ropes. He was pulled into the crowd by a scrum of spectators and members of Bowe's corner, and security people raced toward the scene. The seventh round was going on pause. Bowe's and Holyfield's men wrapped them in towels against the November chill. Miller was booked on charges of "dangerous flying" and dubbed Fan Man, for the motorized pack. His stunt remains a uniquely bizarre moment in American sports.

After a twenty-one-minute delay, the battle resumed. As if nothing had happened, Holyfield raced ahead, putting himself in position to win on the scorecards. At the final bell, they kept punching—the corners flooded into the ring again, and the fighting stopped only when Steward tackled his fighter, Holyfield, bringing him down to the canvas.

Holyfield prevailed by the slimmest of margins: 115–113 and 115–114, from two judges, while the third had the fight even, 114–114. He joined Ali and Floyd Patterson as the only men to regain the title. He had done it as much with his mind as with his body.

So much for Bowe taking the heavyweight reins. As for Holyfield, he had won new stature and respect, though a third and deciding match against Bowe seemed only fair. There was also the matter of Lennox Lewis, whom no one seemed to want to fight. Holyfield said that he would, but he first opted for a title defense against left-handed challenger Michael Moorer. After twelve rounds of lethargic battle on April 22, 1994, the judges awarded the title to Moorer on a questionable decision. Shortly afterward, Holyfield was diagnosed with a heart problem and announced his retirement.

So much for Holyfield starting anew. Did anyone want the heavyweight title?

Moorer hadn't fought as though he wanted it. People remembered his bout with Holyfield not for his performance but for his trainer's. Teddy Atlas exhorted Moorer in the corner between rounds with advice straight out of a motivational speakers' bureau. Sixty seconds between rounds gave Atlas, a Cus D'Amato protégé who had broken with the guru over his special treatment of Mike Tyson, more than enough time to deliver speeches beginning with, "There comes a time in a man's life. . . ." The moody Moorer, who was often short with reporters, brooded further when he found his win upstaged by Holyfield's heart drama and Atlas's rhetorical heroics. So when Moorer chose to defend his title for the first time against forty-five-year-old George Foreman, some noted how the champion resembled the younger, leaner, surlier version of his challenger.

On November 5, 1994, HBO's telecast began with a clip of Foreman, dressed in a tuxedo, reciting the Impossible Dream speech from *Man of La Mancha*. It was a fitting metaphor; Foreman's quest had become quixotic. In the three and a half years that had passed since his loss to Holyfield, he had fought only sporadically, and many wondered why he still wanted to risk getting hurt. Because, Foreman answered, he was obsessed: he wanted his old title back. It all went back to Zaire and Ali. Against Moorer, he wore the same pair of red, white, and blue trunks—now faded—that he had worn on that night in Africa.

His effort against Moorer was noble but only intermittently effective. He used his tree-trunk jab to good effect, and he managed to land some clubbing blows, especially in the fifth, when his uppercuts got Moorer's attention. But for the most part, George took punishment. Always moving forward, he kept eating Moorer's wicked southpaw jab. Moorer picked Foreman apart, even as his trainer warned him to be careful.

"What he's trying to do is set you up for one shot," Atlas told the champion. "He's trying to sneak-punch you. I don't want you standing at the same range." Atlas worried that Foreman was pawing with his jab to disguise the right. But Foreman had yet to get the big punch across.

Well behind on points after nine rounds, Foreman stepped up his pace in the tenth, prodding Moorer over to move him into punching range of his right. Near center ring, Foreman landed the jab and the right hand. Moorer stopped. Foreman landed another right. Moorer tried to circle, but his mobility was gone. He stood in front of Foreman, and Foreman stepped inside and put the right flush on Moorer's chin, dropping the heavyweight champion on his back. Referee Joe Cortez counted ten over him.

"It happened!" HBO's Jim Lampley exclaimed from ringside. "It happened!"

Foreman raised his eyes heavenward and dropped to his knees in prayer. For a few seconds, anyway, he was alone with his thoughts, and what must they have been? He'd achieved the impossible, almost solely through his refusal to believe that it was impossible. Oh, and punching power—that helped, too.

"Always remember that song," he told HBO's Larry Merchant. "When you wish upon a star, doesn't matter who you are, anything your heart desires can come to you, if you just don't give up on your dreams."[6] Who else could make Disney sound like inspiration? Twenty years after his tortured tumble in Africa, George Foreman had become the oldest, most improbable figure ever to wear the American crown.

★

Four months later, on the cold morning of March 25, 1995, a battery of television trucks and curiosity seekers gathered outside the Marion County Detention Center in Plainfield, Indiana. At about 6:15, the doors opened, and a familiar face emerged. Other than the white Islamic skullcap on his head, he looked like the man everyone remembered: it was Mike Tyson. Expressionless, he ducked into a black limousine, bound for the airport and a private jet that would take him to his sixty-six-acre farm in Southington, Ohio. He had served three years and six weeks in prison, during which time he had converted to Islam and taken advantage of an extensive library to read Machiavelli, Tolstoy, Dostoyevsky, Che, Mao, and others, even wielding a dictionary and thesaurus, as Malcolm X had, to look up unfamiliar words. But whether he would come out a better or worse man remained to be seen.

It was a foregone conclusion that he would fight again. "On March 25 boxing will be lifted from the pages of *Ring* magazine and into those of *Newsweek* and *People*—and the *National Enquirer*," wrote Richard Hoffer in *Sports Illustrated*. "The day Tyson walks into his freedom, boxing once more becomes the kind of personality-driven riot that galvanizes globally."[7] Tyson emerged from prison an even bigger figure than before, especially in black urban and hip-hop culture, where he exemplified the outlaw ethos.

By now, the appeal of the bad guy was broad-based. Where Americans had once flocked to athletes with ideal images, even if those images were contrived, they were now increasingly drawn to the dark side, especially since a 24/7 media culture had sprung up on cable television, gratifying every wish—news, gossip, home shopping, true crime, money, sex, sports—but also homing in with gravitational consistency on the shocking and sensational. As Tyson walked through the prison gates, the nation was transfixed by the murder trial of ex–football great O. J. Simpson. Millions would follow its every twist and turn on cable for months, leading up to the sensational and incomprehensible verdict in October 1995: not guilty. For Tyson, this was a very different climate to work in, a different American populace to win over, from, say, the one that Jack Dempsey had faced. Dempsey had been viewed as a bad guy, too—a dirty fighter, an unpatriotic slacker—but he eventually became popular, even a hero, because people forgave him his trespasses. With Tyson, forgiveness didn't really come into it. People had wanted Dempsey to win, and be good; they wanted Tyson to win, and stay bad.

In any case, boxing needed him. The title had become a carnival without a barker. Holyfield and Bowe had fought two classic fights; Lennox Lewis had emerged as a rival to both, while wearing the spurious WBC championship belt; first George Foreman and then Larry Holmes had returned to the ring—and Foreman, in his second try, had won the title. More surprises: Holyfield lost to Moorer, then retired after his heart ailment was disclosed, and then unretired when a "faith healer" remedied the condition. (It turned out that Holyfield had been misdiagnosed.) Lewis lost his title to journeyman Oliver McCall, who knocked him down with one right hand in the second round. When a wobbly Lewis rose, the referee stopped the fight, to the outrage of a London crowd. McCall, in his first title defense, eked out a decision over Holmes, now forty-five, who didn't miss winning by much. Ignoring pleas to retire, Foreman returned to the ring in April 1995, four weeks after Tyson's release, to fight unranked Axel Schulz, the first German to fight for the crown since Max Schmeling. Foreman's handpicked patsy proved uncooperative over twelve rounds, and most observers thought that the German had won. But the judges awarded Foreman a decision victory. For fighting Schulz instead of a top contender, Foreman was stripped of WBA title recognition; for refusing to give him a rematch, he lost IBF recognition, too. No major sanctioning body now recognized him; yet he was the lineal champion, a stubborn reality that hovered over developments for the next few years.

Meanwhile, Holyfield and Bowe were on the comeback trail, and their paths sent them spiraling toward another showdown. Some asked whether Holyfield should be fighting, even if the Mayo Clinic had given him the go-ahead. Against Bowe in their third fight, he looked exhausted by the fourth round. Yet just as Holyfield seemed finished, in the sixth round, he knocked Bowe down with a left hook. For a moment, it seemed that Bowe might stay there, but he struggled to his feet. Holyfield rushed in to finish him, only to find that he had no punches left. He stood looking helplessly at Bowe. He could not fire; it seemed as if he could not get enough air. In the eighth, Holyfield took a short right and fell to the canvas on his face. He got up, but Bowe sent him collapsing into the ropes with another right, and that was all. The deciding match between the great rivals seemed to render a judgment on their futures: Bowe should go on, Holyfield should stop. Yet once again, the script would go sideways. Bowe would be out of boxing within a year, while Holyfield had more races to run.

In Tyson's absence, the failure of any of his would-be successors to emerge as master made them all more or less faceless to the American public, which had always demanded jurisdictional and competitive clarity from the title. The idea was that Tyson would consolidate the fiefdoms of the squabbling princes. Even as the motorcade sped from Indiana toward Ohio, Don King worked feverishly to plan the Tyson Restoration.

★

Tyson started on the way back with quick knockouts of overmatched fighters with semi-distinguished heavyweight pedigrees. On August 19, 1995, in his first appearance in a boxing ring since his rape conviction, Tyson fought Peter McNeeley, son of Tom McNeeley, who had challenged Floyd Patterson for the title in 1961. McNeeley the Younger was gone in eighty-nine seconds, courtesy of his trainer's decision to stop it after he had been knocked down a second time (to collect, some allege, on a bet about how long his fighter would last). Buster Mathis Jr., son of the oversize heavyweight who had fought Ali and Frazier and no hard-body himself, lasted three rounds against Tyson on December 16, 1995. Tyson earned a combined $35 million for his first two comeback fights.

The sanctioning bodies had made an impossible mishmash of the heavyweight championship. As far as general fans were concerned, Tyson could win any of the titles on offer and assume the mantle of champion. Americans didn't know who Frank Bruno was, for example, or that Bruno had won the WBC title from Oliver McCall, who had won it from Lennox Lewis. In March 1996, when Tyson pulverized a clinch-happy Bruno in three rounds to win the WBC title, fans were dutifully told that he had joined Patterson, Ali, Holyfield, and Foreman as the only men who had regained the heavyweight title. He had regained *a* heavyweight title.

When Tyson spurned the WBC's dictates to fight its top contender—once again, Lewis—and the WBC responded by stripping him, Tyson knew that he could go down the block and grab another belt. And he did: on September 7, 1996, he knocked out Bruce Seldon in one round, to win the WBA version, though "knocked out" was a generous description of what happened. Few watching at ringside or on television could identify the punches that brought Seldon down. "Fix, fix!" the crowd chanted.

If the Seldon bout offered no satisfaction, it did please Tyson's friend Tupac Shakur, the rapper who had recorded a new song for him to use on his entrance into the ring. (Tyson sported a tattoo reading "Thug Life," after a Tupac song.) Tupac embraced Tyson after the fight, and the two made plans to meet afterward. They never saw each other again: at an intersection in front of the Maxim Hotel in Las Vegas, Shakur was shot dead from the windows of a car that had pulled up alongside. The murder was never solved. Shakur's death underscored the deadly subculture of rap and hip-hop, and it seemed suggestive of the energy around Tyson as well. The boxer and the rapper were two sides of the same cultural coin. Both had served time for sexual assault; both mined the vein of persecution to channel and excuse their rage; both felt that they wouldn't be in the world for long. To their admirers, they represented purity and defiance of social norms.

Tyson had now earned $80 million for four postprison fights. No boxer had ever approached this kind of earning power, and this money had been made for facing essentially ceremonial opponents. King had expertly orchestrated Tyson's glorious return and made him, at the time, the richest athlete who had ever lived. But the mercenary nature of his comeback struck some as a cynical money grab.

Tyson's next opponent, however, was a man whom everyone respected: Holyfield, who had refused to retire. They would fight on November 9, 1996, nearly five years to the day of their originally intended meeting. Odds opened at 25–1 for Tyson before coming down to a more modest 12 to 1. Conventional wisdom held that Holyfield, thirty-four, was a shot fighter. His stature and diminished skills made him the perfect opponent: safe but lucrative.

But Holyfield had never doubted that he would beat Tyson, if he could only get him into the ring. His confidence traced back over a decade. The two had first crossed paths in the early 1980s, when they met as Olympic hopefuls. Both were outsiders: the Atlanta-based Holyfield was a rare Southerner on a team dominated by northern urbanites; his teammates called him "Country." He kept his distance, preferring Bible reading to trash-talking. Tyson was a shy teenage loner. The two admired each other from afar. He had "never seen anybody work harder than Tyson," Holyfield remembered of their amateur days. "Not ever."[8]

A subtle rivalry developed. Tyson was a heavyweight and Holyfield a light heavyweight, but it wasn't hard to imagine that they might someday meet. One day, the coaches asked Holyfield to work with Tyson. The two fought so furiously that hostilities were halted after just one round. Another time, Holyfield had rights to the next game of pool, but Tyson didn't want to yield the table. Holyfield insisted; Tyson backed down. Between the sparring session and the pool-table confrontation, Holyfield felt that he had sent Tyson a message: everyone else is afraid of you, but I'm not.

But Holyfield's plan relied on more than motivational memories. He had watched every Tyson fight, often traveling to watch Tyson in person—the way Gene Tunney had stalked Jack Dempsey in the 1920s. His plan: "You got to fight Tyson to get his respect, then box him. Then you got to box him to get him in a corner, then fight him."[9] Holyfield would hit Tyson as he rushed in, tie him up, push and maul him. He would yield nothing in ring manners. He'd hit him and keep hitting him until someone told him to stop.

Though most regarded its outcome as preordained, Holyfield–Tyson became a hot ticket. Audiences for Tyson's pay-per-view fights had dropped after his first comeback bout against McNeeley, but now the orders spiked again, driven by the prospect of seeing Tyson in the ring against a brave opponent. Nearly a third of the orders came from fans who had never bought a fight before. More important than the pay-per-view numbers, though, was the undefinable yet pervasive buzz that the event carried among general fans. It was an old-fashioned big fight.

With gospel music playing and his purple robe emblazoned with "Phil 4:13," after his favorite Bible verse—"I can do all things through Christ, who strengthens me"—Holyfield made his way to the ring, smiling. A few moments later, Tyson emerged, surrounded by his now-familiar retinue: scowling men dressed in dark suits, looking like pimps or gangsters. Hip-hop music heralded his arrival. The rivals had settled into their public roles: Holyfield, the Christian gladiator; Tyson, the bad guy who wore black.

Their attitudes toward their personas were as different as the personas themselves. Holyfield genuinely saw himself as a warrior for God. He un-abashedly maintained that he would win because God was on his side. The fight had been "blessed," he said.[10] There was no way that he could lose "if I just trust in God because God is that good."[11]

By contrast, Tyson seemed at odds with his public image. Though still ca-pable of mustering the old fire—"This is not to be taken personally," he told reporters, "but I am just pissed off all the time"[12]—his boxing talk contained little of the passion of the old days. He spoke of upcoming fights as obliga-tions—and paydays. "All I know is that Saturday I'll pick up $30 million," he said, "then Monday I'll sign up for another $30 million."[13] He sought grounding in family life: he would soon marry Monica Turner, a physician, and he now had three children—the first generation of his family, he said, that hadn't been on welfare. His world-weariness didn't harmonize with his role as a ring destroyer. But he was in the ring now, trying to summon the old mojo.

★

At the opening bell, Tyson rushed out and hit Holyfield with a right that drove him backward. It didn't bode well for Holyfield's chances, but he steadied himself and fired back. He had come to fight, not cower. Near the end of the first, the two battled toe to toe, to the delight of the MGM Grand crowd. At the bell, when Tyson landed a right and a left, Holyfield hit him back. Tyson looked at Holyfield quizzically, as if surprised.

In the second round, Holyfield upped the stakes, hurting Tyson with a left hook and getting the crowd of sixteen thousand to chant his name. A pattern took shape: the two would stand near center ring and trade, with Tyson usually initiating and then coming inside to try to do damage. Holy-field would throw his right over Tyson's left hook, and they would clinch, struggling mightily for physical control. It was Holyfield, six foot two to Tyson's five foot eleven, who emerged as the stronger man. Though he outweighed Holyfield, 222 to 215, Tyson suddenly looked too small, just as he had against Buster Douglas.

They battled on close terms through four rounds, with Tyson taking the first and fourth, Holyfield the second and third. But in the third, as both charged in at once, they clashed heads, opening a cut on Tyson's forehead. They would bump heads all night.

Tyson had never been cut, and the sight of the blood seemed to mock his identity as bully in the ring. Still, he pressed forward, fighting a furious fifth round, hurting Holyfield with a right hand to the body and a left hook. But Holyfield stood firm.

Tyson grew frustrated as the rounds passed and Holyfield remained in front of him. He couldn't break Holyfield down. His problems multiplied in the sixth round, when, off balance, he was knocked down by a Holyfield punch to his chest. Though Tyson hadn't really been hurt, the sight of him on the canvas sent the crowd into bedlam, and the cheers for his rival seemed to demoralize him. At the bell, he complained to the referee about Holyfield's head butts, pointing to his cut eye, as if to say, "See what he's done to me!" He looked uncharacteristically whiny.

From there on, Tyson seemed to lose heart. Holyfield would not concede headroom or ring real estate; their heads came together again in the seventh, and Tyson's knees buckled. He was being picked off more easily as he came in. What had been an even fight through six rounds swung decisively in Holyfield's favor. As the battle moved into its final frames, Tyson needed a strong rally to win.

Instead, the surge came from the other side. Near the end of the tenth round, Holyfield hurt Tyson with a right, and then, as Tyson tried a haymaker right of his own, Holyfield beat him to the punch with another right, sending Tyson staggering backward, his head lolling to one side. Only the ropes held him up. The bell sounded just as referee Mitch Halpern leaped between them. Tyson walked half-consciously to his corner as the MGM Grand erupted. In the eleventh, Holyfield swarmed Tyson with another barrage, and Halpern stopped it. Holyfield was the new champion, WBA version. It was the third time that he had won at least a piece of the title.

Holyfield praised the creator. "My God," he allowed, "is the only true God."[14] Such talk was becoming increasingly unwelcome in America, but Holyfield was a popular figure. Buster Douglas's victory over Tyson always had had an air of unreality about it, but Holyfield's triumph suggested a reordering of judgments—perhaps it was he, not Tyson, who was the era's great heavyweight. A rematch would settle that question.

★

The title had remade many men's fortunes, but it couldn't remake the men themselves; that was private work. George Foreman had found that out in the 1970s. In the 1990s, the fruits of transformation continued to come his way.

Though he still claimed the lineal title and hadn't retired, his attentions were increasingly focused elsewhere. A kitchen- and household-products company, Salton, had in storage an indoor grill that could cook on both sides at once and also suck away fat from burgers and steaks. Not long after Foreman beat Moorer, the company's marketing man approached George to endorse the grill, which had never caught on. From the first trade show that he attended to promote the product, Foreman was mobbed by well-wishers. Sales took off after the broadcast of an infomercial wherein George demonstrated the grill, now called George Foreman's Lean, Mean, Fat-Busting Machine. Foreman's naturalness and charm put the product over. During a live spot for the QVC channel, Foreman, feeling hungry, reached over to a plate of burgers and began eating one. Telephone orders exploded. Soon, Foreman began receiving royalty checks in the mail. They reached hundreds of thousands of dollars, and eventually several million, every month. The Foreman Grill, as it came to be known, made George richer outside the ring than he had ever gotten inside it, even in his money-printing second career. He would eventually sell his interest in the grill, which retained his name, for $137.5 million.

Growing happier by the year, the Foreman story contrasted with the Tyson saga, with its dominant chord of despair. Even Tyson's greatest moments seemed suffused with loneliness, as when he poured champagne on Cus D'Amato's grave after he first won the title in 1986. Ten years later, he was prone to visiting the resting place of another figure from the heavyweight firmament: Sonny Liston.

"It may sound morbid and grim," he said, "but I pretty much identify with that life." He felt a kinship with Liston's friendlessness. "I think he wanted people to respect and love him," Tyson said, "and that never happened. You know what I mean?"

Approaching his rematch with Holyfield, Tyson, nearing thirty-one, sounded more conflicted about his life and career than ever before. His inner turmoil and intelligence made him a compelling, unpredictable interview. "Basically, I've been taken advantage of my whole life," he said. "I've been abused, I've been dehumanized, I've been humiliated, and I've been betrayed."[15] (Coddled, glorified, and enriched, too, he neglected to add.) But he also sometimes suggested that he was coming to terms with his own role in things, as when, before the first fight, he said: "I'd like to think I was the way I was because of financial reasons, and I'd like to think it was because of environmental reasons. But I don't really believe that."[16]

Before the second fight, he sounded a hopeful note regarding his growing brood of children. "My children, they've got a mother that's a doctor, a bright loving woman, a father who's rich and takes care of them. I had an alcoholic and a pimp for parents. They're going to have a great life."[17] But not too hopeful: "I know I've got to tell them what I did was bad, but I'm not looking forward to looking like an ass in front of my kids."[18]

He was a man scarred by a past that still owned his psyche and adrift in a present to which he was not committed. Underneath the self-pity and rage, he wanted to build a real life but did not know how. Struggling to break free of the old image, he was about to do something that would imprison him within it.

Holyfield and Tyson fought again on June 28, 1997, at the MGM Grand in Las Vegas. Their second meeting broke records in every meaningful category: a live gate of $17 million, domestic pay-per-view buys of just under two million, netting nearly $100 million; $6 million in closed-circuit showings in the United States and $21 million in foreign sales to ninety-seven countries. Tyson was the draw: as challenger, he made nearly as much ($30 million) as Holyfield ($35 million). In the first fight, when Tyson had been champion, his $30 million purse dwarfed Holyfield's $11 million.

All that money, though, wouldn't change the stubborn fact that Tyson needed something different against Holyfield this time. Though the oddsmakers made him a narrow favorite, his pensive gloom suggested a sense of foreboding. "I read a lot of Communist literature," he said, "and one thing I realized that's so true—the leader is always by himself at a time of doom."[19]

The doom seemed to descend from the opening bell. Holyfield sent a message right away that he was in the ring to win again, perhaps more easily this time: he dominated Tyson physically, tying him up again and beating him to the punch when Tyson tried to get inside. In the early going, he rocked Tyson with a left hook. Holyfield looked more muscular than ever, more powerful than Tyson—and more confident.

In the second round, their heads collided yet again, and Tyson pulled back with a cut over his right eye. The cut infuriated him and probably also caused panic, making him feel that he needed a knockout before the cut got worse and risked a stoppage from the referee. Coming out for the third round, he unleased about thirty seconds of fury that brought spectators to their feet and conjured memories of the young warrior from the 1980s. Now the fight was on.

And then, with the round nearly over, Tyson, moving into a clinch with Holyfield, nuzzled his head close and took a bite out of Holyfield's right ear. Many didn't see it happen. The next thing they knew, Holyfield was leaping into the air, spinning around and hopping as if he had been electrocuted. When referee Mills Lane called time, Holyfield turned his back on Tyson and walked toward his corner. Tyson, who had bitten off and spat out the piece of Holyfield's ear almost in one fluid motion, came up behind Holyfield and pushed him into the ropes. Lane jumped between them. Confusion reigned.

"He bit my ear!" Holyfield said to his corner, pointing to his bloody, gnarled appendage. It looked as though Lane would disqualify Tyson, but then he thought better of it. The ringside doctor, Flip Homansky, inspected the ear and told Lane that the fight could continue. "Put my mouthpiece in," Holyfield said to his men. "I'm going to knock him out."[20]

Lane signaled to the judges to deduct two points from Tyson's scorecard—one for the bite and one for the push. He approached Tyson's corner to inform them.

"That was a punch," Tyson said.

"Bullshit!" Lane replied.[21] He waved the two fighters together. By now, the MGM Grand crowd was on its feet, many not understanding what had occurred. The action resumed. Tyson landed a good left hook and a right. They moved into another clinch. Tyson leaned around Holyfield's neck and bit again—this time, the left ear.

Holyfield hopped away again and glared at Tyson, who held his gloves up, as if to say, "C'mon, fight!" And Holyfield did, throwing wild punches. Both men seemed intent on slugging it out now. The bell sounded.

The millions watching at home or on closed circuit were busy watching replays of the third round when the broadcast cut back to live action. Lane had disqualified Tyson. "One bite, maybe, is bad enough," the referee later said. "But two bites is the end of the search."[22]

The ring announcer had not even had a chance to declare the disqualification to the confused crowd when Tyson and his camp made their way across the ring toward Holyfield's corner, triggering chaos. Tyson threw punches at anyone near him, including police officers (potentially violating the terms of his parole). Only when Holyfield left the ring was it clear that the fight was over. When Tyson left, he was showered with cups and detritus. Someone threw a bottle at Tyson, and he and his men tried to climb into the crowd before they were restrained. The mania spilled out from the arena into the neighboring casino, where a stampede broke out amid rumors of gunshots. The MGM Grand suspended casino gambling for the evening—a fatal blow to its chances of recouping costs for the expensive promotion.

Postfight, an angry Tyson maintained that he had bitten Holyfield out of retaliation for the head butts; who was at fault for all the head banging remained in dispute. But Tyson's legendary ferocity quickly became fodder for parody and jokes. Holyfield was the Real Meal; Tyson was the Heavy-weight Chomp, the Sportsman of the Ear; the bout was seen on Pay Per Chew. It was a public self-assassination.

What became known as the Bite Fight prompted familiar responses: box-ing was a sick and degraded sport and should be banned. Tyson was sick and degraded and should be banned, too. Even the president weighed in: "As a fan," Bill Clinton said, "I was horrified."[23] Others, like Joyce Carol Oates, who had written sympathetically about the young Tyson, reserved her sternest judgment for Tyson's failure to overcome adversity: "He lacked the character, or 'heart,' of a true champion, who will fight even when he knows he might lose."[24]

Others picked up on this theme, seeing Tyson's implosion as a response to being bested in the ring: he couldn't beat Holyfield and knew it, and thus had sought a way out. Teddy Atlas, a harsh Tyson critic, had predicted that if Tyson couldn't score a quick knockout, he would find a way to get himself disqualified. Holyfield concurred. "Everybody knows how to get out of a fight," he said afterward. "All you have to do is foul."[25] On this thinking, Ty-son's surrender resembled that of another ring tough guy, lightweight and welterweight champion Roberto Durán, who threw up his hands and quit against Sugar Ray Leonard in 1980. Durán, with his "No más," and Tyson, with his biting, had something in common: each had made his own demise into such a spectacle that it outshined his conqueror.

Whatever Tyson's motivations, he seemed to understand, in the after-math, that he had passed a watershed. "I know it's over," he said. "My career is over."[26]

★

Holyfield was now recognized as the ring's true "Warrior," an appellation he wore on the waistband of his trunks. He would never attract the obses-sive focus of a Tyson, and—with several out-of-wedlock children from several women and a habit of getting engaged before major fights—he fell short of his godly image. But he was admired for his courage, professional-ism, and graciousness.

Events conspired toward resolving the title confusion of recent years. On November 22, 1997, two months shy of his forty-ninth birthday, George Foreman dominated twenty-six-year-old Shannon Briggs in Atlantic City. It

A moment that lives in boxing infamy: Mike Tyson bites Evander Holyfield in their second fight, June 28, 1997, in Las Vegas.
Associated Press

was, unaccountably, Foreman's best performance in years, but the judges awarded the fight to Briggs, making him—for those still paying attention—the "lineal" heavyweight champion. Perhaps the judges, subconsciously, were sending Foreman a message: go home, George; enough is enough.

Foreman showed no bitterness. He was too busy pitching his Foreman grill. "No home should be without this thing. Go get one," he told Larry Merchant afterward.[27] He was a salesman at heart, he said, almost apologetically. No one who had watched his remarkable decade could question that—even if, like Ali, he seemed to be disappearing into his public persona. He would never step into a ring again, and a generation of Americans would know him only as the winning gentleman who punched hard, not the hard-punching winner devoid of gentleness.

Underwhelming Shannon Briggs did boxing one good turn: in March 1998, he took on Lennox Lewis. When Lewis overpowered Briggs in five rounds— he gave him a fearful beating—he became the legitimate lineal champion. But in the United States, Holyfield was still seen as top man. He had even avenged his 1994 loss to Michael Moorer, capturing another alphabet-soup title belt in the process. Holyfield versus Lewis: as the heavyweight division's madcap decade wore down, they were the last men standing.

It took another year for the fight to come together, but it was finally slated for March 13, 1999, in Madison Square Garden, where the heavy-weights rarely paid visits anymore. The title would be made whole again in boxing's bygone mecca.

The promotion caught on with the public, at least by non-Tyson standards, but the bout itself, which went the full twelve rounds, offered few thrills. It was a commanding boxing performance by Lewis, who, at thirty-three and a half, had reached a late-career peak. His physical tools—standing six foot five, weighing 246, and with a reach of eighty-four inches—along with his boxing skills, stifled Holyfield, who could not harness his chariots. Stuck on the outside, unable to find his way around Lewis's punishing jab, he looked overmatched. The only excited fans were the five thousand loyalists who had flown across the Atlantic to cheer Lewis on in his quest to become Great Britain's first undisputed heavyweight champ since Bob Fitzsimmons in 1897. Incredibly, after twelve rounds, of which Lewis looked to have won at least nine, the judges called it a draw.

A rematch was ordered, and the two fought again exactly eight months later, on November 13, 1999—this time, in Las Vegas. The second fight showed a more active Holyfield, who, after rallies in the sixth and seventh rounds, edged close on the scorecards. But then Lewis took charge, work-ing his jab expertly and mixing in his devastating right uppercut. Lewis was just too much for Holyfield—at least, the thirty-seven-year-old version of Holyfield: he dominated the rest of the way, pulling away in the scoring. This time, the judges got it right, calling the bout unanimously for Lewis, now the undisputed heavyweight champion. The crown had returned to its old home: Great Britain.

It was fitting that the title had once again been unified, its confusions temporarily resolved, in 1999: the American century was near its end. For boxing—and especially, the heavyweight title—it had been an American century, too, with the title becoming a defining property in sports and popular culture. Nearly all its claimants had been Americans, the best of them known to all, symbols of national might.

Lennox Lewis, a Briton, was different. Born to parents of Jamaican descent, he had spent his first twelve years in England, before moving to Kitchener, Ontario, Canada. He won the gold medal in the 1988 Seoul Olympics wearing the Canadian colors. Launching his pro career, he resumed residency in Britain but maintained dual citizenship, irritating some fans. Though Great Britain eventually rallied to him, Lewis never caught on in the United States, and not just because he wasn't an American. His cautious boxing style was the antithesis of Tyson's kamikaze and Holyfield's noble gladiator. His presentation of himself as a sophisticate, especially in ads showing him playing chess and waiting for tea time, didn't help. And he suffered two surprise knockouts that compromised his case for greatness: the 1994 loss to Oliver McCall and a crushing one-punch defeat, in April 2001, against lightly regarded American Hasim Rahman. Lewis avenged both losses, however—he regained the title by beating Rahman in a rematch—and no one seriously questioned his superiority to either man.

The victory over Rahman gave Lewis an open path to the only fight he really wanted: a showdown against Mike Tyson, with whom the American public remained fascinated. Less of a fighter now than a tabloid figure, Tyson had become an avatar of a new cult of authenticity, with its command to "keep it real," which usually meant "keep it outrageous" because anything short of that might be dishonest. Tyson's public career fit perfectly into an age that dissolved the lines between hard news, entertainment, and scandal. The 1990s, yielding the greatest murder trial in U.S. history and a presidential impeachment that introduced intimate sexual terminology into polite company, inaugurated the information overload to which Americans would become so accustomed. The most gigantic figures were those, like Tyson, who could break through the clatter and make you pay attention. However diminished, he still wielded this power.

Since the Bite Fight fiasco, Tyson had fought sporadically, his bouts often becoming bizarre episodes. Against Brian Nielsen, he tried to break his opponent's arm; against Lou Savarese, he kept hitting his opponent after he slid down to the canvas—and then hit the referee as well. Afterward, with drumbeats sounding for a Tyson–Lewis bout, Tyson boasted that he was "the most brutal and vicious and ruthless champion that's ever been" and, thinking of Lewis, said, "I want to eat his children."[28] Trouble persisted outside the ring, too: in 1999, after a traffic accident, he assaulted two motorists and, as a result, served nine months in a Maryland jail.

At the news conference in January 2002 announcing the Lewis–Tyson bout, Tyson rushed his rival and sparked yet another depraved scene. He reprised his cannibal act, biting Lewis in the leg. And he capped it off with a profane rant that made him sound like a psychopath. Yet some portion of his madman act now was contrived to sell tickets. Walking out with Shelly Finkel, his new promoter, Tyson asked: "The fight was big, but this is going to make it bigger, isn't it?"[29] Mired in a $100 million court fight against Don King, and having blown most of a $300 million fortune, he needed a big payday. He, too, was a salesman.

At first, it looked as though he had miscalculated. The press conference fracas brought back unhappy memories of the Bite Fight, and Las Vegas, New York, and New Jersey all turned down the bout. Finally, the Pyramid at Memphis took it on. Even now, Tyson's sullied name remained gold at the box office: the bout broke the pay-per-view record, generating more than two million buys, bringing in $106.9 million. "I'm the biggest fighter in the history of the sport," Tyson said, with some justification. "If you don't believe me, just check the cash register."[30] He and Lewis were guaranteed purses of $17.5 million.

When Tyson climbed through the ropes on June 8, 2002, he was a few weeks from his thirty-sixth birthday and sixteen years past his first glory— beating Trevor Berbick for the heavyweight title. It was nearly the same span of time as separated Ali's defeat of Sonny Liston in 1964 and his fateful comeback try against Larry Holmes in 1980. Observers noted Tyson's placid manner. He looked like a man sent out on an undesired job.

For one round, Tyson looked something like Tyson: he rushed Lewis, and he landed his old left hook, as well as a right hand. He showed some of the head and upper-body movement that had once defined him. But Lewis was not cowed. Backed against the ropes, he jarred Tyson with a right uppercut. It was Tyson's round, but it was all he had.

He'd always been a front-runner. No fighter ever looked better in the first and second rounds; no fighter ever looked more imposing punching the bag or shadowboxing in the gym. But against live competition, it was a different story. From the second round on, Tyson reverted to his latter-day habit of standing straight up, gloves in front of his face, not throwing punches. Lewis, easily managing the distance, punished Tyson with his jab. By the third round, he had opened cuts over Tyson's eyes. Tyson fought with a stoicism that belied his wild persona; he was in the ring not to win but to absorb punishment, and absorb it he did, in perhaps his bravest performance. He could have gone quietly. Instead, he took sickening shots, his mouth filling with blood, his eyes becoming slits. It wasn't quite Ali versus Holmes, but it was hard going.

The end came in the eighth. Lewis kept landing his right; he seemed incapable of missing. Tyson looked wobbly yet resolute. At ringside, George Foreman urged Tyson's corner to intervene. Finally, Lewis landed one more right-hand bomb and, with his body leaning into the exhausted, crouching Tyson, gently eased him over to the canvas. The camera zoomed in on his ruined face as he stared at the ring lights above. He was counted out. Beating his chest in celebration, Lewis could say that he was the only man to beat Tyson and Holyfield, though the three had never fought one another at their best.

Postfight, all of Tyson's fury was gone. He showed respect and affection for Lewis. He cradled his young child. His big purse would help him cover some of his debts, though he wasn't in the clear, financially or personally. It was only clear that the Tyson era, which had been over for years, had finally received its last rites.

He had spent more than half his career as a shadow, always promising to reassume full shape. Was he, as it was now popular to suggest, the most over-rated heavyweight? Or was he a mighty but short-lived force? His place in the lineage would have to be sorted out in time, the way these things were.

★

"This, in effect, was the last big fight of the twentieth century," HBO's Larry Merchant said, signing off in Memphis.[31] It was true. Lewis belonged to the 1990s; whether he or Holyfield stood as the decade's top heavyweight was subject to debate. Tyson belonged not to the 1990s but to the 1980s, an era of cutting-edge technology and consumerism that now looked quaint in a time of cell phones and the Internet. The heavyweight title had spanned more than a century's worth of glorious, American-led technological ad-vances—from the transatlantic telegraph to mass-circulation newspapers and magazines, from radio to television, from cable TV to the web. But in the years that passed after Lewis–Tyson, as the age of social media opened, a realization dawned that the Memphis bout marked something more sig-nificant than the turning of the calendar. As Tyson himself had put it, after the fight that night: "I don't have nowhere to go."[32] He'd found the end of a road, but that road, it turned out, wasn't just his.

EPILOGUE

A Funeral

He was so fast, he used to say, that he could turn off the lights and be in bed before the room got dark. When it came time for the lights to dim for good, it happened almost as quickly. First he was here—and always would be, it seemed, though he grew decrepit before our eyes—and then he was gone. He'd survived several close calls, but this time, there was no reprieve. A respiratory illness hospitalized him, and on the evening of June 3, 2016, Muhammad Ali died at seventy-four in Phoenix, where he had been living in recent years with his wife Lonnie.

Ali's passing set off a frenzy of news coverage befitting that of a world figure or head of state, epitomized by the *New York Times*'s remarkable front-page headline: "Muhammad Ali, Titan of Boxing and the Twentieth Century, Dies at 74." That almost casual add-on—"and the twentieth century"—would have pleased him, confirming his sense of himself as a figure of global importance, far transcending the petty world of sports. This view of Ali remained the institutionalized consensus. Though the Internet offered plenty of room for dissenting views, Ali's death prompted such an outpouring of tributes, from athletes and actors, writers and musicians, foreign leaders and ex-presidents and President Barack Obama himself, that the abstainers had a lonely week. In death, Ali was as triumphant as he had been in Zaire or Miami Beach.

Ali's passing had another effect: it brought the subject of the heavyweight title, and boxing itself, to a prominence not seen in years. With Ali's life and times getting heavy play on cable news, the Internet, sports radio, and newspapers, phones began ringing in the living rooms of men like Larry Holmes, George Foreman, Evander Holyfield, Lennox Lewis, and Mike Tyson. Reporters wanted their thoughts on the passing of the great man. Holmes got more than one hundred calls in one day. Notable for his absence was Joe Frazier, who had died in 2011, thus falling short of his final goal in the never-quite-ended feud. "I'll outlive him, count on it," he had said of Ali.[1] "I'll open up the graveyard and bury his ass when the Lord chooses to take him."[2] Instead, it was Ali, hunched, face contorted into a grotesque shape, moving only with heavy assistance, who showed up to say farewell to Joe. Those who saw him that day would have doubted that he could hang on for nearly another five years.

Some of Ali's admirers in the media tried to make clear that they did not condone boxing—or, at least, they no longer condoned it. Ali, they suggested, was a special case. Ali himself encouraged this instinct with his frequent suggestion that boxing was an opening act of his life, a prelude to his real work. His grandiosity could be expected, but the glorifiers should have known better. Ali had been a warrior through and through, and they had thrilled to his exploits, not just the words and the charm and the beauty but the fighting, too—especially the fighting. It was tiresome to listen to their exculpations. Ali's family did not forget what he owed boxing, however. Tyson and Lewis were named pallbearers, Holmes and Foreman honorary pallbearers.

On Friday, June 10, 2016, the Greatest was laid to rest in Louisville, where his journey had started. Passing through the city, his funeral procession drew one hundred thousand mourners into the streets, where they threw rose petals onto the passing hearse and chanted his name one more time. Others ran after the car, trying to touch it. After the funeral, a three-hour memorial service kicked off at the KFC Yum! Center in Louisville, where fifteen thousand attended. The speakers and eulogizers were legion and multidenominational: Muslim, Christian, Jewish, white, black, Native American. The final speaker was former president Bill Clinton.

And there, somewhere in the vast throng, were Ali's men, the heavy-weight champions: Foreman and Holmes, Holyfield and Lewis, and Tyson, along with other men whom Ali had fought, like the Canadian hard rock, George Chuvalo. Among the dignitaries and famous names, the boxers occupied a unique place. They were integral to Ali's story and yet also somehow estranged from it. For when the funeral was done, it would be a long time, if ever again, that America would remember boxing so vividly. Ali opened up a new world for the American athlete, but that world largely left the American boxer behind. In Louisville, the lords bid the king farewell, but the kingdom had vanished long before his demise.

★

The vanishing had occurred abruptly, at least to the naked eye. In June 2003, one year after knocking out Mike Tyson, Lennox Lewis fought for the last time, escaping with a victory over Vitali Klitschko of Ukraine, whose cut-up face forced stoppage of a bout that, up to that point, he had been winning. In February 2004, Lewis retired a wealthy man and, like few champions before him, stuck to his word, never fighting again. Klitschko, meanwhile, along with his brother Wladimir, soon took control of the various heavyweight titles. Almost as if it had happened when no one was looking, Americans all but disappeared from the heavyweight ranks, replaced by fighters from Eastern Europe and elsewhere. The Klitschkos had little appeal for American fans and rarely defended their titles in the United States. For most Americans, the heavyweight championship—a fixture in popular culture for a century, a title that meant something to millions and defined national sporting achievement—no longer existed.[3]

Taking a longer view, one could see that the vanishing had been a process that played out over more than half a century. Boxing was a poor man's sport; the massive increase in standard of living in the United States throughout the twentieth century, the growth of a huge middle class, made for fewer hungry, hard-up young men willing to put on the gloves. The rise of competitive sports as a commercial industry, a story in which boxing was integral, eventually left the sport trailing badly behind. The advent of television in the 1950s elevated other sports to prominence—especially football, which became a national obsession. Major league baseball and the NFL—and later, the NBA—were rich, well-run sports leagues with lucrative contracts, high-profile stars, well-capitalized ownership, and large, devoted fan bases in major cities. Boxing couldn't compete with that, and its endemic corruption eroded fan support. With its proliferating weight classes, each with multiple champions; its quasi-felonious promoters; its absurd decisions denying fighters honest victories; and its lack of legitimate authority, boxing was just too crazy to follow for fans with a full menu of sports entertainment to choose from. The disappearance of boxing from free television made the sport even easier to ignore, especially when a younger generation increasingly preferred the more sensationalist and far better marketed and managed combat sport of Mixed Martial Arts. Finally, there was the sport's debilitating effect on the human body, especially on the brain. It was boxing, most agreed, that had been responsible for Ali's terrible illness. His ruination, some felt, played a role in driving people away.

Yet ultimately, it was Ali's glories, not his sorrows, that may have done even more to eclipse boxing. He had come along at a dark time for the sport and appointed himself its temporary savior. Boxing would die when he was gone, he promised. No other heavyweight champion would have dreamed of saying such a thing. Before Ali, the title had made modest men into bigger men, but after him, the title seemed somehow smaller.

And smaller still, after Tyson had come and gone. Tyson had arrived as the self-styled inheritor of the lineage, a keeper of its flame, but like Ali, he would prove too big a presence to fit within the title's confines—especially in the modern media age. His critics pointed out, accurately, that he had lost most of his key fights, yet the title, in the end, was about more than just winning or losing; it was about representation. Tyson's global fame made his possession, or nonpossession, of the official title virtually irrelevant. "He got a lot of people interested in Mike Tyson," Larry Merchant said. "I don't know if he got a lot of people interested in the sport."[4] It was ironic that Ali and Tyson, through their giganticism, would help erode the traditional stature of the heavyweight championship, since no two champions thought more about their predecessors or cherished the title more.

★

Before the memorial service began, the pallbearers had filed out of the funeral home, ready to do their final duty: deliver the casket into its hearse, in which it would be driven to Louisville's Cave Hill Cemetery for burial. A group of powerful-looking men, all wearing dark suits, stepped out into the sunshine, among them Will Smith (who had played Ali in the 2001 movie about his life), Lennox Lewis, and Tyson. They formed two lines behind the hearse, with Tyson nearest the vehicle's opened doors. Then the chestnut-colored casket was wheeled out, covered in an Islamic shroud.

Long ago, Cus D'Amato had told Tyson that he could beat any heavyweight who had ever lived—Jack Johnson, Jack Dempsey, Gene Tunney, Joe Louis, Rocky Marciano, Floyd Patterson, Sonny Liston, Joe Frazier. But no matter what you do, Cus said, you could never beat Muhammad Ali. Tyson believed it. Ali had always been a beacon to him. The champ had shown up at Tyson's reform school. Cus put Ali on the phone with Tyson in 1980, when the kid was just fourteen, the outlines of his destiny already sketched in bold colors. Tyson at first declined the Ali family's request to be a pallbearer; he wasn't sure that he could handle his emotions. "God came for his champion," he had written on Twitter, when he heard the news. "So long great one." Finally, Tyson decided that he simply had to attend, and he caught a red-eye flight to Louisville.

Tyson may not have found himself in this position if Ali had died, say, a decade earlier. Yet here he was, nearing fifty, already twice the age he'd expected to reach, and somehow, like Ali, he had found his way to transformation. He'd reached the bottom of his rage and self-destructiveness, after years of drug addiction and personal misadventures, more scrapes with the law, and the loss of a young daughter. Against all expectations, he was engaged in the only comeback that really mattered: to become a decent man, to live "life on life's terms," as he called it. Intensive therapy, a loving marriage, and family life became his bedrocks. In making a go of it, when every smart dollar would have bet that he never could, Tyson had finally become what he had never been in the ring: a sentimental favorite. The story of his struggle and reclamation inspired many, and, as John L. Sullivan had done a century earlier, he wound up on stage as a monologist, giving his testimony. On Broadway, in a one-man show called *Undisputed Truth*, Tyson mesmerized audiences for two hours with the story of his journey from street punk to champion to felon to villain to penitent to entertainer, a man who made his living being himself, laughing at himself but also confessing, making amends, or trying to. It was uneven and herky-jerky and not always consoling; one could sense the potential for cracking. Yet he kept at it, slowly winning goodwill and trust. And so, when Ali died, Tyson was given this dignified honor: to help lay the champion of champions to rest.

"Lift with your body," a man directed at the head of the casket. The big, middle-aged pallbearers obeyed, bending at the knees, hoisting Ali's casket up. "Slowly walk it to the center," the man said. "No hurry." They did not hurry, but the job was finished almost as quickly as it had begun, the casket safely placed inside. "Love you all," one said, and they dispersed, but Mike Tyson bowed his head for a moment before the doors closed.

NOTES

INTRODUCTION

1. Christopher Klein, *Strong Boy: The Life and Times of John L. Sullivan, America's First Sports Hero* (Guilford, Conn.: Lyons Press, 2013), 181.

CHAPTER I

1. Donald Barr Chidsey, *John the Great: The Times and Life of a Remarkable American* (New York: Doubleday, Doran, 1942), 81.
2. Michael T. Isenberg, *John L. Sullivan and His America* (Urbana: University of Illinois Press, 1988), 18.
3. Elliot J. Gorn, *The Manly Art: Bare-Knuckle Prize Fighting in America* (Ithaca, N.Y.: Cornell University Press, 1986), 195.
4. Gorn, *The Manly Art*, 215.
5. "Sullivan's Heavy Blows," *New York Times*, 15 May 1883.
6. Isenberg, *John L. Sullivan*, 152, 160, 225.
7. Chidsey, *John the Great*, 3.
8. Isenberg, *John L. Sullivan*, 152.
9. Christopher Klein, *Strong Boy: The Life and Times of John L. Sullivan, America's First Sports Hero* (Guilford, Conn.: Lyons, 2013), 95, 107.
10. Isenberg, *John L. Sullivan*, 54, 208, 210, 219.
11. Klein, *Strong Boy*, 81.

12. John Durant, *The Heavyweight Champions*, 6th ed. (New York: Hastings House, 1976), 21.

13. Isenberg, *John L. Sullivan*, 202–3.

14. Arthur Brisbane, "Sullivan–Mitchell," in *The Fireside Book of Boxing*, ed. W. C. Heinz (New York: Simon and Schuster, 1961), 49.

15. Stephen Bonsal, *Heyday in a Vanished World* (New York: W. W. Norton, 1937), 52.

16. Brisbane, "Sullivan-Mitchell," 48.

17. "The Big Fight a Draw," *New York World*, 11 Mar. 1888.

18. Richard Hoffer, "Fisticuffs: John L. Sullivan and Jake Kilrain in the Outlaw Brawl That Started It All," *Sports Illustrated*, 6 May 2002.

19. Chidsey, *John the Great*, 165–66.

20. Andrew English, *Ringside at Richburg: America's Last Heavyweight Bare-Knuckle Championship* (Baltimore: Gateway Press, 2008), 65.

21. Isenberg, *John L. Sullivan*, 274.

22. English, *Ringside at Richburg*, 74, 75.

23. Vachel Lindsay, "John L. Sullivan, The Strong Boy of Boston," in *The Fireside Book of Boxing*, 253.

24. Chidsey, *John the Great*, 195.

25. Durant, *The Heavyweight Champions*, 34.

26. Dale A. Somers, *The Rise of Sports in New Orleans: 1850–1900* (Baton Rouge: Louisiana State University Press, 1972), 179.

27. Isenberg, *John L. Sullivan*, 317.

28. Chidsey, *John the Great*, 213.

29. Klein, *Strong Boy*, 221.

30. Somers, *The Rise of Sports in New Orleans*, 179, 185.

31. Klein, *Strong Boy*, 262.

32. Chidsey, *John the Great*, 296.

33. James J. Corbett, *The Roar of the Crowd: The True Tale of the Rise and Fall of a Champion* (New York: G. P. Putnam's Sons, 1925), 171–72.

34. Leo N. Miletich, *Dan Stuart's Fistic Carnival* (College Station: Texas A&M University Press, 1994), 199.

35. Edgar Lee Masters, "The Time of Ruby Robert," in *The Book of Boxing*, ed. W. C. Heinz and Nathan Ward (New York: Total Sports, 1999), 230.

36. Masters, "The Time of Ruby Robert," 230, 233.

37. Monte D. Cox, "Joe Walcott, The Barbados Demon," Cox's Corner, coxscorner.tripod.com/walcott.html (accessed 1 Oct. 2016).

CHAPTER 2

1. Randy Roberts, *Papa Jack: Jack Johnson and the Era of White Hopes* (New York: Free Press, 1983), 61, 68.

2. James J. Corbett, "Jeffries Wins after 25 Terrific Rounds," *New York World*, 4 Nov. 1899.

3. "Jeffries Says He Was Certain of Victory from the First," *New York World*, 4 Nov. 1899.

4. John D. McCallum, *The World Heavyweight Boxing Championship: A History* (Radnor, Pa.: Chilton, 1974), 32.

5. John Durant, *The Heavyweight Champions*, 6th ed. (New York: Hastings House, 1976), 52.

6. Roberts, *Papa Jack*, 35.

7. Richard Wormser, *The Rise and Fall of Jim Crow* (New York: St. Martin's, 2003), 109.

8. "Jack Johnson Wins; Police Stop Fight," *New York Times*, 26 Dec. 1908.

9. Geoffrey Ward, *Unforgivable Blackness: The Rise and Fall of Jack Johnson* (New York: Knopf, 2004), 182.

10. Jack Johnson, *In the Ring and Out* (New York: Citadel, 1992), 239.

11. Ward, *Unforgivable Blackness*, 132, 189.

12. *New York Daily Tribune*, 5 July 1910.

13. *New York Daily Tribune*, 5 July 1910.

14. Finis Farr, *Black Champion: The Life and Times of Jack Johnson* (New York: Scribner's, 1964), 113.

15. Ward, *Unforgivable Blackness*, 209.

16. "Johnson Wins in 15 Rounds; Jeffries Weak," *New York Times*, 5 July 1910.

17. Ward, *Unforgivable Blackness*, 209.

18. *New York Daily Tribune*, 5 July 1910.

19. *Reno Evening Gazette*, 5 July 1910.

20. *New York Daily Tribune*, 5 July 1910.

21. Ward, *Unforgivable Blackness*, 209.

22. "The Fight by Rounds," *New York Times*, 5 July 1910.

23. *Reno Gazette*, 4 July 1910.

24. Roberts, *Papa Jack*, 106.

25. *New York Daily Tribune*, 5 July 1910.

26. Roberts, *Papa Jack*, 110.

27. *Reno Evening Gazette*, 5 July 1910; *New York Daily Tribune*, 5 July 1910.

28. Durant, *The Heavyweight Champions*, 60.

29. "The Battle Round by Round," *New York Times*, 6 Apr. 1915.

30. "Willard Victor; Johnson Retires from Prize Ring," *New York Times*, 6 Apr. 1915.

31. Farr, *Black Champion*, 206.

32. Johnson, *In the Ring and Out*, 230.

33. Bert Sugar, *Bert Sugar on Boxing* (Guilford, Conn.: Lyons, 2005), 269.

34. Nat Fleischer, *The Heavyweight Championship* (New York: G. P. Putnam's Sons, 1949), 153.

CHAPTER 3

1. Randy Roberts, *Jack Dempsey: The Manassa Mauler* (New York: Grove, 1980), 51.

2. Jack Dempsey, as told to Bob Considine and Bill Slocum, *Dempsey: By the Man Himself* (New York: Simon and Schuster, 1960), 11.

3. Dempsey, Considine, and Slocum, *Dempsey*, 31.

4. Jack Dempsey with Barbara Piatelli Dempsey, *Dempsey* (New York: Harper & Row, 1977), 65.

5. Dempsey and Dempsey, *Dempsey*, 117.

6. Bruce J. Evensen, *When Dempsey Fought Tunney: Heroes, Hokum, and Storytelling in the Jazz Age* (Knoxville: University of Tennessee Press, 1996), 33.

7. "Willard Helpless after First Round," *New York Times*, 5 July 1919.

8. Robert Edgren, "Willard's Gameness Stands Out Boldly," *Toledo Blade*, 5 July 1919.

9. "Mrs. Willard Glad Jess Lost Honors" and "Jess Willard Has No Alibi to Offer," *Boston Globe*, 5 July 1919.

10. Dempsey and Dempsey, *Dempsey*, 119.

11. Roger Kahn, *A Flame of Pure Fire: Jack Dempsey and the Roaring '20s* (New York: Harcourt Brace, 1999), 192.

12. Dempsey and Dempsey, *Dempsey*, 160.

13. Frank G. Menke, "Dempsey–Firpo," in *The Fireside Book of Boxing*, ed. W. C. Heinz (New York: Simon and Schuster, 1961), 292.

14. Roberts, *Jack Dempsey*, 187.

15. "Dempsey Whips Firpo in Second Round in Fiercest of Heavyweight Battles," *New York Times*, 15 Sept. 1923.

16. Roberts, *Jack Dempsey*, 188.

17. Roberts, *Jack Dempsey*, 191.

18. Mel Heimer, *The Long Count* (New York: Atheneum, 1969), 19.

19. Heimer, *The Long Count*, 22.

20. Roberts, *Jack Dempsey*, 232.

21. Roberts, *Jack Dempsey,* 222.

22. Dempsey, Considine, and Slocum, *Dempsey*, 198.

23. "Fight Crowds Come by Air, Road, Rail," *New York Times*, 23 Sept. 1927.

24. Heimer, *The Long Count*, 244–45.

25. "Story of Dempsey–Tunney Bout as Broadcast from Ringside," *New York Times*, 23 Sept. 1927.

26. Heimer, *The Long Count*, 255.

27. Gene Tunney, "My Fights with Jack Dempsey," in *The Aspirin Age*, ed. Isabel Leighton (New York: Simon and Schuster, 1949), 167.

28. "Gene Tunney, RIP," *National Review*, 8 Dec. 1978.

CHAPTER 4

1. David Bathrick, "Max Schmeling on the Canvas: Boxing as an Icon of Weimar Culture," *New German Critique* 51, special issue on Weimar mass culture (Autumn 1990): 113–36.

2. David Margolick, *Beyond Glory: Joe Louis vs. Max Schmeling, and a World on the Brink* (New York: Knopf, 2005), 26.

3. Edward J. Neil, "Sharkey Wins from Max, but Verdict Disputed," *Ellensburg Daily Record*, 22 June 1932, news.google.com/newspapers?nid=860&dat=19320 622&id=zNMrAAAAIBAJ&sjid=i4QFAAAAIBAJ&pg=6476,1709788&hl=en (accessed 10 Oct. 2016).

4. Joseph S. Page, *Primo Carnera: The Life and Career of the Heavyweight Boxing Champion* (Jefferson, N.C.: McFarland, 2010), 72.

5. John Kieran, "Weighing in for the Big Bout," *New York Times*, 22 July 1931.

6. Paul Gallico, *Farewell to Sport* (New York: International Polygonics, 1990), 64.

7. Jack Sher, "The Strange Case of Carnera," *Sport*, February 1948.

8. Mike Casey, "Jack Sharkey: Read Him and Weep," Cyber Boxing Zone, www.cyberboxingzone.com/blog/?p=430 (accessed 10 Oct. 2016).

9. Michael C. DeLisa, *Cinderella Man: The James J. Braddock Story* (Preston, UK: Milo, 2005), 136.

10. Jeremy Schaap, *Cinderella Man: James J. Braddock, Max Baer, and the Greatest Upset in Boxing History* (New York: Houghton Mifflin, 2005), 151.

11. Margolick, *Beyond Glory*, 38.

12. Ron Fimrite, "Send in the Clown," *Sports Illustrated*, 20 Mar. 1978, sportsillustrated.cnn.com/vault/article/magazine/MAG1093439/index.htm (accessed 10 Oct. 2016).

13. Schaap, *Cinderella Man*, 47.

14. Schaap, *Cinderella Man*, 98.

15. Mordaunt Hall, "Max Baer, Myrna Loy and Walter Huston in 'The Prizefighter and the Lady,'" *New York Times*, 11 Nov. 1933.

16. Schaap, *Cinderella Man*, 179.

17. Fimrite, "Send in the Clown."

18. Schaap, *Cinderella Man*, 132.

19. DeLisa, *Cinderella Man*, 145.

20. John Durant, *The Heavyweight Champions*, 6th ed. (New York: Hastings House, 1976), 96.

21. DeLisa, *Cinderella Man*, 173.

22. *Cinderella Man*, directed by Ron Howard (New York: NBC Universal, 2005), DVD.

23. Schaap, *Cinderella Man*, 251.

24. Schaap, *Cinderella Man*, 255, 257–58.

25. James P. Dawson, "Braddock Outpoints Baer to Win World Ring Title," *New York Times*, 14 June 1935.

26. Frank Graham Jr., *A Farewell to Heroes* (Carbondale: Southern Illinois University Press, 1981), 67.

27. "Won Title in 3d, Braddock Says; Through with Ring, Declares Baer," *New York Times*, 14 June 1935.

28. DeLisa, *Cinderella Man*, 186.

29. Epigraph to Schaap, *Cinderella Man*.

CHAPTER 5

1. James Dawson, "Louis Knocks Out Carnera in Sixth; 60,000 See Battle," *New York Times*, 26 June 1935.

2. Chris Mead, *Joe Louis: Black Champion in White America* (Mineola, N.Y.: Dover, 1985), 59.

3. Joe Louis, with Edna and Art Rust Jr., *My Life* (New York: Berkley, 1981), 1.

4. Louis, *My Life*, 18.

5. Louis, *My Life*, 27.

6. David Margolick, *Beyond Glory: Joe Louis vs. Max Schmeling, and a World on the Brink* (New York: Knopf, 2005), 64.

7. Louis, *My Life*, 33.

8. Ron Fimrite, "Send in the Clown," *Sports Illustrated*, 20 Mar. 1978, sportsillustrated.cnn.com/vault/article/magazine/MAG1093439/index.htm (accessed 10 Oct. 2016).

9. Richard Bak, *Joe Louis: The Great Black Hope* (Dallas: Taylor, 1996), 95.

10. Mead, *Joe Louis*, 67–68, 119.

11. Randy Roberts, *Joe Louis: Hard Times Man* (New Haven, Conn.: Yale University Press, 2010), 100, 124.

12. Martin Luther King Jr., *Why We Can't Wait* (New York: Harper & Row, 1964), 100–101.

13. Margolick, *Beyond Glory*, 147.

14. Roberts, *Joe Louis*, 128, 124, 120.

15. Louis, *My Life*, 84.

16. John Durant, *The Heavyweight Champions*, 6th ed. (New York: Hastings House, 1976), 111.

17. Bak, *Joe Louis*, 132.

18. Michael C. DeLisa, *Cinderella Man: The James J. Braddock Story* (Preston, UK: Milo, 2005), 222.

19. Bak, *Joe Louis*, 150.

20. Lewis Erenberg, *The Greatest Fight of Our Generation: Louis vs. Schmeling* (New York: Oxford University Press, 2006), 161.

21. Erenberg, *The Greatest Fight of Our Generation*, 139.

22. Jimmy Cannon, "The Joe Louis I Remember," in *The Fireside Book of Boxing*, ed. W. C. Heinz (New York: Simon and Schuster, 1961), 68.

23. Margolick, *Beyond Glory*, 5, 283.

24. Roberts, *Joe Louis*, 165, 166.

25. Margolick, *Beyond Glory*, 298.

26. Clem McCarthy, audio transcript, June 22, 1938. *The American Experience*: "The Fight." www.pbs.org/wgbh/amex/fight/sfeature/sf_radio_pop_1938_01.html.

27. Roberts, *Joe Louis*, 168.

28. After Germany's defeat in World War II, a Hamburg court declared Schmeling "free of Nazi taint," and Schmeling touted his refusal to accept the Nazi Sword of Honor and to join the Nazi Party as proof of his anti-Hitler views. He forged a post-retirement friendship with Joe Louis. By the time he died at ninety-nine in 2005, he was broadly regarded as a man who had been championed by Hitler against his will. That same year, however, David Margolick's exhaustively researched book, *Beyond Glory*, drew a darker portrait of Schmeling as a moral pragmatist who found a way to thrive in Weimar Germany, Nazi Germany, and postwar West Germany by adapting to his circumstances. Margolick made a powerful case. And yet, Schmeling saved two lives at real personal risk. If his worst was opportunistic, his best was goodness itself.

29. John Kieran, "Private Joe at a Public Function," *New York Times*, 27 Mar. 1942.

30. Bak, *Joe Louis*, 199, 200.

31. Durant, *The Heavyweight Champions*, 106.

32. Roberts, *Joe Louis*, 196.

33. Mead, *Joe Louis*, 209, 210.

34. Mead, *Joe Louis*, 271.

35. "Navy Show Draws Crowd of 20,000," *New York Times*, 11 Mar. 1942.

36. Roberts, *Joe Louis*, 224.

37. Durant, *The Heavyweight Champions*, 107.

38. Mead, *Joe Louis*, 243.

39. Arnold Rampersad, *Jackie Robinson: A Biography* (New York: Ballantine, 1997), 92.

CHAPTER 6

1. Russell Sullivan, *Rocky Marciano: The Rock of His Times* (Urbana: University of Illinois Press, 2002), 25.

2. Everett Skehan, *Rocky Marciano: Biography of a First Son* (Boston: Houghton Mifflin, 1977), 80.

3. Skehan, *Rocky Marciano*, 96.

4. Arthur Daley, "For the Championship or Approximately So," *New York Times*, 22 June 1949.

5. W. C. Heinz, "The Strange Case of Ezzard Charles," *Saturday Evening Post*, 7 June 1952.

6. Richard Bak, *Joe Louis: The Great Black Hope* (Dallas: Taylor, 1996), 250.

7. Jack Cuddy, "Had Faith in God, Says New Champion Walcott," *Sweetwater Reporter*, 19 July 1951.

8. Sullivan, *Rocky Marciano*, 21, 19.

9. Sullivan, *Rocky Marciano*, 29.

10. Skehan, *Rocky Marciano*, 97–98, 103.

11. Sullivan, *Rocky Marciano*, 103, 104.

12. Red Smith, "Night for Joe Louis," in *At the Fights*, ed. George Kimball and John Schulian (New York: Library of America, 2011), 94.

13. Sullivan, *Rocky Marciano*, 120.

14. Mike Silver, "Foul Play in Philly?" Boxing.com, 30 Apr. 2014, www.boxing .com/foul_play_in_philly.html (accessed 16 Oct. 2016).

15. Sullivan, *Rocky Marciano*, 126.

16. A. J. Liebling, *The Sweet Science* (New York: Penguin, 1956), 99.

17. Nixon's Checkers Speech, 23 Sept. 1952, *The American Experience*, www .pbs.org/wgbh/americanexperience/features/primary-resources/eisenhower-check ers (accessed 16 Oct. 2016).

18. Thomas Hauser, "Rocky Marciano Revisited, Part Two," Seconds Out, www.secondsout.com/columns/thomas-hauser/rocky-marciano-revisited--part -two?clearcache=1 (accessed 16 Oct. 2016).

19. Skehan, *Rocky Marciano*, 169.

20. Sullivan, *Rocky Marciano*, 135.

21. Red Smith, *American Pastimes: The Very Best of Red Smith*, ed. Daniel Okrent (New York: Library of America, 2013), 215.

22. Sullivan, *Rocky Marciano*, 199.

23. Sullivan, *Rocky Marciano*, 222.

24. Sullivan, *Rocky Marciano*, 225.

25. Arthur Daley, "Too Little, Too Late," *New York Times*, 20 June 1954.

26. Luke O'Brien, "It Looked Like a Butterflied Shrimp: A Cutman's Tour of 12 Terrible Fight Wounds," Deadspin, 5 June 2010, deadspin.com/5554955/it-looked -like-a-butterflied-shrimp-a-cutmans-tour-of-12-terrible-fight-wounds (accessed 13 Oct. 2016).

27. Skehan, *Rocky Marciano*, 245.

28. Skehan, *Rocky Marciano*, 253.

29. Budd Schulberg, "A Champion Proves His Greatness," *Sports Illustrated*, 3 Oct. 1955.

30. Skehan, *Rocky Marciano*, 320–21, 284.

31. Sullivan, *Rocky Marciano*, 286.

32. Larry Schwartz, "Marciano Glorified Boxing," ESPN.com, espn.go.com/ sportscentury/features/00016159.html (accessed 16 Oct. 2016).

33. Joe Nichols, "Marciano Is Killed with Two in Iowa Plane Crash," *New York Times*, 2 Sept. 1969.

34. "Clay's Response: Can't Win 'Em All," *New York Times*, 21 Jan. 1970.

35. Muhammad Ali Talks about Rocky Marciano, YouTube video, 1:55, 1976, posted by Ilia Gvelesiani, 19 Aug. 2010, www.youtube.com/watch?v=GDaw 2QFC1Qg (accessed 16 Oct. 2016).

CHAPTER 7

1. Bob Mee, *Ali and Liston: The Boy Who Would Be King and the Ugly Bear* (New York: Skyhorse, 2011), 29.

2. W. C. Heinz, "The Floyd Patterson His Friends Know," *Sport* magazine, Nov. 1960.

3. Peter Heller, *Bad Intentions: The Mike Tyson Story* (New York: Dutton, 1989), 69.

4. Tom Callahan, "Boxing's Allure," *Time*, 27 June 1988.

5. John D. McCallum, *The World Heavyweight Boxing Championship: A History* (Radnor, Pa.: Chilton, 1974), 272.

6. David Halberstam, *The Fifties* (New York: Villard, 1993), 456.

7. Martin Kane, "Things Will Not Be the Same," *Sports Illustrated*, 9 Feb. 1959.

8. W. K. Stratton, *Floyd Patterson: The Fighting Life of Boxing's Invisible Champion* (New York: Houghton Mifflin Harcourt, 2012), 88.

9. Alan H. Levy, *Floyd Patterson: A Boxer and a Gentleman* (Jefferson, N.C.: McFarland, 2008), 112.

10. Levy, *Floyd Patterson*, 103.

11. Joseph C. Nichols, "Patterson Knocks Out Johansson in Fifth; First to Regain the Heavyweight Title," *New York Times*, 21 June 1960.

12. Gay Talese, "Portrait of the Ascetic Champ," *New York Times*, 5 Mar. 1961.

13. *What's My Line?* Ingemar Johansson; Eamonn Andrews (panel), YouTube video, 26:03, 19 June 1960, posted by What's My Line? 27 Mar. 2014, www.youtube.com/watch?v=ttiAQUKFap41917 (accessed 17 Oct. 2016).

14. Dave Anderson, "Jimmy Cannon, Columnist, Dies; Sportswriter Ranged Far Afield," *New York Times*, 6 Dec. 1973.

15. Frank Litsky, "Ingemar Johansson, Who Beat Patterson for Heavyweight Title, Dies at 76," *New York Times*, 31 Jan. 2009.

16. Springs Toledo, "A Birthday for Sonny Liston," The Sweet Science, 1 Sept. 2012, www.thesweetscience.com/feature-articles/15175-a-birthday-for-sonny-liston.

17. David Remnick, *King of the World: Muhammed Ali and the Rise of an American Hero* (New York: Random House, 1998), 49.

18. William Nack, "O Unlucky Man," *Sports Illustrated*, 4 Feb. 1991.

19. Mee, *Ali and Liston*, 96.

20. Nack, "O Unlucky Man."

21. Nack, "O Unlucky Man."

22. Talese, "Portrait of the Ascetic Champ."

23. Talese, "Portrait of the Ascetic Champ."

24. James Baldwin, "The Fight," in *At the Fights*, ed. George Kimball and John Schulian (New York: Library of America, 2011), 141–53.

25. Stratton, *Floyd Patterson*, 153.

26. Arthur Daley, "At the Crossroads," *New York Times*, 27 Sept. 1962.

27. "Tunney Says Patterson Was Scared of Liston," *New York Times*, 27 Sept. 1962.

28. Mee, *Ali and Liston*, 127.

29. Howard M. Tuckner, "Liston Says He Wants to Prove He Can Be a 'Good and Decent Champion,'" *New York Times*, 26 Sept. 1962.

30. Nack, "O Unlucky Man."

31. Sonny Liston, ESPN Sports Century; see www.youtube.com/watch?v=J6NT 184x93I.

32. Martin Luther King Jr., *Why We Can't Wait* (New York: Harper & Row, 1964), 91.

33. Taylor Branch, *Parting the Waters: America in the King Years, 1954–63* (New York: Simon and Schuster, 1988), 801.

34. Nack, "O Unlucky Man."

35. Remnick, *King of the World*, 45, 142.

36. Mee, *Ali and Liston*, 143.

CHAPTER 8

1. Jack Olsen, *Black Is Best: The Riddle of Cassius Clay* (New York: Dell, 1967), 64.

2. Huston Horn, "Who Made Me—Is Me!" *Sports Illustrated*, 25 Sept. 1961.

3. David Remnick, *King of the World: Muhammad Ali and the Rise of an American Hero* (New York: Random House, 1998), 120.

4. Bob Mee, *Ali and Liston: The Boy Who Would Be King and the Ugly Bear* (New York: Skyhorse, 2011), 136.

5. Jose Torres, *Sting Like a Bee: The Muhammad Ali Story* (New York: Abelard-Schuman, 1972), 104, 109.

6. Mee, *Ali and Liston*, 73.

7. Torres, *Sting Like a Bee*, 125.

8. Thomas Hauser, *Muhammad Ali: His Life and Times* (New York: Simon and Schuster, 1992), 62.

9. Rob Sneddon, *The Phantom Punch: The Story behind Boxing's Most Controversial Bout* (Camden, Me.: Down East, 2015), 139–40.

10. Robert Lipsyte, "Robert Lipsyte Describes How Cassius Clay Met the Beatles," Reader's Almanac, Library of America, blog.loa.org/2011/03/robert-lipsyte -describes-how-cassius.html (accessed 23 Oct. 2016).

11. Mee, *Ali and Liston*, 176.

12. Hauser, *Muhammad Ali*, 61.

13. Remnick, *King of the World*, 148–49.

14. *A.k.a. Cassius Clay*, DVD, directed by Jim Jacobs (Beverly Hills, Calif.: United Artists, 1970).

15. Rob Steen, *Sonny Liston: His Life, Strife and the Phantom Punch* (London: JR, 2008), 169.

16. Remnick, *King of the World*, 190.

17. Dave Kindred, *Sound and Fury: Two Powerful Lives, One Fateful Friendship* (New York: Free Press, 2006), 57.

18. Mee, *Ali and Liston*, 205.

19. Remnick, *King of the World*, 202.

20. Robert Lipsyte, "Clay Wins Heavyweight Title as Injured Liston Fails to Come Out for 7th," *New York Times*, 26 Feb. 1964; Hauser, *Muhammad Ali*, 78.

21. Arthur Daley, "Another Surprise," *New York Times*, 27 Feb. 1964.

22. Robert Lipsyte, "Clay Discusses His Future, Liston and Black Muslims," *New York Times*, 27 Feb. 1964.

23. "Clay Says He Has Adopted Islam Religion and Regards It as Way to Peace," *New York Times*, 28 Feb. 1964.

24. Randy Roberts and Johnny Smith, *Blood Brothers: The Fatal Friendship between Muhammad Ali and Malcolm X* (New York: Basic Books, 2016), 141, 209, 218, 298.

25. Sneddon, *Phantom Punch*, 178.

26. Remnick, *King of the World*, 261.

27. Remnick, *King of the World*, 294.

28. Hauser, *Muhammad Ali*, 139–40.

29. Remnick, *King of the* World, 280–81.

30. Remnick, *King of the World*, 299.

31. Robert Lipsyte, "Clay Reclassified 1-A by Draft Board; Heavyweight Champion Plans Appeal," *New York Times*, 18 Feb. 1966.

32. Kindred, *Sound and Fury*, 102.

33. Red Smith, *American Pastimes: The Very Best of Red Smith*, ed. Daniel Okrent (New York: Library of America, 2013), 370.

34. Hauser, *Muhammad Ali*, 145–46.

35. Arthur Daley, "Clay Halts Williams in 1:08 of Third Round and Keeps Heavyweight Title," *New York Times*, 15 Nov. 1966.

36. Hauser, *Muhammad Ali*, 162.

37. Hauser, *Muhammad Ali*, 167.

38. *Champions Forever: World Heavyweight Champs*, DVD, directed by Dimitri Logothetis (Ridgewood, N.J.: American Home Entertainment, 1989).

39. Eldridge Cleaver, *Soul on Ice* (New York: Delta, 1999), 92–93.

40. *The Trials of Muhammad Ali*, Netflix, directed by Bill Siegel (Chicago: Kartemquin Films, 2013).

41. Mark Kram, *Ghosts of Manila: The Fateful Blood Feud between Muhammad Ali and Joe Frazier* (New York: HarperCollins, 2001), 42.

42. Kindred, *Sound and Fury*, 136.

CHAPTER 9

1. Michael Arkush, *The Fight of the Century: Ali vs. Frazier, March 8, 1971* (Hoboken, N.J.: John Wiley & Sons, 2008), 167.

2. Mark Kram, *Ghosts of Manila: The Fateful Blood Feud between Muhammad Ali and Joe Frazier* (New York: HarperCollins, 2001), 56.

3. Phil Pepe, *Come Out Smokin': Joe Frazier—the Champ Nobody Knew* (New York: Coward, McCann & Geoghegan, 1972), 36.

4. Budd Schulberg, *Loser and Still Champion: Muhammad Ali* (New York: Popular Library, 1972), 162.

5. Kram, *Ghosts of Manila*, 141, 130.

6. Joe Frazier with Phil Berger, *Smokin' Joe: The Autobiography of a Heavyweight Champion of the World, Smokin' Joe Frazier* (New York: Macmillan, 1996), 89.

7. Mark Kram, "At the Bell . . .," *Sports Illustrated*, 8 Mar. 1971.

8. Kram, *Ghosts of Manila*, 143.

9. Arkush, *The Fight of the Century*, 188.

10. Arkush, *The Fight of the Century*, 198.

11. Mark Kram, "The Battered Face of a Winner," *Sports Illustrated*, 15 Mar. 1971.

12. "Ali: It's a Good Feeling to Lose, but I Won," *New York Times*, 10 Mar. 1971.

13. Kram, *Ghosts of Manila*, 149.

14. *The Trials of Muhammad Ali*, Netflix, directed by Bill Siegel (Chicago: Kartemquin Films, 2013).

15. "Ali: It's a Good Feeling to Lose, but I Won."

16. *Champions Forever: World Heavyweight Champs*, DVD, directed by Dimitri Logothetis (Ridgewood, N.J.: American Home Entertainment, 1989).

17. Dave Zirin, "An Interview with George Foreman," Counterpunch, 7 Nov. 2003, www.counterpunch.org/2003/11/07/an-interview-with-george-foreman (accessed 17 Oct. 2016).

18. George Foreman and Joel Engel, *By George: The Autobiography of George Foreman* (New York: Villard, 1995), 89.

19. *Champions Forever: World Heavyweight Champs*, DVD, directed by Dimitri Logothetis (Ridgewood, N.J.: American Home Entertainment, 1989).

20. Richard Hoffer, *Bouts of Mania: Ali, Frazier, Foreman, and an America on the Ropes* (Philadelphia: Da Capo Press, 2014), 156.

21. George Plimpton, "Breaking a Date for the Dance," *Sports Illustrated*, November 11, 1974.

22. Norman Mailer, *The Fight* (Boston: Little, Brown, 1975), 177.

23. George Plimpton, *Shadow Box* (New York: G. P. Putnam's Sons, 1977), 326.

24. Dave Kindred, *Sound and Fury: Two Powerful Lives, One Fateful Friendship* (New York: Free Press, 2006), 201.

25. "Muhammad Ali, Guest on Capitol Hill, Meets President," *New York Times*, 11 Dec. 1974.

26. *Thrilla in Manila*, DVD, directed by John Dower (Darlow Smithson Productions, 2008).

27. Hoffer, *Bouts of Mania*, 186.

28. Kram, *Ghosts of Manila*, 171.

29. *Thrilla in Manila*.

30. Kindred, *Sound and Fury*, 208.

31. Mark Kram, "Lawdy, Lawdy, He's Great," *Sports Illustrated*, 15 Oct. 1975.

32. Kindred, *Sound and Fury*, 209.

33. Kram, "Lawdy, Lawdy, He's Great."

34. Kram, *Ghosts of Manila*, 16.

35. Kram, "Lawdy, Lawdy, He's Great."

36. Kram, *Ghosts of Manila*, 189.

37. Dave Anderson, "For Ali, What Price the Thrilla in Manila?" *New York Times*, 23 Sept. 1984.

38. Kindred, *Sound and Fury*, 204.

39. Foreman and Engel, *By George*, 147–48.

40. John Florio and Ouisie Shapiro, *One Punch from the Promised Land: Leon Spinks, Michael Spinks, and the Myth of the Heavyweight Title* (Guilford, Conn.: Lyons, 2013), 95.

41. Schulberg, *Loser and Still Champion*, 141.

42. Pat Putnam, "One More Time to the Top," *Sports Illustrated*, 25 Sept. 1978.

43. Arkush, *The Fight of the Century*, 11.

44. Putnam, "One More Time to the Top."

CHAPTER 10

1. Joseph Ellis, *American Sphinx: The Character of Thomas Jefferson* (New York: Knopf, 1997), 77.

2. Larry Holmes with Phil Berger, *Larry Holmes: Against the Odds* (New York: St. Martin's, 1998), 25.

3. Holmes, *Against the Odds*, 91.

4. Holmes, *Against the Odds*, 13.

5. Holmes, *Against the Odds*, 130.

6. "Ali Says He Will Fight Holmes," *New York Times*, 17 Apr. 1980.

7. Dave Anderson, "More Thoughts on Ali–Holmes Meeting," *New York Times*, 15 July 1980; "Cairo Out, Vegas in for Ali–Holmes," *The Afro-American*, 19 July 1980, 10.

8. William Nack, "Not with a Bang but a Whisper," *Sports Illustrated*, 21 Dec. 1981.

9. John Papanek, "The Glory That Is Caesars," *Sports Illustrated*, 7 June 1982.

10. HBO, *Legendary Nights: The Tale of Holmes–Cooney*, 2003.

11. HBO, *Legendary Nights*.

12. Tom Callahan, "A Puncher Goes for It: Gerry Cooney and Larry Holmes," *Time*, 14 June 1982.

13. Callahan, "A Puncher Goes for It."

14. Holmes, *Against the Odds*, 199–200.

15. In the years since the fight, a story has circulated that Secret Service agents installed a special phone line to Cooney's dressing room—presumably so that President Ronald Reagan could congratulate him if he won—but had not done the same for Holmes. Cooney and Holmes have often told the story themselves. It may have happened, but Cooney's comanager, Mike Jones, said that he knew nothing about it, and the Secret Service told the *New York Times* that the agency had nothing to do with presidential calls to athletes. See "Editors' Note," *New York Times*, 8 April 1985. Without independent corroboration, the story is best regarded as a legend.

16. William Nack, "The Class of His Class," *Sports Illustrated*, 21 June 1982.

17. Michael Katz, "Holmes Draws Raves for Routing Spinks," *New York Times*, 14 June 1981.

18. Tom Callahan, "Larry Holmes: I Still Have It," *Time*, 21 June 1982.

19. Dave Anderson, "Ali Fogs Holmes's View," *New York Times*, 20 May 1983.

20. "Infamous Holmes–Spinks Postfight Press Conference," YouTube video, 21 Sept. 1985, 14:55, posted by rantplan13, 11 Sept. 2012, www.youtube.com/watch?v=ryLS-KnHsgk (accessed 19 Oct. 2016).

21. Dave Anderson, "Ex-Champ's Bitter Ego," *New York Times*, 23 Sept. 1985.

22. Pat Putnam, "Battle of the Ballot," *Sports Illustrated*, 28 Apr. 1986.

CHAPTER 11

1. Mike Tyson with Larry Sloman, *Undisputed Truth* (New York: Blue Rider, 2013), 19.

2. William Nack, "Ready to Soar to the Very Top," *Sports Illustrated*, 6 Jan. 1986.

3. Tyson, *Undisputed Truth*, 37.

4. Tyson, *Undisputed Truth*, 52, 53, 59.

5. Joyce Carol Oates, *On Boxing* (Hopewell, N.J.: Ecco, 1994), 119.

6. Phil Berger, "Tyson Wins WBC Championship," *New York Times*, 23 Nov. 1986.

7. Dave Anderson, "Tyson Era Is Now," *New York Times*, 24 Nov. 1986.

8. Anderson, "Tyson Era Is Now."

9. Dave Anderson, "Another Knockout for Tyson," *New York Times*, 17 Feb. 1986.

10. Peter Heller, *Bad Intentions: The Mike Tyson Story* (New York: New American Library, 1989), 157.

11. Berger, "Tyson Wins WBC Championship."

12. Nack, "Ready to Soar to the Very Top."

13. Heller, *Bad Intentions*, 73.

14. Pat Putnam, "Only One No. 1," *Sports Illustrated*, 10 Aug. 1987.

15. Mike Tyson–Tyrell Biggs, 16 Oct. 1987, www.youtube.com/watch?v=gCyOGl Y6XWU.

16. Pat Putnam, "The Big Showdown," *Sports Illustrated*, 27 June 1988.

17. Oates, *On Boxing*, 172–73.

18. Mike Tyson–Tony Tubbs, YouTube video, 52:14, 21 Mar. 1988, posted by Lorand, 22 Jan. 2011, www.youtube.com/watch?v=4HxkowX-w4c (accessed 21 Oct. 2016).

19. Jack Newfield, *Only in America: The Life and Crimes of Don King* (New York: William Morrow, 1995), 250.

20. Tom Callahan, "Boxing's Allure," *Time*, 27 June 1988.

21. Otto Friedrich, "Flashy Symbol of an Acquisitive Age: Donald Trump," *Time*, 16 Jan. 1989.

22. Callahan, "Boxing's Allure."

23. *Late Night with David Letterman*, 26 June 1987, pt. 5, YouTube Video, 10:47, 26 June 1987, posted by jerkylfish, 15 May 2011, www.youtube.com/watch?v=1yKGP9P6zJQ (accessed 20 Oct. 2016).

24. Pat Putnam, "'I'm Gonna Hurt This Guy,'" *Sports Illustrated*, 4 July 1988.

25. Ira Berkow, "The Ring of Fear," *New York Times*, 30 June 1988.

26. Pat Putnam, "Smashing!" *Sports Illustrated*, 6 Mar. 1989.

27. Pat Putnam, "The Beatings Go On," *Sports Illustrated*, 31 July 1989.

28. Joe Layden, *The Last Great Fight: The Extraordinary Tale of Two Men and How One Fight Changed Their Lives Forever* (New York: St. Martin's, 2007), 94, 112.

29. Oates, *On Boxing*, 15.

30. Tyson vs. Douglas, HBO broadcast, YouTube.

31. Newfield, *Only in America*, 286.

32. Tyson, *Undisputed Truth*, 220.

33. Robert Seltzer, "The Devolution of Mike Tyson—from Savior of Boxing to Shame of Boxing?" *Seattle Times*, 28 June 1991, community.seattletimes.nwsource.com/archive/?date=19910628&slug=1291587 (accessed 20 Oct. 2016).

34. Pat Putnam edited by Steve Wulf, "On the Ropes," *Sports Illustrated*, 24 Feb. 1992.

CHAPTER 12

1. George Foreman and Joel Engel, *By George: The Autobiography of George Foreman* (New York: Villard, 1995), 148.

2. Richard Hoffer, "Still Hungry after All These Years," *Sports Illustrated*, 17 July 1989.

3. Frank Lotierzo, "Why We Never Saw Foreman–Tyson," Boxing Scene, 7 March 2005, www.boxingscene.com/why-we-never-saw-foreman-tyson--818 (accessed March 6, 2017).

4. Holyfield vs. Foreman (entire HBO program), YouTube video, 1:55:42, 19 Apr. 1991, posted by Sterling Wainscott, 4 July 2014, www.youtube.com/watch?v=DkhTno_nKLY (accessed 21 Oct. 2016).

5. William Nack, "A Leap of Faith," *Sports Illustrated*, 12 Apr. 1993.

6. Foreman vs. Moorer (entire HBO program), YouTube video, 1:37:04, 5 Nov. 1994, posted by Sterling Wainscott, 15 Sept. 2014, www.youtube.com/watch?v=di7PRwl11b0 (accessed 21 Oct. 2016).

7. Richard Hoffer, "Up from the Canvas," *Sports Illustrated*, 27 Mar. 1995.

8. George Willis, *The Bite Fight: Tyson, Holyfield, and the Night That Changed Boxing Forever* (Chicago: Triumph, 2013), 86.

9. Dave Anderson, "The Heart That Helps and Hurts," *New York Times*, 8 Nov. 1996.

10. Richard Hoffer, "Real Deal," *Sports Illustrated*, 18 Nov. 1996.

11. Dave Anderson, "'I Knew I Needed the Spirit,'" *New York Times*, 10 Nov. 1996.

12. Richard Hoffer, "Zero Tolerance," *Sports Illustrated*, 16 Sept. 1996.

13. Hoffer, "Real Deal."

14. Tyson vs. Holyfield I (full fight), YouTube video, 1:12:11, 9 Nov. 1996, posted by Mayur6, 2 Nov. 2015, www.youtube.com/watch?v=F4HXeZi2t3Q (accessed 21 Oct. 2016).

15. Richard Hoffer, "Feeding Frenzy," *Sports Illustrated*, 7 July 1997.

16. Gerald Eskenazi, "Tyson Covers His Long Career from Dark Days to Paydays," *New York Times*, 7 Nov. 1996.

17. Tom Friend, "Tyson a Not So Raging Bull," *New York Times*, 25 June 1997.

18. Hoffer, "Real Deal."

19. Friend, "Tyson a Not So Raging Bull."

20. Tom Friend, "After Biting, Tyson Faces Trouble from All Corners," *New York Times*, 29 June 1997.

21. Mike Tyson vs. Evander Holyfield II, YouTube video, 1:29:49, 28 June 1997, posted by FameKillusion, 1 July 2016, www.youtube.com/watch?v=HXmcy-m994o (accessed 21 Oct. 2016).

22. Hoffer, "Feeding Frenzy."

23. Richard Sandomir, "Tyson Apologizes for Bites, Saying He 'Snapped,'" *New York Times*, 1 July 1997.

24. Joyce Carol Oates, "Fury and Fine Lines," *New York Times*, 3 July 1997.

25. Dave Anderson, "Tyson Inflicts a Wound That Will Not Heal," *New York Times*, 30 June 1997.

26. Willis, *The Bite Fight*, 174.

27. Richard Hoffer, "Born Again and Again and Again," *Sports Illustrated*, 1 Dec. 2003.

28. Mike Tyson–Lou Savarese, YouTube video, 27:37, 24 June 2000, posted by Boxing VHS, 30 Nov. 2015, www.youtube.com/watch?v=1rO2h3cefjI (accessed 21 Oct. 2016).

29. Willis, *The Bite Fight*, 189.

30. Lewis–Tyson preview show (HBO), YouTube video, 25:40, posted by Fehmisual Danny, 22 July 2015, www.youtube.com/watch?v=Ecdkj59uTEc (accessed 21 Oct. 2016).

31. Mike Tyson vs. Lennox Lewis, YouTube video, 1:19:55, 8 June 2002, posted by Борис Самойлик, 1 Mar. 2015, www.youtube.com/watch?v=Vewmp2JigcQ (accessed 21 Oct. 2016).

32. Fox Sports, *Mike Tyson: Beyond the Glory*, 2003.

EPILOGUE

1. Mark Kram, *Ghosts of Manila: The Fateful Blood Feud between Muhammad Ali and Joe Frazier* (New York: HarperCollins, 2001), 19.

2. Joe Frazier, with Phil Berger, *Smokin' Joe: The Autobiography of a Heavyweight Champion of the World* (New York: Macmillan, 1996), 196.

3. This didn't change when, in 2015, American Deontay Wilder won the WBC heavyweight belt. Wilder was not generally recognized as the legitimate champion, and, in any event, it would take more than token American representation to restore the title's cultural power in the United States.

4. Quoted in Joe Layden, *The Last Great Fight: The Extraordinary Tale of Two Men and How One Fight Changed Their Lives Forever* (New York: St. Martin's, 2007), 201.

BIBLIOGRAPHY

BOOKS AND ARTICLES

(Note: Newspaper articles cited in the Notes are not cited again here.)

Abdur-Rahman, Sulaiman. "Former Heavyweight Champ Larry Holmes Remembers Muhammad Ali as 'Great Man.'" *The Trentonian*, 6 June 2016.

Acevedo, Carlos. "Hard Times: The Mystery of the Jack Dempsey–Jess Willard Fight." The Cruelest Sport, 25 June 2015 (originally published in *Undisputed Fight Magazine*). thecruelestsport.com/2015/06/25/hard-times-the-mystery-of-the-jack-dempsey-jess-willard-fight.

Ali, Muhammad, and Richard Durham. *The Greatest: My Own Story*. New York: Random House, 1975.

"Ali Says He Will Fight Holmes." *New York Times*, 17 Apr. 1980.

"Ali Wins in Draft Case Appeal." *New York Times*, 29 June 1971.

Allen, Frederick Lewis. *Only Yesterday: An Informal History of the 1920s*. New York: Harper Perennial, 1964.

———. *Since Yesterday: The Nineteen-Thirties in America*. New York: Harper Perennial, 1972.

"All-Time Rankings." International Boxing Research Organization. www.ibrore search.com/category/rankings.

Anderson, Dave. "Ali Outpoints Bugner and Keeps Title; Champion Decides to Continue Career." *New York Times*, 1 July 1975.

Anderson, Martin. "The Reagan Boom—the Greatest Ever." *New York Times*, 17 Jan. 1990.

Araton, Harvey. "The Night the Ali–Liston Fight Came to Lewiston." *New York Times*, 19 May 2015.

Arkush, Michael. *The Fight of the Century: Ali vs. Frazier, March 8, 1971*. Hoboken, N.J.: John Wiley & Sons, 2008.

Bak, Richard. *Joe Louis: The Great Black Hope*. Dallas: Taylor, 1996.

Baldwin, James. "The Fight." 141–53 in *At the Fights: American Writers on Boxing*, edited by George Kimball and John Schulian. New York: Library of America, 2011.

Bathrick, David. "Max Schmeling on the Canvas: Boxing as an Icon of Weimar Culture." *New German Critique* 51, special issue on Weimar mass culture (Autumn 1990): 113–36.

Berkow, Ira. "Mike Should Still Be Paid Zero." *New York Times*, 1 July 1997.

"The Bigger Brute Won." *New York Times*, 9 July 1889.

Bingham, Howard L., and Max Wallace. *Muhammad Ali's Greatest Fight: Cassius Clay vs. the United States of America*. Lanham, Md.: M. Evans, 2000.

Bonsal, Stephen. *Heyday in a Vanished World*. New York: W. W. Norton, 1937.

Branch, Taylor. *Parting the Waters: America in the King Years, 1954–63*. New York: Simon and Schuster, 1988.

Briggs, Kenneth A. "Town Puts Pride in Holmes Corner." *New York Times*, 17 Apr. 1986.

Brinkley, Alan. "The Fifties." Gilder Lehrman Institute of American History. www.gilderlehrman.org/history-by-era/fifties/essays/fifties.

Brisbane, Arthur. "Sullivan–Mitchell." 48–50 in *The Fireside Book of Boxing*, edited by W. C. Heinz. New York: Simon and Schuster, 1961.

"Bull v. Butterfly: A Clash of Champions." *Time*, 8 Mar. 1971.

Burka, Paul. "Grande Dame of the Gulf." *Texas Monthly*, Dec. 1983.

Cable, Mary. *The Blizzard of '88*. New York: Atheneum, 1988.

Cady, Steve. "Ali Scoffs at Rematch, Urging Norton to Beat Foreman First." *New York Times*, 30 Sept. 1976.

Callahan, Tom. "A Puncher Goes for It: Gerry Cooney and Larry Holmes." *Time*, 14 June 1982.

——. "Larry Holmes: I Still Have It." *Time*, 21 June 1982.

——. "Boxing's Allure." *Time*, 27 June 1988.

Cannon, Jimmy. "The Joe Louis I Remember." 66–72 in *The Fireside Book of Boxing*, edited by W. C. Heinz. New York: Simon and Schuster, 1961.

——. *Nobody Asked Me, but . . . : The World of Jimmy Cannon*. New York: Holt, Rinehart and Winston, 1978.

Carney, Jim, Jr. *Ultimate Tough Guy: The Life and Times of James J. Jeffries*. Westlake, Ohio: Achill, 2009.

Casey, Mike. "Jack Sharkey: Read Him and Weep." Cyber Boxing Zone. www.cyberboxingzone.com/blog/?p=430.

Cashill, Jack. *Sucker Punch: The Hard Left Hook That Dazed Ali and Killed King's Dream*. Nashville: Nelson Current, 2006.

Cashman, Sean Dennis. *America in the Gilded Age: From the Death of Lincoln to the Rise of Theodore Roosevelt*. 2nd ed. New York: New York University Press, 1988.

Cavanaugh, Jack. *Tunney: Boxing's Brainiest Champ and His Upset of the Great Jack Dempsey*. New York: Random House, 2006.

Chidsey, Donald Barr. *John the Great: The Times and Life of a Remarkable American*. New York: Doubleday, Doran, 1942.

Cleaver, Eldridge. *Soul on Ice*. New York: Delta, 1999.

Clifford, Joseph. "The History of Cutmen (Part 3)." FightMedicine. fightmedicine .net/cutman-advice/the-history-of-cutmen-part-3.

Coffey, Michael, ed. *The Irish in America*. New York: Hyperion, 1997.

"Color Line Erased by Jack Dempsey." *New York Times*, 19 July 1920.

Cooper, John Milton. *Pivotal Decades: The United States, 1900–1920*. New York: W. W. Norton, 1990.

Cope, Myron. "Muslim Champ." *Saturday Evening Post*, 14 Nov. 1964.

Corbett, James J. *The Roar of the Crowd: The True Tale of the Rise and Fall of a Champion*. New York: G. P. Putnam's Sons, 1925.

Cortesi, Arnaldo. "70,000 See Carnera Retain Ring Title." *New York Times*, Oct. 23, 1933.

Cox, Monte D. "Were Dempsey's Gloves Loaded? You Decide!" Cox's Corner, 1 Dec. 2004. coxscorner.tripod.com/dempsey_gloves.html.

———. "Did Jack Dempsey Take a Dive?" Cox's Corner (no date). coxscorner. tripod.com/dempsey_dive.html.

———. "Joe Walcott, the Barbados Demon." Cox's Corner (no date). coxscorner. tripod.com/walcott.html.

CPI Inflation Calculator. Bureau of Labor Statistics. www.bls.gov/data/inflation_ calculator.htm.

Crouse, Karen. "Celebrating Joe Louis's Contribution to Golf." *New York Times*, 28 Jan. 2012.

Curl, James. *Jersey Joe Walcott: A Boxing Biography*. Jefferson, N.C.: McFarland, 2012.

Daley, Arthur. "Demise of an Octopus." *New York Times*, 14 Jan. 1959.

———. "A Voice from the Past." *New York Times*, 9 Feb. 1964.

———. "The Might-Have-Been." *New York Times*, 27 Feb. 1966.

Dartnell, Fred. *"Seconds Out!": Chats about Boxers, Their Trainers and Patrons*. London: T. W. Laurie, 1924.

Davies, Richard O. *Sports in American Life: A History*. Oxford, UK: Wiley-Blackwell, 2012.

Dawson, James P. "70,000 See Sharkey Outpoint Schmeling to Win World Title." *New York Times*, 22 June 1932.

———. "Charles Outpoints Louis in Bruising 15-Round Bout." *New York Times*, 28 Sept. 1950.

———. "Walcott Knocks Out Charles in Seventh, Wins Heavyweight Title." *New York Times*, 19 July 1951.

Deford, Frank. "The Boxer and the Blonde." *Sports Illustrated*, 17 June 1985.

———. "Almost a Hero." *Sports Illustrated*, 23 Dec. 2001.

DeLisa, Michael C. *Cinderella Man: The James J. Braddock Story*. Preston, UK: Milo, 2005.

Dempsey, Jack, with Myron M. Stearns. *Round by Round: An Autobiography*. New York: McGraw-Hill, 1940.

Dempsey, Jack, as told to Bob Considine and Bill Slocum. *Dempsey: By the Man Himself*. New York: Simon and Schuster, 1960.

Dempsey, Jack, with Barbara Piatelli Dempsey. *Dempsey*. New York: Harper & Row, 1977.

"Dempsey Knocks Out Carpentier in the Fourth Round." *New York Times*, 3 July 1921.

Di Franco, Philip J. *The Italian American Experience*. New York: T. Doherty Associates, 1988.

DiGiacomo, Frank. "The Esquire Decade." *Vanity Fair*, Jan. 2007.

Doyle, Jack. "Dempsey vs. Carpentier, July 1921." *PopHistoryDig.com*, 8 Sept. 2008. www.pophistorydig.com/topics/dempsey-vs-carpentier-1921.

Dray, Philip. *At the Hands of Persons Unknown: The Lynching of Black America*. New York: Random House, 2002.

Dundee, Angelo, and Bert Sugar. *My View from the Corner: A Life in Boxing*. New York: McGraw-Hill, 2007.

Durant, John. *The Heavyweight Champions*. 6th ed. New York: Hastings House, 1976.

Early, Gerald, ed. *Tuxedo Junction: Essays on American Culture*. New York: Ecco, 1989.

———. *The Muhammad Ali Reader*. New York: Ecco, 2013.

Edwards, Rebecca. *New Spirits: Americans in the Gilded Age, 1865–1905*. New York: Oxford University Press, 2006.

Ellis, Joseph. *American Sphinx: The Character of Thomas Jefferson*. New York: Knopf, 1997.

English, Andrew. *Ringside at Richburg: America's Last Heavyweight Bare-Knuckle Championship*. Baltimore: Gateway, 2008.

Erenberg, Lewis. *The Greatest Fight of Our Generation: Louis vs. Schmeling*. New York: Oxford University Press, 2006.

Eskenazi, Gerald. "The Bully Gets Bullied, and the Underdog Reigns." *New York Times*, 11 Nov. 1996.

Evensen, Bruce J. *When Dempsey Fought Tunney: Heroes, Hokum, and Storytelling in the Jazz Age*. Knoxville: University of Tennessee Press, 1996.

Ezra, Michael. *Muhammad Ali: The Making of an Icon*. Philadelphia: Temple University Press, 2009.

Farr, Finis. *Black Champion: The Life and Times of Jack Johnson*. New York: Scribner's, 1964.

Fields, Armond. *James J. Corbett: A Biography of the Heavyweight Boxing Champion and Popular Theater Headliner*. Jefferson, N.C.: McFarland, 2001.

"Fight Broadcast Heard by Millions." *New York Times*, 22 June 1932.

"The Fight Declared a Draw." *New York Times*, 11 Mar. 1888.

Fimrite, Ron. "Send in the Clown." *Sports Illustrated*, 20 Mar. 1978.

Fitzgerald, Ed. "The Blockbuster from Brockton." *Sport*, Jan. 1953.

Fleischer, Nat. *The Heavyweight Championship*. New York: G. P. Putnam's Sons, 1949.

Fleischer, Nat, and Sam Andre. *A Pictorial History of Boxing*. New York: Bonanza, 1981.

Florio, John, and Ouisie Shapiro. *One Punch from the Promised Land: Leon Spinks, Michael Spinks, and the Myth of the Heavyweight Title*. Guilford, Conn.: Lyons, 2013.

Foreman, George, and Joel Engel. *By George: The Autobiography of George Foreman*. New York: Villard, 1995.

Frazier, Joe, with Phil Berger. *Smokin' Joe: The Autobiography of a Heavyweight Champion of the World, Smokin' Joe Frazier*. New York: Macmillan, 1996.

Friedrich, Otto. "Flashy Symbol of an Acquisitive Age: Donald Trump." *Time*, 16 Jan. 1989.

Gallender, Paul. *Sonny Liston: The Real Story behind the Ali–Liston Fights*. Pacific Grove, Calif.: Park Place, 2012.

Gallico, Paul. *Farewell to Sport*. New York: International Polygonics, 1990.

George, Nelson. *Hip Hop America*. New York: Viking, 1998.

Gorn, Elliot J. *The Manly Art: Bare-Knuckle Prize Fighting in America*. Ithaca, N.Y.: Cornell University Press, 1986.

Graham, Frank, Jr. *A Farewell to Heroes*. Carbondale: Southern Illinois University Press, 1981.

Halberstam, David. *The Fifties*. New York: Villard, 1993.

"Harding Ends War; Signs Peace Decree at Senator's Home." *New York Times*, 3 July 1921.

Hauser, Thomas. *Muhammad Ali: His Life and Times*. New York: Simon and Schuster, 1992.

———. "The Importance of Muhammad Ali." Gilder Lehrman Institute of American History. www.gilderlehrman.org/history-by-era/civil-rights-movement/essays/importance-muhammad-ali.

———. "Rocky Marciano Revisited," Parts One and Two. Seconds Out. www.secondsout.com/columns/thomas-hauser/rocky-marciano-revisited--part-one.

Hawley, Samuel. *The Fight That Started the Movies: The World Heavyweight Championship, the Birth of Cinema and the First Feature Film*. Kingston, Ontario: Conquistador Press, 2016.

Heimer, Mel. *The Long Count*. New York: Atheneum, 1969.

Heinz, W. C. "The Strange Case of Ezzard Charles." *Saturday Evening Post*, 7 June 1952.

———. "The Floyd Patterson His Friends Know." *Sport*, Nov. 1960.

Heinz, W. C., ed. *The Fireside Book of Boxing*. New York: Simon and Schuster, 1961.

Heinz, W. C., and Nathan Ward, eds. *The Book of Boxing*. New York: Total Sports, 1999.

Heller, Peter. *In This Corner . . .!: Forty-Two World Champions Tell Their Stories*. New York: Simon and Schuster, 1973.

———. *Bad Intentions: The Mike Tyson Story*. New York: New American Library, 1989.

Hinckley, David. "From the Start, Big-Time Radio Was a Knockout." (New York) *Daily News*, 25 July 2011.

"History of Cable." California Cable & Telecommunications Association. www.calcable.org/learn/history-of-cable.

Hoffer, Richard. "Still Hungry after All These Years." *Sports Illustrated*, 17 July 1989.

———. "Up from the Canvas." *Sports Illustrated*, 27 Mar. 1995.

———. "Zero Tolerance." *Sports Illustrated*, 16 Sept. 1996.

———. "Real Deal." *Sports Illustrated*, 18 Nov. 1996.

———. "Feeding Frenzy." *Sports Illustrated*, 7 July 1997.

———. *A Savage Business: The Comeback and Comedown of Mike Tyson*. New York: Simon and Schuster, 1998.

———. "Grand Larceny." *Sports Illustrated*, 22 Mar. 1999.

———. "Fisticuffs: John L. Sullivan and Jake Kilrain in the Outlaw Brawl That Started It All." *Sports Illustrated*, 6 May 2002.

———. "Born Again and Again and Again." *Sports Illustrated*, 1 Dec. 2003.

———. *Bouts of Mania: Ali, Frazier, Foreman, and an America on the Ropes*. Philadelphia: Da Capo, 2014.

Holmes, Larry, with Phil Berger. *Larry Holmes: Against the Odds*. New York: St. Martin's, 1998.

Holyfield, Evander, and Lee Gruenfeld. *Becoming Holyfield: A Fighter's Journey*. New York: Atria, 2008.

Horn, Huston. "Who Made Me—Is Me!" *Sports Illustrated*, 25 Sept. 1961.

Houston, Graham. *Superfists: The Story of the World Heavyweight Champions*. New York: Bounty, 1975.

"Huge Dust Cloud, Blown 1,500 Miles, Dims City 5 Hours." *New York Times*, 12 May 1934.

Isenberg, Michael T. *John L. Sullivan and His America*. Urbana: University of Illinois Press, 1988.

"Jack Dempsey, New Heavyweight Champion, Announces He Will Draw the Color Line." *New York Times*, 6 July 1919.

"Jack Johnson Wins; Police Stop Fight." *New York Times*, 26 Dec. 1908.

"Jeffries Still Champion." *New York Times*, 12 May 1900.

Johnson, Jack. *In the Ring and Out*. New York: Citadel, 1992.

Johnson, William. "And in This Corner . . . NCR 315." *Sports Illustrated*, 16 Sept. 1968.

Kahn, Roger. *A Flame of Pure Fire: Jack Dempsey and the Roaring '20s*. New York: Harcourt Brace, 1999.

Kane, Martin. "Things Will Not Be the Same." *Sports Illustrated*, 9 Feb. 1959.

———. "The Art of Ali." *Sports Illustrated*, 5 May 1969.

Kanfer, Stefan. *The Voodoo That They Did So Well: The Wizards Who Invented the New York Stage*. Chicago: Ivan R. Dee, 2007.

Kasson, John F. *Amusing the Million: Coney Island at the Turn of the Century*. New York: Hill & Wang, 1978.

Katz, Michael. "Richest in History." *New York Times*, 15 June 1982.

Khalid, Sunni. Interview with Eddie Futch, Las Vegas, 13 Aug. 2000. sunnikhalid. com/2000/08/13/interview-with-eddie-futch-august-2000.

Kimball, George, and John Schulian, eds. *At the Fights: American Writers on Boxing*. New York: Library of America, 2011.

Kindred, Dave. *Sound and Fury: Two Powerful Lives, One Fateful Friendship*. New York: Free Press, 2006.

King, Martin Luther, Jr. *Why We Can't Wait*. New York: Harper & Row, 1964.

Klein, Christopher. *Strong Boy: The Life and Times of John L. Sullivan, America's First Sports Hero*. Guilford, Conn.: Lyons, 2013.

Kram, Mark. "At the Bell . . ." *Sports Illustrated*, 8 Mar. 1971.

———. "The Battered Face of a Winner." *Sports Illustrated*, 15 Mar. 1971.

———. "Lawdy, Lawdy, He's Great." *Sports Illustrated*, 15 Oct. 1975.

———. *Ghosts of Manila: The Fateful Blood Feud between Muhammad Ali and Joe Frazier*. New York: HarperCollins, 2001.

Lacayo, Richard. "Blood at the Root." *Time*, 2 Apr. 2000.

Lardner, John. *White Hopes and Other Tigers*. Philadelphia: J. B. Lippincott, 1951.

Lauderdale, David. "Voodoo's Heyday Has Passed, but the Gullah Tradition Still Bewitches in SC." *The State*, 27 Jan. 2016.

Layden, Joe. *The Last Great Fight: The Extraordinary Tale of Two Men and How One Fight Changed Their Lives Forever*. New York: St. Martin's, 2007.

Levy, Alan H. *Floyd Patterson: A Boxer and a Gentleman*. Jefferson, N.C.: McFarland, 2008.

Lewis, Anthony. "High Court Ends Boxing Monopoly." *New York Times*, 13 Jan. 1959.

Liebling. A. J. *The Sweet Science*. New York: Penguin, 1956.

Lindsay, Vachel. "John L. Sullivan, The Strong Boy of Boston." 253–55 in *The Fireside Book of Boxing*, edited by W. C. Heinz. New York: Simon and Schuster, 1961.

Lipsyte, Robert. "Clay Wins Heavyweight Title as Injured Liston Fails to Come Out for 7th." *New York Times*, 26 Feb. 1964.

———. "Champion Lauds Foe for Courage." *New York Times*, 23 Nov. 1965.

———. "Robert Lipsyte Describes How Cassius Clay Met the Beatles." Reader's Almanac, Library of America. blog.loa.org/2011/03/robert-lipsyte-describes-how-cassius.html.

Long, Clarence D. "The Course of Money Wages during 1860–1890." 13–38 in *Wages and Earnings in the United States, 1860–1890*, edited by Clarence D. Long (Princeton, N.J.: Princeton University Press, 1960).

Lotierzo, Frank. "Why We Never Saw Foreman–Tyson." Boxing Scene, 7 March 2005. www.boxingscene.com/why-we-never-saw-foreman-tyson--818.

Louis, Joe, with Edna and Art Rust Jr. *My Life*. New York: Berkley, 1981.

Lucas, Bob. *Black Gladiator: A Biography of Jack Johnson*. New York: Dell, 1970.

Mailer, Norman. *The Fight*. Boston: Little, Brown, 1975.

Malcolm, Andrew H. "Ali, Inoki Fight to Draw in Dull Bout." *New York Times*, 26 June 1976.

Marcus, Norman. "Every Punch Was Aimed at Hitler." Boxing.com, 7 Feb. 2012. www.boxing.com/every_punch_was_aimed_at_hitler.html.

———. "The Strange Death of Ernie Schaaf." Boxing.com, 19 May 2013. www.boxing.com/the_strange_death_of_ernie_schaaf.html.

Margolick, David. "Only One Athlete Has Ever Inspired This Many Songs." *New York Times*, 25 Feb. 2001.

———. *Beyond Glory: Joe Louis vs. Max Schmeling, and a World on the Brink*. New York: Knopf, 2005.

Mason, Herbert Molloy, Jr. *Death from the Sea: Our Greatest Natural Disaster: The Galveston Hurricane of 1900*. New York: Dial, 1972.

Masters, Edgar Lee. "The Time of Ruby Robert." 228–33 in *The Book of Boxing*, edited by W. C. Heinz and Nathan Ward. New York: Total Sports, 1999.

Maule, Tex. "Cruel Ali with All the Skills." *Sports Illustrated*, 13 Feb. 1967.

———. "For Ali, a Time to Preach." *Sports Illustrated*, 19 Feb. 1968.

McCallum, John D. *The World Heavyweight Boxing Championship: A History*. Radnor, Pa.: Chilton, 1974.

McCarthy, Clem. Audio transcript, June 22, 1938. *The American Experience*: "The Fight." www.pbs.org/wgbh/amex/fight/sfeature/sf_radio_pop_1938_01.html.

McElvaine, Robert S. *The Great Depression: America, 1929–1941*. New York: Times Books, 1984.

McGrath, Charles. "Cover Story: The King of Visceral Design." *New York Times*, 27 Apr. 2008.

Mead, Chris. *Joe Louis: Black Champion in White America*. Mineola, N.Y.: Dover, 1985.

Mee, Bob. *Ali and Liston: The Boy Who Would Be King and the Ugly Bear*. New York: Skyhorse, 2011.

Menke, Frank G. "Dempsey–Firpo." 291–93 in *The Fireside Book of Boxing*, edited by W. C. Heinz. New York: Simon and Schuster, 1961.

Miletich, Leo N. *Dan Stuart's Fistic Carnival*. College Station: Texas A&M University Press, 1994.

Miller, Nathan. *New World Coming: The 1920s and the Making of Modern America*. New York: Scribner, 2003.

Mitchell, Kevin. *Jacobs Beach: The Mob, the Fights, the Fifties*. New York: Pegasus, 2010.

Molnar, Alexandra. "History of Italian Immigration." www.mtholyoke.edu/~molna22a/classweb/politics/Italianhistory.html.

Myler, Patrick. *Gentleman Jim Corbett: The Truth Behind a Boxing Legend*. London: Robson, 1998.

———. *Ring of Hate: Joe Louis vs. Max Schmeling: The Fight of the Century*. New York: Arcade, 2005.

Nack, William. "Not with a Bang but a Whisper." *Sports Illustrated*, 21 Dec. 1981.

———. "The Class of His Class." *Sports Illustrated*, 21 June 1982.

———. "Ready to Soar to the Very Top." *Sports Illustrated*, 6 Jan. 1986.

———. "O Unlucky Man." *Sports Illustrated*, 4 Feb. 1991.

———. "A Leap of Faith." *Sports Illustrated*, 12 Apr. 1993.

———. "The Rock." *Sports Illustrated*, 23 Aug. 1993.

———. "The Long Count." *Sports Illustrated*, 22 Sept. 1997.

Newfield, Jack. *Only in America: The Life and Crimes of Don King*. New York: William Morrow, 1995.

"New King of the Ring Is a Happy Man." *Taunton Daily Gazette*, 6 Apr. 1915.

Oates, Joyce Carol. *On Boxing*. Hopewell, N.J.: Ecco, 1994.

O'Brien, Luke. "It Looked Like a Butterflied Shrimp: A Cutman's Tour of 12 Terrible Fight Wounds." Deadspin, 5 June 2010. deadspin.com/5554955/it-looked-like-a-butterflied-shrimp-a-cutmans-tour-of-12-terrible-fight-wounds.

O'Connor, Daniel, ed. *Iron Mike: A Mike Tyson Reader*. New York: Thunder's Mouth, 2002.

"Off for the Battle." *New York World*, 8 July 1889.

Olsen, Jack. *Black Is Best: The Riddle of Cassius Clay*. New York: Dell, 1967.

Page, Joseph S. *Primo Carnera: The Life and Career of the Heavyweight Boxing Champion*. Jefferson, N.C.: McFarland, 2010.

Papanek, John. "The Glory That Is Caesars." *Sports Illustrated*, 7 June 1982.

Patterson, James T. *The Eve of Destruction: How 1965 Transformed America*. New York: Basic Books, 2012.

Pepe, Phil. *Come Out Smokin': Joe Frazier—the Champ Nobody Knew*. New York: Coward, McCann & Geoghegan, 1972.

Plimpton, George. "Breaking a Date for the Dance." *Sports Illustrated*, 11 Nov. 1974.

———. *Shadow Box*. New York: G. P. Putnam's Sons, 1977.

Pozzetta, George. "Italian Americans." World Culture Encyclopedia. www.every culture.com/multi/Ha-La/Italian-Americans.html.

Pulford, George R. "Willard Plans Bluff to Scare Dempsey." *Toledo Blade*, 3 July 1919.

Putnam, Pat. "One More Time to the Top." *Sports Illustrated*, 25 Sept. 1978.

———. "Battle of the Ballot." *Sports Illustrated*, 28 Apr. 1986.

———. "Only One No. 1." *Sports Illustrated*, 10 Aug. 1987.

———. "The Big Showdown." *Sports Illustrated*, 27 June 1988.

———. "'I'm Gonna Hurt This Guy.'" *Sports Illustrated*, 4 July 1988.

———. "Smashing!" *Sports Illustrated*, 6 Mar. 1989.

———. "The Beatings Go On." *Sports Illustrated*, 31 July 1989.

Putnam, Pat, edited by Steve Wulf. "On the Ropes." *Sports Illustrated*, 24 Feb. 1992.

Rampersad, Arnold. *Jackie Robinson: A Biography*. New York: Ballantine, 1997.

Remnick, David. *King of the World: Muhammad Ali and the Rise of an American Hero*. New York: Random House, 1998.

Rice, Grantland. *The Tumult and the Shouting*. New York: A. S. Barnes, 1954.

Ritter, Lawrence S. *East Side, West Side: Tales of New York Sporting Life, 1910–1960*. Kingston, N.Y.: Total Sports, 1998.

Roberts, Randy. *Jack Dempsey: The Manassa Mauler*. New York: Grove, 1980.

———. *Papa Jack: Jack Johnson and the Era of White Hopes*. New York: Free Press, 1983.

———. *Joe Louis: Hard Times Man*. New Haven, Conn.: Yale University Press, 2010.

Roberts, Randy, and Johnny Smith. *Blood Brothers: The Fatal Friendship between Muhammad Ali and Malcolm X*. New York: Basic Books, 2016.

Rossinow, Doug. *The Reagan Era: A History of the 1980s*. New York: Columbia University Press, 2015.

Rozen, Wayne. "Great White Hope: Not Great, No Hope." *New York Times*, 3 July 2010.

Sammons, Jeffrey. *Beyond the Ring: The Role of Boxing in American Society*. Urbana: University of Illinois Press, 1988.

Sandomir, Richard. "King's Next Act: A Knockout with Pay-per-View." *New York Times*, 27 June 1997.

"Schaaf Suffered from Brain Inflammation; Ill When He Entered Ring, Tests Show." *New York Times*, 20 Feb. 1933.

Schaap, Jeremy. *Cinderella Man: James J. Braddock, Max Baer, and the Greatest Upset in Boxing History*. New York: Houghton Mifflin, 2005.

Schulberg, Budd. "Win or Lose, Archie Moore's Publicity Campaign for the Title Fight Makes Him the Sport's Communications Champ." *Sports Illustrated*, 5 Sept. 1955.

———. "A Champion Proves His Greatness." *Sports Illustrated*, 3 Oct. 1955.

———. *Loser and Still Champion: Muhammad Ali*. New York: Popular Library, 1972.

Schulman, Bruce J. *The Seventies: The Great Shift in American Culture, Society, and Politics*. New York: Free Press, 2001.

S. D. Trav. (Donald Travis Stewart). *No Applause, Just Throw Money, or, the Book That Made Vaudeville Famous: A High-Class, Refined Entertainment*. New York: Faber and Faber, 2005.

Sher, Jack. "The Strange Case of Carnera." *Sport*, Feb. 1948.

Shipp, E. R. "Tyson Gets 6-Year Prison Term for Rape Conviction in Indiana." *New York Times*, 27 Mar. 1992.

Silver, Mike. "Foul Play in Philly?" Boxing.com, 30 Apr. 2014. www.boxing.com/foul_play_in_philly.html.

——. "The Myth of 'The Thrilla in Manila.'" Boxing.com, 30 Sept. 2012. www. boxing.com/the_myth_of_the_thrilla_in_manilla.html.

Skehan, Everett. *Rocky Marciano: Biography of a First Son*. Boston: Houghton Mifflin, 1977.

Smith, Red. *American Pastimes: The Very Best of Red Smith*. Ed. Daniel Okrent. New York: Library of America, 2013.

——. "Night for Joe Louis." 92–94 in *At the Fights: American Writers on Boxing*, edited by George Kimball and John Schulian. New York: Library of America, 2011.

Smith, Toby. *Kid Blackie: Jack Dempsey's Colorado Days*. Ouray, Colo.: Wayfinder, 1987.

Smith, Tommie, with David Steel. *Silent Gesture: The Autobiography of Tommie Smith*. Philadelphia: Temple University Press, 2007.

Sneddon, Rob. *The Phantom Punch: The Story behind Boxing's Most Controversial Bout*. Camden, Me.: Down East, 2015.

Somers, Dale A. *The Rise of Sports in New Orleans: 1850–1900*. Baton Rouge: Louisiana State University Press, 1972.

Snowden, Jonathan. "91 Seconds: Mike Tyson, Michael Spinks and the Knockout That Shook the World." Bleacher Report, 27 June 2013. bleacherreport.com/ articles/1682639-91-seconds-mike-tyson-michael-spinks-and-the-knockout-that -shook-the-world.

"So. Carolina Legislature Hears Frazier." *New York Times*, 8 Apr. 1971.

Steen, Rob. *Sonny Liston: His Life, Strife and the Phantom Punch*. London: JR, 2003.

Stephens, Mitchell. "History of Television." Grolier Encyclopedia. www.nyu.edu/ classes/stephens/History%20of%20Television%20page.htm.

Stratton, W. K. *Floyd Patterson: The Fighting Life of Boxing's Invisible Champion*. New York: Houghton Mifflin Harcourt, 2012.

Suddath, Claire. "Why Did World War One Just End?" *Time*, 4 Oct. 2010.

Sugar, Bert. *100 Years of Boxing*. New York: Galley Press: Rutledge Press, 1982.

——. *Bert Sugar on Boxing*. Guilford, Conn.: Lyons, 2005.

——. *Boxing's Greatest Fighters*. Guilford, Conn.: Lyons, 2006.

Sullivan, John L. *Reminiscences of a 19th-Century Gladiator*. Frisco, Tex.: Promethean, 2008.

"Sullivan Knocked Out!" *New York World*, 8 Sept. 1892.

Sullivan, Russell. *Rocky Marciano: The Rock of His Times*. Urbana: University of Illinois Press, 2002.

"Sweden Rejoices after Radio Vigil." *New York Times*, 27 June 1959.

"Swedes Knock Themselves Out Celebrating and Toasting Johansson Victory." *New York Times*, 28 June 1959.

Talese, Gay. "Portrait of the Ascetic Champ." *New York Times*, 5 Mar. 1961.

Toledo, Springs. "A Birthday for Sonny Liston." The Sweet Science, 1 Sept. 2012. www.thesweetscience.com/feature-articles/15175-a-birthday-for-sonny-liston.

Torres, Jose. *Sting Like a Bee: The Muhammad Ali Story*. New York: Abelard-Schuman, 1972.

Tosches, Nick. *The Devil and Sonny Liston*. New York: Little, Brown, 2000.

Tunney, Gene. *A Man Must Fight*. Boston: Houghton Mifflin, 1932.

———. "My Fights with Jack Dempsey." 152–68 in *The Aspirin Age*, edited by Isabel Leighton. New York: Simon and Schuster, 1949.

Tunney, Jay R. *The Prizefighter and the Playwright: Gene Tunney and Bernard Shaw*. Buffalo, N.Y.: Firefly, 2010.

Tyson, Mike, with Larry Sloman. *Undisputed Truth*. New York: Blue Rider, 2013.

Walcott, Jersey Joe, with Lewis Burton. "I'll Lick Joe Louis Again." *Saturday Evening Post*, 12 June 1948 and 19 June 1948.

Walsh, Kenneth T. "The First 100 Days: Franklin Roosevelt Pioneered the 100-Day Concept." *U.S. News & World Report*, 12 Feb. 2009.

Waltzer, Jim. *The Battle of the Century: Dempsey, Carpentier, and the Birth of Modern Promotion*. Santa Barbara, Calif.: Praeger, 2011.

Ward, Geoffrey. *Unforgivable Blackness: The Rise and Fall of Jack Johnson*. New York: Knopf, 2004.

White, Thomas H. "Big Business and Radio (1915–1922)." U.S. Early Radio History. earlyradiohistory.us/sec017.htm.

Whitney, Craig R. "3-Year Ring Ban Declared Unfair." *New York Times*, 15 Sept. 1970.

"Wild Celebration if Georges Wins." *New York Times*, 2 July 1921.

"Willard Beaten in Easy Fashion in Toledo Arena." *New York Times*, 5 July 1919.

"Willard Comes to Town." *New York Times*, 30 Apr. 1917.

Willis, George. *The Bite Fight: Tyson, Holyfield, and the Night That Changed Boxing Forever*. Chicago: Triumph, 2013.

Wormser, Richard. *The Rise and Fall of Jim Crow*. New York: St. Martin's, 2003.

Youngblut, Shelly. *The Quotable ESPN: The Best Stuff Ever Said on ESPN in a Compendium for Every Passionate Sports Fan*. New York: Hyperion, 1998.

Zirin, Dave. "An Interview with George Foreman." Counterpunch, 7 Nov. 2003. www.counterpunch.org/2003/11/07/an-interview-with-george-foreman.

VIDEO

YouTube: The overwhelming majority of the fights described in this book are now available, in whole or in part, on YouTube, which has to be the greatest boon to fight fans since the Queensberry rules. I have refrained from citing individual bouts, as they can be found easily through the search engine at www.youtube.com.

A.k.a. Cassius Clay. Directed by Jim Jacobs. Beverly Hills, Calif.: United Artists, 1970.

Champions Forever: World Heavyweight Champs. Directed by Dimitri Logothetis. Ridgewood, N.J.: American Home Entertainment, 1989.

Kings of the Ring. Directed by Jean-Christophe Rosé. La Sept/Arte Canal + D.A. Big Fights, 1995.

Legendary Nights: The Tale of Holmes–Cooney. HBO, 2003.

Mike Tyson: Beyond the Glory. Fox Sports, 2003.

Sonny Liston. Sports Century. ESPN, 2001.

Sonny Liston: The Mysterious Life & Death of a Champion. HBO Home Video, 1995.

The Superfight: Marciano vs. Ali. Directed by Murry Woroner. Mackinac Media, 2005.

Thrilla in Manila. Directed by John Dower. Darlow Smithson Productions, 2008.

The Trials of Muhammad Ali. Directed by Bill Siegel. Chicago: Kartemquin Films, 2013.

Unforgivable Blackness: The Rise and Fall of Jack Johnson. Directed by Ken Burns. Florentine Films, 2005.

When We Were Kings. Directed by Leon Gast. Universal City, Calif.: Polygram Entertainment, 1996.

OTHER SOURCES

BoxRec.com

Cyber Boxing Zone

New York Times web archive

Newspaperarchive.com

Sports Illustrated Vault

Time archives at Time.com

International Boxing Research Organization

I also gained much from Monte Cox's dogged and insightful work on heavyweight history and from Frank Lotierzo's terrifically lucid analysis of fights and fighters.

INDEX

Page references for figures are italicized.

ABOUT THE AUTHOR

Paul Beston is managing editor of *City Journal*, published by the Manhattan Institute. His writing has appeared in the *Wall Street Journal, City Journal, Real Clear Sports, The American Spectator, The American Conservative, The Christian Science Monitor, The New York Journal of Books*, and *The Millions*, as well as on the boxing website The Sweet Science.